Urkesh/Mozan Studies 6

Three-dimensional Volumetric Analysis: the Palace of Tupkish

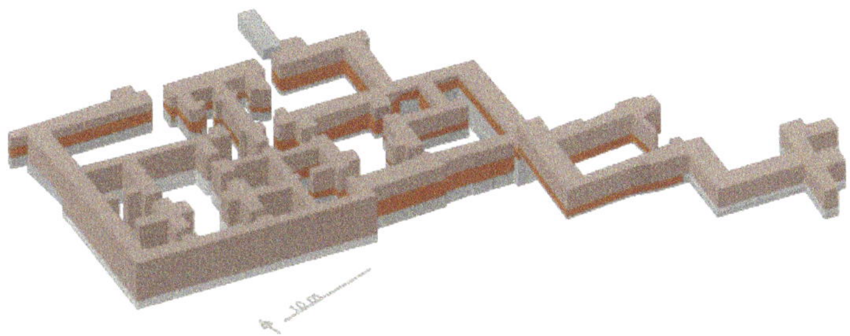

Bibliotheca Mesopotamica

Primary sources and interpretive analyses for the study
of Mesopotamian civilization and its influences
from late prehistory to the end of the cuneiform tradition

IAA

Dual editions
A publication project of the
International Academy of Archaeology

Bibliotheca Mesopotamica
Volume 30

Urkesh/Mozan Studies 6

Three-dimensional Volumetric Analysis in an Archaeological Context

The Palace of Tupkish at Urkesh and its Representation

Federico Buccellati

Undena Publications
Malibu 2016

This research was made possible through the support of:

Deutsche Forschungsgemeinschaft
Graduiertenkolleg 1576 "Wert und Äquivalent"

IIMAS
The International Institute for Mesopotamian Area Studies

The volume offers a detailed architectural analysis of the Palace of King Tupkish, built around 2250 B.C. and of the process of construction by examining the steps in the process through the chaîne opératoire method.

In order to quantify these steps, the volume deals extensively with methodology through a series of algorithms by which the energetic investment in a construction project can be quantified. These algorithms are applicable in general to structures in stone and mudbrick, and can be used to define and compare the cost and value of such structures in a meaningful way. This allows the archaeological record to play a central role in wider theoretical discussions such as questions relating to monumentality and prestige or the economy and the social setting that made the construction possible. This methodology proposes an objective standard of measurement that can be used beyond the case study presented here.

By combining the understanding of the individual steps in the process of construction with the general algorithms and the volumetric measurements from a precise 3D model of the Royal Palace, this study calculates the effort needed to construct the building.

Dual editions are published contemporaneously online and on paper.
The paper edition is sold at a nominal price, to cover only distribution costs.
The online edition is available free of charge at www.undena.com.

Library of Congress Control Number: 2017932337
ISBN 978-0-9798937-2-8

www.undena.com

Excavations at Tell Mozan/Urkesh
and publication of its reports
have been made possible over the years through grants from

The Ahmanson Foundation
The Ambassador International Cultural Foundation
The American Cultural Center, Damascus
The Catholic Biblical Association
The Cotsen Family Foundation
The Cotsen Institute of Archaeology, UCLA
The Council of Research, Academic Senate, UCLA
Fondazione Gianmaria Buccellati
Gulfsands Petroleum Plc
IIMAS – The International Institute for Mesopotamian Area Studies
The Mellon Foundation
The National Endowment for the Humanities
The National Geographic Society
The Office of the Vice-Chancellor for Research, UCLA
Rotary Club Conegliano
The Samuel H. Kress Foundation
The San Carlos Foundation
The L. J. and Mary C. Skaggs Foundation
The Steinmetz Family Foundation
Syria Shell Petroleum Development B.V.
Vartanian Oilfield Services
The World Monuments Fund

with the institutional participation of

The Cotsen Institute of Archaeology, UCLA
The Getty Conservation Institute
The Metropolitan Museum of Art
L'Opificio delle Pietre Dure, Firenze
Università degli Studi e Centro Scavi, Torino

The series *Urkesh/Mozan Studies* evolves directly from an earlier series entitled *Mozan*, of which it continues the numeration. The sequence of volumes is as follows:

Mozan 1 — Giorgio Buccellati and Marilyn Kelly-Buccellati, *The Soundings of the First Two Seasons.* Bibliotheca Mesopotamica 20. Malibu: Undena Publications, 1988.

Mozan 2 — Lucio Milano, with contributions by Mario Liverani, Giorgio Buccellati and Marilyn Kelly-Buccellati, *The Epigraphic Finds of the Sixth Season.* Syro-Mesopotamian Studies 5/1. Malibu: Undena Publications, 1991.

UMS 3 — Giorgio Buccellati and Marilyn. Kelly-Buccellati (eds.), *Urkesh and the Hurrians: A volume in Honor of Lloyd Cotsen.* Bibliotheca Mesopotamica 26. Malibu: Undena Publications, 1998.

UMS 4 — Sophie Bonetti (ed.), *Gli Opifici di Urkesh. Conservazione e restauro a Tell Mozan.* Bibliotheca Mesopotamica 27. Malibu: Undena Publications, 2001.

UMS 5 — Rick Hauser, *Reading Figurines: Animal Representations in Terra Cotta from Royal Building AK at Urkesh (Tell Mozan).* Bibliotheca Mesopotamica 28. Malibu: Undena Publications, 2006.

UMS 6 — Federico Buccellati, *Three-dimensional Volumetric Analysis in an Archaeological Context. The Palace of Tupkish at Urkesh and its Representation.* Bibliotheca Mesopotamica 30. Malibu: Undena Publications, 2016.

UMS 7 — Patrizia Camatta, *The Temple Terrace of Tell Mozan/Urkesh (Syria). Architecture, Typology and Comparative Analysis of Mesopotamian High Temples.* Bibliotheca Mesopotamica 31. Forthcoming.

UMS 8 — Arwa Kharobi, *A Place for the Dead. An Overview of Burial Practices at Tell Mozan in the Middle Bronze Age.* Bibliotheca Mesopotamica 32. Forthcoming.

to my parents

"If I have seen further it is by standing on ye shoulders of Giants."
- Isaac Newton

Table of Contents

Foreword......ix
Preface......xi
Acknowledgments......xiii
1 Introduction......1
1.1 Approach......2
1.2 Architectural Analysis......3
1.3 Elements and Process of Construction......5
1.4 Theoretical Underpinnings of Architectural Analysis......7
1.5 Construction of 3D Models: Methodological Aspects......7
1.6 Application to the AP Palace......9
1.7 Impact and Directions for Future Research......10
2 Architectural Analysis......11
2.1 The AP Palace as a Whole......12
2.1.1 Palace: Position......14
2.1.2 Palace: Chronology......17
2.1.2.1 Pre-Palace......17
2.1.2.2 Leveling and Terracing......17
2.1.2.3 Construction and First Use......19
2.1.2.4 Use as Administrative Building......20
2.1.2.5 Chronology and the Seal Impressions of Tar'am-Agade......20
2.1.2.6 Chronological Phase Chart......22
2.1.3 AP Palace as a Royal Palace......24
2.1.4 Palace: Typology......26
2.1.4.1 Mirrored plan......26
2.1.4.2 Palace Entrance......26
2.1.4.3 Iwans......27
2.1.4.4 Rabbeting......29
2.1.4.5 Proportion of Room Area to Room Perimeter......30
2.1.5 The Perception of Space through the Optic, Acoustic, Haptic, Olfactory Senses......33
2.1.5.1 Sensing the Palace from Outside: Acoustic......34
2.1.5.2 Sensing the Palace from Outside: Optic......34
2.1.5.3 Sensing the Palace from Outside: Haptic......35
2.1.5.4 Sensing the Palace from Outside: Olfactory......36
2.1.6 Palace: in Relation to the Urban Setting......36
2.1.6.1 Elevations......36
2.1.6.2 abi......37
2.1.6.3 Canal and Lower Town to West......37

2.1.6.4 Plaza to East....38
2.1.6.5 Question of Access....38
2.1.6.6 Visibility....39
2.1.7 Building as Synthetic Whole....40
2.2 Analysis of AP Palace: Sectors and Installations....41
2.2.1 Palace Sectors and Rooms....42
2.2.1.1 Sectors A, B, C, D – The Service Wing of the AP Palace....43
2.2.1.2 Sectors E, F – Access to the North and East....49
2.2.1.3 Sector G – Possible Staircase Access....52
2.2.1.4 Sectors H and I – The Formal Wing of the AP Palace....53
2.2.1.5 Sectors Y, X and W – Outside areas of the AP Palace....59
2.2.2 Palace Installations....61
2.2.2.1 The 'Bathroom' Installation in C6....61
2.2.2.2 The Clay Bin in C2....62
2.2.2.3 The Charred Beams in C1....63
2.2.2.4 The Path in F1....65
2.2.2.5 The Kitchen Installations in D1....65
2.2.2.6 The Baked-Brick Platform F1-G1....66
2.2.2.7 The Drainage System in D and C....67
2.2.2.8 The Drain in H4....68
2.2.2.9 Well in H6....69
2.2.2.10 The Stone Courtyard H3....69
2.2.2.11 The Baked Brick Installation Below Courtyard H3....70
2.2.3 Palace Dimensions....71
2.3 Estimated Footprint of the Palace....71
2.3.1 Missing Sectors....71
2.3.1.1 Royal Residence....71
2.3.1.2 Access Point Towards Plaza....72
2.3.1.3 Scribal/Administrative Area....72
2.3.1.4 Religious Area....72
2.3.2 Estimate of Building Footprint....72
2.4 Selected Comparisons....74
2.4.1 Stone as Construction Material....74
2.4.2 Internal Terracing....75
2.4.3 Iwans....75
2.4.4 Mirrored Architecture....76
3 The Elements and Process of Construction....79
3.1 From *Chaîne Opératoire* to *Gedankenexperiment*....79
3.1.1 Applying a *Chaîne Opératoire* to Architecture....80
3.1.2 Sources for the Analysis....83

3.1.2.1 The Ethics of Including the Garshana Texts........................85
3.1.2.2 Postulate 1: Ethnoarchaeological Link................................85
3.1.2.3 Postulate 2: Continuity of Experience................................85
3.2 Materials..86
3.2.1 Stone..86
3.2.1.1 Use of Stone in Construction..87
3.2.1.2 Quarry possibilities near Mozan..88
3.2.1.3 Quarrying Techniques...88
3.2.1.4 Stone Working...92
3.2.1.5 Use of Limestone..93
3.2.1.6 Stone Construction at Tell Mozan.......................................93
3.2.2 Mudbrick...94
3.2.2.1 Use of Mudbrick in Construction...94
3.2.2.2 Process of mudbrick making...95
3.2.2.3 Materials needed to make mudbricks................................105
3.2.2.4 Half-bricks...106
3.2.2.5 Mudbrick Volume and Weight...108
3.2.2.6 'Timing' Mudbrick production..109
3.2.2.7 Storage of Mudbricks..110
3.2.2.8 Mudbricks and the AP Palace...111
3.2.2.9 Mudbrick Production at Mozan...112
3.2.3 Philological Considerations on Mudbrick, Mortar and Plaster. .113
3.2.3.1 Index of Terms..113
3.2.3.2 Sign for Mudbrick, Brickform...114
3.2.3.3 Calculating number of mudbricks needed.........................116
3.2.4 Mud Plaster and Mortar..117
3.2.5 Gypsum and Lime Plasters...118
3.2.6 Chaff...120
3.2.7 Wood..121
3.2.8 Reed matting..121
3.2.9 Fill Material...122
3.2.10 Tools...122
3.3 Know-How...123
3.3.1 Commissioning Ruler...124
3.3.2 Planning Team..125
3.3.2.1 Planning Team: City Planner..125
3.3.2.2 Planning Team: Economic/Manpower Coordinator...........126
3.3.2.3 Planning Team: Architect/Engineer/Surveyor....................128
3.3.3 Execution Team..129
3.3.3.1 Execution Team: Material Coordinators...........................129

3.3.3.2 Execution Team: Master Builder....129
3.3.3.3 Execution Team: Overseers....129
3.3.3.4 Execution Team: Construction Coordinator....130
3.3.4 Know-How and the AP Palace....130
3.4 Manpower....130
3.4.1 Divisions within the Workforce....131
3.4.1.1 Skilled/Unskilled Workers....132
3.4.1.2 Slaves....132
3.4.1.3 Hired workers....133
3.4.1.4 Workers from another locality....133
3.4.1.5 Workers and the Organization of Work....133
3.4.1.6 Worker Pay and Working Hours....135
3.4.2 Organization of Labor....135
3.4.2.1 Work Crews....136
3.4.2.2 Foremen, Forewomen....136
3.4.2.3 Overseers....136
3.4.2.4 Hierarchy Among Specialized Workers....137
3.4.2.5 Builders....137
3.4.2.6 Chief Administrators and Scribes....137
3.4.3 Transportation....137
3.4.3.1 The Transportation of Stone....138
3.4.3.2 Transportation of Mudbricks....142
3.4.3.3 The Transportation of Wooden Beams....143
3.4.3.4 The Transportation of Earth, Mortar, Plaster and Gypsum. 145
3.4.3.5 The Transportation of Reeds and Straw....146
3.4.3.6 The Tools of Transportation....147
3.4.4 Gender....147
3.4.5 Manpower and the AP Palace – a Hypothesis based on the Garshana Texts....148
3.4.5.1 Work-crew Tasks....149
3.5 Putting it all together: the *Chaîne Opératoire*....149
3.5.1 Timeline of Construction....149
3.5.1.1 Step 1: Commissioning of Project....150
3.5.1.2 Step 2: Establishing Planning Group....150
3.5.1.3 Step 3: Determining Constraints of the Project....150
3.5.1.4 Step 4: Building Plan....150
3.5.1.5 Step 5: Initial Pre-Construction Work....150
3.5.1.6 Step 6: Construction....151
3.5.2 Gathering, Processing and Transporting the Construction Materials....151

3.5.2.1 Stone....151
3.5.2.2 Mudbrick....153
3.5.2.3 Mud plaster and mortar....154
3.5.2.4 Gypsum and Lime....154
3.5.2.5 Chaff, Wood, and Reed Matting....155
3.5.3 Constructing the Palace: Putting Together the Pieces....155
3.5.3.1 Preparing the Worksite....157
3.5.3.2 Leveling, Terracing, Filling....158
3.5.3.3 Foundations, Drains....160
3.5.3.4 Stone Placement....161
3.5.3.5 Preparing the Finished Stonework....163
3.5.3.6 Laying the Mudbricks....163
3.5.3.7 Doorways and Windows....165
3.5.3.8 Preparing Wall-Tops for a Roof....166
3.5.3.9 Roof Construction....167
3.5.3.10 Plastering Walls, Laying Floors....172
3.5.3.11 Construction of Installations....172
3.5.3.12 Decoration and Movable Goods within the Building....172
3.6 Beyond the Chaîne Opératoire....173
3.6.1 Applying Algorithms to a Specific Structure....173
3.6.2 Construction and Ritual....175
3.6.3 The 'Who' of Construction....175
4 Theoretical Underpinnings of Architectural Analysis....177
4.1 Postulates....179
4.1.1 Postulate 1: The Ethnoarchaeological link....179
4.1.2 Postulate 2: Continuity of Experience....180
4.2 Context....181
4.2.1 Variables of Design....182
4.2.2 The Influence of Vernacular on Planned Architecture....182
4.2.3 The Role of Architecture in Creating an Urban Environment....183
4.2.4 Architecture and History....184
4.3 Actors....186
4.3.1 The Human Background....186
4.3.2 Palace Architecture: Motivations for Change....187
4.3.2.1 Architecture as a Statement of Disassociation....188
4.3.2.2 Using Architecture to Change the Message....189
4.3.2.3 Affecting the Urban Texture....190
4.3.2.4 Using Architecture to Achieve or Reaffirm Elite Status....191
4.3.2.5 Deciding not to Build a Palace....192
4.3.3 The Architect as Agent....192

4.4 The Search for Meaning in Architecture....193
4.4.1 Style in Architecture....194
4.4.2 The Role of 3D Modeling as a Heuristic Vehicle....195
4.4.3 The Value of Architecture....196
4.4.3.1 Value and Energetics....197
4.4.3.2 Value and Function....199
4.4.3.3 Value and Social Institutions....199
5 The Construction of 3D Models: Methodological Aspects....201
5.1 The *UFO Problem*....201
5.2 The Problem of Interaction: Archaeology and 3D Technology....202
5.2.1 Accuracy....202
5.2.2 Use of the Model....203
5.2.3 The Fourth Dimension....203
5.3 The Need for 3D Models....204
5.3.1 The 3D Model's Ancestor: Hand-drawn Illustrations....204
5.3.2 Goal for 3D Modeling: Communication....206
5.3.3 Goal for 3D Modeling: Visual Interactivity....207
5.3.4 Goal for 3D Modeling: Problematics of Reconstruction....208
5.3.5 Goal for 3D Modeling: Volumetrics....208
5.3.6 Visualizing 3D in Three Dimensions....209
5.3.7 The Power of 3D Models....210
5.4 Current 3D Modeling Practices....210
5.4.1 Extrude 3D from 2D....211
5.4.2 Complex Models....211
5.4.3 Photo-modeling....211
5.4.4 3D Scans....212
5.5 Embracing Simplicity: BlockGen....212
5.5.1 Desiderata....213
5.5.1.1 Precision in Reflecting the Actual Archaeological Record. 213
5.5.1.2 Use, As much as Possible, Data Already Collected in the Field....213
5.5.1.3 Have the Results Available in a Lasting Format....213
5.5.1.4 Allow for the Integration of Stratigraphy as well as Architecture....213
5.5.1.5 Allow for the Inclusion of Objects....214
5.5.1.6 Allow for Change and Expansion of the Data....214
5.5.1.7 Allow for the Inclusion of the Model in Other Programs...214
5.5.2 Data Collecting in the Field: Planning and Methods....214
5.5.2.1 Method 1: Surveying....214
5.5.2.2 Method 2: Photogrammetry and Elevation Measurements. 215

5.5.2.3 Method 3: Extrapolation from Publications....................215
5.5.3 Using Scripts....................215
5.6 Beyond the Architectural Model: Software....................216
5.6.1 AutoCAD....................217
5.6.1.1 Adding to the Model....................217
5.6.1.2 Using the Model....................217
5.6.1.3 Exporting to other Programs....................219
5.6.2 GIS Programs....................219
5.6.2.1 Integrating the 3D Model with Other Data Sources....................219
5.6.3 Animation Programs....................220
5.6.3.1 Specific Lighting....................220
5.6.3.2 Walkthrough....................220
5.6.3.3 Reproduce Camera Images....................221
5.6.3.4 Avatars and Activities....................221
5.6.4 First-Person Interactive Environments....................221
5.6.4.1 Interaction as Communication....................222
5.6.4.2 Programming Example: Cave UT....................222
5.6.4.3 Online Environments....................222
5.7 Beyond the Architectural Model: Concepts....................223
5.7.1 Architecture and Stratigraphy....................224
5.7.2 The Movable and the Stationary....................225
5.7.3 Realtime Representation....................226
5.7.4 3D in a Didactic Context....................227
5.7.4.1 Communication of Meaning: Presenting the Value of Archaeology....................228
5.7.4.2 The Ethical Dimension of Communication....................228
5.7.4.3 Interactivity....................229
6 Application to the Tupkish Palace at Urkesh....................231
6.1 Exploring the 3D Model....................232
6.1.1 The Data....................232
6.1.2 Layers: Stone....................233
6.1.3 Layers: Brick....................236
6.1.4 Layers: Installations....................242
6.1.5 The Precision of the 3D Model....................244
6.1.6 Calculating Volumes....................246
6.2 Using the 3D Model of the AP Palace as a Tool....................246
6.2.1 Combining the 3D Model with the Algorithms....................247
6.2.1.1 Algorithms: Quarry....................248
6.2.1.2 Algorithms: Stone....................248
6.2.1.3 Algorithms: Mudbrick Production....................249

6.2.2 Looking at Visibility....251
6.2.3 Time, Work crews and Volume....252
6.2.4 The Cost of Monumentality....252
7 Impact and Directions for Future Research....255
7.1 Impact....255
7.2 Future Research....256
Bibliography....259
Appendix: BlockGen Vademecum and Program Code....279
AP Palace Wall Catalog....299
Alphabetical Index....351
List of Illustrations....357
List of Tables....363

Foreword

This volume by Federico Buccellati deals with a theme that has developed from his many years of work at the excavation in Tell Mozan (Northeast Syria) – the analysis, interpretation and reconstruction of the AP Palace from the 3rd millennium BC. In general, it should be stated that this monograph is an unusual, very impressive work – here is not a 'compendium of data' of digging results, but a very highly theoretical treatment of an architecture complex at a high intellectual level.

Striking is the use of the *chaîne opératoire* method for analyzing the individual steps of the building of the palace – a method that has increasingly become the focus of archaeological research in recent years, albeit seldom applied to architecture. The method is based on the assumption that technical processes and social actions can be understood in a step-by-step analysis. The implementation here has been highly successful, not only on the technical side but also including the social dimension (commissioning ruler, workers) – in particular the inclusion of the Garshana texts, references to the work process, a consideration of the persons involved and a study of the working time make this study such a success. Thus, it becomes possible to reconstruct not only the society in which the architectural complexes were created, but also the social context, the actions and the ideas connected with the building. As an example, the author uses elements of sociology to consider architectural forms, analyzing the effects of a physical environment on social behavior, such as communication, by means of sensory perception – acoustic, optical, haptic, olfactory.

Striking is also the verification of the analytical and material- or production-related results by means of theoretical models. For this study two 'qualities' are selected and pursued from the multitude of possible approaches: ethno-archaeological and historical analogies. This ability of the author to reformulate the ideas developed in other contexts for his own line of questioning can be seen in the inclusion of the exhibition concept "Shrinking Cities" in the German Architectural Museum, Frankfurt am Main in 2007-08. The ideas developed in the exhibit (which was neither archaeological nor centered on the Ancient Near East) were applied by the author to the reconstruction of the urban texture in the Ancient Near East, in particular for the case of Tell Mozan / Urkesh. The author consistently goes far beyond the presentation of the archaeological findings and attempts to develop approaches which aim to understand the human and social conditions tied to the architecture. In developing these approaches, the value of digital 3D models becomes clear as a heuristic tool for analysis, especially in regard to the interpretation of architecture. A large portion of the volume is thus the presentation of the methodological foundations (BlockGen) and the development of these 3D models. This software is based on AutoCAD and can be integrated into a GIS program, which can be extended by means of animated animation programs (lighting, possibilities for walking through, avatars). This allows the user to experience the 'real' experience of the relevant architecture and its environment, while at the same time providing a deeper understanding of the interpretation of archaeological field work. At the same time, 'primary data' in the archaeological record, such as different stratigraphic observations, can be relatively easily integrated. Thus the 3D model developed can already be supplemented during the course of the excavation and possibly used to alter the excavation strategies in realtime. In addition to providing an environment in which to experience the architecture and integrate diverse archaeological data, it also provides a didactic platform: this tool can be used as a portal for a wider public to encounter and understand archaeological results.

This volume presents an extensive body of excavation material which has been expertly documented, interpreted by means of an impressively innovative approach. This approach, as well as the theoretical considerations, speak to the wide impact that this work will have in our field, while at the same time being a real pleasure to read.

Jan-Waalke Meyer

Preface

My initial interest was in providing a documentary description of the AP Palace, in the excavations of which I have taken part since the beginning. In particular I was responsible, in whole or in part, for the excavation of units A10, A13 and A16. The publication of the AP Palace as excavated is presented in chapter 2.

At the same time, I developed a strong interest in two aspects of architectural analysis that went beyond the "philological" dimension, in two parallel directions.

The first aimed at understanding the architectural process as it took place in antiquity, with regard to the way in which a structure would be both constructed in practice and planned in a design phase. This has involved me in a serious confrontation not only with the underlying theory, but also with a project of experimental archaeology with which I tested some of the inherent assumptions. The use of the *chaîne opératoire* method helps to see the individual steps as a series of linked moments in a complete process of construction. While the *chaîne opératoire* method can aid in understanding the individual steps, what is still needed is a way to quantify the energy (in terms of manhours) needed for each step. Thus the analysis of the process of construction is augmented by a series of generalized algorithms designed to determine the cost in terms of energy for as many of the steps detailed in the *chaîne opératoire* as possible. This is presented in chapter 3.

The second theoretical aspect that I developed pertains to the use of 3D modeling not only as a technical tool, but as the application of a method that impacts the field of archaeology by showing how a 3D model is a tool for research. My main effort in this direction was to show how the development of a flexible tool for creating recursive 3D models in the field would help in a major way to produce a record at a higher level of documentary sophistication, and integrate it with the ethnographic data in order to quantify the specifics of construction. The model of the AP Palace is thus more than documentation: it is a tool with which one can calculate, through the general algorithms defined in chapter 3, the 'cost' in energy of choices made in the construction of the Palace or study questions regarding visibility. I argue for this in chapters 5 and 6.

The ability to link the archaeological data on an epistemological level, with questions on an interpretative level, such as prestige, is a fundamental aspect of the research presented here. Often questions which focus on theoretical, social or interpretative aspects are not directly tied to the archaeological data, and this problem is particularly felt when speaking of architecture: this study presents a method for how to link, on a very specific level, data and interpretation.

In dealing with these aspects of analysis a number of themes arose on a theoretical level which, because of their level of abstraction, were tangential to the discussion being made in each chapter. However, these theoretical themes have influenced the work I have done and help contextualize the material being presented – thus they are included in chapter 4.

I feel that this approach yields rich results for the understanding of an otherwise mute ancient record and for an innovative use of techniques that are typically invoked as an after the fact, *deus ex machina* type of intervention.

Federico Buccellati

Acknowledgments

First and foremost, I would like to thank my parents, whose support as parents and as teachers could not be greater. The pride with which I dedicate this work to them is incalculable.

This study, and my own intellectual growth, have been guided and encouraged by Jan-Waalke Meyer, to whom I owe the unrepayable debt of a student to his teacher. From my first visit to Frankfurt up to the writing of these words he has always had all the time in the world for me – between many a coffee and (his) cigarette, the ideas on which this book rests were discussed.

My thanks also to Pascal Butterlin, whose shared passion for architecture and willingness to better this study is very much appreciated, as well as Ditmar Machule, who came in at the end with infectious enthusiasm.

I owe a great thanks to the people of the Jezireh, modern and ancient. It is difficult, at times, to focus on the distant past when one hears on a daily basis of the horrors of social upheaval. It is my fervent hope that my contribution to the understanding of the ancient past of the area may accompany a pride in the shared history of all those who call the region their home. My thanks in particular to Samer Abdel-Ghafur, Sarkis Balian and Samer Kabawat as well as all the people who have worked at Mozan, uncovering our shared past with intelligence, generosity and pride.

My wife, Maria Gabriella Micale, has encouraged me in every way during the writing and correcting of this volume – her support, moral and practical, made the process easier and the final product better in so many ways. Thank you.

Jack W. Kessler and the trustees of the International Institute for Mesopotamian Area Studies have supported the work done at Mozan for decades, and have taken particular interest in my efforts. Presenting this finished study to them is a moment of pride for me, and it is with regret that Sandy Elster and Hermann Hoeh are not able to share this moment with us.

The Research Training Group "Value and Equivalence" in Frankfurt has provided more than just the financial means which made this work possible: it also provided a stimulating intellectual environment and a group of young scholars who became friends. My thanks to those who made the RTG possible and encouraged my intellectual growth along the way, in particular Annabel Bokern, Hans-Markus von Kaenel, Franziska Lang and Thomas Richter.

Kenneth Judge and Mahdi Sajjad have not yet seen the palace firsthand, but their support even beyond the events of 2010 meant that Mozan could continue, and to see them 'catch the bug' of archaeology at Mozan encourages all of us to reach for greater goals. Souren Vartanian was able to come to Mozan, and he was immediately enchanted with the palace; his passion and support were a great boost to our work.

Thanks to the colleagues and friends who have supported me in this endeavor, particularly Ernestine Elster, Diane Favro, James Sackett, Monica Smith and James Snead at UCLA. A special thanks to Jerry Scordan, who gave me a lot of insights into how to treat my 'muse'. Last but not least, my grandmother Claire, zio Ico and zio Gianmaria: *il sangue non è acqua*.

1 Introduction

Spatial relationships are among the most important aspects of field archaeology, and the ability to discern and define discrete architectural elements within a stratigraphically complex archaeological context is one of the hardest tasks an archaeologist faces. The results of such an understanding are equally difficult to communicate, and only two methods of graphic representation (besides photography) have been widely used. First, two-dimensional drawings (in plan and section) which retain a high degree of accuracy and usefulness in scientific analysis, but do not render volumetric relationships. Second, three-dimensional drawings (or various kinds of models) which allow for a greater perception of the architectural and stratigraphic reality, but are often limited to an artistic, as opposed to an accurate, depiction, and are therefore less useful in a scientific analysis.

This study will approach this set of problems with reference to the Palace of King Tupkish (AP Palace) at Tell Mozan, ancient Urkesh. This palace dates from the latter part of the third millennium B.C., and can be attributed to a specific king, Tupkish, on the basis of seal impressions found within the rooms. The site lies within the Mesopotamian cultural horizon, and can probably be tied to the Hurrian ethnic group (G. Buccellati 2009b). The technological portion of this study goes hand in hand with a detailed architectural study of the palace itself, whereby the construction and particulars of each architectural segment are thoroughly analyzed.

This study first considers (in ch. 2) analytical questions relating to the Tupkish Palace such as function, access, and covered areas vs. courtyards. Next, the material from the archaeological record, parallels drawn from ethnographic analogies and textual evidence are used to explore (in ch. 3) the materials used, knowledge required, manpower needs, as well as the steps taken in the building process. One of the most important tools is the *chaîne opératoire*, which helps isolate production steps and the required know-how.

A discussion of questions related to theory follows, aiming to highlight the postulates underlying this work as well as some of the potential avenues for research (ch. 4). Questions relating to context, actors and meaning as related to the theoretical dimension of architecture are explored.

On the basis of the data presented in the preceding sections, a method for creating a 3D model is proposed (ch. 5). The reasons for a new approach are discussed, and its integration with other programs is highlighted. Two aspects of integration within an archaeological project are explored more in depth: stratigraphy and didactics. This new method relies on tools with which many archaeologists are already familiar (e. g. AutoCAD) and uses spatial data that are, at least in part, already present in the standard documentation. By stressing simplicity and modularity over details of aesthetics, this method can be used by an archaeologist while in the field, instead of being the domain of a 3D specialist.

Finally, the excavated portions of the AP Palace at Mozan are modeled using this method (ch. 6). The 3D model is explained in depth, and the model is queried for volumetric information which is then put together with the data from the previous chapters, in particular chapter 3.

1.1 Approach

The goals of the research rest on three pillars: the *data*, i. e., the archaeological evidence from the AP Palace at Tell Mozan; the *theory*, which explores the volumes in themselves and in relationship to their stratigraphic context, the people who use the space and the broader urban environment; and a new *technique*, that of a simple but effective way through which an archaeologist can build a 3D model and use it to explore research questions. It is through the interplay of these three elements that the goals of this study can be reached.

The Palace of King Tupkish (AP Palace) was built during the Akkadian period, approximately 2250 B.C. This corresponds to the period between the reigns of Sargon and Naram-Sin. The initial analysis will focus on the architectural elements present in the building, looking primarily at questions of access, function and roof/lighting. The building has not been fully excavated, but enough material has been uncovered for a thorough study.

The theoretical dimension is central to this research. While theory is helpful in providing the conceptual framework within which the data can be understood at a higher level of meaning, it is also important to study it on its own merits.

The archaeological record provides both a diachronic view of the life of a building as well as the footprint of the architectural monument. This temporal element, combined with the incompleteness of the architectural record as excavated, means that many steps in the rendering of the construction and use of a building must be postulated, however much these postulates may be grounded in the contemporary sources or ethnographic data. Here questions of theory can help further bridge the gaps in the record, as well as develop questions exploring both diachronic and synchronic relationships. The methods used in this study also benefit from a theoretical underpinning, as well as some consideration as to the inevitable downside to the use of certain methods and models.

Questions of audience, function, individuality vs. tradition and the place of architecture within the urban environment are further theoretical considerations that help explore the larger picture by embedding the data in other conceptual structures.

The primary technique developed in this study is the way in which 3D modeling can better contribute to the scholarship of Near Eastern Archaeology and, in fact, of archaeology in general. Currently, the most common use of 3D models is in the realm of visualization in an *illustrative* setting. Illustrative because such 3D models are most often created for and used during presentations to a larger audience, be it as a digital slide presentation or distributed on paper in one form or another, or at most as a video. This usage of 3D models is a continuation of the tradition of axial drawings that are often used in older publications.[1] Such drawings are very useful for imagining the spatial volume of a building or other architectural environment, but it does not do justice to the potential of this technology.

There is a second technique adapted to the data in this study, namely the combination of *chaîne opératoire* (ch.3) and G*edankenexperiment* (ch.6). These tools have rarely been used to study architecture, if at all, but provide a means to explore the practical realities of such a construction through the archaeological record and ethnographic comparisons.

1.2 Architectural Analysis

The first step in the analysis of the data is a detailed study of the building: the individual sectors, rooms, and construction elements present in the AP Palace. This analysis focuses on the archaeological record, in particular questions regarding function and access. Parallel to and supported by this analysis, broader questions can also be discussed, regarding chronology, the place of the building in the urban texture, and comparable architecture on a local and regional level.

The Palace of Tupkish at Tell Mozan, ancient Urkesh, can be dated to the Akkadian period (approximately 2250 B.C.). The chronology is confirmed by three different dating methods: Radio-Carbon analysis of samples from the palace, the presence of seal-impressions from the daughter of Naram-Sin in one of the levels of the palace, as well as the typological evidence from glyptic and ceramic finds.

1 Two of the best known examples are by Margueron (1982) and Heinrich (1984).

The palace has been only partially excavated, but what has been uncovered allows one to explore patterns in construction and to estimate the extent of the complete palace, as well as give a series of hypothetical models as to what the complete footprint of the Palace looked like.

A question that is of central importance, but is often taken for granted, is the very nature of the definition of the building as a Palace. Even though the case of the Urkesh AP structure seems clearly to offer a *prima facie* evidence for it being so interpreted, a clear case can be made for understanding the structure as a Royal Palace.

Enough of the tell has been excavated so that the place of the palace within the urban texture can be discussed. In particular the relationship between the city-wall, a monumental necromantic shaft (known as the *abi*), the central urban plaza, the temple terrace and the palace gives a unique look into the overall layout of the city.

In addition to studying the various architectural elements of the building, there is a cohesion to the building as a whole that can be studied, both as a synthetic consideration of the sum of the analytic portions studied in the preceding sections, as well as a single unified structure. The building method can be explored through questions regarding the exploitation of sunlight (involving the shape and location of courtyards), as well as rooms used perhaps for storage, and circulation patterns, which show the planning that went into carefully controlling access.

Certain areas of the palace combine rooms around courtyards, and are also tied to certain activities. One of the primary architectural elements which define the various sectors is the positioning of doorways to limit or facilitate access to certain areas of the palace, which also raises questions regarding the line-of-sight between sectors and rooms. On the basis of these considerations, sectors have been defined. This division is based on modern considerations of the archaeological record, but the formal elements that support the theory are clear enough that it is plausible to assume that it reflects the ancient view of the division of architectural space.

The rooms of the AP Palace were designed to fit the needs of the royal court. These functions can be determined based on installations in the rooms, the presence of certain categories of objects in the rooms or the location of the room within the building as a whole. Some of these rooms form identifiable clusters, which in turn are combined with other elements to respond to these needs.

Additionally, it is important to consider the fact that the Palace was not built in a neutral environment – rather, when it was built there were already various topographical constraints posed by earlier settlement levels. To adapt to these constraints, the palace was built on two levels in order to provide the necessary space. These levels were then integrated into the architecture, with the more important sectors of the building placed on the higher terrace. Thus, even if this difference within sectors was conditioned to some extent by the preexisting topography, the way in which the architect adapted to this reality was a distinct choice.

The second constraint was the first city wall (see section 2.1), which had been superseded by a larger city wall enclosing a much larger area. The palace was constructed so that its western edge would sit on top of this older city wall, allowing it to see, and be seen by, the lower city and a portion of the surrounding plains. This too was a distinct choice, not only on the part of the architect but also on the part of the person responsible for defense, since the removal of a part of the city wall negated its defensive nature, meaning the defensive function was then carried solely by the city wall surrounding the lower city.

After this detailed study of the building it is important to see its most marked elements within a wider context, and as such comparative material will be provided, in particular with regard to the use of stone in construction, terracing, the use of *iwans*,[2] and the mirrored elements in the building's footprint.

1.3 Elements and Process of Construction

In order to understand the volumes of the constructed architecture, as well as the process of construction, it is necessary to consider three aspects of the act of building: the materials, the know-how and the manpower needed. These combine to form an understanding of the process in general, expressed in the format of a series of *chaîne opératoire*. These considerations are founded on three different sources: the archaeological record of the AP Palace, ethnographic studies that examine modern practices, and textual data from other sites.

The materials from which the AP Palace was constructed come from the region, and are similar to the materials used in other structures in the city: sun-dried mudbricks, hewn stone, gypsum plaster, wood and straw. Apart from straw, these materials would not have been readily available in the immediate vicinity of the city in the quantities needed for such a large public building, but would have had to have been brought in. Even the soil needed for the mudbricks would have had to come from outside the city, from an area where a large hole would not have disrupted agriculture. Thus, each of these materials had to come from a satellite production facility, and transported to

2 For more on the use of the term *iwan* see section 2.4.3.

the construction site.

Among the laborers at the construction site there would have to be a certain group of people with special skills, comprising the necessary know-how for the construction. One group of people would have been involved in the planning of the building, much like an architect today. These persons would have been the most specialized in the group, since their experience could not be carried over directly from the private sector, rather they would be specialized in the planning and execution of massive public buildings. Another class of laborer would be specialists in administration, organizing the pay/rations of the workers at satellite and local work areas, the transportation of materials and the long term planning of material availability. A third group would be involved in the technical aspects of the construction, such as bricklayers, roofers and so on, all under the control of one or more skilled contractors. The final group would be involved in decoration, for example wall decoration. A further group would have been involved in the transportation of building materials.

The manpower needed for such a project would have been considerable; unfortunately there is little evidence for the numbers of people employed in the construction of the AP Palace, but some inferences can be made, primarily from the textual and ethnographic sources. Using this information, one can hypothesize how many people would have been needed and how long it would have taken to produce materials for the construction of the Palace, as well as aspects of the construction itself.

Each of these elements can be combined and understood as a process, or series of actions. This way of studying the material is called *chaîne opératoire* in the literature, and, while it is primarily used to study lithic artifacts, it can also help in the analysis of architecture. In a way, applying the *chaîne opératoire* method to architecture involves 'nesting' several smaller 'chains' into a single larger one. For example, the making of mudbricks, the transportation of materials and the construction of walls are each a separate 'chain' but are also part of a larger 'chain' which describes the construction of the building.

While the *chaîne opératoire* provides a clear understanding of the individual steps, one needs a way to calculate the cost in terms of energy of each of those steps. A series of algorithms have been developed from diverse sources: ethnoarchaeological experiments, ancient textual material and modern ethnographic experiments.

The consideration of individual elements and their combination into *chaîne opératoire* is a general methodology that can be applied to a great many buildings from this time-period in the Near East. By combining the volumetric data with this general understanding of the process of construction and the algorithms which aid in defining the energetic cost of each step, a hypothetical construction model is generated for the AP Palace with regard to materials, operations, actors, energetic cost and timeline.

1.4 Theoretical Underpinnings of Architectural Analysis

This study raises a number of theoretical questions and, through its analysis, opens the door to several possible avenues of further research. While these theoretical aspects can, and should, be pursued in depth, they are not the focus of this study. Nevertheless they bear mention, since these underpinnings and further avenues of study remain tied to the analysis presented here.

Two postulates are made: first, that there is a link between some modern and ancient practices, also called the ethnographic analogy, and that this analogy can provide information with which one can better understand the past. The second postulate states that on the most basic level there are common perceptual or psychological reactions to interactions with the space around us, which architecture seeks to exploit, and we as moderns can perceive.

Three further theoretical aspects can be tied to the analysis presented here: questions regarding context, actors and meaning. The context of architecture, in a theoretical sense, is tied to the variables of design, the influence of vernacular architecture as well as the interaction with the urban environment and its historical dimension.

The tasks and know-how of the people involved in the construction are described in chapter 3, but there are some actors whose involvement can be considered on a deeper level. The motivations behind the decision to construct a new palace (or not) can be hypothesized, with regard to who makes the decision, as well as the reasons behind it.

There is also the fact that architecture is often studied as if divorced from other art historical studies, limiting the sophistication of analysis (Zevi 1972, 11); thus a study of architectural works from this era is a study of works 'in search of an author'. But the architect is very much an actor in the process of building, even if little is known about the person as such.

1.5 Construction of 3D Models: Methodological Aspects

Too often three-dimensional models are considered graphics, produced by 3D artists after and apart from the process of excavation itself. The practical consensus in archaeology is that a 3D model is to be created at the end of an excavation, as a tool for communicating to a wider public, and is best used to model single architectural complexes in great detail.

This study shows that a 3D model can be much more. First, a 3D model should be worked on during the excavation, adding each piece as a separately documented element. Just as an archaeologist finds a building piece by piece, a 3D model which documents this process should be built in the same fashion. Such a model has as its origin the actual archaeological record; models which are created only once the archaeological process has ended tend to communicate a 'finished' perception or even reconstructed understanding. These are certainly useful aims, but they are scientifically useful only if they arise from accurate documentation and modeling during the archaeological process. This approach has a powerful heuristic value because it is of immeasurable help in projecting potential scenarios relating to a building under excavation, and thus in shaping the day-to-day strategy (F. Buccellati and Kansa 2016).

Second, there is the impression in archaeology that 3D models are primarily useful as a tool for communicating to a wider public. Instead, such models can be an invaluable tool for research in archaeology. With a precise model of the architecture it is possible to measure the structure in the following ways: quantity and quality of materials used, and beyond that the planning and know-how which went into the construction. The form of the structure is dictated by the preexisting urban topography, and this can be well documented in a 3D model that includes the depth of the foundations. Finally, a 3D model allows for an analysis of the rooms and courtyards within the structure with regard to lighting and access.

The third impression is that 3D models are to be used to model single architectural complexes in great detail, as architecture. Here too this study presents an alternative: a 3D model can also be used to show the interaction of several archaeological complexes in use in the same time period, the change in structures over time, or the location of structures under the existing tell surface.

Ideally, a 3D model that serves the needs just outlined should be easy to construct, should show different possibilities for reconstruction, and should be sufficiently modular to allow its expansion alongside the excavation, serving as a real tool in research while being at the same time as realistic as possible. Unfortunately, some of these elements are almost mutually exclusive, such as ease and realism. However, by removing the need for some realistic aspects (textural and surface realism), many if not all of the other conditions can be achieved.

The model proposed here is based on scripts that can be used in AutoCAD. By taking precise measurements in the field, a model built of blocks can be generated whereby the exact coordinates of each of the eight corners of each block can be defined. By combining such blocks, almost all construction elements found in an archaeological context can be recreated. The software used to create such blocks from scripts is called BlockGen, and was programmed specifically for this study, since this function does not exist in current versions of AutoCAD. The technical details and a vademecum of this function will be presented in the Appendix.

As a tool, such a model, combined with an understanding of the process, can help construct hypotheses as to the process of construction of a specific construction project, or the structure can be seen in the context of the remainder of the ancient mound, allowing for hypotheses concerning urban planning and chronological topography to be posited and tested. But it is only because it is the archaeologists themselves who produce the model that it becomes integrated into both the documentation and interpretation of the archaeological record. One example of the usefulness of this three-dimensional approach as a tool is how it renders very visible the impact of orientation to the sun. The process of constructing a three-dimensional model and using it as a tool for analysis means that questions arise that are often not considered when a building is examined in a 2D plan or section.[3]

The model in and of itself is already a tool for research, but it is possible to integrate this kind of model into other programs used in archaeology, such as GIS platforms or animation programs. Additionally, the models can be imported into first-person interactive environments. These programs allow the archaeologist and other users the possibility to visualize the data in new ways and combine it with other information, but it is equally important to look beyond the capability of programs to the conceptual potential that these technologies have: the integration of stratigraphic layers into the model, the inclusion of the find spots for groups of objects, the potential for real-time use of the model in the field and its inherent communication which can be broadened and adapted to reach a wider audience.

1.6 Application to the AP Palace

The 3D model of the AP Palace, as generated with the BlockGen plug-in in AutoCAD, contains 48 wall segments consisting of over 1500 points. Here the model is presented, along with a discussion of the technical advantages and disadvantages of the BlockGen program in this specific case.

The next step in this study is to apply the general understanding of the

3 There are, of course, several notable exceptions, such as the previously cited works of Margueron 1982 and Heinrich 1984.

construction process developed in chapter 3 to the 3D model of the AP Palace. While the *chaîne opératoire* method allows scholars to analyze the technical aspects on a general level of the construction, it is also limited by this focus. The application of this understanding to the specific case of the AP Palace, as defined by the 3D model, might be called a *Gedankenexperiment*. This term highlights the fact that, as archaeologists, one has very limited (if any) evidence of the process of construction in the archaeological record, but by combining the general discussion of construction from chapter 3 with the specific information that the 3D model can give, one can generate a convincing hypotheses as to the specifics of the construction of a certain building.

1.7 Impact and Directions for Future Research

Ideally, this study will have four consequences. The first will simply be to contribute to the comprehensive documentary publication of the Tell Mozan excavations by giving a detailed analysis of the AP Palace. The second is to explore the potential information to be gained from the archaeological record, ethnographic analogies, and textual data, in order to understand the materials, know-how, manpower and process of construction. The third is to provide a discussion of those elements of theory which are tied to the architectural analysis presented here, highlighting aspects of context, actors and meaning. Finally, this study provides a method for creating 3D models (BlockGen), a vademecum to aid archaeologists who want to use the program, as well as a concrete example (the AP Palace).

Future studies may include comparing the 3D model and other palaces in the region in order to examine the relative effort employed, as well as explore questions regarding the materials available and the potential for the expression of prestige and monumentality. The ethnographic analogy might be further explored, and more comparisons (especially from other regions) might be added. The BlockGen plug-in might be adapted for an open source CAD program, so that the models are not dependent on a for-profit platform, and it might be expanded in order to include more complex shapes, vaults for example. Finally, the chapter on theory provides a number of directions for future research.

"We shape our dwellings, and afterwards our dwellings shape us."
W. Churchill, 28 October 1944

2 Architectural Analysis

To investigate the AP Palace from the perspective of the architecture means looking at the palace on several different levels, considered sequentially in the following steps, from largest to smallest.

The first is to look at the palace as a whole, investigating questions such as the 'royal' designation, the position within the ancient city, the chronology and typological considerations. Also, installations will be discussed here, since they contribute to the overall understanding of the palace. Some of the more important installations include the drainage system, a hearth, a bin and a stone-paved courtyard.

The second step is an analysis of the palace in terms of the sectors of the palace, i. e. with regard to how these sectors may be described and to the function and interaction between sectors, followed by the installations found in the rooms of the palace, and finally the dimensions of the various rooms and sectors of the palace. Twelve sectors have been defined for the palace, clustered in five groups: service sectors, access sectors, staircase, the formal wing and the outer areas. When of particular interest, the individual rooms will be referred to, in particular when discussing the installations discussed in the first section, and when they aid us in defining the function of the spaces. It is not the aim of this study to include the finds from each of the rooms, since this material should be approached as a typological study and the vast quantity of finds makes including them here prohibitive.[4] It is my aim to present here the information needed to provide the context for these typological studies, and the 3D portion of this study would be a logical beginning for distribution analyses of such finds.

The third step is to look beyond the excavated portions of the palace to

4 Two studies have already been published relating to the finds in the palace: see Bianchi 2012 and Hauser 2006.

determine what functional spaces are expected to be found within the areas of the palace hitherto unexcavated, as well as hypotheses as to the spatial extension of the palace and its relationship to other urban structures.

Lastly, it is necessary to look at a few select *comparative structures*. The aim here is not to give a complete overview of palaces in the ancient Near East, nor even in the Syro-Mesopotamian area, but only to highlight similarities and differences that other palaces within the region have in relation to the AP Palace. Elements such as stone construction, internal terracing, *iwans* and planning are of particular interest.

It is also necessary to limit the scope of this study – it is meant as an architectural overview, which does not include the finds within the rooms except for two cases (seal impressions in B1 and H1, and the small charred beams in C1) where these objects are fundamental for an understanding of function. This means that a detailed room analysis or *Raumbuch* (Klein 2001, 77) for the excavation areas is not envisioned in this publication, nor is an analysis of the pottery or small finds. The diverse excavation units which lead to the discovery of the palace are being published within the Urkesh Global Record series of digital publication,[5] with the unit directors as authors. Wherever possible the feature and object numbers from these units will be included, so that readers can also refer to those publications. Many of the points here have been published elsewhere in season reports or other publications, and where appropriate these publications have been cited; as such, this portion of the study is, in large part, an overview of work done on the Palace as a whole.

2.1 The AP Palace as a Whole

The first step in our analysis is to consider the AP Palace as a whole. The first question relates to the position of the palace within the urban framework of the city as uncovered to date. To what extent does the placement of the palace influence its function, and how does its placement affect the surrounding structures and the infrastructure, such as the road network and city defenses?

A second question considers the chronology of the building leads to an understanding of the life of the building: how long was it used and how did the activities taking place within the structure change over time?

Thirdly, the function of the structure – why can one understand it as a palace, and is it a 'royal' palace? Was the palace a residence, or an administrative seat? Did it perform both functions?

Fourthly, the palace has elements which fit into a wider typological

5 For the Global Record digital publication series see www.urkesh.com.

understanding. A direct comparison with other similar structures is not intended here, rather a consideration of the palace within the wider context of 'standard' architectural formulae.

The fifth point focuses on the perception of space; the palace was probably considered as a whole only when seen from the outside, and even here it is unlikely that there were many points within the city from which a significant portion of the perimeter of the palace could be seen. Visibility is not the only criteria for perception: the optic, acoustic, haptic and olfactory perception of the palace from the perspective of someone outside of the structure itself also plays an important role in the consideration of the palace as a whole.

The sixth point expands on the consideration of the palace within a context as it were, discussing the relationship between the palace and the buildings around it. While not much has been excavated in the area immediately surrounding the Palace, structures such as the inner city wall, the *abi*, the plaza and the temple terrace all contribute to our understanding of the urban environment.

Illustration 1: AP Palace without the wall coverings, looking North.

The seventh and final point concerns the building as a synthetic whole. The points mentioned up to now concern the palace as an analytic whole: a whole studied with regard to its internal divisions. It is important to pair this view of the palace with a synthetic one – where the palace is seen as a conglomeration of interacting parts which are defined as a single unit. Questions of design, interaction and organization come to the fore in such an approach.

2.1.1 *Palace: Position*

The AP Palace sits on the western side of the high mound, along the southern slope of hill A. A series of soundings on hill A conducted since the beginning of excavations at Tell Mozan have revealed a series of occupation layers above and to the North of the AP Palace.

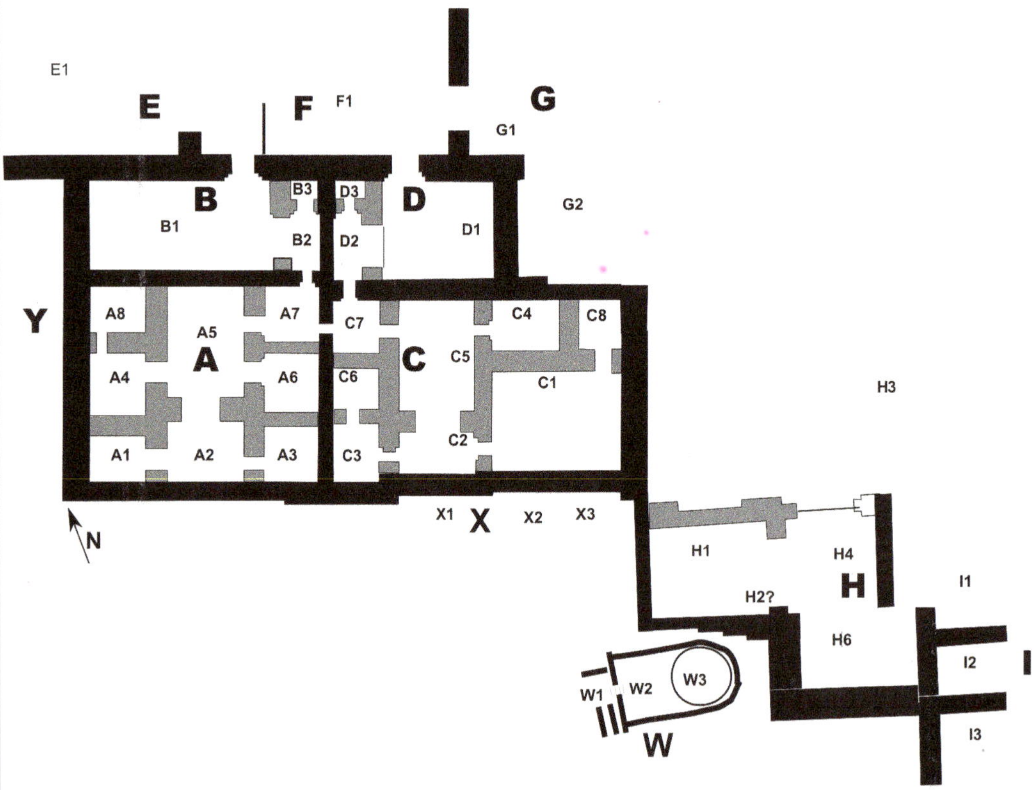

Illustration 2: AP Palace showing Sectors and room numbers.

A total of sixteen excavation areas reached the palace levels: A1, A2, A5, A6, A7, A8, A9, A10, A11, A12, A13, A14, A15, A16, A17, A19. The layout of the AP Palace is clearly affected by preexisting topographic elements. In the first place, there is a difference in elevation of two meters between the floors of sectors A-B-C-D and Sectors H-I. No point of access between the two areas has been discovered to date, but an access staircase has been hypothesized in sector G, which remains largely to be excavated (G. Buccellati and Kelly-Buccellati 2000, 133–41). This difference in elevation can be explained on the basis of preexisting structures that sloped up towards the center of the ancient city (in an easterly direction). In point of fact, the main floor of the service wing is six meters higher than the level of the ancient plain, which, too, implies that there were several layers of preexisting occupation below the palace.

Two important elements of these preexisting structures are in fact known from the excavations. (1) The inner city-wall ran in a N-S direction along the western side of the AP Palace. There is evidence of the city-wall to the north of sectors B and D, but these sectors are clearly built in place of the city-wall. Thus the city-wall, in the area of these two sectors, was removed to make way for the western external wall of these sectors. (2) The *abi* and its associated architectural elements also affect the footprint of the palace, as can be seen in the jog in the southern wall of the palace in sector C.

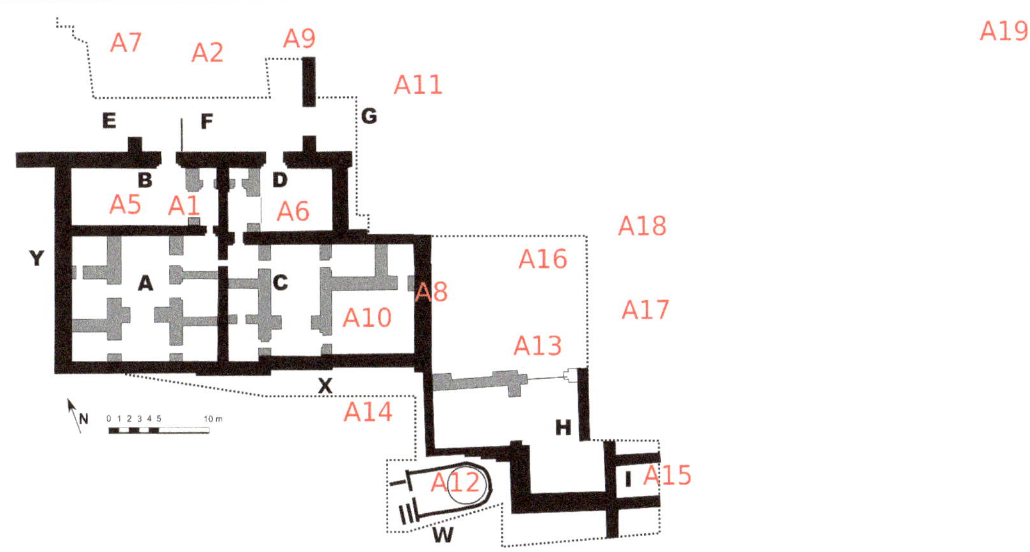

Illustration 3: AP Palace showing excavation unit designations.

A question which is still open is the presence or absence of an earlier city gate to the south of the AP Palace. One topographic factor indicates that some sort of access would have been present here: the valley, cut by a *wadi*, between the two hills. This is the case in the eastern part of the mound, where a geomagnetic survey shows streets converging on a similar valley. This would seem to indicate that the *wadi* (and thus the valley) followed the path of least resistance down from the top of the tell – such a path would have followed an ancient depression, presumably a street. However, to date no evidence for a roadway or a gate has come to light in this area, and the *abi* is positioned in the lowest portion of this valley where one would have expected the road to have run. Unfortunately the sharp slope of the hills, a vineyard and a large quantity of metal detritus in the soil mean that geomagnetics in this area is inconclusive. Further excavations in the area need to be undertaken to clearly show whether the road lies further to the south or if no road was present for the periods in which the AP Palace was in use.

The AP Palace has two levels due to this terracing: the level of the stone courtyard lies at 85 m relative (485 m above sea level), while the level of the service wing lies at 83 m relative (483 m above sea level). When one is standing on these floors looking out over the modern-day plains to the west, the elevation does not seem much higher than the surrounding area. However, due to the deep sounding S2 North of BH that the ancient plain level lay at 75 m relative (475 m above sea level). Thus, even considering the outer city wall, someone in the upper portion of the AP Palace could have looked onto the plain level below, and, vice versa, people on the plain would have been able to identify the palace from extra-mural areas.

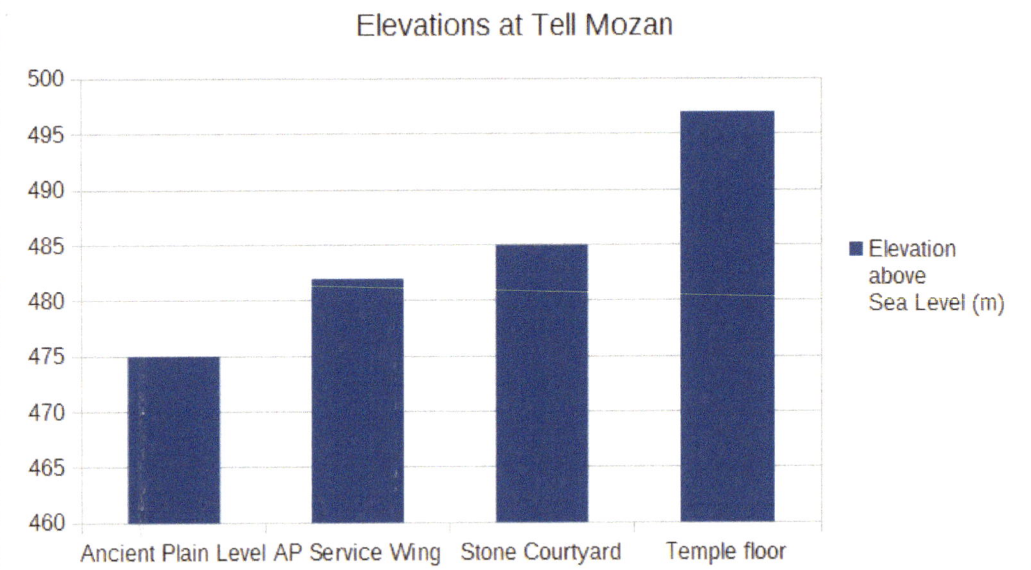

Illustration 4: Elevations at Mozan.

A further question relating to position is the question of how the palace affects the urban layout after its construction. There is little architectural evidence for activities outside of the Palace during the time of its use, but the remains of the Palace itself, after the collapse of the walls, affected the settlement patterns in the immediate area, especially during the Khabur period of occupation. Since this study deals only with the architectural aspects of the AP Palace, these later topographical influences will not be discussed here.[6]

6 There is a great deal of literature which deals with such questions of urbanism; while a complete bibliography is outside the scope of this study, some of the work from which this study has benefited are: Orthmann 1995; Butterlin 2002, 2003; Butterlin et al. 2006; Meyer 2006, 2007a, 2007b; Butterlin 2009; Margueron 2009.

2.1.2 *Palace: Chronology*

The palace was built in an area where there were previous occupation levels, which were exposed in only one small area of the palace. The construction phase and the use of the palace followed; after the palace was no longer used as a royal palace it was still used, probably as an extension of the administration of another palace in the vicinity. Finally, the ruin of the palace affected the topology of the later settlement.

2.1.2.1 *Pre-Palace*

In room D2 there was a deep sounding made (excavation area A1) to determine the chronology of the period preceding the palace, which was determined to be from the latter part of the Early Dynastic period (EBA II-III). A particularly hard packing was found, which during the excavations seemed to have the consistency of cement; this packing was not, however, a foundation for the palace, but belonged rather to a pre-palace level (G. Buccellati and Kelly-Buccellati 2000, 151). This small sounding was the only excavation which went into levels pre-dating the construction of the palace.

2.1.2.2 *Leveling and Terracing*

The first stratum which can be identified with the palace is the leveling and filling of the area to support the structure. Sectors A through F, as well as sectors X and Y were all at a lower level than sectors H and I (G. Buccellati and Kelly-Buccellati 2000, 136–39). Sector G is unclear since so little has been dug, and it is likely that a staircase would have been present in this sector, granting access between the two levels. In the excavated portions, no access between the two levels has been found. In the portion of the palace uncovered to date there is evidence of two levels, but it is possible that the portions of the palace to the north were built on yet another level. It is unlikely that the palace rose to a third level to the east (or sank back down to the lower level) because of the parity of elevation between the plaza and the floor level of the formal wing.[7]

It would have been necessary to construct one wall (from what we know of the excavated portions) during this terracing and filling: the wall between sectors C and H. This wall marked the boundary between the lower and higher levels within the palace, and in order to maintain the step between the two a massive stone wall was needed. It would also have been necessary to have a similar solution in sector G, perhaps a similar wall or the staircase itself, but one can only hypothesize until further excavations in the sector are carried out.

7 For more on the elevations between the palace and the plaza, see 2.1.6 below.

The system of drainage channels present in the palace was built before the walls were constructed – this is clear because in several instances the channels go under the walls – but it is unclear when exactly the drains were installed.[8] They could have been installed while the leveling was done, or they could have been inserted after the leveled surface had been finished. On the

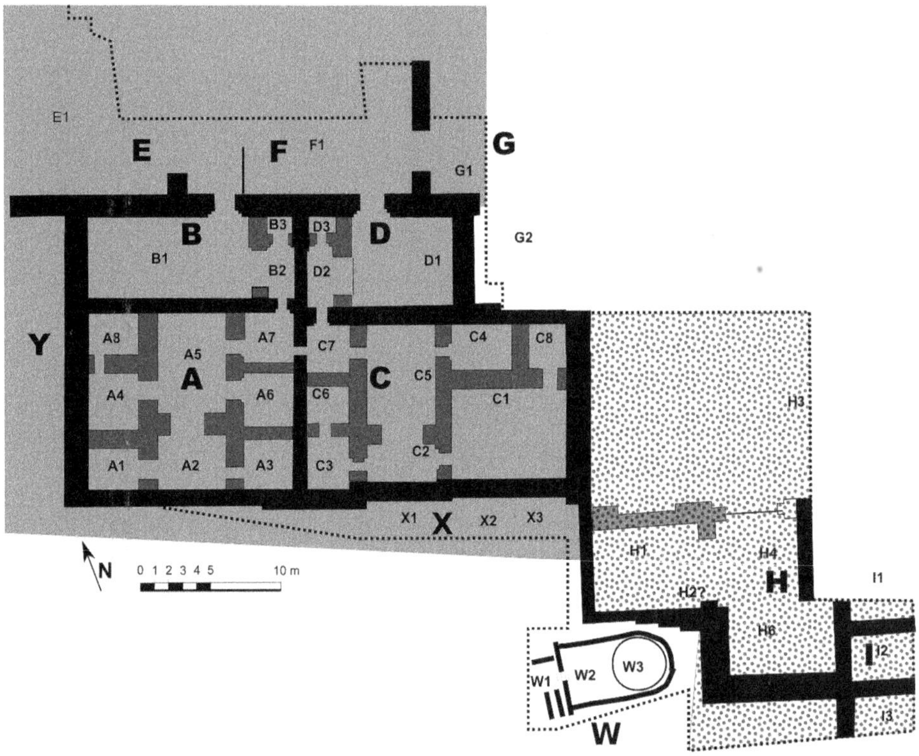

Illustration 5: The AP Palace with shading to indicate differences in elevation. Solid shading indicates the lower level, while dotted shading indicates the raised level.

one hand it would have required less effort to install the drains while the terracing was being constructed, instead of cutting into the new fill which made up the terracing. On the other hand, it would have been simpler to ensure that the drains maintained a constant slope if they were inserted after the leveling material had been placed and had been compacted, thus avoiding the inevitable (and uneven) settling when compaction occurs.

One further installation linked to the water system is the series of baked bricks underneath the stone courtyard, H3 (G. Buccellati and Kelly-Buccellati 2004, 14–18). Only a limited understanding of this installation is possible, since the only evidence is from the portions of the stone courtyard which were

8 The drainage system and the installation below the stone courtyard will be discussed at greater length below in section 2.2.2. They are included here because of the information that they give us in describing the sequence of construction of the AP Palace.

removed by Khabur pits, but it seems clear that the bricks form an interlinked installation underneath the courtyard, and this installation seems to have been hydraulic in nature, probably linked to water storage.[9] In terms of chronology, this installation under the stone courtyard must have been built during the

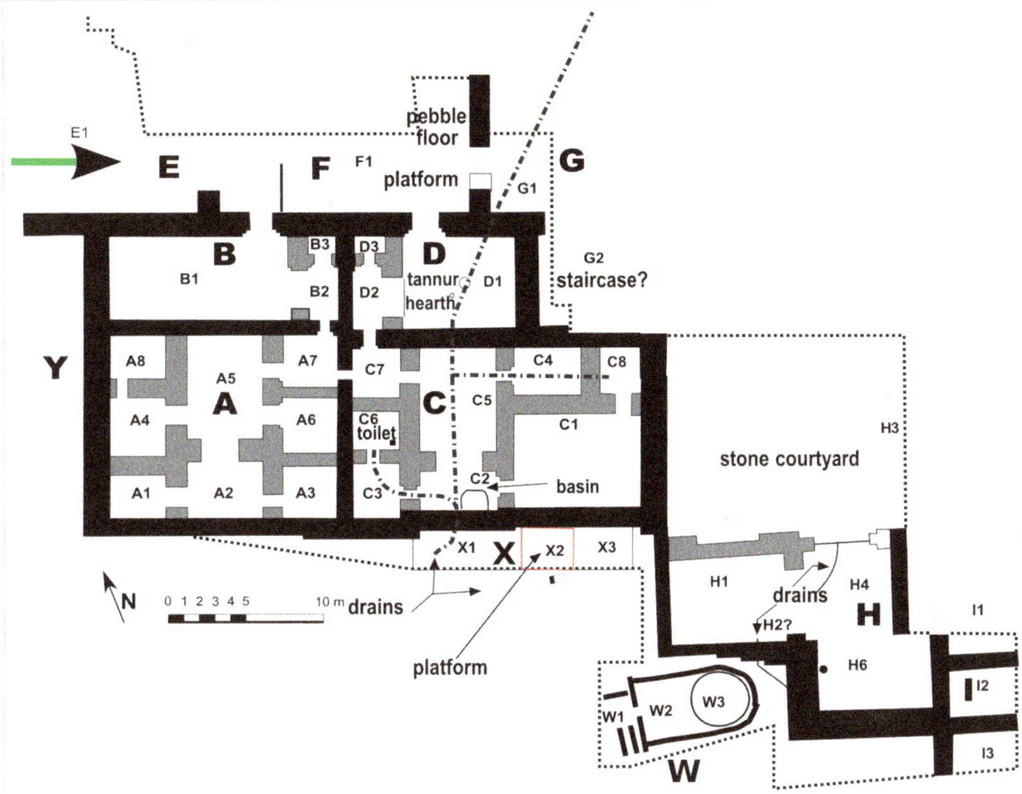

Illustration 6: AP Palace showing the installations; the main drain is marked with a dash-dot line running from NE to S.

buildup of the two terraces on which the palace came to be built, since it presumably would have filled the volume under the stone courtyard (H3) itself, an area which otherwise presumably would have belonged to the lower level. Were the installation to predate the palace, one would expect the east wall of C1 and C8 to also predate the palace, which is not the case due to the bonding with the other palace walls.

2.1.2.3 *Construction and First Use*

After the two terraces were prepared and the hydraulic installations were built, the wall foundations could be cut, the foundations laid, the stone courses built up, mudbrick laid on top, the roof and floors prepared, the other installations built and the walls plastered.

---

9 For more information on the stone courtyard and this installation, see section 2.2.1.4.1 below.

Illustration 7: Seal impressions of Tar'am-Agade and her court (G. Buccellati and Kelly-Buccellati 2002, 14-23).

Once the palace was ready to be inhabited, the king and his court would have begun using the working areas of the royal administration and also the royal living quarters. The accumulations with the seal impressions of Tupkish and his court come from this phase of use of the palace.

2.1.2.4 *Use as Administrative Building*

At a certain point the palace was no longer used as a Royal Palace, probably when King Tupkish's successor came to power and moved into another palace. This is suggested by two considerations. (1) It is clear that at one point the original installations were no longer in use, because they are covered by later accumulations, without any new accumulations taking their place; also a few doorways are narrowed, and cleaning of the prestigious stone courtyard is no longer carried out, allowing for an accumulation to obscure the stones. (2) The accumulations that go with the earlier phase are consistently and exclusively linked to seal impressions belonging to Tupkish and his court, while the accumulations that were deposited on top are associated with seal impressions of other royal figures, primarily Tar'am-Agade.

2.1.2.5 *Chronology and the Seal Impressions of Tar'am-Agade*

But even after the AP Palace was no longer used as a Royal Palace, it still seems to have remained part of the royal administration, since the seal impressions of Tar'am-Agade, the daughter of Naram-Sin, and possibly her husband along with other members of her court were found in the higher accumulations (in room H1) (G. Buccellati and Kelly-Buccellati 2002; Foster

2016, 22, 204).

A happy chance gives us, in addition to the stratigraphic relationships, the proof that the impressions from the Tar'am-Agade cache follow, chronologically, the Tupkish material. A seal was used by Unap-[...], a member of the administration during the time of Tupkish, and the same seal had a figure added that obliterated the writing and was thus used by someone,

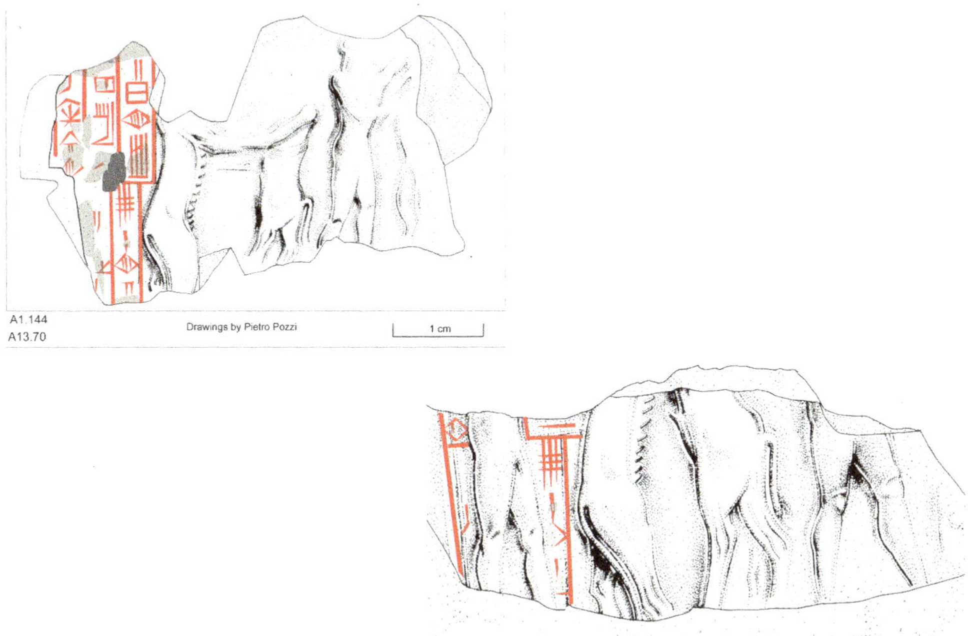

Illustration 8: Unap-[...] impressions showing recutting of seal impression (G. Buccellati and Kelly-Buccellati 2002, 26).

perhaps even the same person, in the administration of Tar'am-Agade (G. Buccellati and Kelly-Buccellati 2002, 25–27). Additionally, this overlap between administrations supports the argument that Tar'am-Agade was present in Urkesh as a Queen.[10]

After the secondary use of the palace as a part of the administration, it was abandoned, and collapsed. In the ensuing period (Ur III and Isin-Larsa), this remains an open area with accumulations indicative of such a use (such as gravel lenses). Nothing was then visible of the earlier Palace, and its very existence seems to fade from memory.

In the early Khabur period, a successive series of pottery kilns were

10 To discuss in depth the corpus of seal impressions found in the AP Palace is beyond the scope of this study. They are included here only because they are fundamental to our understanding of the chronological sequence. A complete series of articles can be found on the project website, www.urkesh.com. Of particular interest here are: G. Buccellati and Kelly-Buccellati 1995; G. Buccellati and Kelly-Buccellati 1996; G. Buccellati and Kelly-Buccellati 1998; G. Buccellati and Kelly-Buccellati 2002.

built in the area that corresponds to the (as yet largely unexcavated) southeastern portion of the AP Palace, which generated large dumps that cover the area of the palace courtyard. Immediately preceding this dumping, and perhaps in function thereof, large pits were cut so deep as to affect portions of the palace structure, most notably the stone courtyard (H3).

There is one final phase of disturbance before our excavations brought the palace to light: portions of the stone walls were exposed in modern times, and the local inhabitants mined the ruins for construction material. Several houses in the nearby modern village of Mozan have stone foundations and lower wall courses visible today, in much the same style as the palace would have been.

2.1.2.6 Chronological Phase Chart

The following chart[11] is a phase chart that was elaborated based on the stratigraphy of the various excavation units. As discussed previously, the stratigraphic and typological considerations behind this chart as well as the relationship between the objects and the stratigraphy are beyond the scope of this work, and will be published within the framework of the Urkesh Global Record, the online publication of the Mozan / Urkesh Archaeological Project.[12] The phase chart is provided here as a guide to the chronology of the palace, since some of the descriptions of the installations and sectors include chronological information by necessity.

The oldest material in the sequence of phases is the material which predates the construction of the AP Palace, and was found only in two soundings within the Palace itself: a small sounding in area A1 in front of room D2; a few other soundings were conducted to determine the extent of the foundations of the palace, including a small sounding next to the platform in the doorway between sectors F and G.

Pre-dating the palace are also the *abi* as well as the platform X, both of which lie south of the southern wall of the palace, as well as the city-wall which was removed to accommodate the construction of the AP Palace in sector Y. It is unclear, however, to which phase these structures belong – while it is known that they predate the Palace, it is not clear that they belong to Phase 1.

The main leveling, terracing and construction of the Palace belongs to phase 2. The first use of the Palace, as the royal residence of King Tupkish, also belongs to this period. This Phase can be dated to the Akkadian period or

11 The chart in Table 2 is based in part on G. Buccellati and Kelly-Buccellati 2000, 151.

12 Please see www.urkesh.com for more information and access to the UGR (Urkesh Global Record).

Phase Sequence (Based on Strata sequence AAC)			
Phase	**Southern Mesopotamia**	**Early Jezira**	**Definition vis-a-vis AP Palace**
6b	Modern		surface wash, erosion, modern burials, removal Of stones from sector A
6a	Modern		ancient *wadi*, brick decomposition where exposed
5c	Late Khabur		great brickfall, late houses, tumuli burials, A15-16 street
5b	Mid Khabur		houses, construction and first floors
5a	Early Khabur		scattered (extramural) occupation, multiple pits, creating depression, dumping in depression, pottery kilns
4b	Ur III	EJ 5	tannurs, pebble lenses, retaining walls, extramural occupation
4a	Ur III	EJ 5	burials, first reshaping of surface after Abandonment of palace
3	Akkadian/ Post-Akkadian	EJ 4	Use of AP Palace as administrative building, no longer royal residence. Narrowing of doorways, Lack of maintenance
2	Akkadian	EJ 4	Construction and use of AP Palace as royal residence and palace
1	Akkadian	EJ 4	Buildings existing prior to construction of AP Palace

Table 1: Phase sequence.

the Early-Jezira 4[13] period on the basis of typological considerations, primarily ceramic and glyptic evidence.

Phase 3 includes the use of the palace as an administrative building, albeit not a Royal Palace. This can be seen in the presence of the cache of Tar'am-Agade seal impressions, as well as in the lack of maintenance of the installations, primarily the fact that the stone courtyard was allowed to be covered in accumulation, and a *tannur* and small hearth were placed in this area.[14]

During Phases 4 and 5 the Palace was no longer visible, and its presence was most likely forgotten. During these phases the palace is damaged by pits and burial shafts which were dug in what was, at the time, the edge of the settlement. Pits dug during phase 5 damaged the stone courtyard, exposing the baked brick installation which lay below.

Phase 6, covering the modern period, is listed here because the erosion and *wadis* exposed the stones of sector A, which were subsequently removed by local inhabitants and used in the construction of the modern village of Mozan, a few hundred meters from the palace. These stones can still be seen

---

13 The Early-Jezira chronology has been developed for the settlements of the northern Jezira. The most recent discussion of this chronology can be found in Lebeau (2011, 12). In this study the Early Dynastic and Akkadian terminology is often used, due to the direct chronological tie (through the Tar'am-Agade seal impressions) with earlier chronologies developed in Mesopotamia.

14 *Tannurs* are cylindrical bread ovens common in the Near East, both modern and ancient.

today in the village, and a few have even been suggested as having come from the roof of the *abi* due to their length and relative thinness.

2.1.3 AP Palace as a Royal Palace

The first question to ask of the palace as a whole relates to its function. Is this building a Royal Palace? Two criteria are at work here: is the AP Palace the administrative seat of a king, and is the AP Palace a residence?[15]

We know from the seal impressions found in and around the palace that several kings – *endan* in Hurrian – had used the structure or the surrounding area. First and foremost is King Tupkish, whose seal impressions were found in great quantity within the accumulations on the first floors of the palace, primarily in sector B. Along with impressions of his seals, a whole series of other impressions have been found. These included impressions from the queen, Uqnitum, the queen's cook Tuli, and the queen's nurse Zamena (G. Buccellati and Kelly-Buccellati 1995, 1996, 1998; Nadali 2014).

Perhaps the most important were the seal impressions of the queen, Queen Uqnitum and the palace officials connected with her. These were more numerous than those of King Tupkish, and, surprisingly, also represented the impressions of a series of several nearly identical seals (G. Buccellati and Kelly-Buccellati 1997; F. Buccellati 2014a). These seals had differences which would probably have been clear to someone who knew what to look for or could place the various impressions side-by-side and compare them, but would have otherwise appeared identical.

While the seals from which the impressions were derived bear the names of the king and his queen, one cannot conclude that these were *royal* seals in the sense of having been used by the king or the queen themselves, for a number of reasons: (1) There are too many of them.[16] (2) They are found in an area that does not suggest a formal use such as would be presupposed had the royal couple personally affixed the seals. (3) They are found together with a number of seals of members of the queen's household (h1-h4). (4) Even though they are finely executed and with a rich iconography, they are small (an average of 2 cm in height). As a result, it is plausible to assume that they were used to seal goods that belonged to the royal couple or members of their households, used, in other words, in their name but not by them personally (G. Buccellati and Kelly-Buccellati 1995, 27–29).

For present purposes, the conclusion seems inescapable that the

---

15 By residence what is meant is that the king would have also lived in the same structure that housed the administrative functions.

16 Six unique impressions for the king and eight for the queen; these were discussed in the previous publication by the author (F. Buccellati 2014a).

building in which they were found was directly linked to the administration of the royal couple.

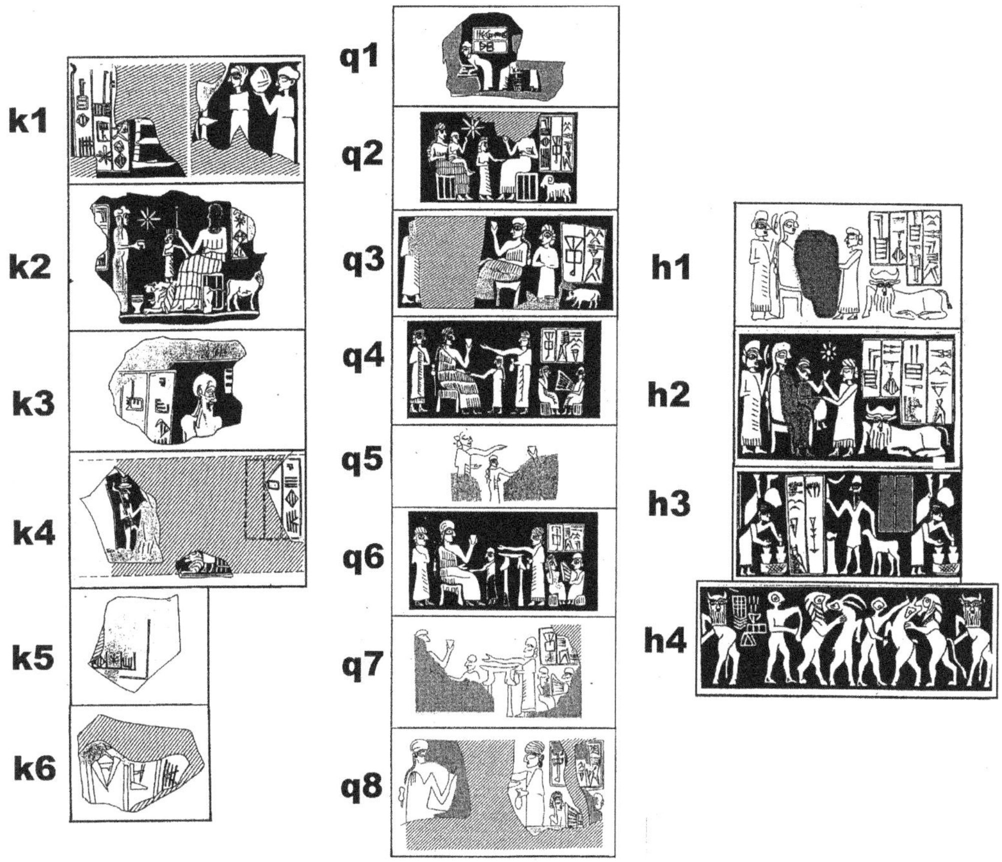

Illustration 9: Administrative seal impressions found within the AP Palace (images are not to scale) (G. Buccellati and Kelly-Buccellati 1997, 81).

In addition to the evidence of the seal impressions connecting the building with the royal administration within the city, the architecture itself aids in determining the function of the spaces in the palace. Directly tied to the question of administration is the function of the extensive stone courtyard, room H3. The investment of resources needed to build such a floor is an indicator that this courtyard was meant as a prestigious space within the building.

Is the palace a residence as well as an administrative center? The fact that the palace had a kitchen as well as installations such as a drainage system and what seems to be a 'bathroom' installation (room C6, see section 2.2.2.1) seems to indicate that the structure did have residential areas, which would be located in the areas to the east and the north, not yet excavated to date.

2.1.4 Palace: Typology

2.1.4.1 Mirrored plan

The only wing of the palace that has been excavated in its entirety is the service wing consisting of sectors A-D. What is unusual with regard to the standard typology of 3rd millennium Near Eastern palace architecture is the fact that this wing is built as a mirrored plan (G. Buccellati and Kelly-Buccellati 1995, 1996; Matthiae 2010a; Pfälzner 2011). The only exception is the foreshortening of sector D and the addition of a room in sector C, C8. Such a mirrored plan is not characteristic of palace architecture; in Leick's study of Near Eastern architecture she states: "A disregard for symmetry and axiality is also characteristic of the monumental form of domestic architecture, the palace" (Leick 1988, 139) Preziosi makes a similar claim for Minoan architecture (Preziosi 1983, 7). Thus the symmetry of the AP Palace is unusual in its regularity vis-à-vis other palaces in the ancient Near East and in neighboring regions.

The formal wing of the palace, consisting of Sectors H and I, is raised in elevation with regard to the service wing by approximately 2 meters. Not enough of this wing of the palace has been explored to be able to see if these sections of the palace are similarly mirrored.

2.1.4.2 Palace Entrance

Unfortunately the excavations to date have also not found an entrance to the palace. Two areas seem likely for an entrance: the western and the eastern sides of the palace. To the west the palace would have access to the western part of the lower town, probably giving access indirectly to the courtyard F and the sectors around it. To the east it is likely that there was access onto the plaza, probably with a more direct access to the formal area than the access to the west.

Access from the south or the north is still possible, but is less likely. To the south there was no road found, and the southern palace wall abuts directly the northern portion of the *abi* (W) and other associated installations (X). Together with the lack of a road, the fact that no doorways have been found in the explored portion of the southern wall[17] means that it is unlikely that there would have been access on this side of the palace.

17 Today, access to the rooms of the palace is possible through the southern wall of room A3, but this does not reflect an ancient access point but rather a modern solution to the problem that no entrances have yet been found.

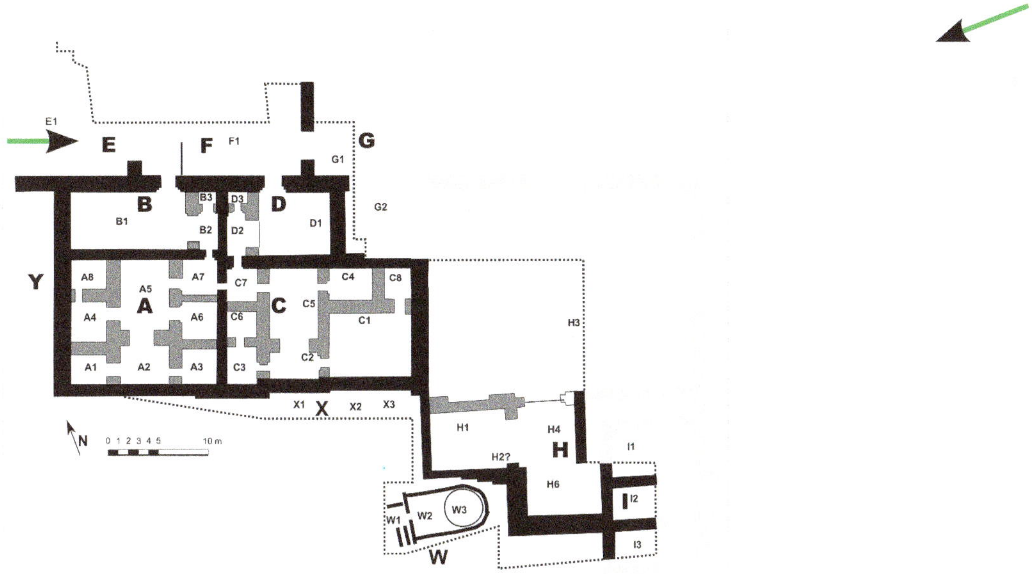

Illustration 10: AP Palace with possible entrances shown with arrows (upper right and upper left).

2.1.4.3 Iwans

A room-pairing which can be found in the palace is the so-called *iwan* type structure (G. Buccellati and Kelly-Buccellati 2000, 141–46). By *iwan* a specific type of room-courtyard pair is meant: a long room which opens with a particularly wide doorway onto a courtyard, which typically lies north of the room. The room is usually as wide as the courtyard, and has no door on the southern side of the courtyard, but often doors on the eastern and western walls are present (Ragette 1974, 88). This configuration is present in two sectors in the palace, the mirrored rooms A5-A2 and C5-C2. The term *iwan* is most often linked to a specific type of Sassanian architecture, a vaulted audience hall, but the concept has been used for earlier periods, including the architecture of Tepe Gawra dating to 3000-2800 BC (Badawy 1978, 87). It has been applied to the combination of a long room and a courtyard in Mozan in particular, since the footprint of the rooms is comparable to that of the later periods. It is important to note that what is meant is not the Sassanian architectural feature, but is used to identify the rooms in the AP Palace with a similar footprint; it has been applied in the literature to this room configuration because of the marked similarities between the two (see also section 2.4.3 below).[18]

There are three further examples of similar room-pairs, but they deviate somewhat from the pattern as described here. These are D1-D2, B1-B2 and

18 The use of an *iwan*-type architecture to such an extent in the palace is one of the elements unique to the AP Palace (Pfälzner 2011, 174).

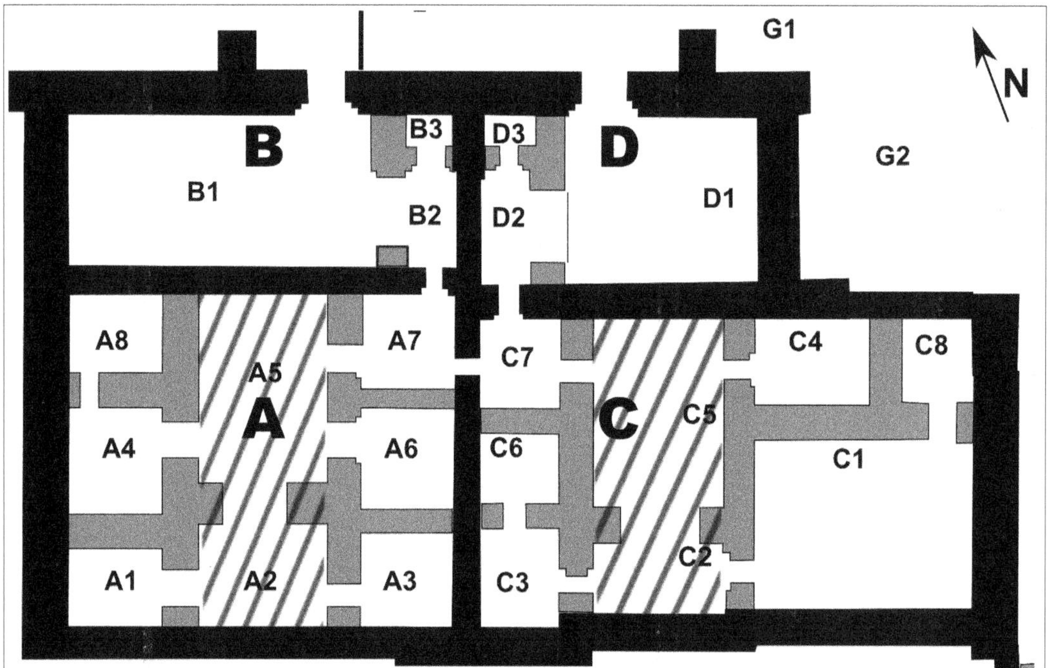

Illustration 11: Service Wing of the AP Palace with hatching to indicate the two iwan room groups A5-A2 and C5-C2.

H3-H4. D1-D2 can be seen on Illustration 11; here one can identify a similarly wide entrance to a room which is (nearly) the width of the courtyard, and other doorways to the sides of the room but no door across from the wide entrance. Two elements deviate however from the standard *iwan*: the wide room entrance is not orientated to the north but rather to the east, and it is unlikely that room D1 was a courtyard, even if it is likely that some sort of opening was present at roof level to allow smoke to escape. One reason against D1 being a courtyard is that the adjacent space in sector F is definitely a courtyard and it is unlikely that two courtyards would have been adjoining. Also the accumulations in D1 pointed to a closed rather than an open area.

The second room-pair is B1-B2, which is, as previously described, the mirror of room-pair D1-D2, and thus the same argument as in D1-D2 holds here. What changes is obviously that the wide room entrance points to the west instead of the east due to the mirrored nature of the layout.

The third and final room-pair is the H3-H4 entrance. Here a courtyard is certainly present, but the other doorways and the shape of the room varies from the standard *iwan* pair.

Room H4 is quite large and deep for a room in an *iwan* room-pair. Its southern boundary with room H6 is ill defined, and it may be that H4 and H6 are actually a single room with a jog in the eastern wall. This would be the only case of such a jog within the AP Palace. Furthermore, the doorway between H1 and H4 is also a very wide entrance, presumably to have more light in H1. The eastern wall of H4 also is without a doorway, which is normally the case with *iwan* room-pairs.

2.1.4.4 Rabbeting

A further aspect of the AP Palace which is present in many rooms, and which is typical for similar constructions, is the presence of rabbeting in doorways. By rabbeting a slight inset in the wall on either side of a doorway is generally meant, typically only on one side of the doorway. Such an inset is present from the top to the bottom of the wall, and remains at the same depth in both the mudbrick and stone portions of the walls. Most of the rabbeting is reflected in the stonework by using two stones, but in a few cases a single stone is shaped to provide the inset.

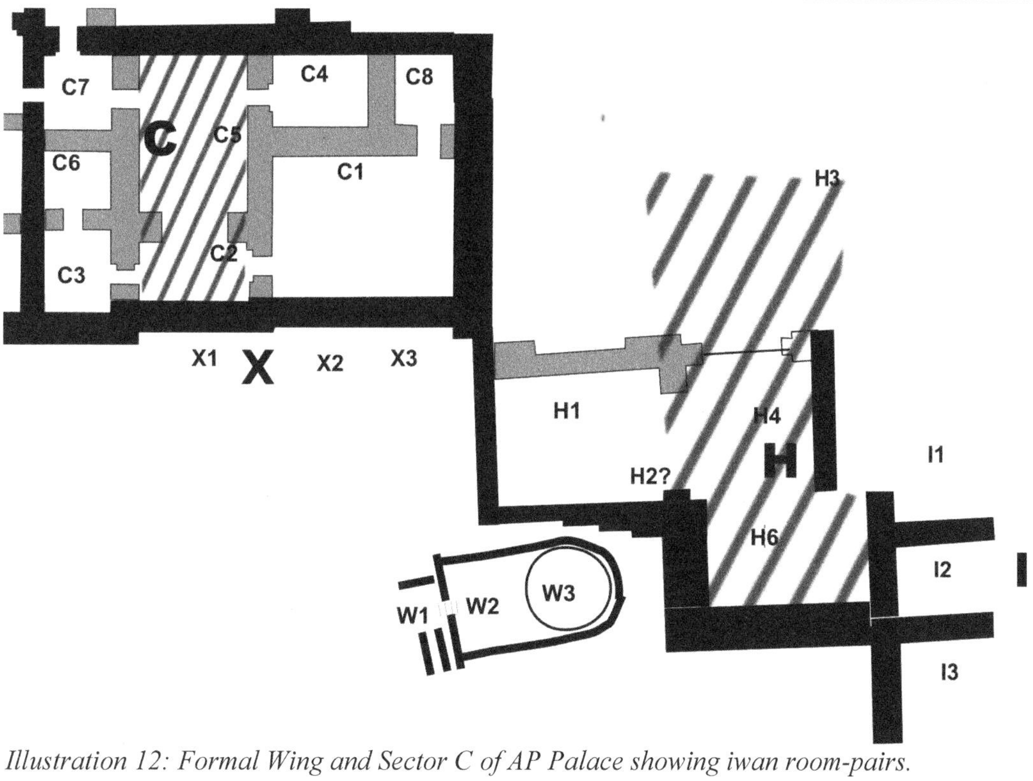

Illustration 12: Formal Wing and Sector C of AP Palace showing iwan room-pairs.

In the reconstruction presented here, this rabbeting is not ornamental but is rather functional – providing enough room for a door (presumably wooden) to rest in the insets when closed. It is unlikely that the insets were deep enough for the door to be flush with the wall when closed, considering that the few doorsockets discovered indicated that door posts were wider than the inset of the rabbeting.

2.1.4.5 Proportion of Room Area to Room Perimeter

Room	Room Function	Area (in m²)	Perimeter (in m)	Proportion Area/Perimeter
A1	room	10.1	12.8	0.79
A2	iwan	18.1	17.5	1.04
A3	room	10.1	12.7	0.79
A4	room	10.6	13.0	0.81
A5	courtyard	36.9	24.5	1.50
A6	room	11.3	13.5	0.84
A7	room	10.6	13.1	0.81
A8	room	11.3	13.5	0.84
B1	workroom	67.2	34.9	1.93
B2	iwan	7.0	11.4	0.62
B3	storeroom	2.9	6.9	0.41
C1	room	33.3	23.5	1.42
C2	iwan	11.4	15.1	0.76
C3	room	14.2	15.1	0.94
C4	room	10.4	12.9	0.80
C5	courtyard	26.7	20.7	1.29
C6	room	7.9	11.4	0.69
C7	room	10.0	12.7	0.79
C8	room	7.2	10.8	0.67
D1	workroom	50.0	28.5	1.75
D2	iwan	9.4	12.9	0.73
D3	storeroom	2.9	6.9	0.42

Table 2: Proportion between the area and perimeter, sorted by room.

It is difficult to tie typological categories to mathematical formula, especially within the context of architecture. One index that is useful in this case, however, is the proportion between the area and perimeter of groups of rooms. This is not an index which is found in the literature dealing with architectural analysis, but it seems an excellent way to quantify space in a fashion that supports a typological division of rooms. The following table lists the rooms of the four sectors A-D which make up the service wing of the AP Palace. The spatial data includes only the rooms themselves, ignoring the doorways.

Listed is the room label, the function of the room as defined in this thesis, the area of the room in square meters, the perimeter of the room and the proportion of the area to the perimeter. This proportion describes the relationship between the sum of the sides of the room and the total floorspace. This does not indicate the size of the room per se, but rather how much open space is available in a room.

As an example, a square room which is 5.5 by 5.5 meters has a total area of 30.35 square meters (5.5m x 5.5m); the perimeter of this room is 22

Room size (in m)	Area (in m^2)	Perimeter (in m)	Proportion Area/Perimeter
5.5 x 5.5	30.25	22	1.38
10 x 1	10	22	0.45
30.25 x 1	30.25	62.5	0.48

Table 3: Proportion between the area and perimeter, examples.

meters (5.5m + 5.5m + 5.5m + 5.5m); the proportion of the area to the perimeter is 1.38 (30.25m^2 / 22m). This proportion does not reflect a spatial reality (since it is a proportion between square meters and linear meters) but instead serves as an index. A corridor with exactly the same perimeter, for example, has a very different value for this proportion – a corridor which is 10 meters long and one meter wide also has a perimeter of 22 meters, however the area is only 10 square meters. Thus the proportion between area and perimeter is quite different: 0.45. A further example to clarify would be a corridor 30.25 meters long and one meter wide: thus the area of this second corridor is 30.25 square meters, the same as the 5.5 x 5.5 meter room. The perimeter of such a room is by consequence 62.5 meters – and thus the proportion between area and perimeter remains low: 0.48. This proportion is thus a good index of the 'openness' of a room, and can be of use in checking the proposed room typology.

Table 4 shows the same data from the AP Palace, this time sorted by the proportion between area and perimeter of these rooms. I have organized the data into four groups according to the proportion between area and perimeter: 2-1.5, 1.5-1.0, 1.0-0.5, 0.5-0. The first group (2.0-1.5) includes only two rooms, the workrooms of B1 and D1. These rooms are defined as workspaces, B1 as an area where containers were opened and D1 as a kitchen.

The second group (1.5-1.0) includes four rooms, A2, A5, C1 and C5. A5 and C5 are the courtyards in A and C, respectively. Thus the proportion reflects the open spaces of these courtyards. Room C1 is particularly large, and thus is the only room within this second group. This may seem an anomaly, but room C1 seems to have been used as a workspace, considering the burnt logs found here (see section 2.2.2.3).

Thus this high proportion may reflect the fact that the room was conceived as a workspace even during the architectural planning phase. The final room of this group is room A2, which is the *iwan* linked to courtyard A5. This *iwan* is somewhat larger than its parallel in sector C (C2) perhaps because the southern external wall of the palace is notched between C3 and C2, reducing the space in the *iwan*, as well as the fact that the wall and opening

Room	Room Function	Area (in m^2)	Perimeter (in m)	Proportion Area/Perimeter
B1	workroom	67.2	34.9	1.93
D1	workroom	50.0	28.5	1.75
A5	courtyard	36.9	24.5	1.50
C1	room	33.3	23.5	1.42
C5	courtyard	26.7	20.7	1.29
A2	iwan	18.1	17.5	1.04
C3	room	14.2	15.1	0.94
A8	room	11.3	13.5	0.84
A6	room	11.3	13.5	0.84
A4	room	10.6	13.0	0.81
A7	room	10.6	13.1	0.81
C4	room	10.4	12.9	0.80
A3	room	10.1	12.7	0.79
A1	room	10.1	12.8	0.79
C7	room	10.0	12.7	0.79
C2	iwan	11.4	15.1	0.76
D2	iwan	9.4	12.9	0.73
C6	room	7.9	11.4	0.69
C8	room	7.2	10.8	0.67
B2	iwan	7.0	11.4	0.62
D3	storeroom	2.9	6.9	0.42
B3	storeroom	2.9	6.9	0.41

Table 4: Proportion between area and perimeter, sorted by area/perimeter proportion.

separating A2 from A5 is farther north than the wall and opening separating C2 and C5, further enlarging the *iwan* A2. This larger size means that it is the only *iwan* within this second group, having an area/perimeter proportion of 1.04.

The third group (1.0-0.5) consists of eleven rooms and the remaining three *iwans*, C2, B2 and D2. It is worth mentioning that six of these rooms are nearly identical in size: A1, A3, A4, A7, C4, C7 all have an area of within 0.6 m^2 of each other, and differ by a maximum of 0.3m in perimeter. Rooms A6 and A8 are identical in both area and perimeter.

The fourth and final group (0.5-0) consists of two rooms, both of the small storerooms in sectors B and D (B3 and D3). They are identical in both area, 2.9m^2, and perimeter, 6.9m. Comparing B3 to the larger workroom, B1, of the same sector, one can see that the workroom has just over 23 times the area and five times the perimeter.

2.1.5 The Perception of Space through the Optic, Acoustic, Haptic, Olfactory Senses

The consideration of the perception of space due to what one can see, hear, touch or smell is a very important aspect in the analysis of architecture because of the great differences that these forms of perception communicate (Ankerl 1981, 45–46).[19] For obvious reasons the fifth sense, that of taste, is not discussed in reference to architecture.

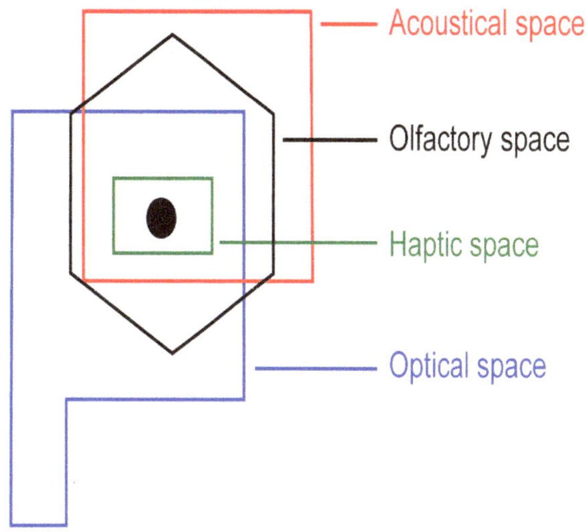

Illustration 13: A graphic representation of the acoustic, haptic olfactory and optical spaces of perception. These do not completely overlap, thus, for example, what can be heard is not necessarily visible or touchable. A singing dancer (black dot in center) is perceived by various people through different senses in different spatial areas (adapted from Ankerl 1981, 156).

In the AP Palace, it is important to consider these differences because of the diverse impressions that these senses give the viewer. As an example, sectors A through D are characterized by relatively small rooms placed as close as possible to each other: 19 rooms of these four sectors (out of 22) could fit into the projected expanse of the courtyard H3, and they are laid out in a large square, as opposed to a linear fashion, whereby the rooms would be chained one after another. Thus the high number of small rooms increases the haptic space and decreases the optical space by increasing the number of walls. Put another way, the visitor cannot see very far, but has a lot of surface area within reach. The high level of surface area means that there is more space along the walls for storage, be it for shelving or larger objects on the floor along the wall.

The third sense, that of sound, is much more difficult to project based on the architectural footprint as we have it, since sound would be most affected by the elements of the building which are no longer present: doors,

19 *pace* Preziosi, who limits perception to optical perception: "In connection with the nature of its perceptual address, architecture employs visually palpable means to broadcast its messages" (Preziosi 1983, 211).

the roof, windows and the presence of textiles in the rooms which would have affected how sound traveled as well. The compact nature of the plan of the building, and the relatively small size of the rooms would have meant that sounds within the rooms would not have carried far. Thus people would have been able to walk up to the outer walls of the palace, and presumably hear some of the sounds emanating from inside, primarily from the courtyards.

The final sense to be discussed here is that of smell. The placement of kitchen or workshop areas would have had a direct impact on portions of the structure which would have been affected when the wind carried in smells of cooking, smelting or kiln fires. As wind direction is often determined by the topography of the city and by local geography, it is possible to estimate the space in which wind conditions might have carried such odors.

These elements, considered for various portions of the building can help understand how architecture shapes and is shaped by social space. Such an approach, in addition to studies on interaction and space syntax (Hillier 1988; Deblauwe 1992, 1994, 1997b; Seamon 2013), can lead to a deeper understanding of not only the architecture itself but also of the uses for which it was designed as well as how changes over time show shifting functions of the rooms.

2.1.5.1 Sensing the Palace from Outside: Acoustic

Within the palace sound would have carried from the courtyards to the adjacent rooms, in particular those linked to the courtyards by an *iwan*-type room chain. It is also important to consider how sounds from the courtyards would have affected activities being carried out on the roofs or upper stories. The exterior of the palace is just as important in terms of perception, and thus it is just as important to consider it using the same parameters. Sounds would have carried outside of the AP Palace, beyond the outer walls and affect how people perceive the palace and related activities. To the south of the palace there is the *abi*, which would presumably not have been used often and when it was used only few people would have actively participated.[20] Thus the acoustic impact of the palace in this direction would have affected only a few people. To the west it is unclear what would have been present in the urban landscape, and the space to the North and East is as yet unexcavated, even if it is assumed that the palace bordered on the JP Plaza to the east.

2.1.5.2 Sensing the Palace from Outside: Optic

The AP Palace would have been visible from outside of the walls, and

20 One of the indications of the fact that only few people would have participated is the limited access available through the doorway (F. Buccellati 2010).

three points are worth discussing here: the outer walls, activity on the roofs and the possibility of seeing into courtyards from the outside. The outer walls of the palace would have been visible to visitors to the city, at various distances: up close, the stones would have been visible and the plastered mudbrick up to the roof. It is also possible that the stones would have been covered in similar plaster, but unfortunately the archaeological record does not preserve any. Further, someone seeing the palace from the outside would have seen the doorway (or doorways) which gave access to the palace, and would have possibly also seen through the doorway to the first interior spaces. At a farther distance it is conceivable that the palace could also have been seen, both from the plaza area to the East of the palace as well as the urban area of the lower city to the west. The Plaza area would have been open and the wall of the Palace (assuming that the Palace fronted on the Plaza) would have been visible. It seems also evident that a doorway would also have been present on this side, granting direct access to the Plaza and the structures around it. The urban area to the West of the Plaza would also have seen the Palace, but from farther away, and, due to the topography of the earlier settlement, the Palace would have sat at a higher elevation from the structures in this area. Thus someone looking at the palace from the lower city to the West would have had to look slightly up at the palace, and would have seen little of it, as the roof areas would have been obscured for the most part by the elevation. It is also possible that the elevation difference between the Palace and the structures in the lower city would have been enough so that the Palace would have been visible from outside the city, even if only from the western approaches.

While there is no direct evidence of activity on the roof spaces of the Palace it is very likely that these areas would have been used for various activities. Most of these activities would have been visible to people standing both inside and outside of the Palace, unless blocking screens had been set up.

Thirdly it may have been possible to see into the courtyards of the palace from certain locations which would have overlooked the palace. While areas of the Palace now may lie lower than some of the cultural layers now present on the Tell, it is most likely that all of these higher spaces are formed by later cultural levels; thus the courtyards would probably not have been visible from outside the palace. The only exception to this would have been the temple terrace, which may have been high enough to see activity on the roofs of the palace, even if seeing into the courtyards themselves would probably not have been possible.

2.1.5.3 Sensing the Palace from Outside: Haptic

Physical contact with the Palace from the outside would have been the most limited sense that someone remaining outside the Palace would have had with the structure. The only real reason for someone to touch the palace would be if they were walking along its outer wall, or if they were going into the structure through one of the doorways.

The difference between the visibility of the Palace from a large portion of the city and the small number of occasions where one would enter it or even touch it might be one way in which the architects and planners indicated the monumental nature of the structure. A modern example might be a skyscraper, which is seen by most of the city, yet very few of the inhabitants have been in or have touched the skyscrapers themselves (see also section 2.1.6.6).

2.1.5.4 Sensing the Palace from Outside: Olfactory

A further sense, which is not considered in the example brought by Ankerl above (see Illustration 13), is the sense of smell. The drain exiting the AP Palace to the south, running under the southern wall of room C2 and emptying onto the walking surface, carried dirty water (as evidenced by the link of the drain from the toilet/washroom in C6 – see also section 2.2.2.7); the smell from the run-off would certainly have been perceptible to passersby, and perhaps even to those using the platform in area X.

The kitchen elements in use in area D1 would have also produced smoke (on the kitchen installations see section 2.2.2.5), and it is possible that on windy days the smell would have carried to other parts of the city. In our experience flying a parafoil kite to take overhead pictures it is more common for the wind to come from the east, which (assuming the pattern was true in ancient times as well) would have carried the smoke towards the outer city areas.

2.1.6 Palace: in Relation to the Urban Setting

The AP Palace is situated in a context that is already in part known from excavations to the south and the east which continued outside of the perimeter of the palace itself. This larger context has been described as a monumental urban complex, since the palace, plaza and temple terrace are all spatially linked (G. Buccellati 2005).

2.1.6.1 Elevations

A sounding (excavation area S2) in the north of the high mound, north of area BH, showed that the ancient plain level was at 475 meters above sea level. The level of the plaza is the same as the stone courtyard (AP Palace room H3) i. e. is ten meters above the ancient plain, at 485 m above sea level, while the service wing lies at 482 m above sea level. Thus there are ten meters of cultural material below the plaza and the formal wing of the palace. For reference, the floor of the temple on top of the temple terrace is at 497 m above sea level, 23 m above the ancient plain level.

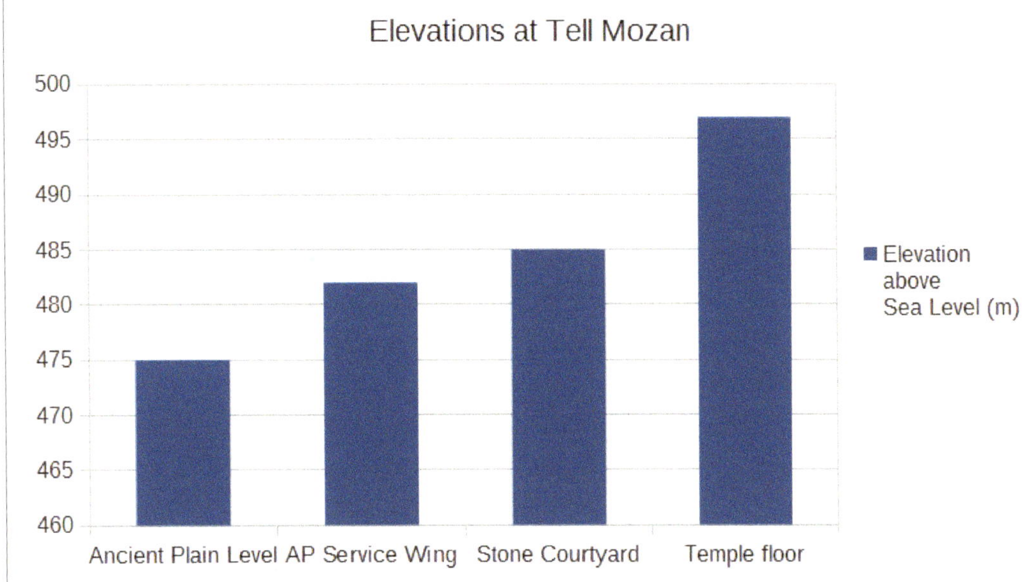

Illustration 14: Elevations at Tell Mozan.

2.1.6.2 *abi*

To the southeast of the palace a further structure was found, which was identified as an *abi* on the basis of the finds and the architectural elements (Kelly-Buccellati 2002). The *abi*, during the time when the AP Palace was in use, would not have been very visible, with the cupola at ground level. The *abi* would have been roofed over during this period, and the entrance was most probably blocked when the structure was not in use.

2.1.6.3 *Canal and Lower Town to West*

To the west of the AP Palace there is a wide portion of the lower city, extending to what is the modern village of Mozan. Combining data from the Corona images, apparent gaps in the lower town's city wall (visible in the topography), as well as the fact that the modern village sits on a small tell raised higher than most of the lower city, one can hypothesize that a canal passed through the lower town from north to south; also evidence for a canal was found in sounding OP.

The Corona images give us a view of the lower town which is no longer visible today: since the images were taken between 1959 and 1972, mechanized plowing has leveled many of the topographic features then visible.

On these Corona images a *wadi* bed is clearly visible running through the lower town to the west of the AP Palace.[21] This *wadi* bed matches two points in the lower town's city wall, where the canal would have entered and exited the urban space.

The mound of ancient cultural material on which the modern village of Tell Mozan sits is one of the highest points in the lower town, forming a small tell. A sounding showed that cultural material from the Middle Assyrian period lay directly under the surface,[22] indicating that the mound was primarily formed in the ancient periods and not as a result of the modern village. One cannot exclude the fact that the *wadi* was formed after the city was abandoned, and does not reflect an ancient canal, but the evidence points strongly to the *wadi* being a continuation of an ancient topographic feature. This canal would have been of great use during the construction of the palace, since the wood and stone needed could have been floated down from work-sites in the mountains to the north of the city.

2.1.6.4 Plaza to East

To the east of the Palace there is the JP Plaza, and it seems clear from a deep sounding (excavation area A19) that the palace bounded directly onto the plaza itself. It would seem obvious that an entrance would have been located on this side of the palace, allowing access to and from the Plaza, but none has been found to date due to the Khabur and Mittani period occupation levels which cover this portion of the palace. The elevations of the floor level of the plaza and the elevation of the stone courtyard in the palace match, further supporting the hypothesis that the two areas were linked, and red brickfall found in area A19 was at the same elevation as comparable brickfall found on the stone courtyard (h3).

2.1.6.5 Question of Access

Access to the AP Palace remains an open question, since only one possible point of access has been found, and no roads have been uncovered in the vicinity. One surprising discovery lies to the south of the AP Palace, where one might expect to find a road leading from the lower town to the plaza, matching the modern *wadi* valley between the two mounds. Instead, the presence of sectors H and I, as well as the *abi*, seem to block the expected

21 See in particular the Corona Front and Aft image pair from 9 Aug 1968: DS1104-1025DA012_12_b and DS1104-1025DF006_6_c as well as the image DS1047-1088DF065_65_d.

22 This material (from excavation area OJ2) has been published in a recent PhD Thesis by C. Chaves Yates (2014).

east-west access to the south of the Palace. It is still possible that a road lies farther south, but the mound present to the south seems to indicate that another large building or city quarter may have been directly adjacent to the southern extent of the AP Palace (see also section 2.1.1 above, which presents the same argument vis-à-vis a possible city-gate, also 2.1.4.2 which considers access from the point of view of the room divisions within the Palace).

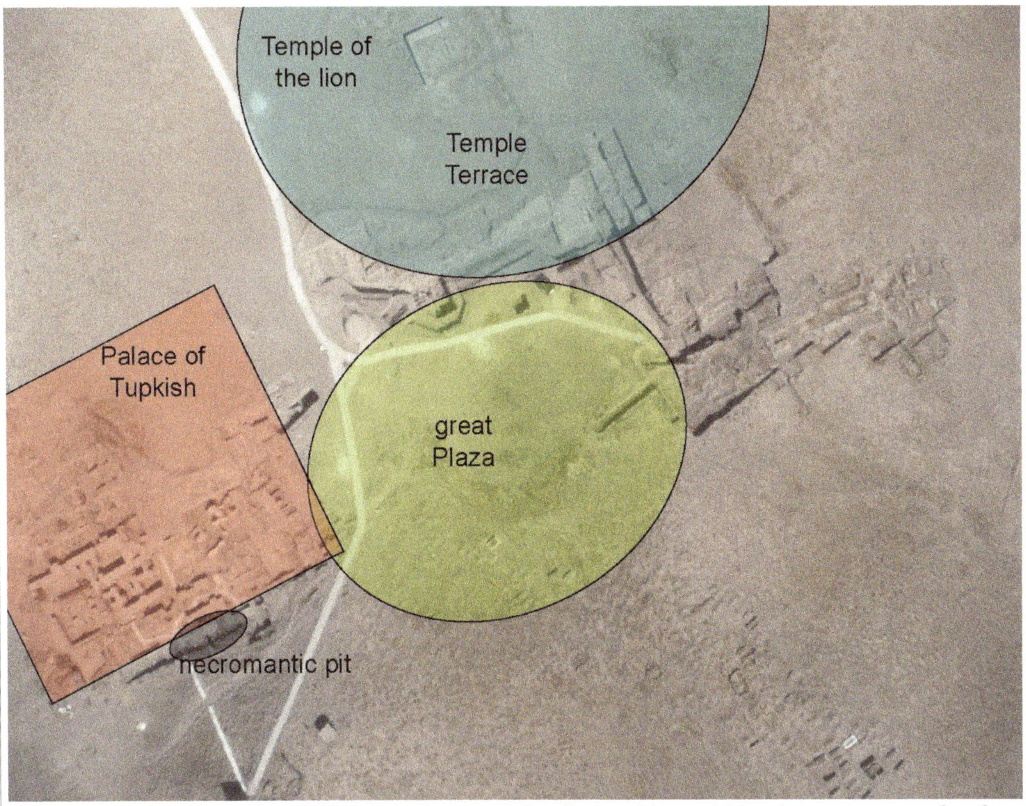

Illustration 15: Kite photo showing the spatial relationships within the monumental urban complex.

2.1.6.6 *Visibility*

The visibility of the palace from other parts of the city as well as from the immediate extra-urban environment would have meant that, much like the temple, the AP Palace would likely have been representative of the city as well as of the power of the king.[23]

The visibility between Palace and the surrounding city and countryside is important to underline, since this relationship highlights the impact that the

23 Unfortunately there are no artistic representations of the AP Palace, but this tie between the image of the palace (however realistic) and the concept of the city as a whole can be clearly made in later times (Micale 2011, 23–25). Thus the visibility of the AP Palace might have also underlined the building's role as an emblem of the city, as perhaps a *pars par toto*.

architect aimed to achieve.[24] The Palace would have been seen from a large swath of the region to the west of the city, and perhaps even some activities on the roof of the palace would have been seen in the lower town.

Only one other structure, that has been found to date, commanded such a view of the surrounding area – the structures on top of the temple terrace.[25] These would have had a complete 360 degree view of the lower town and the hinterland, and they might have even been visible from the lowlands of the Tur Abdin mountains to the north, especially at night if there were fires on the temple terrace. With regard to the AP Palace, it is probable that from the temple terrace one would have been able to see into at least the stone courtyard, H3.

2.1.7 Building as Synthetic Whole

This chapter has analyzed the AP Palace, looking at the individual parts. However, it is also important to consider the structure as a synthetic whole. Three things point to an understanding of the palace in such a light: the plan of the palace as a whole, the presence of a drainage system which links several different sectors, and a tablet found in sector H.

The plan of the AP Palace is a grid-pattern (Aurenche 1981, 206–8), with east-west and north-south lines present in the excavated portions. This plan runs with only minor variations through the various sectors of the palace, maintaining the same pattern in both the service and formal wings. Interestingly, some of the variations which are found are due to the presence of preexisting structures, namely the platform in sector X to the south of sector C, as well as the *abi*, sector W, to the southwest of sector H. Both of these structures necessitate adapting the grid pattern of the palace: the southern wall of C3-C2-C1 is set slightly to the north, while the south wall of H1 becomes thinner as it goes to the west in order to accommodate the *abi*, and one might even imagine that the southern wall of H1 might have otherwise been situated several meters south as a continuation of the southern wall of H6.

The drainage system will be discussed in more detail below (2.2.2.7), but it is also pertinent here, in a discussion of the palace as a synthetic whole. The drainage system links not only sectors D and C, but seems to come from

24 The work of Richard Bradley (1997) shows, for a completely different region and type of material, how the correlation between viewpoint and landscape can be understood within a semantic framework, and a similar approach might yield interesting results with palaces of the Bronze Age in Syro-Mesopotamia. However, such a study would go beyond the scope of this study. For a comparison for the architectural use of terracing and courtyards, see Ragette 1974, 89.

25 For further reading on the temple terrace, see: F. Buccellati 2010; G. Buccellati 2010; Kelly-Buccellati 2013; Camatta forthcoming.

portions of the palace farther to the north, in areas as yet unexcavated (G. Buccellati 2005, 19–21). This drainage system runs under the walls of the palace, and serves a series of installations in the excavated portions. This indicates a very detailed level of design, and an ability to plan drains which ran across the whole building and serviced several branches which were linked to installations in diverse sectors of the palace.

One of the finds in the palace points directly to our understanding of the building as a synthetic whole: the tablet A15.231 (G. Buccellati 2005, 14–19).[26] This tablet is an architectural sketch, probably used by an architect to communicate the measurements of a specific portion of the palace to the responsible work crew. Once the foundations had been laid, the tablet was discarded within the wall itself, close to the rooms it presumably depicted. These considerations relate directly to the argument being developed here. It is already apparent from the way in which the Palace has been built that this massive construction was carried out all at once. This implies a very careful planning on a large scale, and a unitary architectural conception of the whole. The tablet confirms the implications already drawn from the excavated remains of the palace and tells us a great deal about the care and the awareness with which such large construction projects were undertaken and carried out.

2.2 Analysis of AP Palace: Sectors and Installations

The palace is divided into sectors, which are determined by three architectural elements: (1) access and circulation; (2) the presence of courtyards; (3) the mirrored plan. The division of the palace into sectors is thus based on the analysis of the structure as excavated: the ancient descriptions that might aid us in defining the individual sectors are unfortunately missing. Interesting is also the difference between the sectors and known room-configurations in private houses.

Access to the various parts of the palace is possible through doorways, and the placing of these doorways help define the sectors of the palace; this is particularly the case in sectors A-D. The two walls separating these sectors are the two longest continuous walls in this part of the palace: the wall separating B and D from A and C, as well as the wall separating A and B from D and C. Despite their length, there are very few doorways allowing for circulation: the wall between A and B and C and D has a single doorway allowing access between A7 and C7, while the wall separating B and D from A and C has two doorways but positioned directly next to each other, allowing access between B2 and A7 as well as D2 and C7. The fact that these long walls have only one or two doorways limits circulation between the various parts of the palace, and

26 See section 2.2.1.4.2 below for a detailed description of the tablet.

thus aids us in defining the sectors.

Because of the light and air that courtyards provide to the rooms surrounding them, courtyards traditionally form the nucleus of room-groupings. Functional descriptions are difficult for the courtyards themselves, since they are shared among the various rooms, and evidence (objects as well as installations) would be affected by weather. The *iwan*-shaped rooms are a specific room type always associated with a courtyard.[27]

Illustration 16: Oblique kite view of the excavations showing the excavated portions of the AP Palace (MZ V14k5042).

One distinct feature of the AP Palace is that a portion of the building's plan is reflected along a north-south running axis. This feature was described above (in section 2.1.4), but is worth noting here again since it helps define the parts of the building thus mirrored as sectors.

Perhaps because of this mirrored plan, the sectors seem to diverge more than usual from typical house-plans. This is reflected in two ways: the proportion between the long and short sides of the individual rooms, and the overall composition of the sector vis-à-vis standard house types.

2.2.1 Palace Sectors and Rooms

As excavated so far, the AP Palace consists of twelve sectors, which

27 See section 2.1.4.3 for a more detailed description of the *iwan* room-courtyard pair.

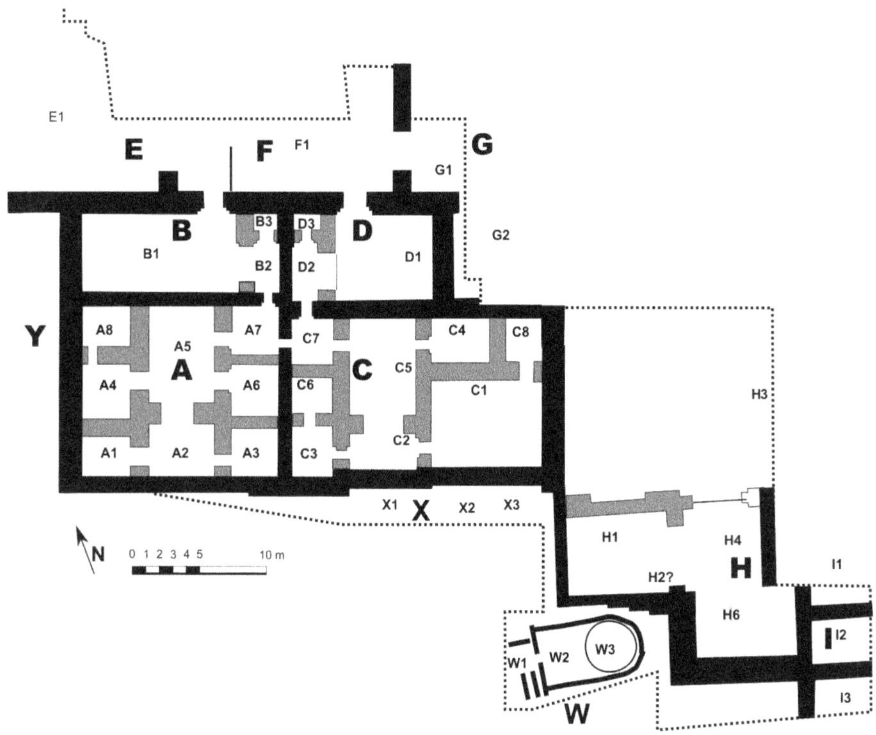

Illustration 17: Complete Plan of excavated portions of AP Palace showing sector and room designations.

have been separated into five groups or wings. The first group consists of four sectors, sectors A C B and D, which make up the service wing of the palace. The second group of sectors, sectors E and F, reflect the access to the north, which remains unexcavated due to later cultural deposits dating to the Khabur and Mittani periods. The third group consists of a single sector, sector G, which is the most probable location for a staircase linking the service and formal wings of the palace. The formal wing of the palace with sectors H and I forms the fourth group, while sectors Y X and W lie outside the palace but are important to consider in relation to the structure.

2.2.1.1 Sectors A, B, C, D – The Service Wing of the AP Palace

Sectors A, B, C, D form a 'wing' of the palace, forming a unit because of the way in which the architecture conditions access, with only two doors giving access to 21 rooms. The excavators have identified it as primarily tied to service functions because of the lack of decorative elements and the small finds present in the various rooms.

Furthermore, the walls in this sector are not plastered, and there is evidence of storage in the presence of seal impressions, the size of the rooms, and in the limited access to the various sectors in this wing. The lower elevation of this wing vis-à-vis the formal sector may also indicate that it was a service rather than a public area of the palace.

The large number of broken seal impressions scattered over the accumulations in B1 indicate that a number of containers were opened in this room, suggesting that administrative recording activities might be tied to this wing.

The two doors leading into the service wing both lead off of the same space, a courtyard, F1. The map below shows an analysis of the access to the service wing, with a number circled with a dotted line in each room. This number represents the number of rooms through which one must pass to reach that point, beginning in courtyard F1.

Thus, room C2 is the fifth room one reaches when one starts in courtyard F1. Such an analysis is useful because it highlights both the similarities and differences in the architectural patterns present in this part of the AP Palace.

Furthermore, what is interesting is the relative lack of variability in the pathways which can be chosen to reach the rooms. In a sociological study of architecture, Ankerl writes (Ankerl 1981, 157): "Another basic feature of the architectural space system is the fact that spaces are not made in a row like words in spoken language. If the parallel existence of the difference sensory spaces gives a simultaneity, the tridimensional arrangement (not unilinear alignment) of spaces allows the 'reader' of architecture not only to reverse his direction, but also to choose alternative 'readings' with a completely different string order." The service wing has, however, a distinct lack of alternative readings. In no case is it possible to reach a room in the same number of steps following a different path: in illustration 18 it is obvious the rooms through which one passes to arrive at the number of steps given. If, however, one were to want to follow a longer path but not re-trace ones steps (walking into and then back out of the same doorway) then only one variation is possible: to enter the doorway from courtyard F which is farther from the goal and use the single doorway between A7 and C7 to cross the sector wall separating B and D and A and C.[28] As an example, to reach A5 from F1 the shortest path is: F1-B1-B2-A7-A5, consisting of four steps. No other four step route is possible. The length of this route is 22.1 meters, while the direct distance (as the crow flies) is 12.5 meters. Only one longer route, is possible without retracing one's steps: F1-D1-D2-C7-A7-A5. This route consists of five steps.

The longest route within the service wing is from F1 to C8, passing through F1-D1-D2-C7-C5-C2-C1-C8, a total of seven steps. The pedestrian

28 On control rooms, see Aurenche 1977, 60.

distance traversed is 43.5 meters, while the direct, as-the-crow-flies, distance is only 16.9 m.[29]

This lack of variability emphasizes the control over the access patterns, since 'avoiding' someone, such as a guard, would be nearly impossible due to

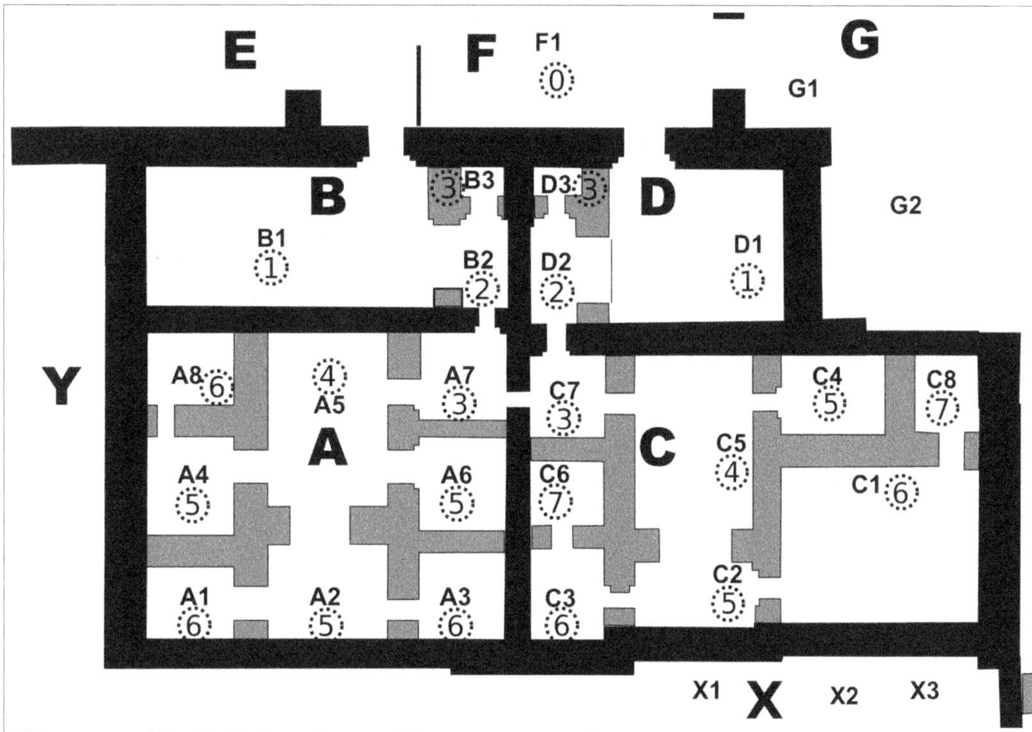

Illustration 18: AP Palace Service Wing, access analysis.

this architectural configuration. This very linear grouping then highlights the "isolating nature of the envelope" (Ankerl 1981, 155) as Ankerl describes the way architecture limits the perceptive spheres.

A further consideration is that the distance from the courtyard F1 to any given room may also be an indicator of the function of the room vis-à-vis the multi-functional space F1 or other courtyards.

2.2.1.1.1 Sector A

Sector A is the most damaged of all of the sectors in the AP Palace. This is due to two factors: erosion and modern stone removal. The erosion was particularly bad in this sector of the palace because it was the area least covered by later deposits, as well as a particularly strong *wadi* running along the southern edge of the palace, coming down from the east.

Upon excavating the rooms of this sector, the excavators came across a strange feature: where a stone wall was expected, there was instead a trench

29 An interesting take on this type of analysis has been done by F. Deblauwe (Deblauwe 1992, 1994, 1997a, 1997b).

filled with jumbled *wadi* wash and modern garbage, including tin cans and

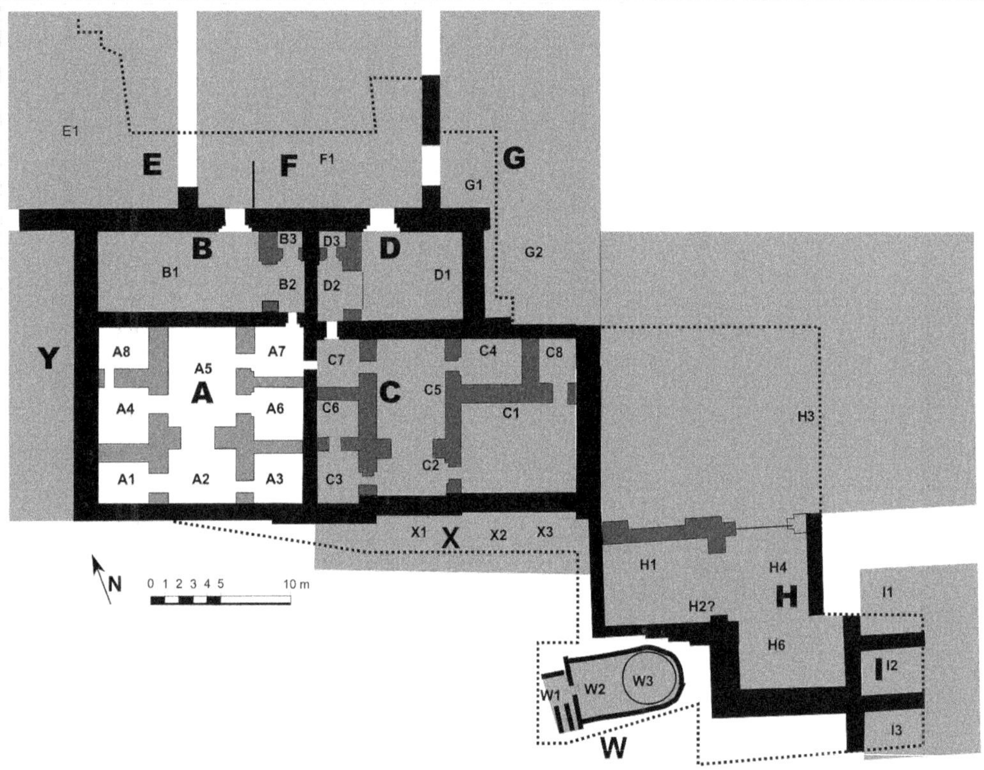

Illustration 19: AP Palace with sector A highlighted.

plastic. These 'modern' trenches were the width of the ancient walls, and sometimes were in a position across from one side of an ancient doorjamb. The most plausible reconstruction which explains this phenomenon is this: at some point when the modern village of Mozan was being built, some of the stones of this sector of the palace were removed. A few of the stones were visible due to the cut of the *wadi*, and were identified and used by families building houses in the nearby village. As they were removing the visible stones from the *wadi* cut, they must have seen that behind these initial stones there were further stones. Thus a 'mining' of the ancient stone walls began, to reuse them in the modern buildings of the village. When there were no more stones visible, the mining stopped – thus in the excavations there are door-jambs with one side marked by a modern trench and the other side by ancient stones. Such reuse is not limited to modern times; the stone pavement in sector H was similarly damaged by pits dug during Phase 5, and in Phase 6[30] some of the buildings in units A18 use stone which might have been similarly recuperated in their construction.

30 For more on the chronological phases, refer to section 2.1.2.6 above.

2.2.1.1.2 Sector C

The room configurations of sector C reflect the configuration in sector

Illustration 20: AP Palace showing 'negative' sector A walls (MZ V13d8233).

A, along the sector wall dividing sectors A and B from sectors C and D.

The mirror-configuration of the two sectors has three exceptions. First, the size of the two sectors is slightly different: sector C is longer along the east-west axis than sector A is, and sector C is slightly shorter on the north-south axis. This can be explained when considering the possibility of a staircase in sector G.

The second difference can be seen in rooms C6-A6. Room C6 has what can be understood as a toilet installation (small vertical shaft lined with baked bricks) as well as a drain, while room A6 has no installations which can help give a functional description to the room. Also, Room C6 opens to the south, into room C3, while room A6 opens to the west, into courtyard A5. This change in doorways may be in function of the toilet and drain installations.

The third difference can be seen in rooms C4/C8 and A4/A8. In sector C room C1 is a much larger size than any other room in sectors C or A, larger than even the two courtyards. This affects the two rooms C4 and C8 in that C4 is 'pushed' up to the northern limit of the sector, while C8 is moved to the east

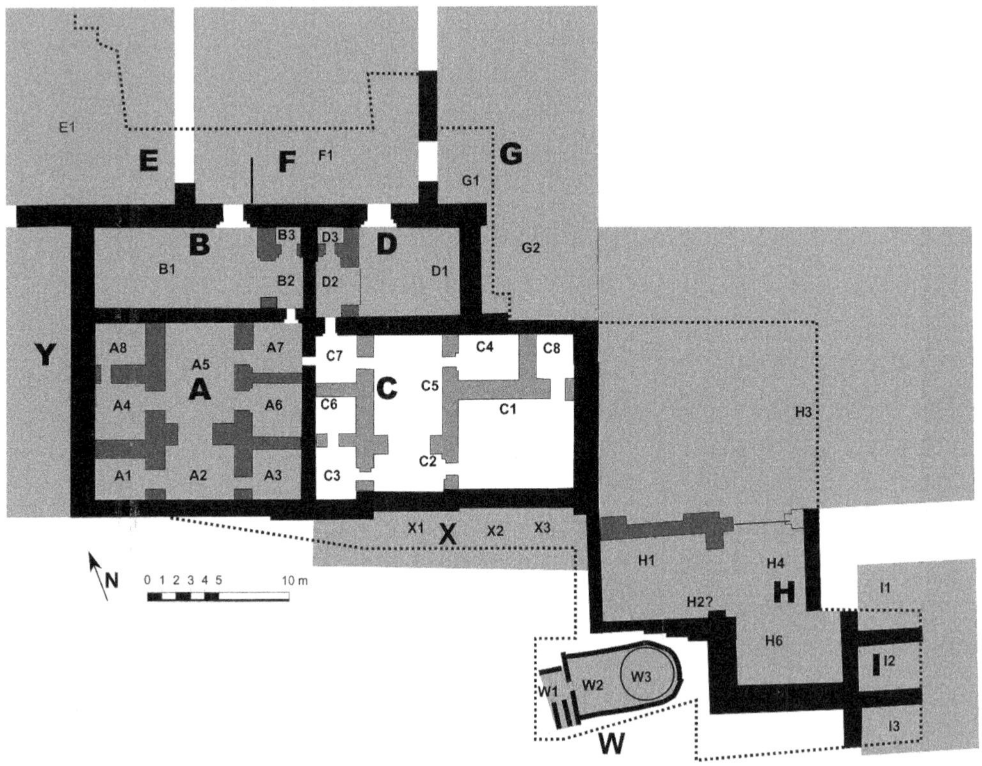

Illustration 21: AP Palace with sector C highlighted.

of C4 with an access to C1. Because of the size of C1, this arrangement would mean that C8 was the farthest room in sectors A and C from a courtyard (C5 through C1 and C2), therefore the room with the least natural light coming from a courtyard. Also, looking at the access analysis above in Illustration 18, it is the only room which is 7 rooms removed from courtyard F – in the other sectors the farthest room is only 6 rooms removed from the courtyard.

The walls of C1 have high stonework compared to other walls in the sector. The eastern wall is very high because of the courtyard of the formal wing of the palace (H3), the floor level of which is 2 meters higher than the floor in C1. One of the stones shows signs of pounding, which is very unusual for the AP Palace. The eastern wall bonds with the southern wall, but not with the doorjamb between C1 and C8.

2.2.1.1.3 Sector B

Sector B consists of only three rooms, but was the richest sector of the service wing of the palace in terms of small finds. In room B1 the majority of the seal impressions from the palace were found.

B is organized along the same mirror principle with D, just as A and C mirror each other. There are only three rooms, one a large hall or courtyard (B1), one an *iwan* (B2), and the third a small room, B3, which might have served as a small storage area within this sector.

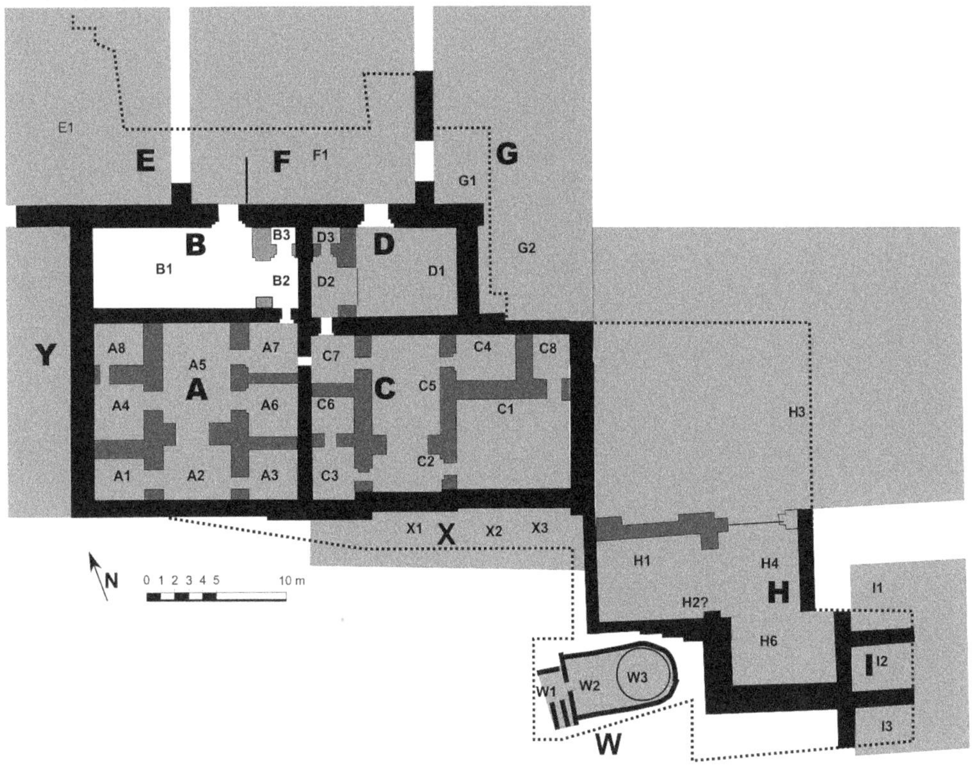

Illustration 22: AP Palace with sector B highlighted.

2.2.1.1.4 Sector D

Sector D mirrors the architecture of sector B, with the exception of room size, primarily D1. The archaeological record indicates that D1 served as a cooking area, with a *tannur* and a cooking hearth situated in the middle of the room, and ash deposits in the vicinity.

In this area a sounding was conducted below the floors to determine what lay below – a very hard packing was uncovered, but it was unclear if this packing was related to the construction of the palace or dates to a previous occupation layer.

2.2.1.2 Sectors E, F – Access to the North and East

Sectors E and F lie to the North of sectors B and D, and are accessed through two doorways to these sectors which formed the service wing. These two sectors provide the only access to B and D (and through them to A and C).

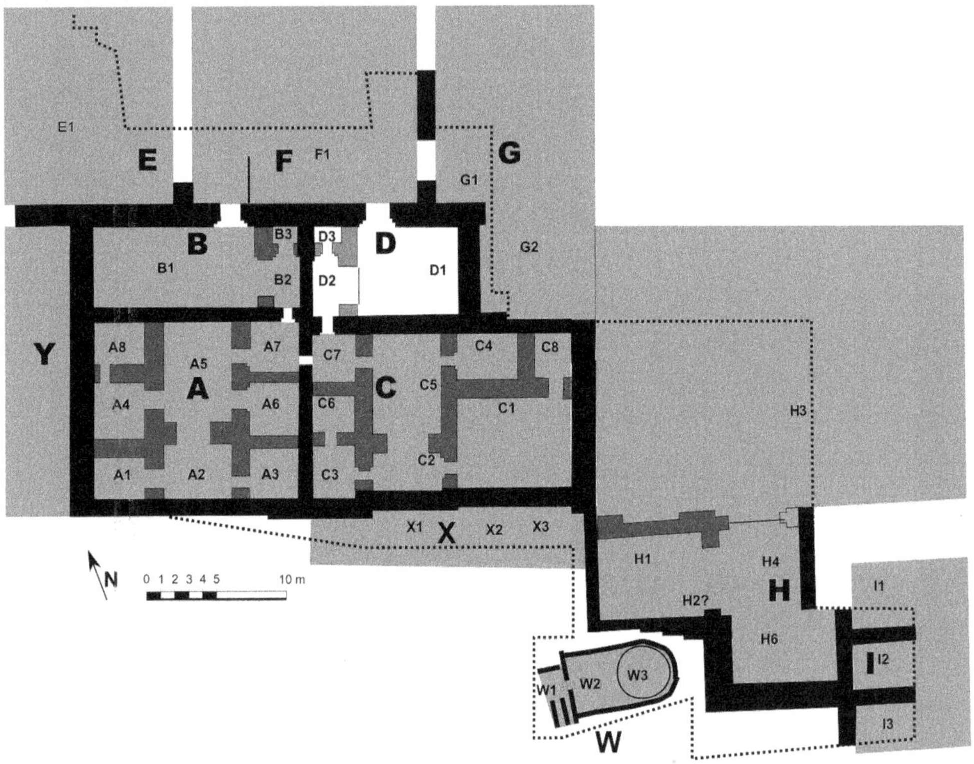

Illustration 23: AP Palace with sector D highlighted.

2.2.1.2.1 Sector E

Sector E lies to the west of sector F, north of sector B. This sector was excavated only in part; later houses and burials were found in the excavation area to the north, which limited the exposure of the AP Palace levels.

Only two walls were found in this area, a small wall running north-south, bonded with the north wall of B1 and just to the west of the doorway between B1 and sector F. This short wall defines the boundary between sectors E and F. It is significant because it suggests a wide opening rather than a doorway. This leaves two possibilities for the interpretation of sector E: as either an *iwan* or as an entrance to the palace.

As an *iwan* (see sections 2.1.4.3 and 2.4.3 for more on the concept of *iwan*), sector E would have an opening facing east, which is unusual (D2 being the only comparable room). It would have been considerably larger than either of the *iwans* in the service wing, rooms A2 and C2. If this room were an *iwan*, one would also expect a doorway along the wall shared with B1, as the other *iwans* in A2 and C2 lead to rooms to either side.

The second and more likely interpretation is that sector E (of which, again, only one room has been excavated to date) is part of an entrance to the palace from the western side. The fact that the southern wall of room E1 (northern wall of B1) runs further to the west than any other is an indication that the entrance may have been stepped out from the palace towards the west.

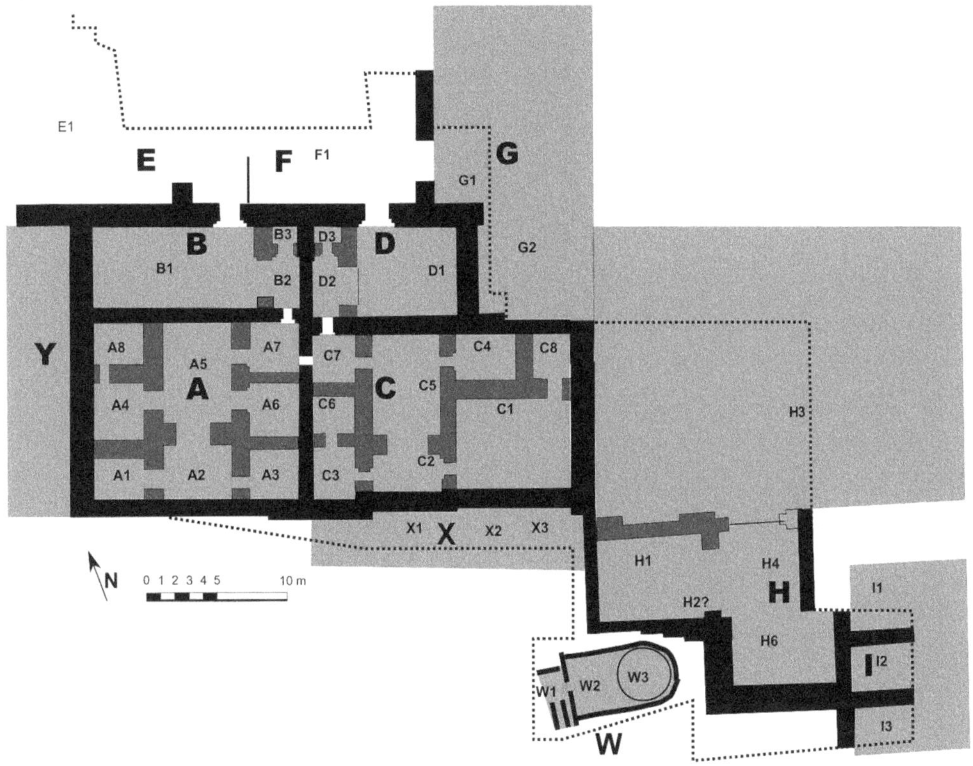

Illustration 24: AP Palace with sectors E and F highlighted.

The southern wall of E1 is also significant because it clearly is set on top of the earlier city wall, indicating first that the city wall was no longer used as a defensive structure, and that the palace was designed with a 'viewshed' looking over the lower town and the immediate outer town just outside the outer city wall (F. Buccellati 2014a).

2.2.1.2.2 Sector F

Sector F lies to the north of sector D, and the excavated portions show that it forms a central node for access within the palace. No other sector gives access to as many different areas of the palace as sector F, at least in the portions excavated to date. Sector F comprises a single courtyard, F1, but has not been completely excavated, with the unexcavated areas lying to the north, where more rooms might be found.

F1 allows access to sectors B and D to the south, sector E to the west, and sector G to the east. A pebble floor lies in the eastern part of the courtyard, while a platform of baked bricks forms part of the access between sectors G and F. One interesting element is a small retaining wall running north-south between the doorways to sectors B and D. Its purpose is unclear, since it does not form a border between specific areas, nor does it appear to have helped with water. It would have been a hindrance when passing from B1 to D1, since the most direct route would not have passed through B2-A7-C7-D2 but would have simply gone through F1. It seems unlikely that a retaining wall would have been built in such a central area for the purpose of limiting access, but the possibility bears mentioning.

2.2.1.3 Sector G – Possible Staircase Access

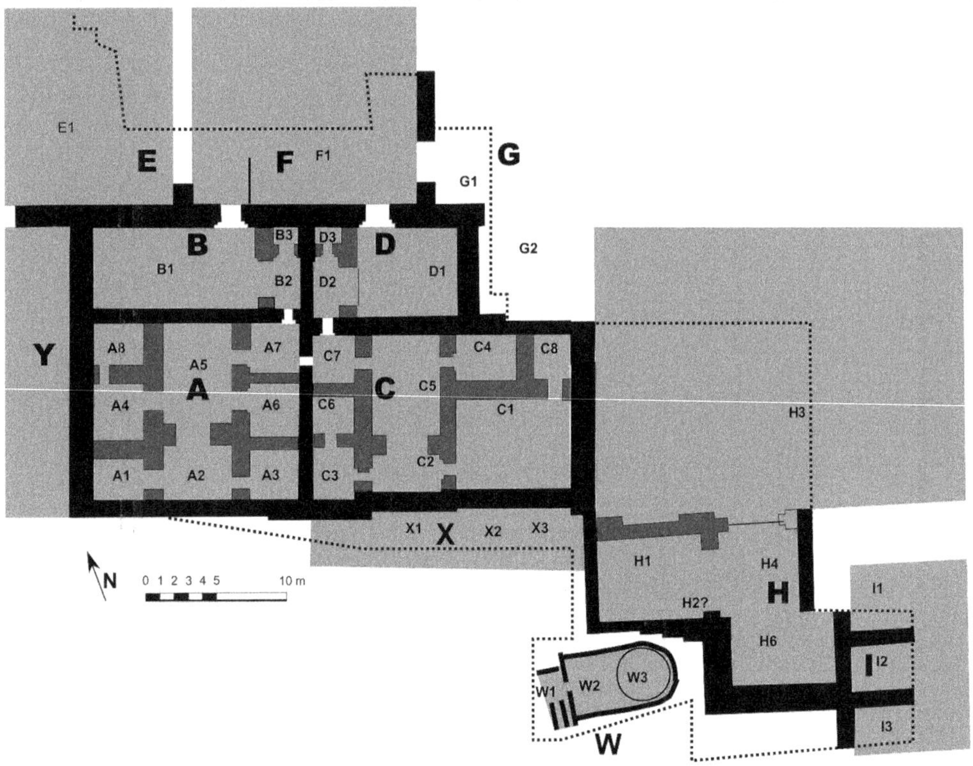

Illustration 25: AP Palace with sector G highlighted.

Sector G is the least excavated of all of the sectors found to date, even if it is one of the most tantalizing. It is here that one might expect to find the access between the formal wing (sectors H and I) and the service wing (sectors A to D). This access would be made directly from courtyard F1, and would lead (probably through another room) to the courtyard of the formal wing, H3. It might not have been the only access between these sectors, depending on how much the palace extended to the north. It seems odd that the staircase in sector G would have probably been the access used when passing from the kitchen area in D to the formal wing, traversing the courtyard F, but no access routes were found.

Sector G seems to consist of two potential rooms, G1 and G2. These two appear to be divided by the extension of the North wall of D1 towards the east. No doorway has been found between these two rooms, but it seems likely that there would be a doorway along this east-west running wall.

2.2.1.4 *Sectors H and I – The Formal Wing of the AP Palace*

At present there is no indication of reciprocal access between the two wings, although it seems plausible to assume, as previously mentioned, that the unexcavated portion of area G may contain a staircase linking the two. It should further be pointed out that while in the service wing there were considerable accumulations with material attributed to King Tupkish and his court, the formal wing was kept perfectly clean, also on account of the hard surfaces that characterize its pavements, as a result of which there was practically no accumulation which would allow one to correlate the two wings in terms of the deposition within them. There are, in any case, two main reasons why it seems certain that the architecture presented here was a single structure, namely a palace with (at least) two wings. The first is that the two wings share the same wall (the north-south running wall between C1 and H3), which is extremely well constructed. The second is that a stepped layout for palaces is found elsewhere in the region, notably at Tell Beydar and Tell Chuera (for a slightly earlier period).[31] Accordingly, there seems to be no reason to doubt that here a single overall structure can be hypothesized, and that the sectors may be properly articulated as belonging together.

2.2.1.4.1 Sector H

Sector H forms the main excavated portion of the formal area of the palace, consisting of three rooms (H1, H4 and H6) and the large stone courtyard (H3). Two elements support the idea that this sector is part of the formal area of the palace: the wall-plaster in H1 and the extent of the stone courtyard H3. H1 has a portion of the mudbrick wall in the NE corner of the room which had white gypsum plaster. The walls of the service wing were clearly not plastered, because the ashy accumulations within the rooms left a definite mark on the vertical surface of the walls which would not have been possible if they had been plastered. This makes this find an important indicator of a more representative function for these rooms. Rooms H4 and H6 are not separated by a doorway, but are rather distinguished by a narrowing of the space on one side; they might be better considered two linked areas rather than two rooms.

31 For more on these comparisons see section 2.4 below.

Two drains are present between the rooms H1 and H4, with the openings to the two located only a few meters apart. This peculiarity for the palace must be tied to a particular function, but neither objects indicating what this might be nor a parallel in the ethnographic metaphor or texts shed light on what activities might have taken place here. The first drain goes from room H2

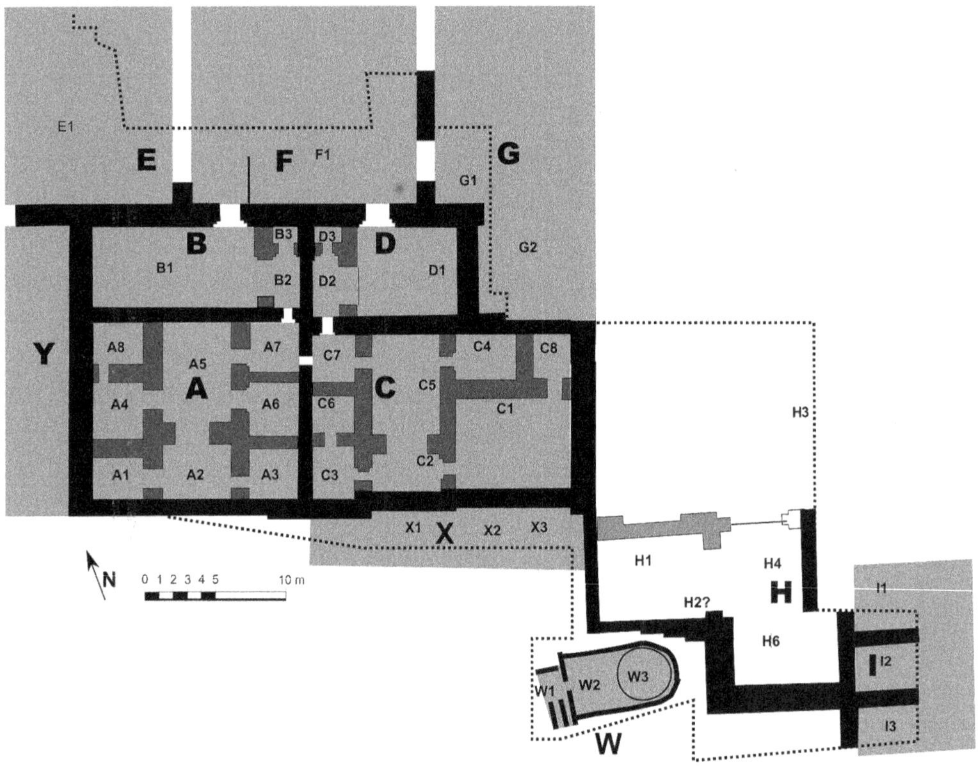

Illustration 26: AP Palace with sector H highlighted.

and passes through the southern wall, draining outside the palace quite near the *abi*. The second drain was located in room H4 and went through the doorway leading to the courtyard H3, emptying immediately onto the paving stones next to the doorway. The opening of the drain (in H4) had a broken piece of pottery serving as a catch-all basin, and the drain itself was constructed of baked bricks.

The stone courtyard H3 is the second reason for considering this sector of the palace as being part of the formal wing. The size, quality and quantity of the stones and their preparation are not seen anywhere else in the AP Palace, and such a large and energy-intensive architectural element is an indicator of the monumentality of this sector of the palace. Such a large effort in construction can only be seen in one other construction at the site, temple area JP.

The stone courtyard was damaged by a series of pits which were dug from the Khabur levels above. When the pit-diggers encountered the stones of the courtyard, in most cases they removed them. Certainly these pits were not dug to mine the palace levels for stone, but once discovered they were occasionally removed. In one case a stone was left at the bottom of the pit, in other cases a few stones were removed. These stones were not reused in the immediate vicinity of the pits, because the Khabur structures found directly next to the area from which the pits were dug did not use stone in their construction.[32]

The holes in the stone courtyard which were made by the Khabur period pits gave us an unexpected look into the material below the stone courtyard. One might have expected a very hard fill on which the stones rested, due to their weight and the fact that the area was an open courtyard and thus particularly affected by water infiltration. Instead, baked bricks were found, which seemed to be connected together in a larger hydraulic installation underneath the stone courtyard. With only a few areas of this installation exposed it is difficult to definitively determine its function, and impossible to see the entirety of the installation. Despite these limitations one can hypothesize that the installation was linked to the collection of rainwater under the stone courtyard. The use of baked brick, as opposed to stone as is the case in sectors B and D, indicates a function different from the drainage channel in the service wing of the palace. Furthermore, the fact that baked bricks were found in several spots under the courtyard indicates that the installation is not merely a single drainage channel coming from an undiscovered portion of the palace to the North or East of the courtyard.

One can further speculate that perhaps a portion of the installation lead to the southernmost portion of the courtyard's western wall. The fact that the perimeter wall of the stone courtyard has an area outside of the palace behind it is a quite rare feature in palatial and residential structures. Typically, courtyards are surrounded by the rooms of the structure on all sides; in the few cases where one perimetral wall of a courtyard is not also the wall of a room, then one typically sees a main doorway in that wall. Here one has the unusual situation where a portion of the courtyard's perimetral wall backs onto a space which lies outside of the palace itself. It seems likely that this would have been a deliberate choice by the architect, since the wall of the room to the south (H1) could easily have been moved a few meters north to be in line with the southern wall of room C1.

Since it seems clear that a space was intentionally left along the

32 For more information on the Khabur period settlement see the forthcoming publication on excavation unit A16 by the author in the Urkesh Global Record online publication series.

courtyard's perimetral wall, one can ask why? It is a small segment, at most one meter wide, and it may simply be the result of adapting the layout of the entire building to the preexisting complex of the platform (X) and the *abi* (W) (for more on this see section 2.1.7).

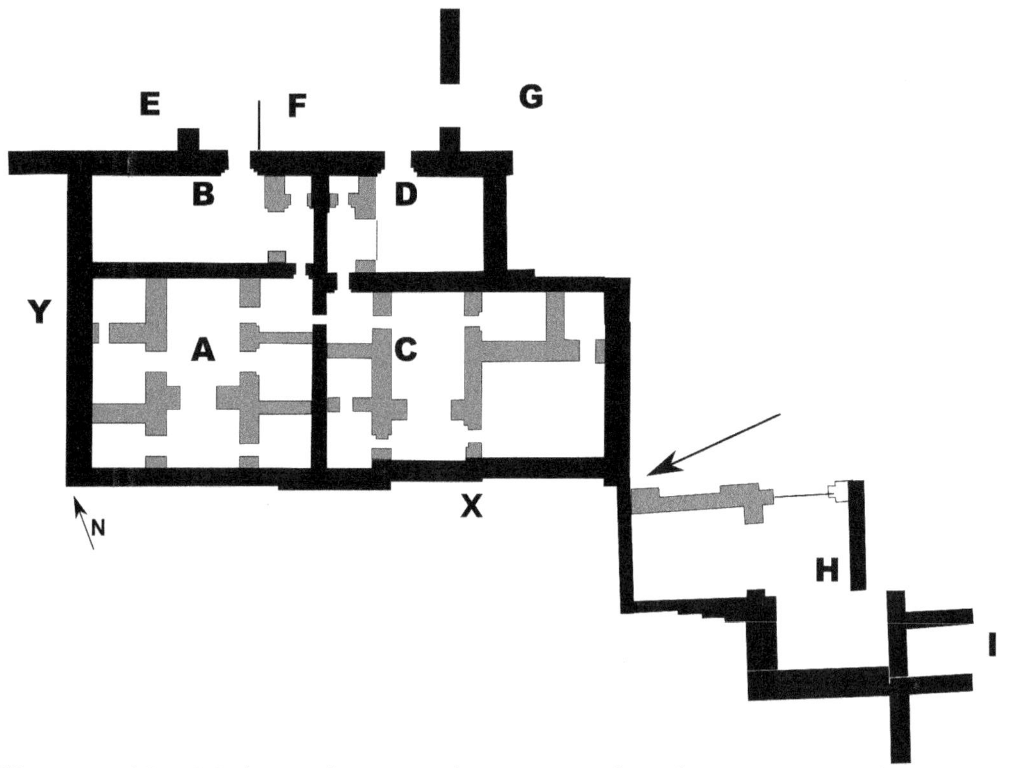

Illustration 27: AP Palace with arrow indicating spot where the stone courtyard's perimeter wall backs onto area X outside of the palace.

Rooms H1, H2, H4 and H6 seem to be accessible only through a doorway leading to the stone-paved courtyard, H3. A possible interpretation is that this was a dependent area in function of events that would take place in the courtyard. The presence of a drain in H2 and of a small well in H6 may indicate that water could be drawn to be served to people in the courtyard H3, for ablutions or for drinking.

2.2.1.4.2 Sector I

Sector I has been excavated only to a limited extent, and it is especially tantalizing because it most likely opens onto the eastern portion of the AP Palace, where access to the palace from the plaza may have been located, and may have held the king's residential quarters as well. This suite of three rooms is especially interesting because it may be interpreted as the actual implementation of an architectural sketch drawn on a small tablet (A15.231) found in the debris of a wall in the nearby room H4.

This tablet does not have cuneiform signs on it (two wedges in a cross-pattern probably are a marker, not a cuneiform sign), but rather portrays an architectural drawing. This drawing is not, however, a detailed architectural plan, due to its small size and the lack of detail or written information. The hypothesis can thus be made that the plan is a sketch for a work-crew or a subordinate architect, who would have been responsible for the construction of a part of a building.

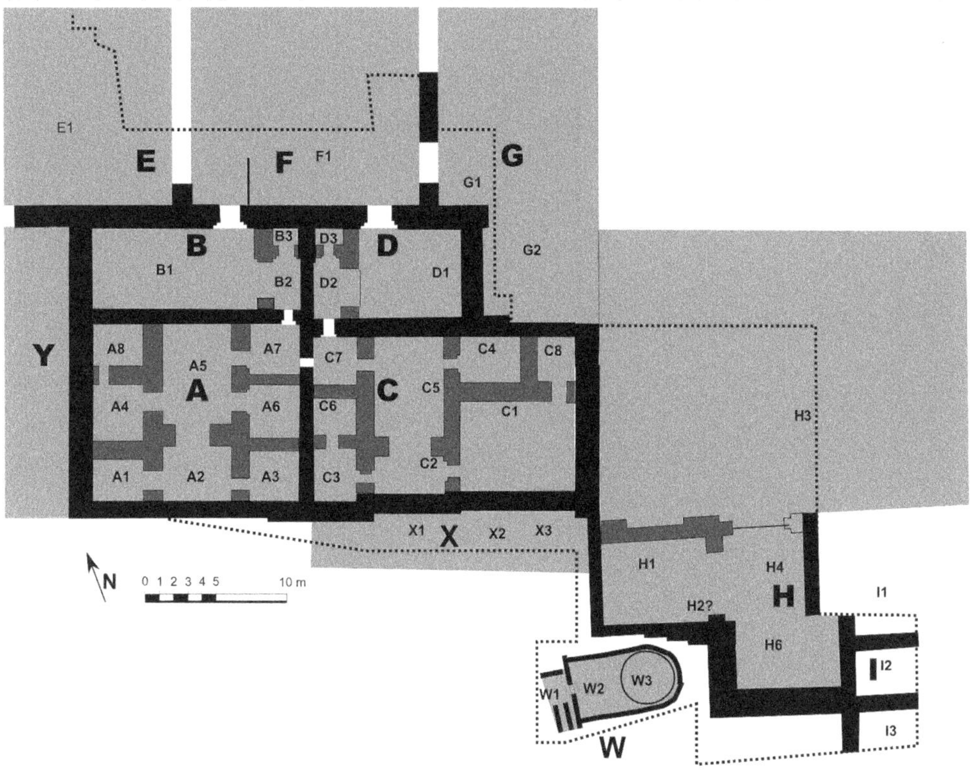

Illustration 28: AP Palace with sector I highlighted.

The drawing was found in room H4, but it was not found in the floor accumulations or the abandonment fill – instead it comes from the wall collapse from the wall along the Eastern side of the room. This leads to the conclusion that the tablet comes not from the use-period of the palace, but rather was placed in the wall itself while the construction was taking place. The most logical place for this deposition would be in the layer of sherds and other debris between the stone and mudbrick layers of the wall.

No measurements are given on the tablet, but on the basis of the hexagesimal system which was current in Mesopotamia,[33] one can correlate

33 Hexagesimal refers to a base 60 system of counting – one unit can be broken down into 60 smaller units, and 60 smaller units can be combined to make one larger unit. Our way of

quite well the three excavated rooms in sector I with the drawing. Assuming a scale 1:240 (4 times 60), the distance of 300 cms on the ground between the two walls as excavated corresponds to the distance of 1.25 cms on the tablet (300/1.25 = 24). If one can further take the two wedges on the lower right of the tablet for something other than a cuneiform sign, but the location of the

Illustration 29: Tablet A15.231 showing 1) measurement on tablet 2) equivalent in hexagesimal system and 3) possible relationship to measurement points (G. Buccellati 2005, 17-19).

benchmark on the ground, the distance of 3.60 cms between point a and b on the tablet would correspond to 864 cms on the ground between a presumed benchmark and the corner of the room as shown (864/3.60=240) (G. Buccellati 2005, 17–19).

The Akkadian word for surveyor is *abu aslim* "the father of the rope", and this appellation may suggest how the tablet was used. The tablet might have been entrusted to a surveyor who would have taken the proper distances from the benchmarks, and marked the spot on the ground for the work crew to use in laying the stone substructure of the wall. At that point, the tablet was no longer needed, and would have been tossed into the fill between stone and mudbrick portions of an adjacent wall, whence it fell to the floor when the wall collapsed.

The importance of such 'blank' architectural plans is evidenced by a detail of a statue of Gudea (slightly later than the AP Palace): on his lap, there is an architectural plan with a graduated scale below the plan, which cannot be adequately explained, but which seems to refer to some aspect of measurements associated with the plan itself.

---

counting time is hexagesimal: 60 seconds make up a minute, and 60 minutes make up an hour.

2.2.1.5 Sectors Y, X and W – Outside areas of the AP Palace

Three sectors lie outside of the palace proper: Y, X and W. They are included in this study since they border on the palace itself, and each has marked the palace in its own way. Sector Y borders the palace to the west, lying to the west of sectors A, B and E. Sector X lies south of sector C and west of sector H. Sector X contains a platform which was probably connected to the *abi*. Sector W lies south of sectors H and X, and contains the *abi*.

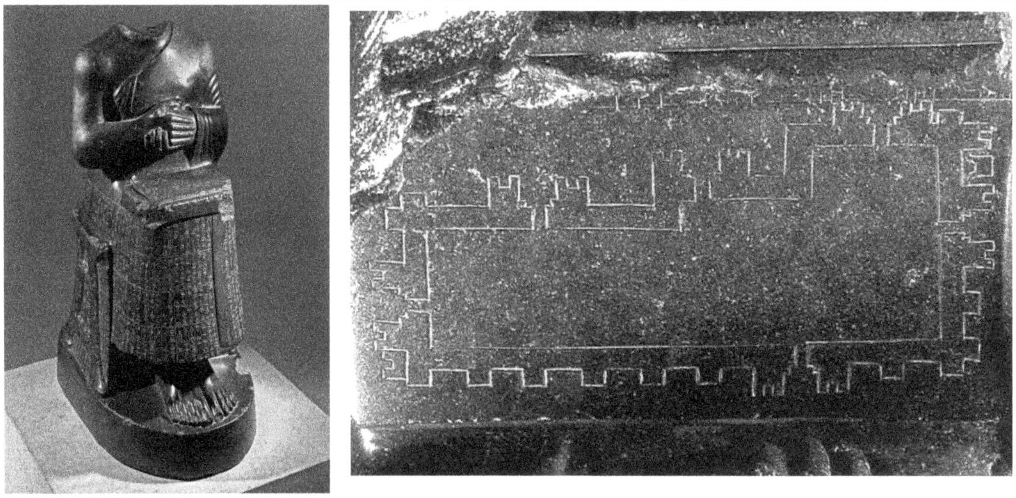

Illustration 30: Statue of Gudea with plan of temple (Musée du Louvre).

There is one possibility which is worth considering at this juncture, vis-à-vis the open area to the south of the palace. Instead of being a space outside the perimeter of the palace, it is possible that the palace area extends south of sector I, and was closed with a perimeter wall to the west. This would mean that the *abi* and the platform (sector X) would not have been outside the confines of the palace, but would have been enclosed by the palace complex (while remaining outside in the sense that they were not in a roofed space) to the south and to the west, as well as to the north and the east. This is a very interesting hypothesis with regard to the perception of social space during the time of the construction of the AP Palace, and begs the question of how this space was organized before the AP Palace was built.[34] Only further excavation will be able to give more evidence for the organization of this space.

2.2.1.5.1 Sector Y

Sector Y lies west of sector E, in an area where the inner city-wall

34 This idea, in particular, was explored together with Jan-Waalke Meyer, during one of many fruitful discussions.

would have run before it was removed to make room for the palace. If sector E was indeed an entrance to the palace (for further discussion of this see 2.2.1.2.1) then sector Y would have been the area directly adjacent to this

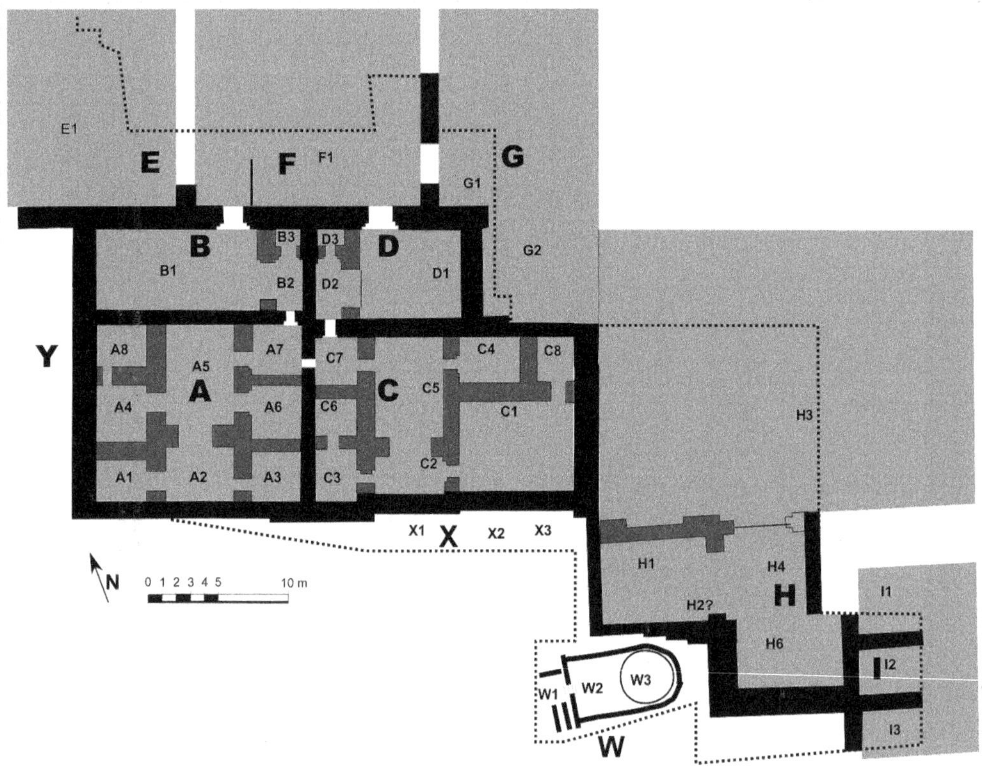

Illustration 31: AP Palace with sectors Y, X and W highlighted.

entrance.

2.2.1.5.2 Sector X

Sector X bordered directly on the southern wall of the palace. The drain which ran through the palace (see 2.2.2.7) emptied into this area, directly south of room C2. A further element in this area is a platform with several layers of phytoliths, indicating that the platform was covered with organic material, perhaps reed matting. There was no direct access from the palace, so it is unclear how one would have accessed this area from the palace itself.

It is worth noting that sector X must have been little used in ancient times, at least based on the evidence present: the walls of sector C and H closed the area to the North and the East, while the abi lay to the South-East. The presence of the platform shows that there was activity, but the access to the sector seems to have been rather limited.

The southern wall of sectors C and A are one of only two walls in the palace which change width (the other is the southern wall of H1), and it is likely that this is an expedient adaptation to the fact that the platform in sector X was already there when the palace was being built.

2.2.1.5.3 Sector W

The final sector, sector W, lies outside the palace and includes the *abi*, which was located to the south of room H1. This structure has been published elsewhere (Kelly-Buccellati 2002), but it is worth mentioning here in regard to the palace, in particular access to the *abi* and the southern wall of sector H.

As with sector X, the access from the palace to the *abi* is as yet unclear. It is possible that from sector I access would have been possible, but such an access has not yet been found. One further indication (in addition to ceramic evidence) that the *abi* pre-dates the palace is the fact that the southern wall of room H1 narrows as it runs west towards the *abi*. This wall, along with the southern wall of sectors C and A, is the only case in the whole palace where a wall changes in width.

2.2.2 *Palace Installations*

There are nine major installations present in the palace of varying types: a 'bathroom' installation in C6, a bin for clay in C2, a set of small charred beams in C1, the kitchen installation in D1, the drain in H4, a pebble path in F1, a baked-brick platform between F1 and G1, and finally the drainage system present in sectors D and C.

Illustration 32: Drain coming from C6 (lower left) and progressing through C3 to C2. Note change from baked brick to stone covering as drain goes deeper (V16d1172).

2.2.2.1 *The 'Bathroom' Installation in C6*

In C6 an installation was uncovered consisting of two baked-brick elements: a lined vertical shaft and a drain. The lined vertical shaft had been presumably covered in antiquity, since it was discovered empty of accumulations; it was likely used as a toilet. No sign of the covering could be found, suggesting that a wooden or textile cover had been used. The drain was similarly made of baked brick for the first portion, and then once a certain depth was reached, it was lined with stone. The drain passed from room C6 to the south, into room C3, and from there it passed to room C2, where it exited the south wall of the palace.

It is worth mentioning that this path is rather unexpected, since other drains in the palace went under walls, begging the question if this installation was a later addition to the palace; however there is no evidence that could lead us to answer this question. The installation was certainly used in phase 2 (use of the structure as a royal palace) and was subsequently abandoned in phase 3, since the accumulation covering the lined vertical shaft dated to phase 3.

Illustration 33: Clay bin in room C2 (MZ V12d1408).

2.2.2.2 The Clay Bin in C2

In room C2 an installation was found against the southern wall of the palace. This installation was rectangularly shaped, and in form resembled a bin. Striking was the material used in its construction: the bin, at least the surface, was covered in thin layers of high-quality clay (uniform in texture, fine particles, no inclusions). Additionally, around the bin a large quantity of clay balls were found, measuring one to two cm in diameter. These were too small and too round to be slingballs, and were made of the same high quality clay as was found in the bin itself.

Illustration 34: Detail of bin, showing layering of clay (MZ V12d1429).

A possible interpretation of this material is that the installation was a storage bin for high quality clay used by scribes. Note that the clay used for sealings was not this high-quality clay, so the material here would not have been used for sealings. In addition to the quality of the clay is also the placement within the palace itself – room C2, where the bin was found, is an *iwan* located south of the courtyard C8. Such an area would have had ideal lighting for scribal activities. It had also been hypothesized that the small room C8 (which 'violates' the mirroring of the eastern portion of the building) might have served as the archive room. However, no evidence was found for any scribal activity in this sector, and the presence of the charred logs does not fit with the scribal hypothesis.

2.2.2.3 *The Charred Beams in C1*

In room C1 a series of small charred beams were found, lying scattered

Illustration 35: Reconstruction of log position in C1 (MZ V16d1084).

about the room. While an initial interpretation might point to the collapse of a burnt roof, the archaeological data collected did not bear out this interpretation. First, no other burnt material was found: one would also expect to find burnt roofing material with mat impressions, but none was found. One would also expect the accumulations in which the beams rested to show traces of a conflagration: burnt soil, large quantities of ash and charcoal. These were also absent from the archaeological record. The beams would have been badly

Illustration 36: overview of charred logs in room C1 (MZ V14d1205).

charred, so as to leave little trace of the original wood. This was also not the case, and several of the beams still showed the texture of the wood. Finally, the beams were embedded in different accumulations, and were resting at different angles within the soil matrix. This suggests that they were used in connection with different, repetitive episodes, where a log would be set on fire, which was then intentionally put out. The interpretation of this collection of charred logs might point to their function as part of an installation, but the purpose of such an installation is difficult to determine.[35]

Illustration 37: Detail of one of the logs in C1, showing lack of burning in surrounding accumulation and on wall (left) (MZ V12d0929).

Illustration 38: Pebble path in F1 along southern and eastern edges of the courtyard (MZ V12d2913).

35 One possible interpretation is that the logs were used in the processing of woolen textiles – the author has observed rugs being treated by brushing them with fire in the *souk* in Damascus, but no direct evidence in the ancient record was found which might support such an interpretation.

2.2.2.4 *The Path in F1*

A path (A9f80) made of gravel was discovered along the southern wall and the eastern wall and doorway of courtyard F1, leading from just east of the doorway between B1 and F1 to the baked brick platform in the doorway between F1 and G1 (G. Buccellati and Kelly-Buccellati 2000, 139–41).

2.2.2.5 *The Kitchen Installations in D1*

In room D1 two installations were found: a *tannur* and an andiron; these two installations suggest that room D1 was a kitchen. The position of D1 near the storage areas, as well as the (presumed) staircase to the formal wing in area G, would have facilitated the movement of supplies to the kitchen and the distribution of prepared food to the various areas of the palace, primarily the formal wing with the royal apartments. There was no opening in this room onto the water channel which ran directly under the floor (for more on the drainage system see section 2.2.2.7); this may be a further indication that the channel was used to remove dirty water rather than as a runoff of clean water.

Illustration 39: Brick platform between F1 and G1. Note that bricks have been sprayed with water to enhance the coloring of the baked bricks (MZ V12d2714).

2.2.2.6 The Baked-Brick Platform F1-G1

On the south eastern side of the courtyard F1 and connected with a

Illustration 41: Brick platform looking SW (MZ V12d2715).

Illustration 40: Inside of the drain. Note stone lining above, on sides, and as bottom of the channel (MZ V16d1173).

doorway leading into room G1, a platform was discovered which used baked bricks with alternating colors of red and yellow, A9f163. It is connected with a pebble pavement A9f80 and slightly above a similarly colored baked brick pavement (A9 f84) of which only a small portion has been excavated.

2.2.2.7 The Drainage System in D and C

Illustration 42: Exit of drain to south of room C5 (MZ V16d1167).

Illustration 43: Drain channel in room C5 (MZ V16d1151).

A drainage system was discovered under the floor of sectors D and C, and appears to originate in as-yet unexcavated areas north of sector F, while emptying into the open area outside the palace south of room C2.

This drain was built of large stone blocks, much the same as those used in the construction of the walls of the palace. These rectangular blocks completely lined the channel, with the top and bottom laid perpendicular to the flow of water, while the sides were laid parallel. The blocks used were very roughly hewn, even less squared than the blocks used in the palace walls.

Two installations were linked to this drainage system, the bathroom installation mentioned previously (2.2.2.1) and an opening in room C8. This opening was subsequently sealed with bricks, whether in phase 2 or 3 was unclear due to the lack of clear phase 2 material in the accumulation directly above the drain itself. It is possible that this access was constructed but never used during the life of the palace. It is worth mentioning that there was no access from either the kitchen area (D1) nor from the courtyard C5. No similar drainage was found running through sectors B or A, indicating that the installations using water were centered in the eastern portion of the service wing.

Illustration 44: Closed drain access in room C8 (MZ V16d1166).

Due to the lack of access from the kitchen, its link to the 'bathroom' installation as well as the drainage outside of the building it is more likely that this system drained dirty water from the palace rather than acting as a runoff for clean water.

2.2.2.8 The Drain in H4

The drain in room H4 is a small channel made of baked brick running from room H4 into the stone courtyard H3. Interestingly, half of a pottery vessel, probably a jar, was used as the catch-basin for the drain, which then continued to the north as a channel made of baked bricks. The channel then empties into the baked brick installation below the stone courtyard.

Illustration 45: Drain in room H4, seen on right of image (MZ V14d3334).

The function of this drain is unclear, but it seems quite different from the other drains in the palace, for example the one in C6, for two reasons: the presence of the ceramic catch-basin and its location in the formal wing.

The ceramic catch-basin indicates that the drain was not used for either rainwater runoff nor for sewage, but perhaps smaller quantities of liquid. The drain is located in a very prominent spot, since it would have been visible from most of the stone courtyard as well as the rooms H1 and H6.

2.2.2.9 *Well in H6*

In room H6 a well was found in the center of the room, which may have been functionally linked to the drain in H4.

2.2.2.10 *The Stone Courtyard H3*

Included here among the installations is the stone courtyard (H3) because it represents a particular architectural feat, and helps describe the

Illustration 46: Stone Courtyard (H3) of the AP Palace (Photo: MZ V15d4117 Drawing: MZ W15d4510).

function of this space and the sector of which it is a part.

The courtyard as excavated represents only a portion of the complete space. It is likely that only about a third to half of the courtyard has been uncovered – for more on the projection of the stone courtyard, see section 2.3.2.

The stones used in the courtyard are prepared more carefully than the stones used in the construction of the walls in the palace sectors. While the stones of the palace walls were squared but not shaped, it the stones of the courtyard were also shaped using a pounder so that the surface of the courtyard was as flat as possible. This was most likely done *in situ* since the pounded portions of the stones do not cover the stone, but only the areas needed to form a flat surface.[36]

2.2.2.11 *The Baked Brick Installation Below Courtyard H3*

Perhaps the most tantalizing installation found in the palace area is the series of baked bricks found under the stone courtyard H3. These came to light only because pits, dug during the Khabur period when the palace was no longer visible, reached the stones of the courtyard and removed them for reuse in other structures. In removing these stones, however, a series of baked bricks under the stones came to light. These baked bricks seem to be part of a single, large installation underneath the stone courtyard, based on the distribution of bricks where revealed by these later pits. With only the evidence from the damaged areas of the stone courtyard it is very difficult to determine the function of this installation, or even to show that it is a single installation and not several. Three possibilities come to mind: either the installation is a sub-floor for the stone courtyard, or it is part of a structure which pre-dates the palace and is not linked to it, or the installation in some way is linked to the use of water, perhaps water storage.

(1) It is possible that the baked bricks form a sub-floor for the stone courtyard, as a way to strengthen the courtyard floor and keep the stones from sinking into the soil during heavy rains, thereby making the floor of the courtyard uneven. However, in other areas of the palace soil was used for packing below floors, and the use of baked brick seems too much, since sun-dried bricks would serve the same purpose with much less effort.

(2) The second possibility is that the baked bricks form part of a structure which pre-dates the palace, and the removal of the paving stones merely revealed portions of this previous structure. However, no similar structures – consisting of a large expanse of baked brick – are present at the site or in parallels from the region.

(3) The third, and most likely, possibility, is that a structure under the stone courtyard is a structure built for the palace. Since it is constructed of baked brick, it seems likely that the structure was built to contain water, and its size under the stone courtyard seems to indicate that a large cistern lies below the stone courtyard.[37]

Further excavation in this area is not possible, since opening the

---

36 For more information on the tools and on the preparation of the surface of the stone courtyard, see 3.2.1 and 3.4.3.

37 There is yet another possibility, which should be mentioned, however unlikely it may seem: that the area under the stone courtyard is the location of the royal tombs.

installation to determine its function would most likely destabilize the stone courtyard itself.

2.2.3 *Palace Dimensions*

The length of the palace as excavated along the east-west axis is 50 meters, while the length along the north-south axis is 49 meters. The north-south axis is an estimate, since there is no continuous line along this axis: the 49 meters is a hypothetical line between the northernmost point of G to the southern point of I.

Sector	m^2
A	234.4
B	128.7
C	250.6
D	98.3
E	62.8
F	109.3
G	38.7
H	166.8
I	89.1
Total	1178.6

Table 5: Square meters by sector.

The total area of the AP Palace as excavated is 1178.6 square meters, including the walls. The total area of the service wing (A,B,C,D) is 711.9 square meters, while the excavated portion of the formal wing (H, I) covers 255.9 square meters.[38]

2.3 Estimated Footprint of the Palace

The palace uncovered to date is not complete, since excavations to the north and east did not find the perimeter wall of the palace, as was found to the south and west. The boundary of the palace to the east is known even if it has not been found, since the central plaza of the site would have been the natural border for the palace to the east. The northern perimeter is wholly unknown, and can only be estimated as a minimum extent based on a presumed set of rooms around a courtyard north of courtyard F.

2.3.1 *Missing Sectors*

In addition to considering the space which the complete palace would have occupied, it is equally important to consider the sectors of the palace which are missing in terms of function: the royal residence, a point of access towards the plaza, an administrative sector, and possibly a religious area.

2.3.1.1 *Royal Residence*

To date, there is no evidence for the royal living quarters, but these would have been attached to the formal wing, and so probably lay to the north of sector H. The area to the north of courtyard F would also be a possibility, albeit less likely because of the greater distance to the formal sector. Three indications of the 'household' being present in the building are: the presence of the kitchen (D1), the large quantity of seal impressions relating to both king

38 For an interesting examination of the relevance of the areal dimensions of buildings in Uruk and Mari see Butterlin 2010, in particular with regard to the significance this had for the establishment of diverse 'proto-urban' settlements.

and queen, and the presence of functionaries who were tied to the more familial aspects of the royal couple, such as the wet nurse Zamena.

2.3.1.2 Access Point Towards Plaza

A second sector which is most likely present in the unexcavated portions of the palace is an access point leading to the east, towards the plaza and the temple terrace beyond it. The entrance in sector E (if indeed it is an entrance, see 2.2.1.2.1 above) would lead to the lower town, and would not have been convenient for the king to access the plaza, considering also the fact that there is no evidence as yet for a street running along the southern edge of the palace leading into the plaza. Thus an access point leading from the formal wing towards the plaza is very likely.

2.3.1.3 Scribal/Administrative Area

It would also be possible for a scribal or administrative area to be located within the palace, perhaps north of sectors E and F. However this is not necessarily expected: the Tar'am-Agade seal impressions which were found in the post-palace period (phase 3, see 2.1.2 above) seem to indicate that the AP Palace was used for some administrative functions while the king and queen inhabited another palace as yet undiscovered. If this practice was carried over from previous administrations, it is possible that the administration of King Tupkish was located in the previous king's palace, and thus not in the AP Palace. The Tar'am Agade seal impressions were found on the original floor of a room of the formal wing, presumably because the floors were kept clean during the use of the rooms in the reign of Tupkish.

2.3.1.4 Religious Area

Finally, it is possible but unlikely that a religious area would have been present within the walls of the AP Palace. There are several examples of palaces which contain a chapel or even a small temple, but in this region it is not common, and a palace-chapel may have been superfluous considering the presumed access to the plaza and the temple situated on top of the temple terrace. It is possible that sectors X and W were linked in some way to the palace, and as such made up the religious area of the palace (see section 2.2.1.5).

2.3.2 Estimate of Building Footprint

In addition to these sectors which one might find in a Palace, one can make some estimates as to the physical dimensions of the unexcavated portions of the palace. The following diagram shows some projections, as well as several circled numbered points which will be further described below.

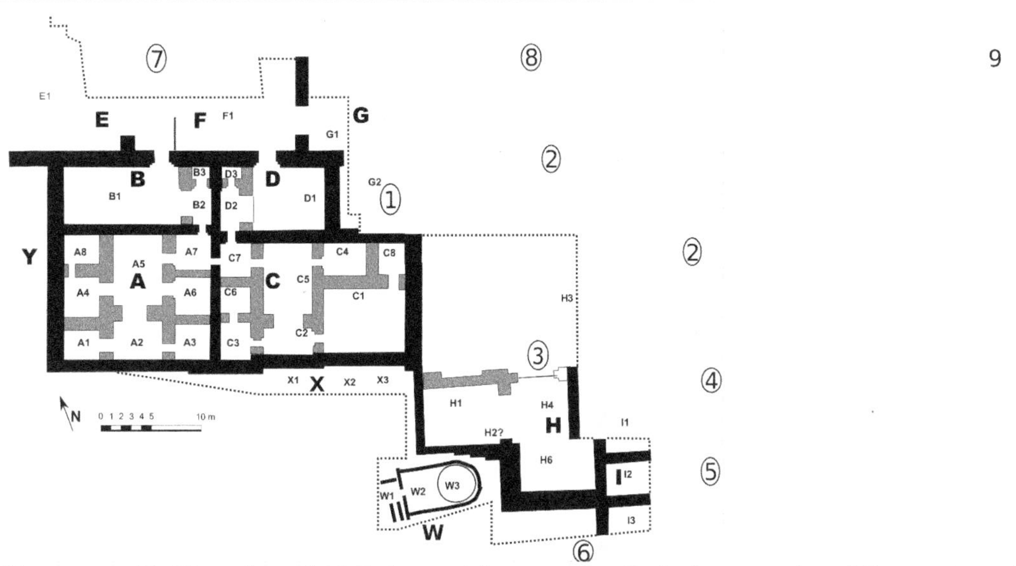

Illustration 47: Floorplan of AP Palace, with excavation limit shown as dotted line, projected walls in light gray.

1 – Point one marks the area where it is thought that a staircase might be found, sector G. This position between the courtyard F and the service and formal wings would have been ideal for access between these parts of the palace. In addition, this position straddles the difference in elevation between the service and formal wings, north of the wall between sectors C and H.

2 – Point two marks a possible access to the east and to the north from the stone courtyard: one east towards the plaza, onto which the temple terrace also fronts, and one north towards other areas of the palace.

3 – Point three marks the southern wall of the stone courtyard. Assuming that the doorway between H3 and H4 (the southern entrance to the stone courtyard) is in the middle of the southern wall, then the total estimated length of the southern wall would be 23 meters.

As for the northern limit of the of the stone courtyard, it had been thought that the northern limit might be an eastern extension of the wall between sectors C and D. Excavations showed that this is not the case, and the next likely northern limit might be the extension of the sector wall between D and F. The total length of the eastern limit of the stone courtyard would then be 20 meters.

Thus the current excavated portion of the stone courtyard is approximately 175 square meters, while the estimated area, following these parameters, is 460 square meters, meaning that 38% of the stone courtyard has been uncovered so far.

4 – The area in between sector I and the stone courtyard shows a problem in the projection, since the projected south wall of the stone courtyard does not match the projection of sector I as based on the tablet discovered in H4. It is possible that a staircase might be found here, but only further excavation will clarify this situation.

5 – The fifth point marks the projection of sector I based on the tablet found in H4.

6 – This point marks the southern limit of sector I, and it is likely that this is the southernmost limit of the AP Palace. The tell topography rises to the south at this point, and if there is an access point or road here, then it is most likely that the AP Palace does not continue to the south.

7 – The area to the north of the service wing, north of sectors E and F, would have also been part of the palace, but there is no information as to how far the palace would have continued to the north. It is also unclear the elevation of this area: sectors E and F remain at the level of the service wing, but it is possible that the palace changes elevation further to the north.

8 – The same is true for point 8, the area to the north of the stone courtyard, although this area would most likely remain at this higher elevation, since it would have formed the western side of the plaza.

9 – A sounding was made in area A19, east of the plaza, at a point where the palace was thought to meet the plaza, based on a geomagnetic survey of the plaza area. This sounding uncovered brickfall consisting of the same brick material of which the palace wall are built, and at the right elevation. It seems likely therefore that this is the eastern limit of the palace, where it fronted onto the JP plaza.

2.4 Selected Comparisons

A comprehensive study of palace architecture in the third millennium is beyond the scope of this study, and has been covered extensively in other publications (Margueron 1982; Heinrich 1984; Tamm 2008; Pfälzner 2011). The aim here is to provide comparative examples for some of the particularities of the AP Palace, including stone architecture, internal terracing, *iwans* and mirrored architecture.

2.4.1 Stone as Construction Material

The best example of the use of stone as a construction material comes from Tell Chuera (Orthmann 1995; Meyer 2006, 2010), Palace F.[39] This palace predates the AP Palace at Tell Mozan – the excavators date the construction of

39 For the most recent overview of Palace F of Chuera, see Tamm (2008, 69–89). My thanks to A. Tamm for the updated plan in Illustration 48.

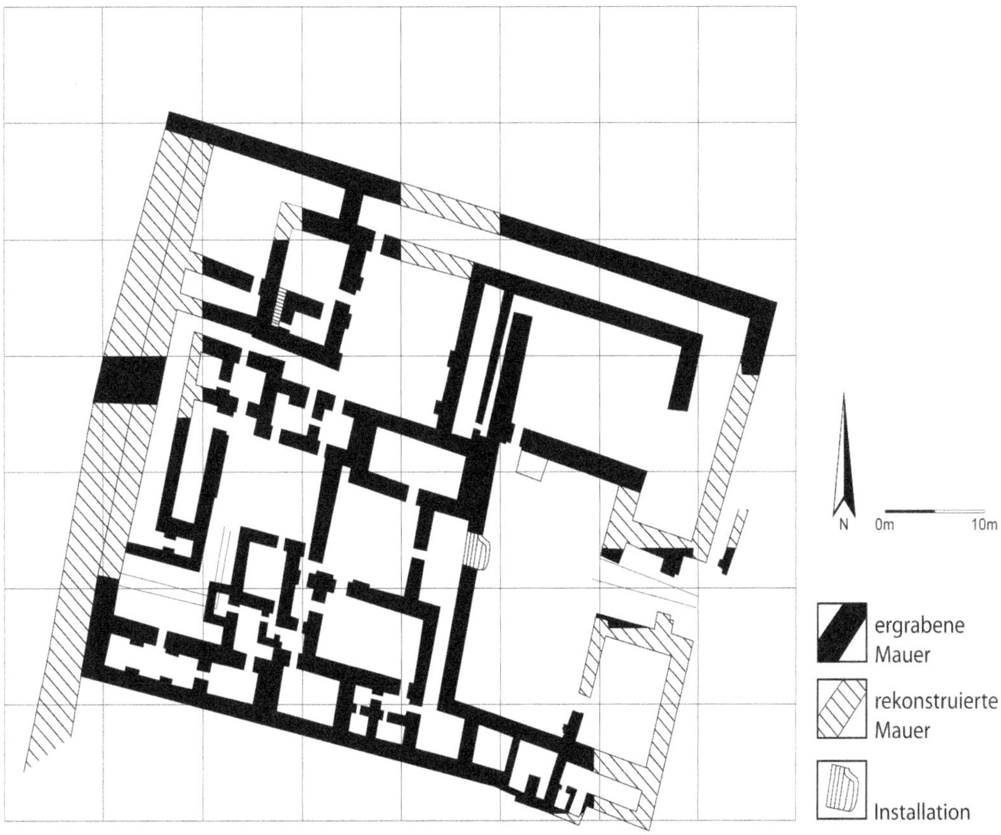

Illustration 48: Tell Chuera, Palace F (Tamm 2008, 101).

the palace to the EB IIIa (EJ IIIa) period, phase Chuera 1C.

Stone was widely used in the construction of public buildings in Chuera, and as such is not isolated to Palace F; this is the same as construction methods in Mozan, where stone is also used in the temple terrace. Perhaps the most notable use of stone in Palace F is the "eye-catching semicircular stone-paved staircase" (Pfälzner 2011, 171). This staircase, visible on the plan directly in front of the principal entrance, links courtyard 3 to room 7.

2.4.2 *Internal Terracing*

Internal terracing is present in several palaces in the region. In addition to the staircase just mentioned in Chuera's Palace F (Tamm 2008, 101) there is the example of Tell Beydar, with a staircase between the courtyard 6233 and room 6326.

2.4.3 *Iwans*

The architectural form of the *iwan* is not common in palatial architecture of this period in the area, but can be found in Beydar in an earlier period, albeit with a column in the middle of the *iwan*'s wide doorway (Lebeau and Suleiman 2003). Two examples can be found linked to courtyard 6233 – to the North, with room 6249, and to the East, with room 6130 (Pfälzner 2011, 172).

2.4.4 Mirrored Architecture

As Foster notes, architecture in the Akkadian period tends more towards symmetry in plan (Foster 2016, 206). Perhaps the best parallel to the mirrored architecture of the AP Palace can be found at a site at some distance: Eridu. The interim publication of the palace mentioned a mirrored plan (Safar 1950), but initially it was unclear as to how the published portion was mirrored (Margueron 1982, 107–19). A later publication made clear the mirrored portion of the palace was not actually mirrored, but rather was copied (Margueron 1983), meaning that instead of being reflected over one axis, the same plan was reproduced next to the first instance. Note that the northern copy of the palace is slightly smaller on the east-west axis.

Illustration 49: Palace in Tell Beydar, Area F Level 3a (Lebeau and Suleiman 2003, Architectural Plan 6).

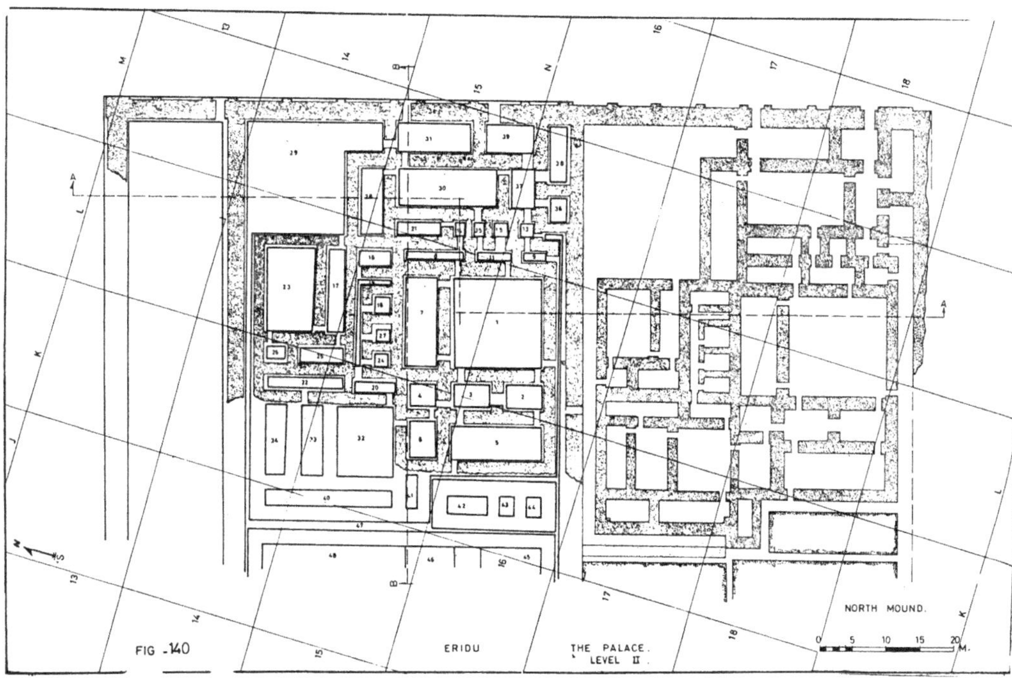

Illustration 50: Plan of Eridu from final publication (Margueron 1983, 227).

"We must not only consider how things are, but how they came to be so. 'Tis pleasant to look upon a tree in the summer, covered with its green leaves, decked with blossoms, or laden with fruit, and casting a pleasing shade under its spreading boughs; but to consider how this tree with all its furniture, sprang from a little seed; how nature shaped it, and fed it, in its infancy and growth; added new parts, and still advanced it by little and little, till it came to this greatness and perfection, this, methinks, is another sort of pleasure, more rational, less common... to take in pieces this frame of nature, and melt it down into its first principles; and then to observe how the divine wisdom wrought all these things out of confusion into order, and out of simplicity into that beautiful composition we now see them in; this, methinks, is another kind of joy, which pierceth the mind more deep, and is more satisfactory."

- *Thomas Burnet*[40]

3 The Elements and Process of Construction

3.1 From *Chaîne Opératoire* to *Gedankenexperiment*

The next step in this study is to examine the process of construction as activity, describing the building as the result of a series of decisions, technological possibilities and functional necessities. The study of a building from an archaeological perspective normally entails looking at the floors and accumulations that grow over time after the building has been completed. In this chapter the approach is different – what is being considered is the time leading up to the building's completion, beginning with the realization that such a structure is needed.

The actual process of construction can be analyzed by considering three main aspects: materials, know-how and manpower. By studying the interaction of these three aspects one can analyze the questions of 'who, what, where, why and how' which, despite their apparent superficiality, can act as a guide in describing the building in a very profound way.

40 Burnet 1965, 54.

Once the elements pertaining to materials, know-how and manpower have been extrapolated, then their interaction, or at least a hypothetical model of their interaction, can be posited. This can best be done through a timeline, logically chaining the steps together as a temporal sequence. The method used in this analysis is the *chaîne opératoire*, allowing for a discussion of each of the elements and its relation to the whole. Since this model is merely hypothetical, it is a form of *Gedankenexperiment*[41] which attempts to reconstruct the process that is inherently behind the *chaîne opératoire*, while at the same time deriving general algorithms which can be applied to the specific case of the AP Palace at Tell Mozan.

3.1.1 Applying a Chaîne Opératoire to Architecture

Before looking at these various elements and then at their interaction, it is important to consider the reasons for the methodological choices. The major portion of this analysis can be described as a *chaîne opératoire* applied to architecture, with most of the steps either extrapolated from the final product as recorded from the archaeological record, carried over from the ethnoarchaeological experiment, extracted from ethnographic studies or inferred from textual sources. The final portion of the analysis goes beyond the *chaîne opératoire* method, since the building of a timeline over such a long period, the multiplicity of actors and the analysis of the effects on the physical urban landscape are all aspects that study the unfolding of the architectural process beyond the compass of the *chaîne opératoire*.

Chaîne opératoire is a well-known method for investigating the process of production, behavior and use of technology; it is primarily applied to objects, particularly lithics (Lemonnier 1986; Bar-Yosef et al. 1992; Gamble 1998; Bleed 2001; Martinón-Torres 2002; Schlanger 2005; Bar-Yosef and Van Peer 2009). One of the strengths of this method is the combination of technological process and the production organization which reflects social processes.[42] A term used in English is 'operational sequence', and is often used as a synonym for *chaîne opératoire* despite a few differences.

One aspect of the *chaîne opératoire* method which differentiates it from the 'operational sequence' or 'operational chains' of English language literature is the focus on the cognitive processes involved (Julien and Karlin 1994; Bleed 2001, 105–8). Bleed (2001, 118) suggests that the *chaîne opératoire*, arising as it does from the French Humanist tradition, places more emphasis

41 An experiment which cannot be carried out in the physical world, but which can be postulated. What is being employed here can be described as a variation on a 'retrodiction' thought experiment.

42 For more on 'technological process' and 'production organization' see Udy 1959, 3.

on the cognitive aspect of such modeling, as opposed to the sequence models more prevalent in the American tradition: such sequence models tend to focus more on material aspects (Bleed 2001, 114).

A further term which is sometimes used in conjunction with *chaîne opératoire* is 'behavioral chain' but this term refers to an analysis of the activity which brings time and space into the analysis (Schiffer 1975a), which produces a specific study of a specific event in a specific space,[43] as opposed to the *chaîne opératoire* which produces a more general sequence which can be applied to various events in various places. Behavioral chains reach this level of abstraction in a second stage, in their contribution to the formation of cultural transformations ('c-transforms') and the interaction of humans or objects through natural agents ('n-transforms' – the cases in behavioral chains where the energy source is non-human, for example) (Schiffer 1975b, 1999). The *chaîne opératoire* methodology was chosen for this study in lieu of behavioral chains because, in analyzing architecture, the areas where the actions take place are dispersed between the collection of raw materials and the construction site itself, and because of the lack of detritus from production steps, such as the quarrying or forming of the blocks themselves.

The understanding of process which these types of analysis make possible would be of great interest if the method could be successfully applied to architecture.[44] The greatest difficulty lies in the availability of data regarding the various steps in this process: while with a lithic ensemble there are finds which can be used to document each step, architecture as process tends to be much more complex.[45]

The first major difference between lithics and architecture when attempting to apply the *chaîne opératoire* method is the diverse end-products: in a sense, lithic production can be compared to the production of each of the individual elements making up a building – mudbricks, roofing beams, stone blocks, plaster etc. These elements are, however, not really 'understood' within an operational chain[46] unless their role in the larger construction project is also analyzed, as if a series of smaller chains 'participate' in forming our

43 Selectionist archaeology and evolutionary ecology are further methods for analysis of such processes (Broughton and O'Connell 1999), but are less focused on the sequence of the process.

44 To my knowledge, only three studies approach architecture with such a methodology: V. Izzet for Etruscan Architecture (Izzet 2007), Karen Ryan for Dorset Architecture (Ryan 2009) and Smith for the Egyptian Pyramids (Smith 2006).

45 For a recent study using *chaîne opératoire* with lithics tied to economic aspects of society, see Helms 2013.

46 For readability I am referring to operational chains when speaking of specific analyses, but will continue to use *chaîne opératoire* when referring to the method in general.

understanding of the process of constructing, *nested* as it were within the greater process. These *nested* operational chains can and should be considered first in isolation, because they do 'participate' in other activities, such as shipbuilding in the case of wooden beams or the making of statues in the case of stone quarrying. Once the operational chain has been understood, then the role of the nested chain within the greater whole can be analyzed, as well as any initial criteria that the overall project imposes on the nested chain; an example would be the need for a special stone quality and size for a sculptor, which conditions the use of the operational chain but not the process itself (or only to a very limited extent).

The second difference between lithics and architecture is the diversity in the skills of the actors and the materials that they use, even when considering the 'nested chains'. While in lithic production actors, tools used, operation locations and materials are rather limited, the study of architecture entails a much greater diversity. As an example, the production of mudbricks requires a specialized team using a mudbrick form, in a place where water, straw and good loam are available. The production of lithics, instead, is much more portable, and the raw material needed usually comes from only one source.

Thirdly, the final link in an operational chain dealing with lithics is the moment of discard; the final link when applying this method to architecture is more difficult to distinguish. The moment of 'discard' of a building can be specifically pinpointed on only two occasions: first when it collapses, or when the roofing beams are removed or destroyed, or second, when excavating a building that was not finished – in that case one may find material piled up (e. g., bricks) that was not in the end used during construction. In the case of the AP Palace, one may consider one important case of discard that is highly pertinent, though quite uniquely unusual, namely the architectural tablet with a plan of a three-room suite discussed in the previous chapter. However, it may be more pragmatic and useful for this study to consider the end of the operational chain as the beginning of the life of the building rather than the end. If our goal is to understand the process of construction, then the use and collapse of the building is not pertinent. One could argue that by excluding the 'life' of the building post construction, one limits the scope of the *chaîne opératoire* to merely a study of technology, excluding what one can learn about behavior and social patterns. The *chaîne opératoire* is, however, a method for developing an understanding of a specific process, and it is in studying this result that questions of behavior and social patterns can bear fruit. In our case, the design proposed by the architect reflects the need to influence behavior and to embed the structure within the social and urban fabric; in this way the result of the *chaîne opératoire*, even if limited in scope, can be used to further investigate questions that reach beyond the level of technology and production. Thus this analysis of the process of construction will end with the last moment of construction before the building is inhabited – what is called the turn-key moment in modern contexts.

Finally, when using a *chaîne opératoire* to study lithics, the objects created can be studied as movable items within a social framework; architecture can and should be studied within the social fabric, but also as a stationary structure within a physical urban framework. An architectural construct fills a preexisting urban space that had to be created for the new structure, either by removing older buildings or enlarging the urban area. The new building has a much greater effect on tangential aspects of urban life than a lithic object: pedestrian patterns, line of sight and hydrology are examples of this.[47]

One further consideration may be pertinent here. A constructional or developmental analysis of architecture is a field in its own right, known also as 'archaeology of architecture' (*Bauforschung* in German and *archéologie du bâti* in French). It is in some ways similar to a study dealing with the identification of the *chaîne opératoire*, since it aims at defining the constructional stages, understood in the sense of a temporal succession as it can be understood from an examination of the finished product. However, this approach, which has been used in the study of another important architectural structure in Mozan, the Temple Terrace,[48] does not pursue the full dynamics of the operational process that the *chaîne opératoire* entails.

3.1.2 Sources for the Analysis

In this study, four sources will be used to re-construct the elements and process of construction: the archaeological record, ethnographic parallels ethnoarchaeological experiments and textual sources. Of these four, the archaeological is by far the most important, but the understanding of the archaeological record is greatly enhanced when considered concomitantly with the other two sources.

The archaeological record includes information collected from a wide variety of sources, from publications considering comparative material on the regional level to specific samples from excavations at Mozan. Since this study deals primarily with the AP Palace at Mozan, this structure is the primary archaeological example.

47 Architecture is also very much an historical construct, but this facet is developed in chapter 4, particularly 4.2.4.

48 See Camatta forthcoming.

The ethnographic analogy, or metaphor, is the second source of information used to form the *chaîne opératoire*. Contemporary local building traditions appear to produce construction elements that are remarkably similar to construction elements found in the archaeological record. By studying these modern practices scholars can form a hypothesis as to the operations required to produce the ancient construction elements.

The third source comes from ethnoarchaeological experiments; while linked to the ethnographic analogy just mentioned, it should be discussed separately because of the diverse aim. In these experiments archaeologists attempt, through experimentation, to use the same materials and tools available to the ancients in order to arrive at a finished product which is as close to that found in the archaeological record as possible.

The final source of information comes from ancient textual sources. None of these sources come from, or refer directly to, building activities at Mozan, nor do the majority of them refer to the building of monumental architecture. Despite this 'distance' from the data used, textual sources are still of great use in this study when seeking to understand the role of the building elements in the linguistic and social framework. The words and context for words concerned with building can help in defining the use and perception of the elements under study. One study in particular has been fundamental for this research: the archive describing construction at Garshana, which gives a wealth of information as to the day-to-day process of administration for construction projects (Heimpel 2009). This group of texts provides a fascinating look into the details of a construction project in southern Mesopotamia, as seen through the records of the administrators of the project. Garshana was an Ur III period military camp next to a town of the same name (Heimpel 2009, 2–5). Both are located somewhere in the vicinity of Umma. The categories of persons given in these texts are: a 'general' *shagina,* a person who is second in command, soldiers, workers, and slaves. The slaves were involved in making leather goods, including 'boots' for the soldiers. But they also produced textiles, were launderers, and were extensively involved in the major building projects carried out in the camp. These building projects consisted in constructing a palatial residence, craftsmen's houses, barracks, utility buildings, and the erection of a surrounding ringwall for the camp of which 216 meters were completed. These texts are particularly helpful in understanding the manpower aspect of the process, and will be further discussed section 3.4 below. Another fascinating architectural study linking texts, ethno-archaeological data and archaeological evidence is Stone's investigation of houses in Nippur (Stone 1981, 1987).

One overlap of all three sources can be found in the transportation of earth, see section 3.4.3.4. This overlap is particularly important as it speaks to the validity of the method and the combination of the three sources being used.

3.1.2.1 The Ethics of Including the Garshana Texts

The use of the Garshana texts poses an ethical dilemma, since these texts come from illegal and undocumented excavations. While I am strongly opposed to the looting of ancient sites and to the publication of stolen cultural material, I have decided to include the published material from the Garshana archive, since its exclusion from this work would not be an impediment to future looting. But while reading this analysis, I would ask the reader to consider how much information has been lost due to the lack of context for the tablets, as well as a detailed archaeological study of the structures described in the texts. Were we to have this correlation between the texts and the archaeological evidence, the analysis presented here would be stronger and the conclusions more certain and complete. An analogous case can be made for the tablets from Drehem, ancient Puzrish-Dagan: every single one of them comes from early looting, and our understanding of the archive as a whole would be immeasurably enhanced were we to have the archaeological context; yet it would be inconceivable to have a history of Mesopotamia which does not refer to this epigraphic material. A great deal of literature has been written regarding this dilemma, but a detailed bibliography would be outside the scope of this study; for one example, see Renfrew (2009).

3.1.2.2 Postulate 1: Ethnoarchaeological Link

Two postulates lie behind this analysis, and should be stated explicitly: first, there is the postulate stating that the physical act of building and the engineering problems that arise when using similar materials are the same in antiquity as can be seen in modern local villages. This is based on the empirical similarities between the bricks and other materials which can be found on the excavations at Tell Mozan as well as the local villages, such as Mozan or Umm Ar-rabia. This allows one to postulate that techniques, problems and timeframes collected within a modern framework can be applied to the ancient situation. It is of course important to eliminate as much as possible the influence that modern improvements have exercised, directly or indirectly. The usefulness and dangers of this ethnoarchaeological link will be further discussed in chapter 4.

3.1.2.3 Postulate 2: Continuity of Experience

The second postulate is that of the continuity of the human experience. This may seem obvious, especially on a broad level; however, it is also the greatest source of possible error in such an experiment. This is particularly true of assumptions on the social level, or elements that are unknown but which influenced the physical record as found. This will also be further explored in the theory portion of this study (see section 4.1.2), in particular with regard to the concept of uniformitarianism, i. e. the unbroken continuity across time and space of certain laws (Gould 1987). This concept comes from the tradition of New Geology, and its application to human experience and cultural processes are what is postulated here.

3.2 Materials

Based on the archaeological finds and on the ethnographic evidence, a variety of materials were needed in order to construct the palace of Tupkish. The primary materials needed are stone, mudbrick, wood, gypsum, straw, mud and fill material. To render the top of stone portions of the walls flat and even so that the mudbricks would sit securely on top of the stones, sherds and pebbles were utilized. In some cases large walls have interspersed layers of reed matting to prevent water from forming inside the structure; this is seen especially in the construction of ziggurats in the south. The production and procurement of each of these final construction materials is a process which in turn needs material-specific tools and one or more raw materials.

In addition, the placement of the palace within the city had an effect on the use of materials in two important ways. First the palace was relatively near the plain level so that ground water would be closer to the level of the foundations than, say, the temple and its enclosure wall. The second has to do with the possible presence of a canal on the western side of the mound that would ensure not only a higher level of ground water in this area but more importantly for transportation of building materials.

As the first step in the analysis of the construction, each of these materials will be analyzed with regard to the construction of the AP Palace at Mozan, and from this analysis a *chaîne opératoire* can be developed for that element.

3.2.1 Stone

All of the walls of the AP Palace have both foundations and the lower courses of the walls built from stone blocks[49] and boulders. Several questions arise: what is the most likely area for the stone quarry from which these stones came? How were the stones quarried?[50] Were the stones further hewn after

49 In this study the term 'stone blocks' is used instead of 'ashlar masonry' (Hult 1983) as the stone blocks used in the AP Palace were not sufficiently squared after quarrying.

50 "Quarrying" vs "mining" - quarrying refers to the removal of stone, gravel or sand from an

quarrying? How were the stones transported to the construction site? What preparation was necessary before the stones could be placed? How were the stones put in position? What was used as filling between stones? How was the top of the wall prepared for the mudbricks?

3.2.1.1 Use of Stone in Construction

Upstream from these points regarding the use of stone is the basic question of why the architects and builders of the AP Palace decided to use such a large quantity of stone. What properties of this material encouraged the architect to select it, and nothing else, as the foundation and lower wall courses for all the walls in the building? There seem to be three reasons on the practical side:[51] humidity, salt and structural stability.

By placing a stone sub-structure, the mudbrick superstructure is insulated from the ground and the resulting humidity (Peters 1972; Lechevallier 1978, 22; Aurenche 1981, 35). A further advantage of this hydraulic barrier is the fact that humidity often carries salt from the surrounding terrain up into mudbrick walls, as if a wick. The saturation of the mudbrick walls with salt greatly contributes to their deterioration, in addition to the damage done by the humidity itself. The three most common processes of mudbrick deterioration are the wet/dry cycle (salts from ground causing erosion), the freeze/thaw cycle (moisture in walls expand when frozen, damaging walls) or capillary rise (water rises in the walls, and in evaporating cause the adobe to flake).[52] These three processes can be mitigated, for the most part, through the use of stone foundations and the lowest courses of the walls. In the case of the AP Palace in Tell Mozan the problem of salt does not exist[53] but the problem of water is clearly present. The high level of rainfall, the placement of the palace relatively close, in terms of elevation, to the ancient plain level, and the presence of a *wadi* near it were clearly factors necessitating strong measures to avoid water problems. The local architects knew of these problems with monumental constructions in the city because of previous experiences with flooding problems and implemented solutions at the base of the revetment wall surrounding the temple terrace. They also knew of the various attempts to solve these problems.

open cut into the earth's surface, and as such is a specific kind of mining ("Quarry" 2010).

51 There are, of course, other possible factors, such as those tied to monumentality and prestige. These will be discussed below and in chapter 4.

52 See Cornerstones Community Partnerships 2006, 54. This book is an excellent practical guide to Adobe conservation, and is quite useful for anyone involved in preserving mudbricks.

53 The soil has generally little salt, and several meters of earlier cultural deposits formed a further barrier to the natural salt present in the soil.

The last consideration is the stability of the construction itself. In several particular cases the stone sub-structures vary in height, apparently in response to stresses that the rest of the structure placed on them, both vertical and, in one case, horizontal. These walls were discussed individually above, where the individual architectural elements of the AP Palace were considered.

3.2.1.2 Quarry possibilities near Mozan

While it is impossible at the moment to pinpoint the precise quarry from which the palace stones were taken, more recent quarries are present in the area of Mozan, the most visible exploitation of which dates from the Byzantine and modern periods.

The Byzantine quarry of Dara (the village of Oguz/Dara in modern Turkey) was used to build the fortified city of Anastasiopolis in 505 AD and approximately ten years later by Justinian to strengthen the fortification walls and build a convex dam. This quarry from a much later period shows the availability of good stone in the area, even if the chronological period and quarrying technology are completely different from that of the AP Palace. A walking survey of this quarry shows that the stone formations protrude from the soil, indicating that the stone was probably visible from the surface even in ancient times. This quarry lies approximately 14 kilometers from Tell Mozan, on the other side of the modern-day Syro-Turkish border.[54]

Modern quarrying for gravel can be seen presently at several sites in the area on both sides of the border, ranging from 9 to 15 kilometers away. The gravel seems to be made from crushed rock similar to that used for the discrete blocks in the AP Palace.

The stone used in the AP Palace is sedimentary rock, based on the presence of fossils in the stone matrix, the relative softness of the stone and through comparison of the ancient stone to local geological formations of sedimentary rock.

An analysis shows that the rock from Mozan and samples taken from the surface near the Dara quarries are petrographically very similar — both samples are almost entirely composed of calcite, with traces of quartz (study undertaken by Dr. E. Frahm; personal communication, Oct 4, 2010).

3.2.1.3 Quarrying Techniques

We know little about stone quarrying techniques in ancient

54 An interesting comparison can be found at Uruk, where only two structures in the early periods used stone in their construction: the Temple of level 5, and one phase of the Anu ziggurat. The stone used here was probably brought from a source 60 kilometers away (Heinrich 1934, 46; Eichmann 2007, 15).

Mesopotamia, since it is a material so seldom used in the south. Two neighboring regions, modern Turkey and Egypt, may provide information as to the techniques that might have been used in Syro-Mesopotamia, and at Urkesh in particular.

In general, three types of quarrying were used in the ancient world: cutting a rock face, undercutting[55] and shaft mining. Where present, geological layers can be exploited to produce a nearly perfect flat surface by removing (presumably by pulverizing or chipping) four channels on the four sides of the block to be used down to the softer geological layer, and then prying the exposed block free. The reconstruction of quarrying in Göbekli Tepe, further explained below, is an example of this. In addition, the collection of stones from natural rockfall is a further means of getting stones without actual quarrying activity (Protzen 1985). The closest example of similar stonework is at Tell Chuera, where several monumental stone structures, i. e. Steinbau I-VI (Orthmann 1995, 9), have been excavated over the last several decades. No study has been undertaken as to sources of stone or quarrying activities, but the region has been extensively explored, and limestone can be seen even at the surface.[56]

The major neighboring region with a prominent use of stone in architecture is ancient Egypt, where quarrying techniques and stone-working were developed already in prehistoric times (Helck, Otto, and Westendorf 1982, 260; Klemm 1993), and became a fundamental material for major public works. The quarrying, transportation and finishing of stone blocks became a major industry, and a highly developed skill (Smith 2006, 143–46).

The tools used in ancient Egyptian quarries can be divided in three categories: measuring tools, hammering tools and chisels (Smith 2006, 83; Harrell 2008). Measuring was accomplished through the ingenious use of wooden sticks or frames and ropes; straight lines, angles and the flatness of surfaces could all be calculated with great precision.

Hammering tools came in two types: mauls and pounders. Mauls are made of hard stone which come to a slight point, and could be used with or without a wooden handle. Pounders were rounded, and could have a handle much as with a mace. Both of these tools worked by chipping or pulverizing the surface of the stone being worked, and as such had to be made from a relatively harder stone. While this process may seem inefficient, modern

55 These two methods are mentioned in Protzen (Protzen 2008, 2027) albeit in a different cultural context; in general, J.-P. Protzen and S. Nair's studies on Incan stoneworking provide a very useful comparison (Protzen and Nair 1997, 2013); Protzen also draws parallels between Incan and Egyptian stoneworking (Protzen 1985, 165–66).

56 Personal observation near the *Stelenreihe* - my thanks to Tobias Helms for bringing me out to this portion of the site on a visit to Chuera in 2010.

experiments using the same techniques proved surprisingly effective: by varying the angle of impact, it was possible to chip the stone being worked with these tools, and shape the stone to a large degree (Protzen 1985, 2008). These experiments were conducted in the context of Inca construction, in the Andean region of Peru, but the technologies employed, the materials available and the end results make the comparison plausible. Further attempts at experimental archaeology show that the method is certainly viable, even if not very efficient (Coles 1973, 82–84); one author claims that shaping limestone boulders into usable blocks is "a lot like splitting wood, but it doesn't go quite as quickly" (McRaven 1999, 13).

The third group of tools used in Egypt were chisels, which were probably made from metal (copper-alloy initially, later iron-alloys) or chert. There is no archaeological evidence for the use of chert as a chisel, but its use in woodworking, its ubiquity in other aspects of daily life and modern experimentation all point to the use of chert chisels in ancient stoneworking (Harrell 2008). The relative absence of metal tools for stone-working in the archaeological record is perhaps not surprising: the majority of stonework would have been done at the quarry, and, because of the relative softness of copper-alloy tools, they would have been badly damaged through use. C. Smith indicates that copper (presumably a copper-alloy) tools were used extensively in the construction of the pyramids, such as chisels and even saws (Smith 2006, 82–84).

Protzen's enlightening experiments using only hammer-tools show that no chisels are needed to produce a finely shaped block (Protzen 1985), but illustrations from Egyptian tombs show that stonecutters did use chisels, perhaps for more detailed work (Harrell 2008, fig.s 1 and 4).

A further ethnographic study is detailed in Abrams' book on Mayan architecture, where he compares the speed with which modern masons work with steel and stone tools. The difference is less than what one might imagine: using stone tools made the finishing of a block take 50% more time, so that a ratio of 1 : 1.5 can be used when comparing time efficiency between steel and stone tools (Abrams 1994, 45). As to the volume produced, Abrams' experiments show that a modern quarryman using stone tools can produce one cubic meter of stone in 11.6 person-days.

One particularly useful site for comparison is the Neolithic settlement at Göbekli Tepe (Schmidt 2006). This is the first known example of quarrying in the region, and one of the oldest in the world. The technique employed is one which utilized the geological layers as breaking points, excavating all around the desired rock segment with stone tools, down to a softer or more friable layer. Once the rock segment was completely detached from the surrounding

Illustration 51: A Stone construction element which was abandoned half excavated in a stone quarry near Göbekli Tepe (Schmidt 2006, 103).

layer and rested only on the softer or more friable layer, it could be removed and transported to the construction site (Kurapkat 2009).

Illustration 52: A reconstruction of stone quarrying near Göbekli Tepe, showing excavation, loading and transportation of a stone construction element (Kurapkat 2009, 75).

The stones used for the AP Palace are at best roughly squared, with the majority of the stones showing a single flat face. The flat surface was positioned as the visible portion of the stone, making the wall faces relatively flat, while the faces of the stones which were inside the wall tend to be much less geometric. Such 'one-sided' stones tend to suggest that the technique employed in the quarry was that of exploiting flat geological layers, perhaps in combination with the collection of stones from such a layer which were readily available as loose rocks.

The relative lack of finishing remains a question, however. It is likely that the tools and techniques were available to the stonecutters who produced the stone for the AP Palace, as demonstrated in the earlier quarries of Göbekli Tepe and the contemporary and later quarries in ancient Egypt. The reason may be circumstantial. The two major areas where stone masonry is present *in situ* at Tell Mozan are the AP Palace and the Temple Terrace. One should note, however, that the walls in the AP excavations so far belong only to the service wing, hence the lack of finishing may be due to the non-formal quality of this particular wing. The Temple Terrace, on the other hand, may have been intended specifically as an imitation of the mountainous landscape (G. Buccellati 2009a), in which case, too, the unfinished condition of the individual stones would have been preferred.

Because of the need for transportation from the quarry to the construction site and their relative weight by volume, the choice of stones entailed a greater effort in procurement than mudbricks (see below, 3.4.3).

3.2.1.4 Stone Working

Were the stones used in the AP Palace further hewn after being quarried? One result of the hammer-technique described above is that it makes producing 90 degree corners impossible (Protzen 2008), but such angles can be found in the AP Palace, leading one to wonder if chisels were employed to produce these stones. There are two other possibilities to consider: either the stones were selected from natural rockfall as having the appropriate shape with a 90 degree corner and were then further flattened on the exposed face, or geological formations were followed in the quarrying process (as in Göbekli Tepe) which produced blocks with one flat side with 90 degree corners on the four edges.

The corners of walls would need to use stones that had at least one corner which was approximately 90 degrees. The extensive use of rabbeting in the doorways of the palace meant that a much higher number of corner-stones was needed, or single stones cut specifically so as to be rabbeted.

Abrams' study of stone block manufacture gives estimates of

manufacture times for masonry blocks and rougher cobbles used in construction. As mentioned above he estimates that, using stone tools, a stonemason can produce 1 cubic meter of finished stone blocks in 11.6 person-days (the finished material represents 55% of the original raw material) and 1 cubic meter of rough hewn cobbles in 1.6 person days (Abrams 1994, 45–48). The stones from the AP Palace are probably closer to the estimate for cobbles, which were finished on only one side; the specific evidence of stone-pounding in the AP Palace has been discussed in section 2.2.2.10.

The stones of the stone courtyard H3 were worked in order to give the courtyard a smooth surface. This was presumably done with pounder and/or maul after the stones had been placed as flat as possible in the sub-floor. Heimpel suggests that a text from Mari (ARM 23 525) uses the verb 'tamping' for stone (sum. saḫar sè-ge/ke$_4$ akk. sapānu) (Heimpel 2009, 282), although this verb is normally associated with dirt floors; it is possible that this describes the leveling process which was carried out on the stones of H3.

3.2.1.5 Use of Limestone

The stone used for the AP Palace at Tell Mozan was limestone,[57] a type of sedimentary rock composed primarily of calcium carbonate (CaCO3) known to be present in the area. This type of stone is particularly suited to wall construction, since it breaks more easily into blocks than other types of stone (McRaven 1999, 5).

3.2.1.6 Stone Construction at Tell Mozan

During the 2006 and 2010 seasons, an ethnoarchaeological experiment was carried out at the Mozan excavation house. A boundary wall was needed near the main gate, and it was decided that the wall would be built using stones removed from erosion layers of the site, and to document the construction so as to have a model of the process that would be similar to what one would expect ancient builders to have undertaken.

The stone for the experiment was brought to the worksite by tractor, since the stones were too heavy to justify the effort of carrying them all over long distances. However, the placing of the stones was done only by hand, by a crew of workmen. During this part of the experiment:

4 people
in 7.5 hours
carried 42 stones weighing 5.1 tons
with a volume of approximately 3 cubic meters.

57 Not basalt as claimed by Foster (2016, 79).

Thus:
approximately 10 man-hours are needed
to place 1 cubic meter of stone – (4*7.5)/3

These figures give an indication of the effort which would presumably have been needed to construct the walls of the AP Palace.[58]

3.2.2 Mudbrick

3.2.2.1 Use of Mudbrick in Construction

The first question to ask is why mudbrick was chosen as a material for construction.[59] This may seem self-evident, since mudbrick is by far the most prevalent material used throughout history in Near Eastern architecture, but the reasons bear repeating. The first is the availability of the raw material. The soil is readily available, water is present in settlements in any case, and the straw is a byproduct of several crops which were grown for food consumption. The second factor is the thermic property of mudbrick. A wall of 40 cm thickness can hold a difference in temperature between inside and outside environments for up to twelve hours, after which there is no difference in temperature (Doat et al. 1979; Aurenche 1981, 46). Considering these factors, it is not surprising that mudbrick was, and remains, the primary material for construction in the area.

Two other methods of construction using the same raw materials can be found in the Near East: *pisé* and wattle-and-daub constructions. Neither of these construction methods would be more advantageous than building out of mudbrick. Construction in *pisé* would actually take longer than building in mudbrick; layers can be added in 30-50 cm thick sections, and each layer takes 3-5 days drying time (Aurenche 1981, 54–55). To construct a wall that is 3 meters high (reasonable, when taking foundations into consideration) one would need between 18 and 50 days. The advantage of *pisé* lies in the ease of production – while brick making requires several people and a longer planning time, *pisé* can be done by one person sporadically when time is available. Wattle-and-daub constructions need a much larger amount of wood, primarily to support a roof; the roof of such a construction would also not be strong enough to support a working space on the roof, which was normally the case.

---

58 For a comparison between the use of stone in the AP Palace construction and the construction of the settlement wall of Kenan Tepe, see F. Buccellati and Kansa 2016.

59 For an interesting introduction to the origins of mudbricks, see Aurenche 1993.

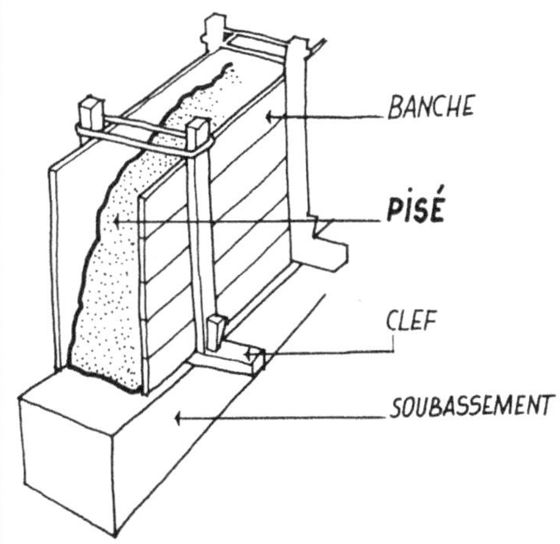

Illustration 53: Pisé construction technique with framing walls (Aurenche 1977, 138).

Another important advantage of mudbrick is that it is, in a certain sense, prefabricated building material: as such, the bricks can be produced at a different time, by different crews and in a different place from the actual construction of the building. Each brick is standard in two ways: each brick can be inserted into any portion of the building instead of being made for a specific location, and the bricks made for this project are the same as other bricks used in other constructions, so that bricks are interchangeable between projects, or rather can be made ahead of time and used in any project. The making of bricks at some distance from the construction site has a further advantage in that the bricks transported have a difference in weight between a dried brick and the same volume of wet mud. The plano-convex bricks used in constructions in previous periods in Mesopotamia were not nearly as standardized (Foster 2016, 205–6), and, due to their uneven upper surface, required a much larger amount of mortar.

3.2.2.2 *Process of mudbrick making*

The process of making mudbricks involves several steps, and even with all the needed materials present, requires several days (Wulff 1966); a mound of mud must be prepared, then wooden forms employed to make bricks on the ground. After a few days the bricks need to be stood upright so as to thoroughly dry, and then they must be either stored in a dry place or transported to a worksite.

Between 2006 and 2010 a series of ethnoarchaeological experiments were done at Mozan within the framework of a project to reconstruct the portions of the AP Palace which were completely destroyed. The following draws on this experiment, which is described in detail in section 3.2.2.9.

Illustration 54: Pit dug to mine dirt for mudbricks (Aurenche 1977, 129).

The first step in the process is the procuring and transportation of the soil (if necessary) which will be used for the bricks (Aurenche 1981, 48–49). The place from where the soil is to be taken is important,[60] since it must be near both water and as near to the construction site as possible (Heimpel 2009, 239). The only other material needed is straw (technically chaff, see section 3.2.6 below), which can be easily transported because of the lightness of the material.

A further consideration is the number of bricks which will eventually be needed: a large number of bricks needs a commensurately large hole, which poses a series of problems for the project planners. Ideally, the dig-site for the bricks would be quite close to the building to be constructed. However, since the building is within the urban environment, it is not practical to dig such a hole directly next to the building site. When choosing the site, then, it is important to be either as close as possible to the construction site as practical (Aurenche 1981, 48–49), or else to be close to the most efficient means of transportation for the bricks to the build-site.

The second consideration concerns the dimensions of the hole to be made when making the bricks. The relationship between the width and depth

60 A discussion of the chemical properties of the soil is beyond the scope of this analysis, but a good introduction can be found in Minke (1994, 27–31).

of the hole is important when considering both the impact on the local agriculture and the quality of the bricks produced.

A narrow but deep hole has two disadvantages: the effort required to lift the dirt from a deeper hole and the lower quality of the soil below the bioturbation layer. This deeper layer has a higher percentage of clay, a much lower percentage of organic matter and is often red in color, as opposed to the brown color of the bioturbation layer. The advantage of a deep and narrow hole, however, is that there is less horizontal impact, meaning that less agricultural area (the bioturbation layer) is sacrificed.

A wide and shallow hole, on the other hand, has the disadvantage of a large impact on the available agricultural area, but the advantages are that less effort is needed to raise the dirt out of the hole, and that the quality of the soil used is better than the lower strata. In order to preserve the agricultural area close to the urban environment while having a wide and shallow hole, it is possible to locate the hole at some distance, but then a transportation system must also be put into place to bring the bricks to the construction site. Transportation will be discussed in a following section.

The hole made in the production of bricks may also have a secondary purpose, such as a storage-pit or a dump-area (Aurenche 1981, 49). This eventual secondary use may play a role in the choice of location for the pit itself.

There are calculations from the ethnographic parallels as to the volume of dirt which can be excavated using wooden tools: an estimate of 2.6 m^3 excavated volume in 5 hours (Erasmus 1965, 285; Abrams 1994, 47).[61]

With regard to the AP Palace, it may be noted that there is a marked difference between two types of bricks, respectively red (used in the original construction, phase 2) and gray (used in the remodeling of phase 3). The assumption is that the red bricks used at the time of the first construction came from large holes in the Outer City or even the open countryside, due to the large quantity of bricks needed. The gray bricks, on the other hand, of which a lesser quantity was needed, would have come from the mound itself or the immediate countryside, the gray color being due to the organic and inclusions resulting from normal cultural deposition at the site itself or the bioturbation

61 It is interesting to note the comment of Erasmus, written in 1965, as to the reaction of the workers employed in the experiment: "The initial reactions of workers to the idea of excavating with wooden tools or to carrying rocks was usually one of amused incredulity. But once the objective was explained, interest in the project was high. The Mayas are understandably proud of their past and are interested in any kind of investigation related to it. I definitely felt that there was a desire on the part of the Maya workers to excel at their tasks as well as to earn the high wages I was paying. This fact was borne out by the tendency for effort to increase during the last hour of the carrying experiment rather than to decrease as it did in Sonora" (Erasmus 1965, 286)

layer.[62]

Illustration 55: Mud mixture for mudbrick production; note AP Palace in background (MZ V22i2235).

The second step in the production of mudbricks involves making a mixture of mud made of dirt, chaff and water.[63] In illustration 55 one can see the hose on the right which provides the water, the white sacks of chaff in the background on the right, as well as the dry dirt in the upper left. These components are mixed with shovels and also by pressing with feet. The procedure is not unlike kneading dough: a pile of dry dirt is made with a depression in the middle, water is poured into the depression, and the dry dirt is 'folded' into the center. After a few minutes of 'folding' the chaff is added by distributing it evenly over the top of the wet mound so that the particles adhere to the mud, and mixing continues. The proportion of dirt to water to chaff is

62 The phenomenon of red bricks has had quite an impact on our perception of ancient architecture. Some tells, such as Brak and Hamadiyah, have a very visible wide red band in the side of one of the mounds, often indicative of a large public building: see Oates 1990, 388–89. This red color has also influenced how archaeologists name structures they uncover: Massif Rouge and Maison Rouge (Mari), and the Tempio Rosso (Ebla). Interestingly, the Rotes Haus in Sheikh Hamed is not named for the brick color (which are, nevertheless, in places reddish) but rather for the color of the plaster on the walls of the first rooms to be uncovered (my thanks to J. Kreppner for pointing this out) (Kreppner and Schmid 2013, LXXXI).

63 The first bricks made are considered the ground-breaking moment of a construction project, at least during the reign of Gudea – see the passage in Gudea Cyl. A XIX 3-5 where the king makes a brick (Heimpel 2009, 239).

not fixed, primarily because the amount of dirt with which one starts cannot really be exactly calculated. The various elements of the mixture are added until the mixture has the correct plasticity, is not lumpy, and has enough chaff. By plasticity, the quantity of water which has been added is meant, enough so that the mixture is evenly moist and not lumpy, but not so much that the material does not adhere together in clumps, becoming more like a liquid (Doat et al. 1979; Aurenche 1981, 47). It is worth noting that the amount of organic material directly affects the ability of the bricks to resist transmitting warmth: the more chaff used, the more warmth resistant the bricks become (Minke 1994, 55–56, 89–92).

The quantity of mud-mixture made is a factor of the speed with which it is going to be used in the second part of the process, filling the forms. If the mixture begins to dry out it forms a crust, and water needs to be added and the

Illustration 56: Adding the mud-mixture to the brick form (MZ V22i2159).

whole mixture then must be re-mixed. Thus the quantity of mud-mixture is, along with the availability of materials, dependent on the quantity of bricks which can be made before this drying-out begins. Aurenche suggests that the mixture be made the day before (Aurenche 1981, 53–54), but in the ethnoarchaeological study in Mozan this was true only of mud-plaster, not the brick mix.

Illustration 57: A trowel is used on the top (MZ V22i2161).

The third part of the process is to fill the brick forms with this mixture. The brick form itself poses a difficult question, since there is little indication of how ancient brick forms were made (Salonen 1972, 36, 87, 100). Modern villagers near Mozan use a square box made of wood on four sides with a dividing wooden slat down the middle. Each side of the box is 60cm, so that each form then produces two bricks which are 60x30 cm. The sides of the box are approximately 12 cm high. The same method was employed to construct the brick form used in Mozan, but altered the dimensions to produce bricks which are the same size as those found in the palace: the bricks in the palace are about 40x40x10 cm, so the form used is 80x40x10 cm, thus making two bricks.

This brick form is most likely very similar to the ancient ones:[64] wood would have been readily available, and any other available material can be excluded for practical reasons.[65] Metal would have lost its shape through time in addition to being very expensive; a textile mould would also not have been able to keep its shape, and the mixture would have stuck to the sides of the form when removing it; stone would have been heavy and difficult to shape

64 Of course there was a complex spectrum of brick sizes used in different periods in ancient times; for an interesting discussion of the use of bricks to date architecture, see van Ess 2001, 1:18–20; what is meant here are the ancient bricks used in the construction of the AP Palace.

65 In Garshana wood was set aside to make wooden brick moulds (Heimpel 2009, 198).

into a precise square.

There is a term in Akkadian for a double-brick form, *kiskirru* (Salonen 1972, 100), of which there is no image; however, from my personal

Illustration 58: Pressing mud-mixture into the form (MZ V22i2236).

observations, it seems plausible that the form would have looked very much like the one used in the ethnoarchaeological experiment at Tell Mozan. Such a double form is the largest form a single person can handle: a triple or quadruple form would need two or more workers to lift straight up from the bricks. The technique of lifting the form from the wet bricks is explained below.

The area where the bricks are to be formed and left to dry has to be prepared ahead of time. The space has to be large enough for the number of bricks which are to be made over a three-day period, which is the usual drying time during the summer in the area around Mozan. The space necessary is dependent on the length of time it takes for the bricks to dry, and this time period for drying is, in turn, conditioned by region and time of year. Thus brick making in an area where bricks take twice as long to dry would require double the area for drying, assuming daily production of bricks.

The space must be relatively flat, clean of stones, sherds or plants, and easily accessible from the mud-mixture area. It is not important for the area to be swept clean, if anything, dust helps avoid the bricks sticking to the surface of the workspace.

Illustration 59: Removing the brick form (MZ V22i2162).

To fill the brick form a wheelbarrow was used to transport the mud-mixture, which in ancient times would not have been available. Instead, baskets, sleds or carrying-shelves would probably have been used. Ceramic vessels could have also been used, but that seems unlikely because of the weight and the danger of breakage and the relative plasticity of the mixture (could not be poured from such a vessel). Before beginning to fill the brick form, it must be thoroughly cleaned. In the ethnoarchaeological experiment done at Mozan the forms were washed but where water was scarce they could be carefully scraped clean. The reasons for careful cleaning are twofold: first, old, dried mud must be removed from the form so that it does not stick to the new bricks, and second so that the wooden parts of the form do not stick to the mud-mixture, making removal of the form difficult. At this point the mud-mixture is pressed by hand into the form, in order to minimize air pockets forming and weakening the brick.

Once the brick is a solid mass of mud without air pockets, a trowel is used on the top of the brick form to create an even surface. Note that the brick form is filled to the top, so that the height of the form determines the height of the bricks produced. A similar trowel may not have been available in the 3rd millennium, but a piece of wood could easily have been scraped across the top of the brick form, both pressing and flattening the top of the mud-mixture, achieving the same effect.

Once the tops of the bricks have been flattened, the form can be immediately removed by pulling it straight up. The technique of removing the form straight up means that it is easier to pull up and guarantees that the sides of the wet bricks will not be deformed by pulling the form diagonally. It can now be used for the next pair of bricks, repeating the process from the beginning.[66] Because of the contact with the ground on the bottom of the brick, and the scraping of a tool across the top, it seems that it would be possible to identify the tops and bottoms of bricks found in an archaeological context. Sometimes the bricks found in other areas of Tell Mozan have three parallel groves pressed into the brick face. These are probably created by drawing three fingers across the top of the brick, in order to improve the stability of the wall by giving a more irregular surface to which the mortar could adhere (J. Oates 1969, 121; Hole 1977, 88; Aurenche 1981, 59; Sauvage 1998, 42–44). Such groves could only be drawn on the top of the brick, just before removing the brick mould.

Illustration 60: Stages of drying – fresh bricks in background, lighter bricks are a day old, vertical bricks nearly dry (MZ V22i2702).

66 Interestingly, mudbricks are still used in some modern construction projects, for example in Australia. A company in New South Wales, *Make it Mudbricks* produces mudbricks on an industrial scale, and the images that they have on their website are strikingly similar to those shown here (Jirgens 2009).

In illustration 60 one can see several day's worth of brick production drying under the sun. The farthest bricks are the most recent, thus the darkest. Closer are series of bricks which have been drying longer, and lighter in color. The closest bricks have been drying for two days, at which point they are stood up on one side so that the underside of the brick dries as well. Enough space is left between the brick rows so that each day's series of bricks can be easily accessed.

Once the bricks are thoroughly dried, they can be used immediately in construction, or stacked. For reasons having to do with the time frame in which one can produce mudbricks (this will be explained in more detail below) it is more likely that the bricks were at least stacked before they were used in construction, if not stored for a longer period of time. Of course the large number of bricks needed for the palace construction would probably require stacking or storing of most of the bricks.

Illustration 61: Stacked bricks, ready for use, transport or storage (MZ V22i2237).

Stacking entails moving the dried bricks from the drying field and placing them in some sort of order in which they can be easily accessed, but do not take up much space. Modern brick makers had a rather elegant method: first a double column was made of stacked bricks, then a double row of leaning bricks were placed against it; against this section further rows of leaning bricks were placed. With such a pattern the bricks could continue to dry, and the 'stack' could be enlarged as much as necessary by adding to the first and then to the second leaning rows. It is surprising how similar this method of stacking is to the early forms of wall construction, the so-called herring-bone pattern. Sauvage notes this as well when discussing brick storage (Sauvage 1998, 78).

3.2.2.3 Materials needed to make mudbricks

The soil used for mudbricks are composed of three kinds of particles: silt, clay and sand (Minke 1994, 30). There is a high divergence in the percentages of each of these elements among mudbricks, even those found within the same settlement, but in general sand should be below 20% for stability, and the clay content is directly proportional to the durability of the mudbrick, but bricks with a high clay content are more difficult to make than bricks with more silt.

Clay	Sand	
5-30%	>40%	*United Nations guidelines*
25-45%	55-75%	*Schultz*
<20%	>45%	*Bardou & Arzoumanian*

Table 6: Various suggested mudbrick compositions (Aurenche 1981, 46).

Aurenche suggests a practical method to discern between clayish and silty soils: while washing dirty hands, clayish soil will become sticky and seem soapy, while silty soil, forming a powder similar to flour, and is more easily washed off (Aurenche 1981, 47). Another simple test used on the excavations is based on whether or not mud can be kneaded into pellets, in which case it has a high clayish component. In general, it may be noted that the quality of the mud used for bricks in the AP Palace is not necessarily fine, since one can often note the presence of pebbles, sherds and even small bones within the matrix of a single brick.

Sand plays the role of a bonding agent, but can be substituted with chaff, which has the added advantage of contributing to the water-resistance of the brick (Rosen 1986) as well as its ability to resist heat. When speaking of sand it is worth mentioning that a specific mineral is not meant, but is a "particle-size category" (Rice 1987, 72). As mentioned above, the bricks used in the AP Palace and the bricks produced in the ethnoarchaeological experiment used chaff instead of sand. The advantage of sand as temper is that the particles are angular, thus bonding the clay together in a cohesive matrix. Chaff as temper, instead, "corrects stickiness, increases porosity, reduces shrinkage and decreases drying time" (Rice 1987, 74). The use of an organic temper gives the mudbricks a compression strength of 5-20 kg/cm^2, and a standard structure in mudbrick needs only approximately 1 kg/cm^2 (Aurenche 1981, 51; Birschmeier and Gasche 1981, 4–5), so a chaff temper provides more than enough structural support. In an ethnographic comparison in Egypt where both sand and straw was available, straw was the preferred temper (Clark 2003). Since straw is a byproduct of grain harvesting, and is so light in comparison to sand, it is the ideal temper for mudbrick production.[67]

Water is the third element needed when creating mudbricks. Here again the number of bricks to be produced is a factor in considering the importance of water access. If a relatively small number of bricks need to be made, then a nearby source can be used even if getting the water is not very efficient, such as a well. If, however, a large number of bricks were needed, then the availability of a large quantity of water is an important consideration as to the location for brick production.

It may perhaps have been possible to accumulate rainfall in a specific area to use as water for brick making, by channeling rainwater into pre-existing depressions or pits. If timed correctly, one could use the rainwater to create the mud-mixture needed, and then dry the bricks immediately afterwards. It is however unclear how long bricks would take to dry in such a humid environment, and there is no way to demonstrate the use of such a process through the archaeological record.

3.2.2.4 *Half-bricks*

One problem in construction is that of overlapping mortar-lines. In order to prevent the wall separating either longitudinally or latitudinally (parallel or perpendicular to the length of the wall) it is important that the spaces between the bricks do not overlap either in the visible mortar-lines or in the lines which are 'inside' the wall, parallel to the face.[68] By laying overlapping bricks in a staggered pattern each brick covers the space between the two of a previous run; this is often called bonding.

With square bricks, such as those used for the AP Palace, this means that half-bricks need to be produced; with rectangular bricks, where width is half the length, there is no need to use half-bricks, since the brick layer can switch the direction of the bricks for each brick run. With square bricks, however, bonded walls can only be constructed by using half-bricks.

It is impossible to determine, on the basis of the archaeological record,

---

67 There is even philological evidence of cattails (a kind of weed) being used as temper in mudbricks (Salonen 1972, 47).

68 This phenomenon is a considerable problem in wall restoration, where new bricks buttress older constructions, because by doing so they don't create a bond between the two.

how or when these half bricks were produced. On the basis of the ethnographic analogy there are two possibilities: cutting fresh bricks or breaking dry bricks.

Once the form has been removed, but while the brick was still fresh, it is possible to further separate a brick in two, giving two half-bricks (Sauvage 1998, 22). This would probably be done by pushing a wood slat into the brick once the mould has been removed. The disadvantage is that there are now two bricks to carry instead of only one; this may have been harder on the brick carriers and/or more costly, making a difference especially if the bricks are to be transported over a long distance.

The second possibility provided by the ethnographic analogy is the breaking of dry bricks. This was the method used in the conservation/re-construction work at Mozan. In order to break the brick cleanly, a pole or thick straight stick was laid on the ground, and a brick was dropped from a height of 20-40 cm so that the line of the brick which is to be broken lands on the pole. The disadvantage of this method is that several half-bricks are lost due to breakage, either breaking unevenly (not along the pole-line) or in more than two pieces. In about 10% of the cases did this happen with one of the half-bricks, and only very seldom were both sides of the broken brick unusable resulting in a 5% - 10% loss rate.

There is, of course, a third possibility. It is conceivable that a second brick mould was employed by ancient brick makers, which would have produced the half-brick size needed for construction. The fact that this possibility did not arise through the ethnographic analogy gives one pause as to the results provided through this method of investigation. This possibility did not arise in the ethnographic analogy because of the parameters given (an interesting example of the limitations and danger inherent in the ethnographic analogy). Unfortunately it was not possible to determine, on the basis of the edges of the half-bricks within the archaeological record, if the half-bricks used in the AP Palace were made in their own mould or if they were made by breaking a whole brick. It would be very interesting to carefully dismantle an ancient wall to determine if the half-bricks were mould made, cut or broken. The difference between mould-made bricks and cut or broken bricks would be the ability of the mortar to adhere to the brick: if mould made, the mortar should flake evenly off of all 6 sides of the brick, while if cut or broken one side should have mortar inseparably embedded in the brickface.

Modern mudbricks in the area around Mozan are rectangular in form, with width half that of the length of the bricks. These are much more practical when building a bonded wall, since only one size is needed. In producing square bricks for the purpose of archaeological conservation/re-construction, the problem was a new one to the local masons, and the solutions which arose were *ad hoc* and did not reflect modern traditions of construction. In textual

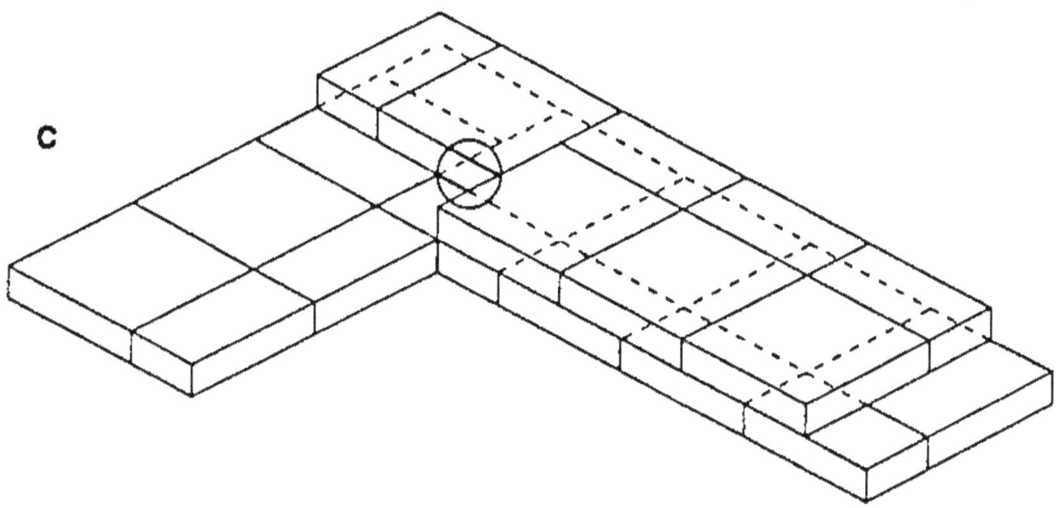

Illustration 62: Bonding along both longitudinal and latitudinal axes in a wall constructed using square and half-bricks (Sauvage 1998, 62).

sources there is a word for 'half-brick' in Akkadian (*arḫu*),[69] but it is unclear to which of these three possibilities it refers (Salonen 1972, 158–60).

The question of why the square brick was used so long in construction is one worthy of further consideration. Two possibilities come to mind: either the square-bricks were a tradition passed on from mason to mason, or the use of half-bricks gave a broader selection of choices in regard to wall width. An additional consideration is that the weight of a standard square brick of the size used in AP Palace with a brick weight of 22 kg was probably best suited to be moved around and raised high by a single workman without excessive incidence of breakages.

3.2.2.5 Mudbrick Volume and Weight

Based on an average value of 1450 kg per cubic meter (Minke 1994, 55), a brick that is 40x40x10 would weigh approximately 23.2 kg.[70] The new bricks from Mozan weighed somewhat more than this figure, an average of 1502 kg per m^3, while the bricks from the excavations weighed somewhat less, 1392 kg per m^3.

69 For further discussion of philological terms see section 3.2.3.

70 A 40x40x10 cm brick would have a volume of 16000 cm^3, equaling 0.016000 m^3. To determine the weight, 1450 kg * 0.0160 = 23.2 kg.

	width (cm)	length (cm)	height (cm)	weight (kg)	volume in cm3	volume in m3	weight of 1 m3 of brick
New bricks							
#1	40	40	9	22	14400	0.014	1527.778
#2	40	40	10	21	16000	0.016	1312.500
#3	39	38.5	10	22	15015	0.015	1465.201
#4	40	40	9	23	14400	0.014	1597.222
#5	39.5	39	10	20.5	15405	0.015	1330.737
#6	40	39	8	19	12480	0.012	1522.436
#7	39	39	10	24	15210	0.015	1577.909
#8	40	39	10.5	24	16380	0.016	1465.201
#9	39	39	8	20	12168	0.012	1643.655
#10	40	39.5	9	22.5	14220	0.014	1582.278
average:	39.650	39.300	9.350	21.800	14567.800	0.015	1502.492
Ancient bricks							
#1	41	33	12	22	16236	0.016	1355.014
#2	41	32.5	11.5	21	15323.75	0.015	1370.422
#3	40	33	12	23	15840	0.016	1452.020
average:	40.667	32.833	11.833	22.000	15799.917	0.016	1392.485
					% vis-a-vis new bricks:		92.68%

Table 7: Volume and weight calculations based on modern and ancient bricks from Tell Mozan.

3.2.2.6 *'Timing' Mudbrick production*

Mudbricks cannot be produced year-round, but are rather dependent on two direct factors: drying-time and availability of straw. During late fall, winter and spring the conditions for drying mud-bricks are poor because of the chances for rain and the relative humidity of the surface on which the bricks are placed. As seen when making bricks during the ethnoarchaeological experiment in Mozan, during dry months the surface has low humidity and the bricks dry within three days. If the days are shorter and the earthen surface gains some humidity over the course of the night as dew, then the bricks can take up to a week to dry. If the drying-time takes any longer, it is felt that the brick making season is over.

The second direct factor in the timing of brick making is the availability of straw. Straw can, of course, be stored over a whole year; however, it is the rigidity, water-absorption and relative lightness of the straw which makes chaff (cut straw) viable as temper for mudbricks. All of these qualities deteriorate when the straw is stored over a longer period of time.[71]

There are many indirect factors which influence the period in which mudbricks are made. The two most important are the need for workers for other tasks and the demand for bricks. Both harvest-time and occasional periods of conflict are moments when the fewest number of workers are available for construction projects. The demand for bricks may seem an obvious factor in producing bricks, but the task of making enough bricks

71 *Pace* Nippa 1991, 33. Workers at Mozan confirmed that they prefer new straw over old for these reasons.

during the right time to last a construction project until the next period of brick making would certainly not have been an easy task, since construction can continue even in the months when bricks cannot be made.

3.2.2.7 Storage of Mudbricks

Mudbricks can be either used immediately, stacked temporarily for use in the near future or stored for a longer period. The choice between stacking and storing is determined by the length of time before the mudbricks are to be used, and the period of the year. If there is the danger that the mudbricks get rained on for any length of time, then it is necessary to store rather than merely stack them.

There is a difference between stacking and storing in the way bricks are placed as well. Stacked bricks, in the ethnoarchaeological experiment done in Mozan and explained above, seldom reach higher than two bricks placed vertically one on top of another, reaching a height of 80-100 cm (see also page 104 above). Space is left between the bricks so that they remain dry and are also easier to lift. Also, by stacking them in a herring-bone pattern the chances of damage through cracking is lessened (Cornerstones Community Partnerships Staff 2006, 81).

Storage of bricks, on the other hand, requires a plastering of the brick stack to prevent rain or snow damage over the winter (Heimpel 2009, 80). Reed matting may also have been placed over the bricks before the plaster cover in order to further protect them. Because of the plastering, the bricks need to be stacked higher and with as little space between them as possible.

In the Garshana texts, bricks were also stored in many brick piles, built in different years. Heimpel suggests that "the choice of the verb 'construct' indicates that the bricks were laid in a bond" (Heimpel 2009, 227). The fact that the bricks were laid in a bond seems, however, unlikely; attempting to remove bonded bricks from the stack after a year would result in many more damaged bricks than if the bricks were merely placed on top of each other and then the stack itself was plastered over. Interesting is also the fact that there were 'master builders' involved in creating these brick stacks, indicating that there was a very specific method to their construction (Heimpel 2009, 228). Heimpel also asks if storing the bricks in such a way would lock in the moisture. The bricks would have been presumably dry when they were removed from the mudbrick production area, so moisture in the bricks would probably not be a problem. However the question leads one to ask about water absorption from the ground; since this is such a problem in the conservation of mudbrick walls, would stored bricks have also suffered? Perhaps a layer of stone or gravel could have been placed, much as in the walls of the AP Palace, or perhaps a layer of reed matting or straw would have been enough to protect the bricks[72]. Texts mention a layer of straw or reed matting being "deposited for use as a bottom" which may indicate a form of insulation (Salonen 1972, 112; Heimpel 2009, 230). Unfortunately, apart from this brief mention of straw, neither the archaeological record nor the texts give an indication as to whether this was a problem and what solutions would have been employed.

We have some idea as to the shape of brick stacks from a series of mathematical texts which pose the question of how many bricks are present in a truncated pyramid or a parallelepiped of certain dimensions (Nemet-Nejat 1993; Heimpel 2009, 227). The fact that such a mathematical problem is present in a series of teaching problems shows how often bricks were stacked for future use, and also shows that part of a scribe's training focused on administrative questions dealing with construction projects.

3.2.2.8 Mudbricks and the AP Palace

The bricks used in the construction of the AP Palace are square, approximately 40 cm on a side and 10 cm high, at an average weight of 22 kg. This size corresponds to brick type #9 as described by Sauvage (1998, 408).

Chaff and not sand was used as a temper; any mineral inclusions in the soil were present at the time of extraction, since the same inclusions can be seen in the earth used for seal impressions found within the same structure. The soil used for the mudbricks is very reddish in color, and does have some mineral inclusions, which would indicate that the soil used was taken from below the bioturbation layer. This would indicate that a deep and narrow hole was created when extracting the earth for the bricks, and could then have been relatively close to the construction site itself (see section 3.2.2.2 above).

Illustration 63: Opening a brick pile after a year (MZ V23i1102).

It is difficult to estimate the time it would take to make a certain number of bricks. The ethnoarchaeological

72 The book on Adobe Conservation does not directly speak of what to place under (modern) adobe bricks in storage, but the illustrations show either wood or gravel (?) under brick piles (Cornerstones Community Partnerships Staff 2006, 81).

experiment carried out at Tell Mozan used wheelbarrows and had a ready supply of water from a storage container which was filled by a pump, which makes a time estimate for ancient mudbrick production more of an educated guess than an estimate. The Garshana texts give an estimate of 240 mudbricks per person per day, with a pay-rate of 5 liters of barley per day (Heimpel 2009, 223–24). Aurenche suggests a higher number, 350 bricks per person per day (Aurenche 1981, 66). These numbers help give an estimate, but the bricks in both of these cases were smaller than the bricks used in the AP Palace, which would have presumably lowered the number of bricks per day. It is also unclear if the mud mixture was part of the work-day of these workers, or if their only task was the moulding of the bricks.

3.2.2.9 Mudbrick Production at Mozan

During 2010 an ethnoarchaeological experiment was carried out at the excavations; a portion of the AP Palace was completely destroyed due to mining of stone for the houses in the village. This presumably took place during the last few centuries, but had stopped by the time excavations began at the site. Since the wall was completely destroyed in this area (the SW corner of sector A) it was decided to rebuild the wall using stone found in erosion fills, and to make mudbricks in the 40x40x10 cm size. The pictures in this study come in part from this experiment.

Illustration 64 shows an overhead of the workspace: A is the storage area for dirt and straw (in white bags) – B is the mixing area, with a large water trailer – C is the brick drying area – D is the brick storage area – E is the area where the stones for the construction are placed.

On the basis of this ethnoarchaeological experiment, the following could be determined:

4 People
in 12 hours (over 3 days)
produced 1000 mudbricks (40x40x10 cm)
with a volume of 19.2 cubic meters.
Thus:
approximately 2.5 man-hours are needed
to produce 1 cubic meter of mudbrick – (4*12)/19.2

These figures assume that the dirt and straw are already at the worksite, and that water is readily available without added effort. Also, a large area for the drying is needed. The 12 hours over 3 days is due to the drying time of the bricks – most of the work is done on the first day, while the next days require only that the bricks be turned on their sides during the drying process.

Illustration 64: Overhead of workspace at Mozan (MZ V22i2238).

3.2.3 Philological Considerations on Mudbrick, Mortar and Plaster

At this point, having dealt with the production of mudbrick, mortar and plaster, a list of ancient terms associated with these materials and tasks as well as a discussion of some of the most important signs may be helpful. The goal is not to explore the philological side of the process, which would stray from the aim of this study, but merely to explore relevant ancient terminology.

3.2.3.1 Index of Terms

An index of the tools and tasks is important to include as a part of the discussion relating to construction, even if not complete or with an adequate discussion of the various meanings and references to literature. Such an index further bolsters the ethnographic analogy by showing that distinctions seen in modern practice were also present as terms in the language of the ancient builders. The list is derived from the book by A. Salonen on the bricks and associated tasks in the Ancient Near East (Salonen 1972). When several words for the same term were given, the one closest to Sargonic Akkadian is listed.

3.2.3.2 Sign for Mudbrick, Brickform

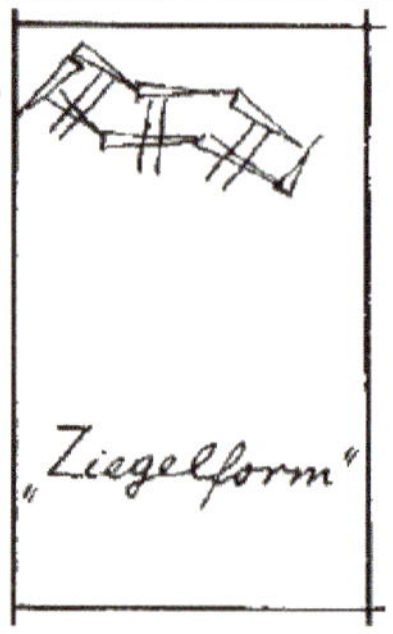

Illustration 65: SIG$_4$ after Deimel 1922.

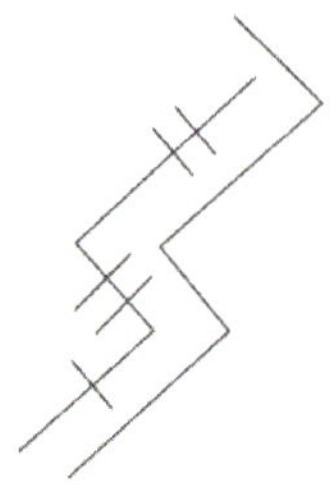

Illustration 66: SIG$_4$ after Labat 1976.

The pictographic sign for mudbrick, SIG$_4$, is also worth discussing at this point. SIG$_4$ seems to depict a series of mudbricks laid out in a wall pattern in its earliest forms (Daimel 1922, 22; Burrows 1935, 53; Labat 1976, 232; Green and Nissen 1987, 2:271). It is unclear what some of the elements of the sign are meant to represent, particularly the short lines crossing perpendicularly to the longer lines. These may represent mortar lines if the picture is meant to reproduce a wall, or they might represent architectural elements if the picture is meant to reproduce the architectural drawing of a wall.

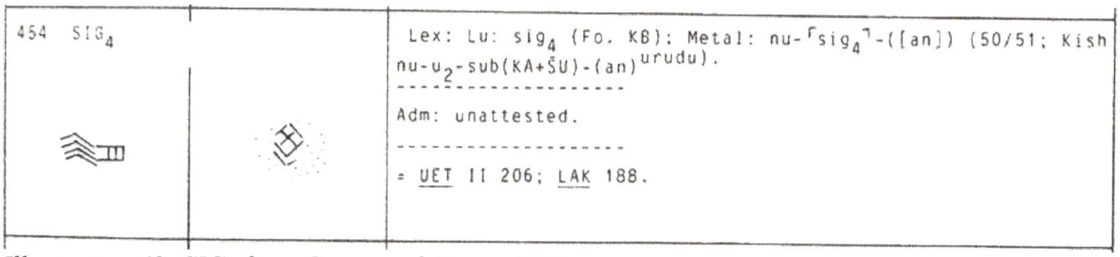

Illustration 68: SIG$_4$ from Green and Nissen 1987.

Illustration 67: SIG$_4$ from Burrows 1935.

Illustration 69: SIG$_4$ from text#272 in Burrows 1935 – one of the earliest attestations of SIG$_4$, from the EDI-II period (Cropped from CDLI image).

Term	Meaning	Page
	<u>Workers involved in Brick Production</u>	
GAL.IM	Master of Clay (chooses place and oversees brick production)	169
ša allim	pickman (preparing soil for brickmaking)	172
nāši marri	Shovelman (both turning the earthen mix and filling the form)	173
kerṣu	Clay-mixer	169
lu$_2$-im	Clay-mixer (or = GAL.IM?)	172
im-ila$_2$	Soil-carrier	169
lābin libitti	Brick-maker	172
agru	Hired Worker	168
aḫānu	unassigned workman	172
ṣārip agurri	brickburner (baked bricks)	173
	<u>Workers involved in Secondary Production</u>	
ēpiš qappāti	weaver of baskets of palm leaves	169
	<u>Workers involved in Brick Transportation</u>	
malāḫu	Boatman	173
nāši tupšikki	Brick-carrier (by means of basket or harness)	173
mušassik tupšikki	Overseer of brick-carriers (?)	173
zābil libitti	Brick-carrier	174
lu$_2$-ila$_2$	Brick-carrier	172
	<u>Workers involved in Construction</u>	
bānû	mason, master mason	168-169
itinnu	mason	169-172
rab itinnī	master mason	173
lu$_2$-sig$_4$-ba-na$_2$-a	Brick-layer (unclear if in brickyard or at construction-site)	173
	<u>Tools used in Demolition</u>	
ḫaṣṣinnu	ax for removing old bricks	115-117
maḫlašu	scraper for removing old plaster	117
ḫalašu, neṣu	to scrape off plaster (verb)	183, 193
	<u>Tools used in Brickmaking</u>	
marru	spade	73
naḫbašu	tool used to chop straw	76
naḫpû	pick for digging	76-77
namsû	bucket for transporting water	77
qappatu	big basket for transporting clay	77
nalbanu, nalbattu	Brick form (without baseplate)	87
kiskirru	Brick form for two bricks	100
kuradu, ṣirru, ṣerru	tool for flattening top of brick while in form (trowel? Scraper?)	104-105
sapānu	to level the surface of the brick in its mould (verb)	196
	<u>Brick Terms</u>	
libittu	mudbrick	136-146
agurru	baked brick	146-157
arḫu	half brick	158-160
	<u>Tools used in Transportation</u>	
gigurdû	carrying basket. Perhaps carried by 2 people over a stick.	106
eleppu ša libitti	boat used to transport mudbricks	107
ṣumbu, ṣubbu, ṣabbu	2 wheeled wagon	108
nazbālum, kudurru	device used to transport bricks on shoulders or around neck	113
	<u>Brick Storage</u>	
amāru	brick pile, to stack bricks in a pile (verb)	108
	<u>Tools used in Construction</u>	
^{giš}dub-ila$_2$	mortar board (for working with mortar and plaster)	117
naspanu	trowel for applying mortar	117
supinnu	blade (used in shaping bricks?)	118
uraku	container for mortar?	118

Table 8: Page numbers (right) refer to Salonen (1972).

One of the meanings of SIG_4 is *murgu*, with meanings of "shoulder" or "drawing". This meaning is already attested in Early Dynastic times, in the Ebla archives.[73]

The sign for 1/2 brick, SIG_4-ÁB, is also of interest: in the *AHw*,[74] the logogram, which corresponds to *arḫu* in Akkadian, is rendered as "cow-brick," but this need not be taken literally, since one can hardly see why a half-brick would be described with such a term; it could be a question of homonymy. In the *CAD* the term is found along with the measurements of the half brick: 2/3 of a cubit by 1/3 of a cubit by 5 fingers height (CAD A2 264). The relationship between SIG_4-ÁB, SIG_4-dili ("alone-brick") and SIG_4-tab.ba ("twin-brick")[75] might also be a fruitful discussion, but would also not contribute directly to this study.

The sign for brick mold, ĝešu$_5$-šub, is also present in the late EDIII, attested in the tablets from Umma/Zabala (Bartash 2013). This may be the earliest reference to date for molds of this type. A slightly later attestation can be found in the Ebla archives (Civil 2008, 145), while a discussion of the sign in these early periods can be found in Steinkeller's (1987, 194) review of Foster's *Umma in the Sargonic Period*.

3.2.3.3 Calculating number of mudbricks needed

With the large number of mudbrick sizes that were in use in various periods in the ancient Near East (Sauvage 1998), one might wonder how ancient builders knew how many bricks of a certain type were needed. Scribes in the Old Babylonian and Ur III periods used a sophisticated method for performing this calculation: they developed the concept of *nabālum*, which represents the ratio between *brick-sar* (720 bricks) and the *volume-sar* those bricks occupied (Robson 1996, 182). Thus the number of bricks needed could be calculated easily given the *nabālum* of the bricks to be used and the size of the wall:

number of *brick-sar* needed
= wall length *x* wall width *x* wall height *x* *nabālum* (Robson 1996, 182)

Of course one has no idea if the scribes or builders in Urkesh knew of this formula, or even needed it, since brick sizes vary little in the archaeological record at the site. However, it remains an interesting and

73 "murgu = SIG_4 = gur-gi-num$_2$" in Archi line 89 (1987).

74 "nach wz. = *arḫu* II = also Kuhziegel?" (von Soden 1965, 67).

75 My thanks to V. Bartash for several fruitful discussions regarding these philological considerations.

elegant solution to the problem of the variety of brick sizes used in construction in other regions and/or other periods.

3.2.4 *Mud Plaster and Mortar*

Illustration 70: Mixing dirt and water for plaster.

The mud-mixture used for plaster is different from the mixture used for making mudbricks in that it has a much higher percentage of chaff, and is

Illustration 71: Adding chaff to the plaster.

much more liquid. The first step in making plaster is the mixing of dirt and water. Once there is a mud mixture, chaff is added; the chaff is the same as that used for mudbricks.

Since so much chaff is added to the mud-mixture, the most efficient way to begin mixing it is to use feet, while adding water to keep the particles from blowing away. In Illustration 72 note the two workmen on the left who are ready to transport the plaster to the area where it will be placed.

There is a difference between mortar and mud plaster, but only one of proportion: mud plaster has a much higher quantity of straw than the mortar, because the straw is much better suited to protect the walls against rainfall. Also, straw is used (longer pieces) rather than chaff (shorter pieces) because the longer pieces give a higher surface area and better surface cohesion than chaff would. The proportion of straw to the quantity of mud varies greatly between the various ethnographic examples. The soil used for mortar and plaster is the same as that used for bricks (Salonen 1972, 47, 50–51; Sauvage 1998, 70).

One component which is sometimes added to mortar is ash, which contributes to hardness and resistance to humidity (Aurenche 1981, 72; D. Oates 1990, 389).[76] This has however not been attested in the mortar present in the AP Palace, nor in the nearby modern constructions. A possible explanation for this lack might be the presence of stone substructures, which serve the same function.

A component which is sometimes added to plaster is lime, which increases the water-resistance. This is also not attested in the archaeological record at Mozan, and modern constructions tend to use cement when waterproofing is necessary. Gypsum is also sometimes used as a final coating on walls, but is normally a thin layer added after the mud-plaster is completely dry.

3.2.5 Gypsum and Lime Plasters

Two types of white plaster can be found in archaeological excavations: gypsum plaster and lime plaster (Gourdin and Kingery 1975; Aurenche 1981, 23–30; Kingery, Vandiver, and Prickett 1988; Kurapkat 2009).

In the ethnographic comparisons, gypsum is applied on top of wall plaster as a paint; the ancient method of application is unknown, but was probably similar, since the application of gypsum while dry would be very difficult, if not impossible. The plaster is renewed after a time, and these various layers of gypsum can be seen in the archaeological record when

76 Ash was also placed as a damp course under the second millennium mudbrick walls in the Ninkarrak Temple at Terqa (G. Buccellati, personal communication).

layered against undamaged wall remains (Aurenche 1981, 138). Gypsum ovens are similar to brick ovens, needing to produce between 100-200 degrees Celsius (Wulff 1966, 126). It is also possible to bake gypsum directly in the ground: a strip of dirt is removed, exposing the gypsum ($2CaSO_4 \cdot 4H_2O$) below. Fuel for the fire is added on top of the limestone, and lit: this removes the water content, which is released as steam. Further fuel is added until the limestone has becomes a powder ($2CaSO_4 \cdot H_2O$); the area is then cleaned of fire residue, and only at this point is the powdered form of gypsum can be removed. Once water is added, the powder returns to its hardened state ($2CaSO_4 \cdot 4H_2O$).

In the AP Palace in Mozan, only gypsum was used. Lime is preferable from a materials point-of-view because it hardens uniformly in a chemical process, but requires a much higher firing temperature: a minimum of 900 degrees Celsius for at least 36 hours. Lime plaster creates a hardened surface through a chemical process: in firing quarried limestone ($CaCO^3$), CO^2 is released, leaving quicklime (CaO). Water is added shortly before applying the

Illustration 72: Mixing the plaster with feet.

plaster, altering the chemical composition further ($Ca(OH)_2$); when the lime dries, carbon dioxide is absorbed, returning the plaster to its original state ($CaCO^3$), giving a uniform, hardened surface (Cornerstones Community

Partnerships Staff 2006, 133). This cycle is summarized graphically in Illustration 73.

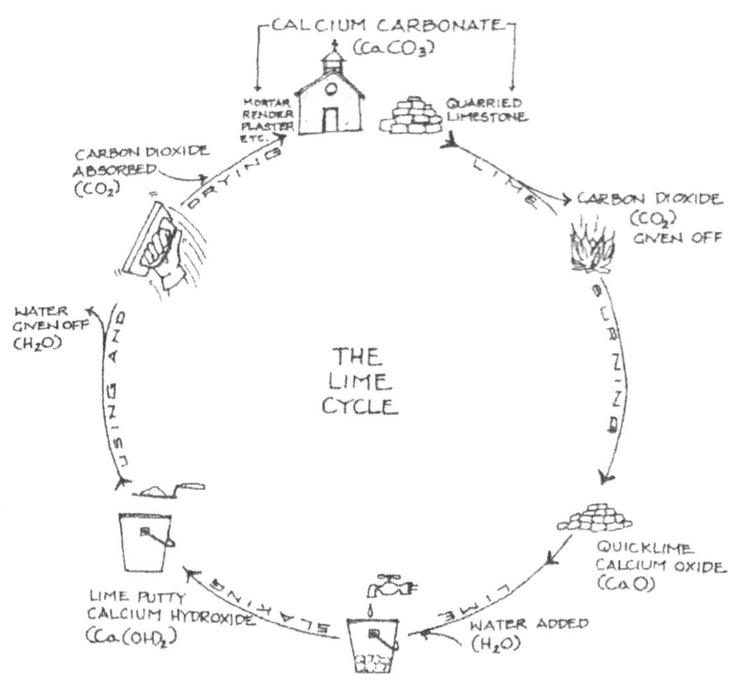

Illustration 73: The lime cycle (Cornerstones Community Partnerships 2006, 133).

3.2.6 Chaff

The chaff used does not have to come from a certain plant, in modern times both wheat and barley are used (Aurenche 1981, 135–36). One difference between kinds of chaff is the size: longer pieces of chaff (sometimes called straw) are ideal for brick making since the function is to bind the soil: 1-1.5 in or 2.5-4 cm (Cornerstones Community Partnerships Staff 2006, 132). Shorter pieces of chaff, instead, are better for mortar, giving a finer mix for use. Plaster, on the other hand, uses longer pieces of chaff, which gives the surface covering the wall better water-resistance. There is even evidence of cattails being used as temper instead of the chaff from harvested grains (Salonen 1972, 47).

The quantity of chaff needed is perhaps underestimated when considering the quantities of material needed to make bricks, mortar and plaster. David Oates asked modern villagers near Tell Brak, who stated that for 100 bricks approximately 1½ sacks of chaff were needed, about 60 kg (D. Oates 1990). About 1/8 of a hectar was needed to produce 1½ bags of chaff (D. Oates 1990), giving the parameters for a rough estimate of the agricultural area needed to provide for a known number of bricks.[77] Extrapolating from D. Oates' figures, one hectar planted with a grain (unclear which grain was used in the calculation, but it was most probably wheat) produced 12 bags weighing a total of 480 kg. The bags used in the ethnoarchaeological experiment in Tell Mozan held more chaff than those used at Tell Brak, each weighing about 53 kg.[78] When making such calculations one should bear in mind the fact that the chaff is otherwise used as fodder for domesticated animals, particularly during the winter months, so that the chaff used in construction must be in surplus vis-à-vis the needs of the livestock of the community.

3.2.7 Wood

Wooden beams are the most important part of the roof, since their length determines the width of the rooms. Depending on availability, palm,[79] poplar or any other tree trunk can be used.[80] The beams are seldom squared in section in the ethnographic examples, but are left as round trunks, only stripped of the bark. Groves were probably tended by foresters, as in other regions (Foster 2016, 123–24).

3.2.8 Reed matting

Reed matting is needed especially for the roofs, placed directly on the wooden beams. Reed matting is further used in construction as flooring under the brickpiles (Salonen 1972, 112; Heimpel 2009, 230). The reeds would have been collected along riverbanks (Foster 2016, 124–25), and would most likely have been woven into mats near the rivers, since the mats would have been much easier to transport than bundles of reeds.

---

77 Unfortunately D. Oates does not mention the size of the bricks made in this example; in my own experience, the bricks in the Mozan area (which is geographically quite close to Tell Brak, where D. Oates was working at the time) are 60x30x14 cm. Thus they would have a volume of 25200cm^3, 6000cm^3 more than the 40x40x12 cm size or 31.25% larger.

78 Five bags were weighed in April 2013: 51 kg, 56 kg, 49 kg, 54 kg, 58 kg for an average of 53.6 kg. These are the white bags seen in the photographs of the ethnoarchaeological experiment carried out in Mozan.

79 Palm trunks as construction material were obviously more prevalent in southern Mesopotamia, where palm trees were much more common. One example of their use can be found in the *weissen Tempel* in Uruk (Heinrich 1934, 27; Birschmeier and Gasche 1981, 2–3).

80 For an anthracological (wood charcoal) study at Mozan giving evidence for local tree types, see Deckers 2010.

Illustration 74: Reed mats (Aurenche 1977, 155).

3.2.9 Fill Material

One further material used for construction is a simple earthen mix, possibly the same as what is used to create the mudbricks, if the pit is located nearby. This fill material is used to level the construction area, and is also used in the laying of the roof. A clean fill is much better for both uses because cultural material tends to be different in compaction, settling in different degrees; this might make, over time, the roof or floor uneven.

3.2.10 Tools

Tools for each of these tasks would have been readily available to the workers at the construction site, possibly with each skilled worker bringing his or her own tools to the job. A discussion of tools currently in use can be found in ethnographic and technical texts (Doat et al. 1979; Cornerstones Community Partnerships Staff 2006). Several of these tools are also shown on the stele of Ur-Namma of Ur (Canby 2001), carried on his shoulder; a basket, adze and ax are among the tools carried.

Illustration 75: Detail from stele of Ur-Namma; note tools in lower register (Canby 2001, Plate 31, fig. 14).

Illustration 76: Detail from drawing of Ur-Namma stele showing tools (after Canby 2001, Plate 33).

3.3 Know-How

In addition to the materials used, there is a need for specific know-how when constructing a large building such as the AP Palace. These tasks are specific skills, as opposed to 'manpower' which is the organization of large groups of people with limited skills, and will be discussed in section 3.4 below.

Here it should be pointed out that these are working areas of expertise, not necessarily specific persons. It is thus possible that the same person is responsible for both the architectural planning and the city planning. The tasks have been identified on the basis of the understanding of modern divisions, and also loosely following the definitions established in the book by C. Smith (Smith 2006).

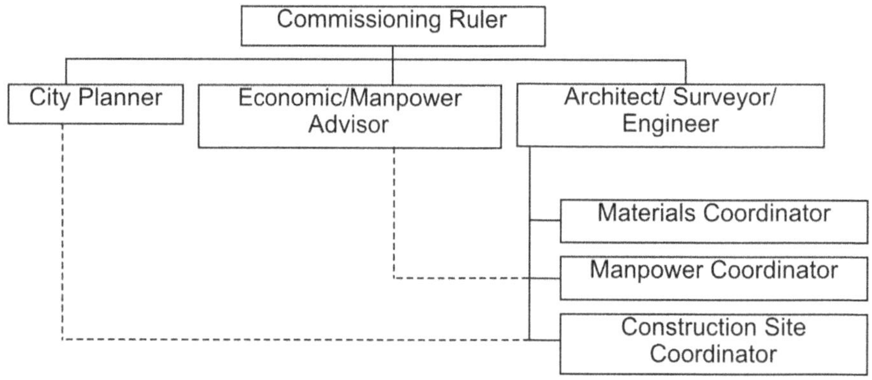

Illustration 77: Flowchart describing hypothetical working groups needed when building a palace.

In the following sections there is a certain overlap with the points which will be made under the section discussing manpower, particularly the section on Organization of Labor (3.4.2) below. However these two sections approach the organizational structure from two different perspectives: the portions discussing Know-How consider what skill sets might have been needed, while the portions discussing the organization of labor are concentrated on the hierarchical structure, drawing in particular on the textual evidence from the Garshana archive.

3.3.1 Commissioning Ruler

The beginning of any palatial construction project starts with the commissioning ruler. This is not necessarily the person who is going to inhabit the palace:[81] it may be that an aging ruler commissions a new palace for the prince who is to follow, or that the prince is integrated enough in the public administration during the reign of his predecessor to begin such a project.

Before discussing these possibilities, the question of the need for a new palace needs to be confronted. There are two categories of reasons: structural and political. Structural reasons are based on the condition of the architecture of the existing palace. Water damage, weakened wooden beams and structural weakness due to unstable foundations are the most likely problems which could affect a preexisting palace. Political reasons are, of course, much more complicated to identify, nearly impossible to discern in the archaeological record, and what is known comes primarily from philological evidence. These

81 In this study the palace being discussed is a royal palace, which is reflected in the terms used for the actors (such as 'commissioning ruler'). If this analysis were applied to another building, not royal, the terms referring to the actors would have to be appropriately modified.

reasons will be discussed to a greater extent in the theoretical chapter,[82] but the primary causes are the need to distance oneself from the previous ruler, to change the semiotic message and/or psychological impact of the palace, or to affect the urban texture. Of course these possibilities are not mutually exclusive.

There are then three likely possibilities as to the commissioning ruler: a new king, an old king for his successor, or the king-to-be while his predecessor still lives. The main question here is the length of time it takes to build a new palace: if five years are needed, then the new king will have reigned for those five years from a pre-existing palace. If the need for a new palace is based on the political reasoning outlined above, then such a long wait would seem counter-productive to that message. Also, if an old king or a king-to-be is the one commissioning the palace, the question arises of who is the real author of the semiotic and ideological messages contained therein.

3.3.2 Planning Team

When first setting out, three types of skilled persons are required: the City Planner, the Economic/Manpower Coordinator and the Architect. This group plans the construction of the palace over the long-term, taking the decisions and making the preparations needed before the actual building can begin.

3.3.2.1 Planning Team: City Planner

The City Planner is responsible for the urban texture into which the palace is going to be embedded. Three main questions need to be asked: how big of a footprint will the palace have, and what existing structures need to be removed, if any? To what extent does the palace rely on and affect the infrastructure of the city? What is the impact of the palace within the city-scape and the surrounding landscape?

The size of the palace is primarily affected by the amount of resources available, but the urban space is also an issue. The location of the new palace within the city is affected by the size of the proposed structure, so that a give-and-take between location and size may be necessary. If the commissioning ruler wants the palace in a certain area of the city, perhaps because of visibility, access or closeness to other important structures, then the area available for construction might be a limiting factor when planning the building.

The relationship of the palace to the urban infrastructure is a further factor. Access to the palace by means of streets or paths is an important factor

82 See section 4.3.2.

in location, since the king and visitors will be using them on a daily basis. Access is also necessary during the building phase for the delivery of building materials. In addition it is important for the functioning of the palace subsequently because goods needed in every-day activities in the palace need to be efficiently delivered. To this end it should be noted that the AP Palace is placed on the western side of the city and near a canal, facilitating water-borne deliveries during months of high water levels. The access to fresh water and the removal of waste water is also an important factor; the palace, as home for the king and a focal point if not home for the court, would rely on good access to both of these water systems. Storage is a further consideration; the palace may have large storage areas contained within its walls, but it would have to rely at least in part on storage areas within or near the city limits.

The last major consideration is the location of the palace within the 'city-scape'. This is more of an ideological component, and depends on the relationship of the palace to structures lying outside of the palace confines. Examples of this might be the location of an important temple or the ability for visitors to see the palace even from outside the city walls when approaching the city.

3.3.2.2 Planning Team: Economic/Manpower Coordinator

The second main task of the planning team is the need for an economic[83] plan and the organization of the manpower to be employed in the construction effort.

The economic aspect of the project is one of the most difficult to discern within the material evidence present in the archaeological record, and a modern monetized economy is far too different from what is known of ancient systems to provide an adequate ethnographic parallel. What one can postulate is that there was someone within the planning team who was responsible for the manpower, and this person had to take into consideration the effect of manpower choices on local households and the city economy.[84] Thus it may be germane to discuss first the aspects of manpower, and then to infer what is possible about the economic considerations necessary.

The timing of the work schedule is one of the most important tasks leading up to the actual beginning of work. The season in which the actual construction takes place is important under two aspects: the climatic

83 By using the term *Economic* I do not mean to suggest that there was the awareness of the complexities often associated with the term today; I am thinking more of the term in its etymological sense, that of the organization of a household (*oikos*), as discussed by Gelb (1979, 3–4).

84 Again, as seen on a practical level as a super-household and thus without the complexities inherent in the modern term.

conditions under which building can be undertaken efficiently, and the other tasks that might limit the availability of the majority of the skilled and unskilled laborers to work on the project (Abrams 1994, 43).

The construction needs to take place during the dry period of the year, otherwise the mudbricks absorb moisture, which hampers their ability to bond with the mortar and increases greatly their weight, which in turn increases breakage during carrying. The straw (long pieces, as opposed to chaff) and wood used for the roofing would have also been much more difficult to place during the rainy season, in part because of the added weight and in part because of the time it would take to wait for the walls to be dry enough to support evenly the weight of the roof beams.[85]

The second factor is the availability of workers, both unskilled and skilled. The agricultural and pastoral work of the city's workers have to take precedence before construction projects, but these work intensive tasks are restricted to specific seasons, primarily during the planting and harvest time. These tasks would require the large numbers of unskilled laborers available, and many of the skilled laborers would also be needed, depending on their skills.

Manpower is also affected by the conditions in the urban and rural environments of the city in addition to the direct needs of the project. Thus this task requires knowledge of the details of the project as well as the wider economic and planning considerations of the local administration, and it is here that one returns to the economic aspect.

The *corvée* system, discussed below in section 3.4.1.5, describes the availability of workers for public projects, but not the effect on the city economy. Thus the planning team must calculate the period when the call-up of the workers is best for the project and hampers the city-economy least.

The difference between skilled and non-skilled workers requires further consideration when discussing the *corvée* system: to what extent can skilled workers be called up in this system, or do they need to be hired separately? Unfortunately further textual evidence would be needed to be able to posit an answer to this question.

While most of the material needs of the palace can be produced by employing manpower, e.g. in the stone-quarries to quarry the required stone, some of the material may have had to be imported from outside the economic sphere of the city, and specialized labor may have also been called from outside this sphere. As an example, a furniture maker using special wood would have to be 'imported' along with the wood needed for his work. The question of how much of a burden on the city's economy this might have been

85 In fact, the Garshana archives list rain-days as “free-days” (Heimpel 2009, 66).

and how the surplus needed was accumulated also falls outside of the framework of this study, but is a question which might be pursued in a situation where more information, primarily textual, was available. For instance, the two Old Akkadian tablets found at Tell Mozan in unit F1 list four villages, with a total which probably reached one hundred individuals between the two tablets (the exact figure is unknown because of breaks): they are divided in groups, under the supervision of an "inspector" called *nu-bànda*. The villages from which they come are mentioned by name (only four are extant in the texts as preserved), and one text refers to a "workshop" (*giš-kin-ti*) in a given village, to which the individuals apparently belonged (Milano 1991, M2 2 VI 1').

3.3.2.3 Planning Team: Architect/Engineer/Surveyor

The last aspect of the planning team is the person or persons directly responsible for the planning of the physical construction. One can divide these responsibilities into three categories: architect, engineer and surveyor. However it is important to realize that this division of tasks is dependent on how buildings are constructed today, and ancient planners may have seen a different division of the tasks, or no division at all. Nevertheless the problems and questions that arise and that is associated today with these professions are still very pertinent to any construction, no matter when it was built. Thus while the division of tasks between architect, engineer and surveyor may have been alien to ancient workers, the tasks themselves must have been accomplished by someone in the planning stages of the work, regardless of specific titles.

The tasks needed to be accomplished are:[86]

building plan including design elements (A)
ceilings/roofing (A)
functional needs (A)
ornamentation (A)
interior installations (A)
foundation strength (E)
major structural installations such as sewers (E)
stone/mudbrick heights and considerations of stability (E)
measurements matching plan to work-site (S)
division of parts of work-site into crew-tasks (S)

In this list the various responsibilities have been labeled in parentheses after the task, to give an idea of the skill set required to complete the task: for example, a different skill set is needed to produce a building plan than that needed to determine the foundation strength needed; this does not preclude

86 Taken in part from Smith (2006, 67–68).

that one person has several or all of these skill sets, as was stated in the beginning.

3.3.3 Execution Team

The second category of responsibilities regards the person or people responsible for the practical execution of the construction job – again, what is being described here are tasks, not specific people, so that the same person could (and probably did) fulfill multiple tasks. These responsibilities have been divided into four groups: material coordinators, construction coordinator, builder and overseers. There is by necessity an overlap with the planning team described above.

3.3.3.1 Execution Team: Material Coordinators

Material coordinators are responsible for the timing and quality of the materials needed at the construction site. They would be located at the place where the materials are gathered or made, such as at the stone-quarry or mudbrick pit. There would be the need for a coordinator for each of the materials used in the construction, and possibly one for tools and another for transportation as well. These coordinators would have timetables regarding when to deliver specific materials, presumably given to them by the planning team.

3.3.3.2 Execution Team: Master Builder

There would have been a primary builder at the site who saw to the division of the work-crews and the sequence in which the various parts of the building would have been built. Their task would have also included the quality of the construction as it was being erected and interfacing with the planning team when the unexpected arose, for example when foundations seem to be insufficient or the construction is hampered by the presence of earlier buildings.

3.3.3.3 Execution Team: Overseers

A group of overseers would have answered to the master builder, each in charge of a group of workers, skilled or unskilled. These overseers[87] might have been experts at a specific task, and then would lead a group of workers who were 'specialists' in that task. This division can be seen in the Garshana archives (Heimpel 2009, 67–76), but it would be going too far to assume that this case would apply to all construction sites. Overseers are different from foremen – overseers do not actively participate in the work being done, while

87 For more on overseers see also sections 3.4.2.2 and 3.4.2.3 below.

foremen are the leader of a work-crew, and work along side the other members of the team.

3.3.3.4 *Execution Team: Construction Coordinator*

The construction site would have needed a coordinator for the incoming materials, the work done by the crews not directly involved in the construction (e. g. brick carriers), the site security and the needs of the workers. This might correspond to one of the chief administrators[88] of the project; in the Garshana archives it seems that one of the main differences between the builders and the administrators is that the builders carry responsibility for the construction[89] while the administrators are scribes.

3.3.4 *Know-How and the AP Palace*

The AP Palace is a product of a group of people having the skill sets described here. Each of these tasks would have been accomplished by the administrative staff tied to the (existing) palace or directly to the construction project.

If these skilled workers are local, as seems more than likely, then questions have to be asked as to how these skills were acquired. Obviously there is a long tradition in the whole of Syro-Mesopotamia of building in mudbrick. Major mudbrick construction projects in Urkesh from earlier than the AP Palace include the inner city wall and the temple BA which date to the Early Dynastic period. The experience of constructing monumental buildings, including the transfer of knowledge and skills to make mudbricks, construct walls and roofing could have been made without a steep learning curve. Also the experience in Urkesh from the Early Dynastic III period of constructing monumental architecture in stone (the temple terrace in particular) would have facilitated the organization of the work on the AP Palace on the level of quarrying, stone preparation, transport of wood and stone, in addition to the actual construction techniques. Additionally, the earlier large building projects must have utilized the skills of a surveyor. The tablet with the architectural plan of three rooms from A15 attests to the knowledge and skill of such a specialist in the building of the AP Palace (see the discussion of this tablet at 2.2.1.4.2).

3.4 Manpower

One of the most difficult questions archaeologists ask is in regard to the

---

88 See also section 3.4.2.6 below.

89 See for example laws 228-233 of the Code of Hammurabi (Johns 1904).

manpower[90] behind the structures and objects found in the archaeological record. There is a considerable amount of information which can be obtained or deduced from the record, but it is really only in combination with text sources that an understanding of the workforce as system can be presented. It is here where the texts from Garshana (Heimpel 2009)[91] can be used to create a hypothesis as to the structure of the workforce involved in building the Palace at Tell Mozan.

On the face of it, the Garshana texts have little to do with the situation at Tell Mozan. First, the texts are from a different time period; the Garshana archive dates to the Ur III period, while, as has already been stated, the AP Palace at Mozan dates to the Akkadian period, presumably the reign of Naram-Sin. Additionally, the Garšhana texts are written in Sumerian, so the titles and tasks named in the texts would not necessarily have corresponded to the Akkadian much less the Hurrian terms that might have been used by the workforce in ancient Urkesh (although either Hurrian or Akkadian would have been in any case be represented by Sumerian logograms, as is known from the administrative texts found at Mozan). Geographically, Garshana lies in the heartland of Mesopotamia, not far from the ancient city of Umma (the exact location of Garshana is unknown, but enough evidence is present to locate it with some degree of specificity). This geographic difference plays a larger role in the availability of materials, but is of interest to some extent because of the onomastic analysis to which the texts can contribute. The texts from Garshana do not describe standard urban structures, since the texts come from a compound which was dependent on a military structure.

Despite these differences, the texts from Garshana give an unparalleled look into the organization of manpower for a construction project. In particular the relationship between slaves and hired workers, the required specializations and the administrative structure give a point of departure from which one can build a hypothesis as to the role of manpower within the construction of the AP Palace. There are also indications that the system in place during the Ur III period had its origins in Akkadian practices (Foster 2016, 93–95), which might well have been the praxis at Urkesh as well.

3.4.1 *Divisions within the Workforce*

The workers in the Garshana archives can be divided into skilled and unskilled workers who can be hired, are slaves or come from another locality.

---

90 I use manpower as a term relating to the (primarily unskilled) workforce involved in a project, irrelevant of the gender of the people engaged in the construction project.

91 For a remark on the ethical considerations of publishing texts from illegal excavations, see 3.1.2.1.

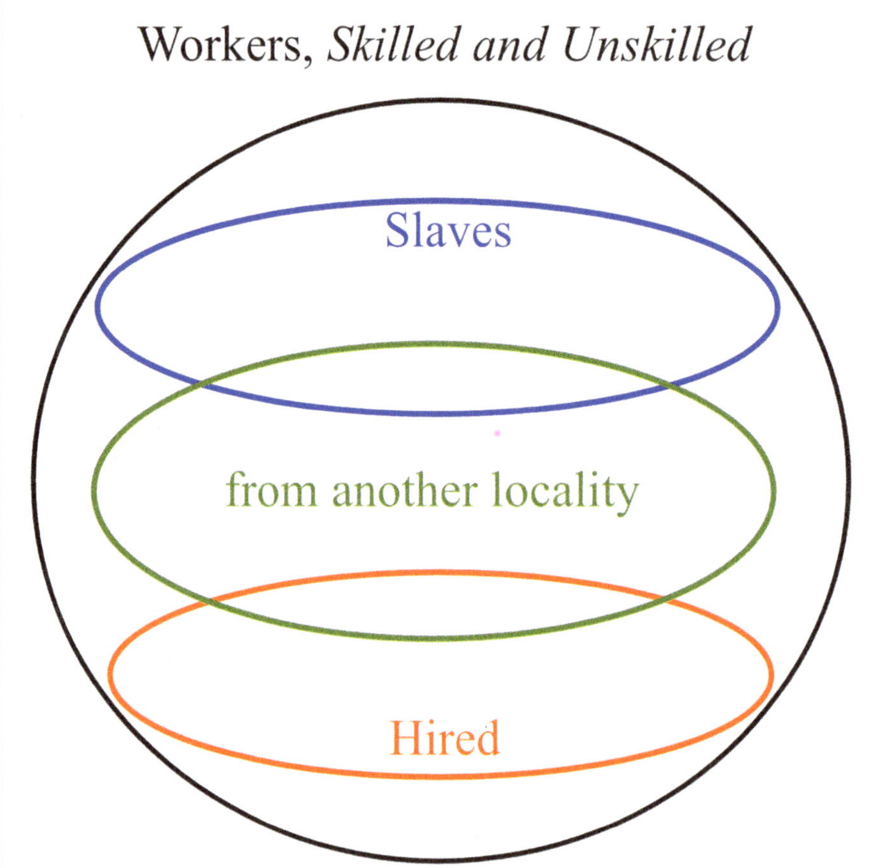

Illustration 78: Worker divisions within the texts from Garshana.

3.4.1.1 Skilled/Unskilled Workers

The vast majority of the workers engaged in the construction projects at Garshana are unskilled workers, such as brick carriers. A cadre of skilled workers form the core of the construction project; their skills are either directly tied to construction, such as master builders, or are tied to common tasks which are also needed in the construction process, such as ox-cart drivers.

3.4.1.2 Slaves

Some of the workers in Garshana were assigned to the construction project, and are referred to as being 'of the house'; Heimpel indicates that these are slaves who are allotted to this task. There seem to be indications that slaves are also 'leased' from other households (Heimpel 2009, 52).

The relationship between slave and the two households involved is unclear: it is possible that the slave is "in the service of" a household (Gelb

1979, 7) implying a looser relationship, but it is also possible that a more rigid form of slavery is meant (Diakonoff 1976). Most likely different forms of dependence or slavery were practiced in different regions or time periods.

The relationship between household and slave has also been the focus of recent research, particularly for the Ur III period (Neumann 2011; Culbertson 2011). Neumann claims that "slavery never played a dominant role in the production spheres of ancient Near Eastern cultures" (Neumann 2011, 21). This seems, however, to contradict the numbers of slaves at work in the Garshana construction projects, which may suggest that either the temporal or regional situation of Garshana was marked by a greater number of slaves, or that the slaves were sent as a part of the system by which public works were built, suggesting that a *corvée*-system might be at work.[92] The number of slaves may have also been higher in the Ur III period, and less in the Akkadian (Foster 2016, 95).

3.4.1.3 *Hired workers*

A series of workers are 'hired' from other households or even other cities (Heimpel 2009, 51). These workers are paid more than the wage paid for slaves, so are presumably free citizens. Many of them are specialized workers, who are hired because other workers with their skill set were not available within the household directly involved in the construction project, primarily builders (Heimpel 2009, 52).

3.4.1.4 *Workers from another locality*

A further group of workers comes from 'another locality' as described in the Garshana texts. These workers are not necessarily skilled workers, but may come to bolster the current workforce. There seems to be many more problems with these workers not showing up for work, which may indicate that the 'other locality' indicates that the origin of these workers is outside of local control (Heimpel 2009, 48–49). Some of these workers are runaways, and 'pursuers' are even sent after them (Heimpel 2009, 60–63).

3.4.1.5 *Workers and the Organization of Work*

Many of the workers at the Garshana construction projects did not come from the household directly involved, and many came from other settlements. These workers are labeled as coming from a different settlement, and often they come in groups which are then treated as work-crews with someone from the group as foreperson.

There are several ethnographic studies detailing how workers can be

92 For more on the *corvée*-system see section 3.4.1.5 above.

organized within pre-industrial societies, and some textual information from the Old Babylonian period in particular (Burke 2008, 146). Without detailed records it is difficult to propose specific models for individual construction projects at 3rd millennium sites in the ancient Near East, and in this case the palace construction at Tell Mozan. However, these studies do give general parameters for various systems, and can be useful when considering the general parameters of worker organization at Tell Mozan.

Two primary systems were probably at work: the *corvée*-system and slavery. These two systems can be identified in the Garshana archives (Heimpel 2009, 45–90), and it is very likely that the work at Urkesh was organized along similar lines. It is important to keep in mind, however, that the *corvée*-system is a modern term which is used to define a work relationship which predates the term by millennia, and is thus to be seen as an analogy which should be used only in so far as it helps understand this ancient work relationship.

The *corvée*-system is considered a form of 'custodial recruitment', and is sub-divided into two types: 'American' and 'African' *corvées* (Udy 1959, 79–81). 'American' *corvées* are more common in North and South America, and are primarily a political organization, with only minimal or no economic support. Thus a political figure can command the participation of members of the society in public projects; each person normally is obliged to contribute only a certain amount to public projects over a set period of time. 'African' *corvées*, on the other hand, are more tied to the economic control of the official over the resources of the community. Thus the people working in an 'African' *corvée*-system contribute to the economic resources which belong to the community, for example in tilling command land or as a shepherd of communal flocks.

The Garshana archives indicate that at least a part of the workforce came from a *corvée*-system, most likely of the 'American' type, since the control over the workers seems to be primarily political as opposed to economic. In this type of *corvée*-system the workers possessed their own means of production for the periods when not working for the state (Schloen 2001, 263).[93]

One difference in the *corvée*-system which seems to be at work in Garshana is that it draws from family-structures as opposed to directly from single individuals. Further evidence of the *corvée*-system in the Ancient Near East can be seen in the Old Babylonian period (Yokoyama 1994) and in the Amarna texts.[94] Some similar variation of the 'American' *corvée*-system was

93 *pace* Diakonoff (1972, 1976).

94 Moran 2000 EA 365, Biridiya Letter 7 of 7.

most likely the system for getting the necessary labor-force in constructing the AP Palace at Mozan.

The second group of workers participating in the work were slaves (Udy 1959, 86–87; Heimpel 2009, 45–90), who belonged directly to the political organization of the state or to the families who supplied workers under the *corvée*-system described above. Thus the use of slaves is not in parallel to the *corvée*-system, but is rather integrated as a part of the workforce, be it under the *corvée*-system or directly as state-controlled labor.

3.4.1.6 Worker Pay and Working Hours

The differences between various workers can be seen in both the titles that they have, as well as in the amount that they are paid. Heimpel, basing his analysis primarily on the study of rations by Gelb (1965), discusses the difference between 'cost' and 'pay' of the workers, suggesting that the various households were given in liters of barley as the cost, but then that the workers were then paid by the household in "ready-made food" (Heimpel 2009, 90). This is not directly pertinent to the aim of this study, but the relationship between the households and the construction project itself is of interest when considering pay relationships within the political structure related to the palace construction. In particular this relationship between households as opposed to specific workers, and the presence of slaves who are highly specialized may shed light on discussions of labor markets.[95]

A standard daily wage for the hired workers is, for men, 5-6 liters of barley, 3 lt for women (Heimpel 2009, 121). A maximum of 8 lt is paid to some workers, and male brick carriers are paid the same as their female counterparts, 3 lt (Heimpel 2009, 64, 121–22). A standard monthly ration for a slave is 60 lt of barley, while a scribe is paid 90 lt (Heimpel 2009, 90–96). These barley rations made up the majority of the pay, but there were supplemental rations as well, such as a yearly wool ration and a portion of rams for the scribes.

There are no indications in the Garshana texts as to the number of hours that an individual worker had to work in a day for the daily wage. Abrams' calculations estimate a working day of 8 hours for 'normal' tasks and 5 hours for 'strenuous' tasks (Abrams 1994, 43). This also matches the results of experiments done in other contexts (see section 3.4.3.4 below).

3.4.2 Organization of Labor

The workers in Garshana[96] were organized into work-crews that had a

95 See Postgate 1992 for the Old Babylonian period.

96 For a discussion of the tasks involved from the perspective of the skillsets needed in such a

foreperson leading the crew. Groups of crews were given tasks by an overseer, who controlled many crews doing various tasks.

3.4.2.1 Work Crews

The tasks to be completed were assigned to work-crews, which were comprised of a group of workers, averaging twenty-three people (Heimpel 2009, 69). The brick carriers form an exception to this, since brick carrier crews average only twelve people (Heimpel 2009, 72). These crews had tasks that they were normally assigned to, such as the brick carriers.

3.4.2.2 Foremen, Forewomen

Foremen and forewomen were responsible for a work-crew, but at the same time were working members of that crew. They therefore had a supervisory role as well as contributing their labor to the task of the team (Heimpel 2009, 59, 72–7f). As Heimpel also notes, this dual function would probably have been a fluid give-and-take between the foreperson and their work-crew, as well as between the foreperson and the overseers.

3.4.2.3 Overseers

Overseers[97] in Garshana were directly responsible for paying the workforce and foremen/women, distributing barley and then returning the extra to the granary (Heimpel 2009, 82). The divisions between foreperson, supervisor and overseer are unclear (Heimpel 2009, 67), and there is one case where one person, *Beli-ili*, fulfills all three tasks over the course of a project (Heimpel 2009, 52). The reasons behind these changing assignments are unclear, and may just arise from the need of the moment rather than being a series of promotions.

Three of the overseers of hired workers formed a core group, remaining with the construction projects throughout the documented period (Heimpel 2009, 75). All of the overseers controlled a wide variety of groups, thus administering many if not all aspects of a portion of the construction (Heimpel 2009, 76). Overseers were thus not responsible for a skill set, rather were probably responsible for an area of construction. In addition to the work-crews, overseers presumably interacted directly with the specialized workers, such as the master-builder. Sometimes the Chief Administrators are also involved directly with the master builders, but it is unclear what the working relationship between the master builders and the overseers versus the chief administrators was (Heimpel 2009, 57, 75–76).

construction project see 3.3 Know-How.

97 For more on overseers, see section 3.3.3.3 above.

3.4.2.4 Hierarchy Among Specialized Workers

In addition to the crew-foreperson-overseer-administrator hierarchy in Garshana, there is a separate hierarchy within the specialized workers based on ability/experience: builder-boys (Heimpel 2009, 54), builders (Heimpel 2009, 47) and master builders (Neumann 1996, 162–63; Heimpel 2009, 49). These specialized workers are not necessarily hired workers: see for example the case of *Mashum*, a 'slave of the house' who is a master builder (Heimpel 2009, 102, 385).

3.4.2.5 Builders

The most important of the specialized workers was the builder,[98] who was responsible for many aspects of the construction process: much more than just brick layers, they oversaw the making of bricks and were responsible for the stability of the buildings. In the Late Babylonian period, the apprenticeship of a builder was eight years, the longest apprenticeship attested for that time (Neumann 1996, 154). While the AP Palace was built in a much earlier time than these Late Babylonian texts, further indications such as the Hammurapi code (Neumann 1996, 153) indicate the importance and responsibility of the builders.

3.4.2.6 Chief Administrators and Scribes

A further group of administrators is labeled as 'chief administrators', and one of these, *Adad-tillati*, seems to be the chief administrator in charge (Heimpel 2009, 25). These administrators were either scribes themselves or worked closely with scribes; a large part of their tasks seems to have been creating and auditing lists dealing with workers and supplies.

3.4.3 Transportation

In discussing transportation, the first material to be considered is stone, which is the heaviest of all of the materials, and the one which was probably transported the farthest; the only possible material to have traveled farther than stone are the wooden beams. The carrying of mudbricks is one of the most energy-intensive parts of the construction, because of their number and relative fragility. The transportation of earth, mortar, plaster and gypsum will all be treated together, since the technique is the same for all. Finally the transport of straw and reeds will be considered.[99]

98 The term builder, Akkadian *itinnu*, Sumerian *šidim*, seems to have been used for both architect and mason (Neumann 1996); see however CAD "neither the translation 'architect' nor 'mason' quite fits".

99 Heimpel groups the transport of various goods (as well as messages) into a single category,

Abrams employs a formula to calculate the transportation of materials which can be useful in quantifying some of the work discussed in this section (Aaberg and Bonsignore 1975; Abrams 1994, 47):

$$Output(m^3) = Q \cdot \frac{1}{(L/V)+(L/V')} \cdot H$$

Table 9: Formula to calculate transportation of materials.

whereby Q is the quantity of material (in cubic meters); L is the distance to be transported; V is the loaded velocity; V' is the unloaded velocity; and H is the number of hours. If one assumes a load of 22-26 kg per trip when using baskets then the formula can be used for earth-carriers and the transportation of small stones. According to Smith, the maximum load for a worker per trip when working a full day is 45 kg (Smith 2006, 205). With more specific information as to the capacity of the boats, rafts or wagons used, this formula could also be used to estimate transport times for those vehicles.

3.4.3.1 The Transportation of Stone

Sleds (also sledges, boats) are one of the principal means that large stone blocks were moved overland in ancient times. For transporting larger stones short distances over land, sleds would have been the only possibility. These have been attested in Egypt (Smith 2006, 173), and are still in use today (Vivian 1978, 68).

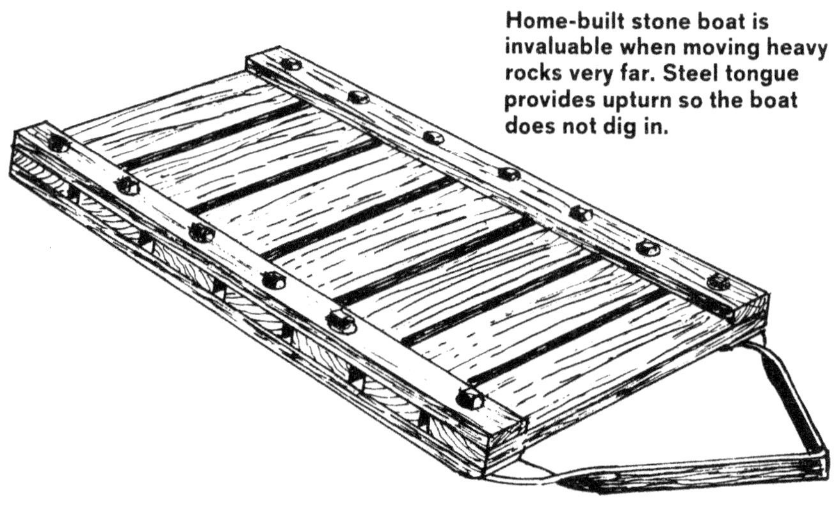

Illustration 79: Stone sled (boat) (Vivian 1978, 68).

which he labels "Escort Service" based on the verb $tum_{2\text{-}4}$ "to bring" (Heimpel 2009, 320).

Depictions of such sleds can be found in ancient art; an example from Egypt has been studied by Coles and describes a team of 172[100] people using a sled to move a statue estimated at 60 tonnes (Coles 1973). A further study suggests a ratio of sixteen persons pulling for every tonne of stone (Coles 1973, 88). Factors which would vary this ratio and the distance that could be covered include the use of rollers, the harness and the slope of the terrain being covered. One might also ask if the use of a sled is necessary, if the stone is large and flat: Kurapkat's representation of stone-transport to Goebekli Tepe shows workers pulling a stone slab which rests directly on rollers (Kurapkat 2009). This would probably have only been feasible for rocks with a very smooth bottom surface, a hard and even terrain, and a short distance to cover. A further question is whether sleds were used to transport other construction materials. This seems unlikely on the basis of the Garshana texts, where fill-soil, mortar, mud-plaster and gypsum seem to have been carried in baskets (Heimpel 2009, 250), and brick carriers were paid individually to carry a number of bricks over a fixed distance (Heimpel 2009, 83). The Garshana texts seem to differentiate between 'carrying' and 'hauling' earth, but what this distinction entails is unclear (Heimpel 2009, 250).

To place the larger stones in the walls, a simple system of rolling or tipping the block up a wooden beam might have been used (McRaven 1999, 9). Here a wooden plank is employed, but it is also possible that an earthen ramp was used to reach the top of the wall, and the stones would have then been carried along the top of the wall to their resting place.

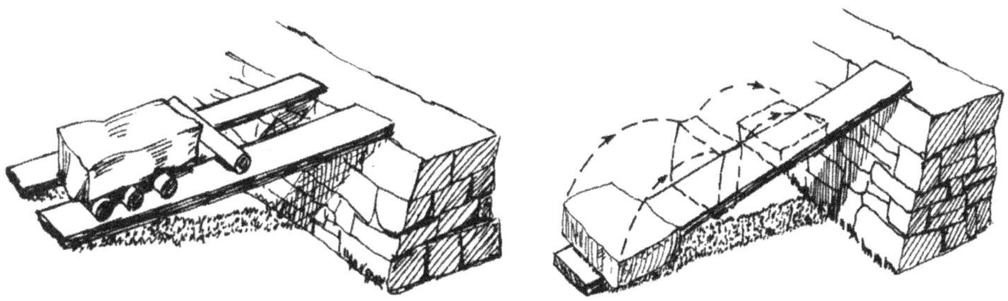

Large stones can be rolled or flipped end over end up a plank ramp to the top of your wall.

Illustration 80: Modern example of how to place heavy stone on top of a wall (McRaven 1999, 9).

100 This number includes everyone engaged in the operation, not only those directly pulling. He comments: "Possibly as essential for the continued progress of the sledge are 6 groups of 10 soldiers with whips and clubs" (Coles 1973, 84).

Transportation of large stones over water routes seems to be the most efficient means of conveyance for those areas where water-routes are available.[101] One might assume that such transportation required large vessels and a considerable amount of water; but this is not the case. A study done in England demonstrates that "a replica of one of these bluestones [used in the construction of Stonehenge] weighing just under 2 tonnes, was crane-loaded onto wooden planks over 3 canoes. The craft was easily manipulated by 4 schoolboys with poles up river, and the total weight of about 2 tonnes drew only 23 cm of water; it could have been poled up very shallow creeks and streams" (Coles 1973, 87).

There is, today, no year-round stream in the vicinity of Mozan, but there are a series of *wadis* which would most likely have allowed for the transportation of stone to the city from the Tur-Abdin in the north, where stone was present (see section 3.2.1.2). A *wadi*-bed is visible on satellite data, and the author has seen this bed filled with water in modern times. The *wadi*-bed is even more visible on older Corona images, before the widespread use of mechanized farming softened such topographic features (see also 2.1.6.3 above). It is interesting that the *wadi*, and thus presumably an ancient canal or stream-bed, runs through the lower city, on the same side as the AP Palace itself. Further archaeological excavations in the area of the outer city wall and along this *wadi*-bed will certainly yield more information as to the presence of such a stream or canal and any associated buildings.

101 This is especially true in Southern Mesopotamia (Foster 2016, 97–98), but would most likely have also been the case here, considering the advantages mentioned here.

Illustration 81: Google image with overlay showing the outer citywall of Urkesh and the wadi-bed (accessed December 2016).

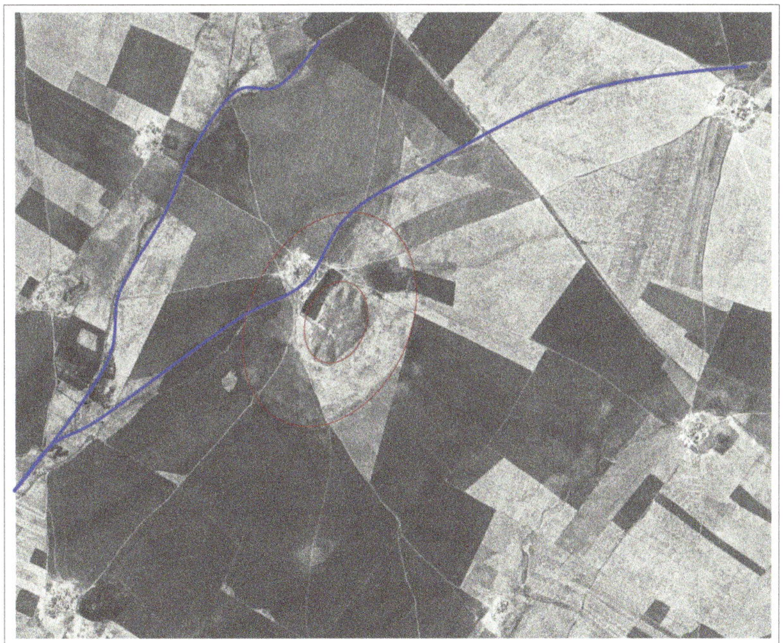

Illustration 82: A Corona satellite image showing wadi-bed (Corona DS1104-1025DA012_12_b – cropped image).

3.4.3.2 Transportation of Mudbricks

Mudbricks, once dry, can be readily transported to another location – how this is done depends on the distance to be traveled. In the Garshana texts, brick carriers are given a day's wage, equivalent to 3 liters of barley (Heimpel 2009, 64, 121), to transport a certain number of bricks a certain distance irrespective of how long it took them (Heimpel 2009, 192, 348–49). The proportion between number of bricks and distance remains a constant, called 'carriage', so the greater the distance the fewer bricks one is expected to transport and vice-versa.

Over 6.5 million bricks were carried in a single year for the Garshana construction projects (Heimpel 2009, 349). Assuming a carriage of the median of 150 bricks carried 432 meters (Heimpel 2009, 83, 190), such an enormous number of bricks would have taken 43,333.3 person-days, at a cost of 130,000 liters of barley, assuming 3 liters per person-day. Since these bricks were carried all in one year, a minimum of 119 people working every day would have to accomplish all the carrying in a single year; since the carrying was probably limited to periods of construction, 100 days may be more realistic, needing a total of 433 persons.

As mentioned above, Smith suggests that the maximum a person can carry over a period of time is 45 kg (Smith 2006, 205). The Garshana texts mention that the brick load for one person is 1 brick of 1 cubit^2 or 6 'normal' bricks (Heimpel 2009, 226), which should be 25 kg.[102]

Wagons and or boats would have been used for longer distances, but there is little information regarding these modes of transport vis-à-vis mudbricks. The Garshana texts mention a device used for transporting bricks, *maššûm ša libittim*, but it is not known what this device was (Heimpel suggests a rack placed on the back), nor (clearly) if it was used in the AP Palace construction (Heimpel 2009, 226).

102 The calculation here seems the best possible one, but is still more of an informed guess than a reliable estimate. The brickweight used by Heimpel is from Old Babylonian mathematical texts, and the parallel given from UET 5 881 and based on Powell's brick types may not support the calculation made: this depends on the weights for Powell's Bt classes. If Bt 2 weighs 7.5 kg each, then the figures in UET 5 881 come a lot closer to Smith's 45 kg load.

Illustration 83: A workman at Mozan carrying two mudbricks on his back. Note the use of a cloth belt to support the back and the base of the bricks (MZ V22i2239).

3.4.3.3 *The Transportation of Wooden Beams*

The most efficient way of transporting wooden beams is to use them as rafts to carry other construction materials to the work-site. This would be particularly effective when stone is one of these materials, with the wooden beams replacing the canoes and planks in the ethnographic example from Coles above (3.4.3.1). By using the beams as both a tool for transportation and a material in the construction, there is no need to return the beams to the quarry for a further load of stone: these beams would be set aside, and new beams would be logged for the next batch of stone. The other possibility is that there were specific boats used for transport, either rented or constructed for this purpose; in addition to rafts (Potts 1996, 132), two variants are known from other sources: reed-boats and wooden craft (Potts 1996, 122–37).

In the case of the AP Palace at Mozan, this scenario of logging going hand-in-hand with quarrying seems to be the most likely reconstruction of transportation methods. This combined means (wood first used as rafts to carry stone, then used in the construction as roofing beams) would be more efficient, less expensive, and faster than any other form of transportation. Today, the valleys upstream of the quarries (or the areas where ancient quarries were most likely located, see above) are one of the main logging sites in the area, and poplar trees are planted specifically for the purpose of logging. Since the topography and the access to water would have been the same (if not better) in ancient times, it seems logical that this scenario is the most plausible. Also, the two other types of watercraft mentioned above, reed-boats and wooden boats seem unlikely. There are no reeds in modern times in these valleys, and it would seem likely that the conditions in ancient times would be similar or even colder, making the presence of the heavy reeds needed for

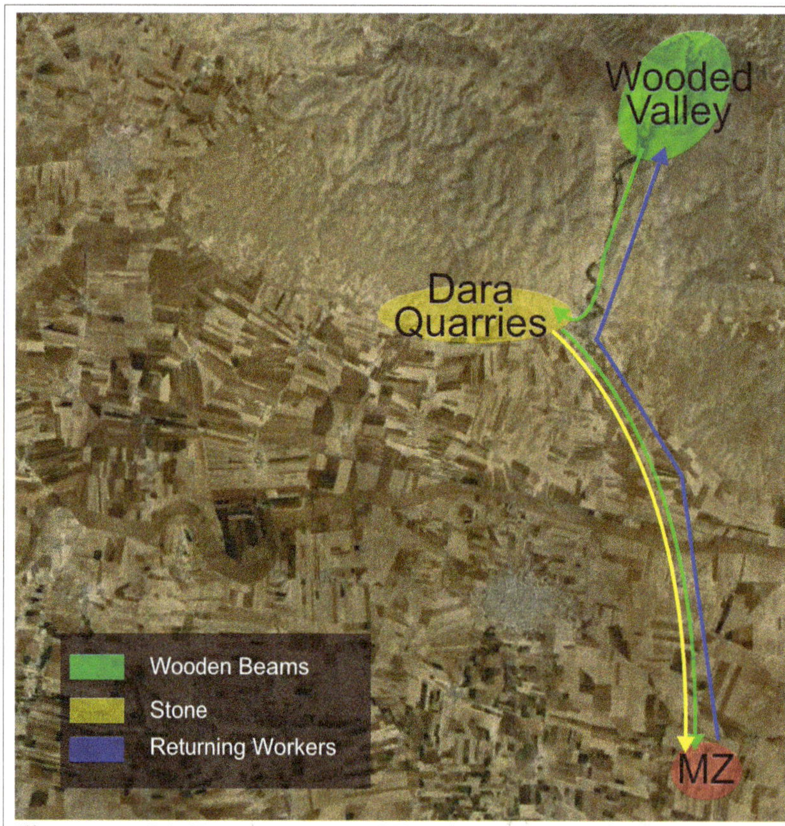

Illustration 84: Transportation of Wooden Beams and Stone near MZ (hypothetical model) (Google Earth image, accessed December 2016).

boats unlikely. Wooden boats seem also unlikely, as these tend to have deeper keels than either reed-boats or rafts, reducing the days these deeper draft boats can travel on the seasonal streams. To guide the rafts punting sticks would have been used, which are attested in other sources during this period (Potts 1996, 125–26, 132). Presumably this skill was hard to master, as the price of a slave skilled as a boatman was quite high (Foster 2016, 98).

Since transport on the waterways could only be used seasonally, it is possible that the loads were prepared by smaller teams of skilled workers during the part of the year when the streams were impassable to watercraft. Then, when the streams were passable (presumably in the spring) they or other workers would transport the prepared loads to the city and the construction site for use.

3.4.3.4 The Transportation of Earth, Mortar, Plaster and Gypsum

Earth, mortar, plaster and gypsum are all materials which are transported in 'loose' form, and as such carried in baskets or some similar sort of container.

The transportation of dirt over a fixed distance has been studied within the framework of 'Experimental Archaeology', showing the results for two haulers transporting a similar dirt container (a 5 gallon can, slightly over 20 kg) over two different distances:

	Distance per trip m	*Total Trips*	*Total Distance km*	*Total Weight kg*	*Total Volume m³*
I	50	206	20.6	4151	3.17
II	100	116	23.2	2313	1.76

Table 10: Earth carriage over a 5 hour day (Coles 1973, 95).

This data is an excellent parallel to the records from Garshana, where a 'boy' is paid a day's wage to move 1.8 m^3 of dirt 180 m (Heimpel 2009, 83). Additionally, a female worker is said to carry 22.5 kg per trip on her head (Heimpel 2009, 250), which was presumably standard for all the workers. On the basis of this data one can roughly estimate that it might take the 'boy' in Garshana about eight hours to complete his task. This working-day reflects the estimates for stonework and construction suggested in Abrams' work discussed above in section 3.4.1.6 (Abrams 1994, 43). This calculation is particularly important for this study, since it is the only point in which data from the ethnographic metaphor (Coles) textual evidence (Heimpel) and the estimate from the point of view of a project manager (Abrams) all overlap. The fact that these three sources come to roughly the same conclusion as regards quantity and time lends credence to the correlation being made in this study.

Illustration 85: Two workmen at Mozan carrying a bucket using a stick (MZ V22i2242).

Illustration 86: Ur-namma of Ur carrying a basket of construction material (OI-Chicago website, accessed December 2016).

The ethnographic analogy described above refers a 5 gallon can, but in ancient times a reed basket was used. These baskets take on an iconographic significance in the representation of kings as related to construction projects they undertake: associated with such a project, Ur-namma of Ur portrays himself carrying a basket of what appears to be mortar.[103] Such a gesture might be comparable to a ground-breaking ceremony at a modern construction site.

3.4.3.5 The Transportation of Reeds and Straw

Reeds and straw can be carried in bundles, wrapped in cloth or put into bags. The difficulty in transportation is not one of weight, but of volume; a large quantity of straw weighs very little, as compared to earth or stone. Once the reeds are made into mats, these can be rolled and carried as such.

103 See also Sievertsen 2014.

3.4.3.6 *The Tools of Transportation*

Besides sleds, wagons would have been one of the most common means of transportation for medium and long distances. The maximum load of a four-wheeled wagon is estimated at 1350 kg.[104]

Pack animals would have also been used, presumably donkeys or other equids. These animals were capable of transporting great weights over long distances, and under certain circumstances donkeys can carry twice as much as humans. Evidence from the Old Assyrian archives is pertinent here because they are only a few hundred years later than the construction of the Mozan palace and because one of the major routes went through the area of Mozan to the modern pass of Mardin. In these texts men are said to be able to carry 30 kg while donkeys carry 75 kg.[105] On average the distance traveled in one day for each type of transport is 25 km. It should be pointed out again that the distance to Urkesh from either the proposed stone source or the proposed wood source is less than this.

Hired transportation workers involved in the Garshana construction projects were paid a surprisingly high wage, the equivalent of spearmen (Heimpel 2009, 122).

3.4.4 *Gender*

While there is no evidence regarding the role of women as opposed to men within the workforce within the archaeological record, the Garshana archives paint a fascinating picture. Women are present as workers, as forewomen and as overseers for the construction projects. In fact, while some tasks (eg. 'builder') were performed only by men, there were more women than men in the Garshana workforce, because so many women were employed as brick carriers (Heimpel 2009, 47). Pay was different between women and men, with men being paid between 30 and 50 percent more than what women were paid for the same tasks (Heimpel 2009, 121). Women overseers were responsible for crews which included men (Heimpel 2009, 75).

One puzzling aspect of the Garshana texts is that all brick carriers, regardless of gender, were paid 3 liters, the wage normally paid to female workers. Heimpel indicates that another group of brick carriers was paid 5-6 lt

---

104 This estimate is given in Lamberg-Karlovsky 2009 but a further reference for the figure is missing.

105 Based on Dercksen's study of the Old Assyrian tablets looking at data of specific shipments (tin and textiles) and the number of donkeys the Old Assyrian merchants used to carry specific loads, he calculated that a single donkey carried as much as 75 kg. Dercksen based his estimates of the distance the donkeys could walk carrying such a load in a day on 19th century British Army records; donkeys could walk on average 25 km per day loaded (Dercksen 2004, 255, 260, 278; Algaze 2008, 55–57, 66–68, 141–42).

per person, and suggests that perhaps this team was comprised entirely of men, thus they were then all paid the rate for males as opposed to the rate for females that an all female or a mixed crew would receive (Heimpel 2009, 64, 121–22). This question remains open, as the texts from Garshana do not provide enough information to arrive at a definitive conclusion.

3.4.5 Manpower and the AP Palace – a Hypothesis based on the Garshana Texts

The Garshana texts give an insight into the day-to-day administration of an Ur III construction project. On the basis of these texts one can form a hypothesis describing the manpower employed in the construction of the AP Palace in ancient Urkesh.

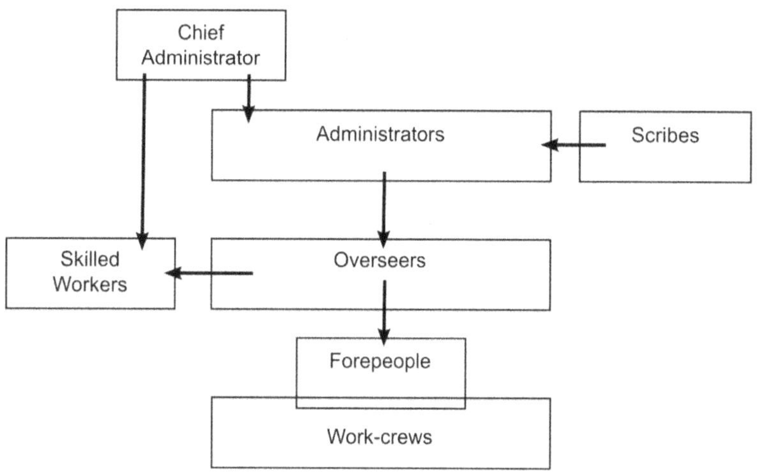

Illustration 87: Hypothetical administrative hierarchy for AP Palace construction.

It is important to understand that the Garshana archives represent the documents created by and for the administrative structure of the construction project. The administrative structure is a fundamental one, but must be understood within a wider framework: both planning and execution would have had similar structures that were both parallel to and intertwined with the administrative structure. For example, there is no mention in the Garshana archives as to the estimates for materials to be used, nor are there discussions as to where in the settlement to put the structures being built. The tasks assigned to the work-crews are mentioned, but not the steps necessary nor the order in which the various tasks need to be completed. The planning and execution structures will be further discussed in sections 3.5 and 3.6.

3.4.5.1 *Work-crew Tasks*

It is useful at this point to list the tasks assigned to various work-crews in the Garshana texts (Heimpel 2009, 65, 76–77).

carry bricks
hand bricks to builders
raze walls
carry roof beams
construction
pounding malt
moving dirt
molding bricks
hoeing

These tasks can be found in the sections above, distributed between materials, know-how and manpower, and are reflected in the *chaîne opératoire* found in section 3.5 below.

3.5 Putting it all together: the *Chaîne Opératoire*

The final step needed in this analysis of the elements and process of construction is a timeline and a series of *chaîne opératoire* which help consider the planning and actions needed to construct a building such as the AP Palace.

The process of creating a structure can be divided into four general steps: procurement of materials, manufacture, transport, and construction/assembly.[106] In describing the process in terms of a *chaîne opératoire*, one can separate the first three steps from the last, since in the first three each material should be treated separately, while in the last step the disparate materials come together to form the building.

3.5.1 *Timeline of Construction*

While considering the construction of such a palace, it is important to see the various steps or clusters of decisions that follow chronologically by necessity. The analysis of aspects of the construction process has been greatly helped by the insightful book by C. Smith on the construction of the Egyptian pyramids (Smith 2006). The following is meant to give a sense of the timeline for the construction of the AP Palace, not explain the expertise of the

106 Abrams puts manufacture in third place, which is at first a bit counter-intuitive. One might think that to reduce transportation costs the manufacturing step would take place at the place where the materials are collected, as has been postulated here. It seems, however, that the Mayans transported raw material (primarily stone) and then finished the material at the construction site; this is probably because they could use the discards from the manufacturing process as fill (Abrams 1994, 43).

individuals: for a detailed look at the tasks of the people mentioned here, see section 3.3.

3.5.1.1 Step 1: Commissioning of Project

The first step in a construction project is that a commission-giver decides to build a palace and so allocates financial and political capital for such an endeavor. The commission-giver can be one of several people: a crown prince, a newly installed king, an old king on behalf of crown prince, the vassal of a liege-lord or, finally, the governor of a king.[107]

3.5.1.2 Step 2: Establishing Planning Group

Commission-giver or his administration decides to hire an architect and so decides the general style of building (local, regional, foreign). A surveyor and an engineer are also assigned to the project. A city-planner is also involved in choosing the site for construction. Also, several coordinators are chosen.

3.5.1.3 Step 3: Determining Constraints of the Project

Architect and city-planner decide where the building will be placed and so determine what should be removed, since the palace will occupy presumably important local spaces where other structures are already present.

The architect and economic-administration decide on basic size of the building, thereby deciding what will be needed in terms of time and effort. The space allotted for the building as well as the availability of materials also limit the scope of the project.

3.5.1.4 Step 4: Building Plan

The architect makes plan for building taking into account constraints determined in the previous step. Architect works with coordinators, surveyor and engineer to determine suitability and feasibility of plan. Materials coordinator establishes sites and transportation routes for construction materials. Manpower coordinator estimates need for workers from outlying areas.

3.5.1.5 Step 5: Initial Pre-Construction Work

Satellite production of construction material begins if necessary, transport and construction staff is hired if needed, 'manpower' comes into the picture for the first time, along with the associated questions of pay, rations

107 For an analysis of the motivations behind the construction of a new palace, see above 3.3.1 and section 4.3.2.

and lodging. Off-site, many of the construction needed construction materials, eg. wooden beams and stones, would begin in this phase. These steps are detailed in a series of *chaîne opératoire* in section 3.5.2.

At the work site, existing buildings are destroyed and removed, leveling and terracing are done as needed. These steps may begin later, but may also overlap with the steps mentioned above. For the *chaîne opératoire* detailing these steps and those in step 6, see section 3.5.3.

3.5.1.6 Step 6: Construction

Construction Coordinator decides when to begin construction, based on arrival flow of material and weather considerations. Economic/manpower coordinator is also involved in decision, so that the impact on other tasks is limited (harvest, conflict etc.).

3.5.2 Gathering, Processing and Transporting the Construction Materials

3.5.2.1 Stone

The quarrying of stone is the most difficult process to describe, since there is no evidence for stone quarrying during the period of the AP Palace in Syro-Mesopotamia, very little from the same time period for the region, and the ethnographic material comes from very distant cultures.[108]

The most plausible hypothesis regarding the process of quarrying is presented here in illustration 88. The tools used would have been pounders and mauls, as well as chisels and wooden wedges. (1) The first step would have been to prepare the site, freeing the top of the stone from organic material, and cleaning it so that the initially exposed rock would be the top of the first blocks. (2) The blocks would then be excavated by using pounders and mauls, as well as chisels and wedges.[109] (3) Once removed, the block would need some initial squaring to remove protrusions or particularly sharp edges. This 'squaring' would be necessary in order to use the block in the construction of a building, and is thus a practical necessity and not an aesthetic step. (4) The block would possibly (but not necessarily) have been further finished, providing smother faces and rounded edges; this 'finishing' would have been a more aesthetic step.

108 Refer to 3.2.1 and 3.4.3.1 for more specific information regarding quarrying.

109 See 3.2.1.3 for more detailed information on the tools used.

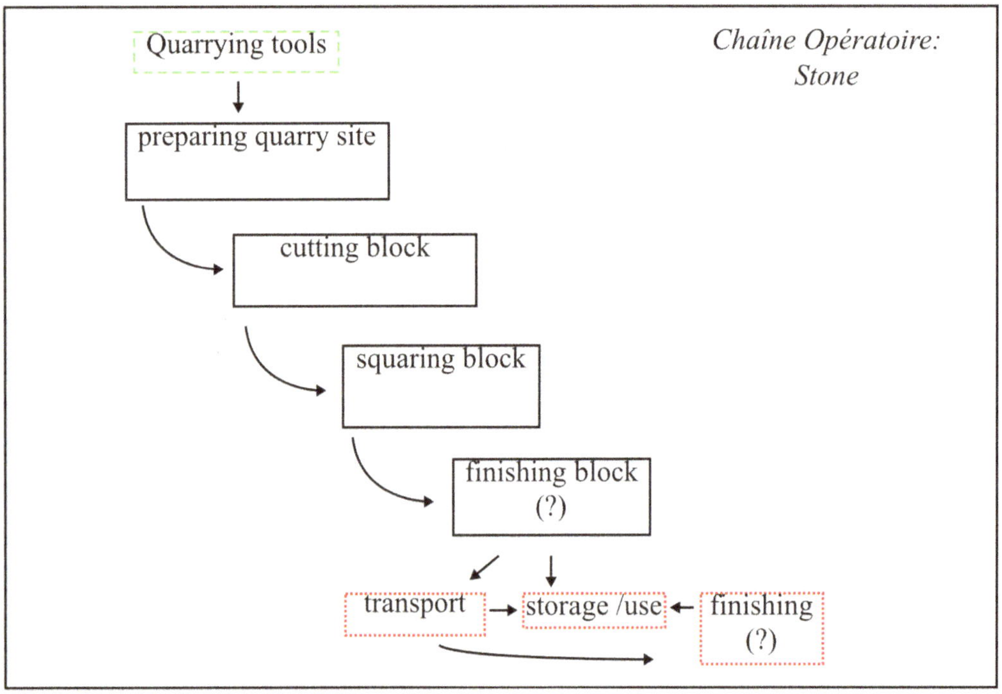

Illustration 88: Chaîne opératoire *for the quarrying of stone. Materials needed during the various steps are indicated by boxes with a dashed line, link to further* chaîne opératoire *indicated by boxes with a dotted line.*

At this point the stone is ready for transport, which, in the case of the AP Palace, was probably done on rafts using a seasonal stream.[110] The blocks could then be used immediately or stored for later use. It is also possible that the blocks were further finished at the construction site, or even after they had been placed in the building, as is the case with the stones used in the stone courtyard, H3.[111]

110 For more on the transport of stone, see 3.4.3.1.

111 See section 2.2.2.10 above for more information regarding the stone courtyard.

3.5.2.2 Mudbrick

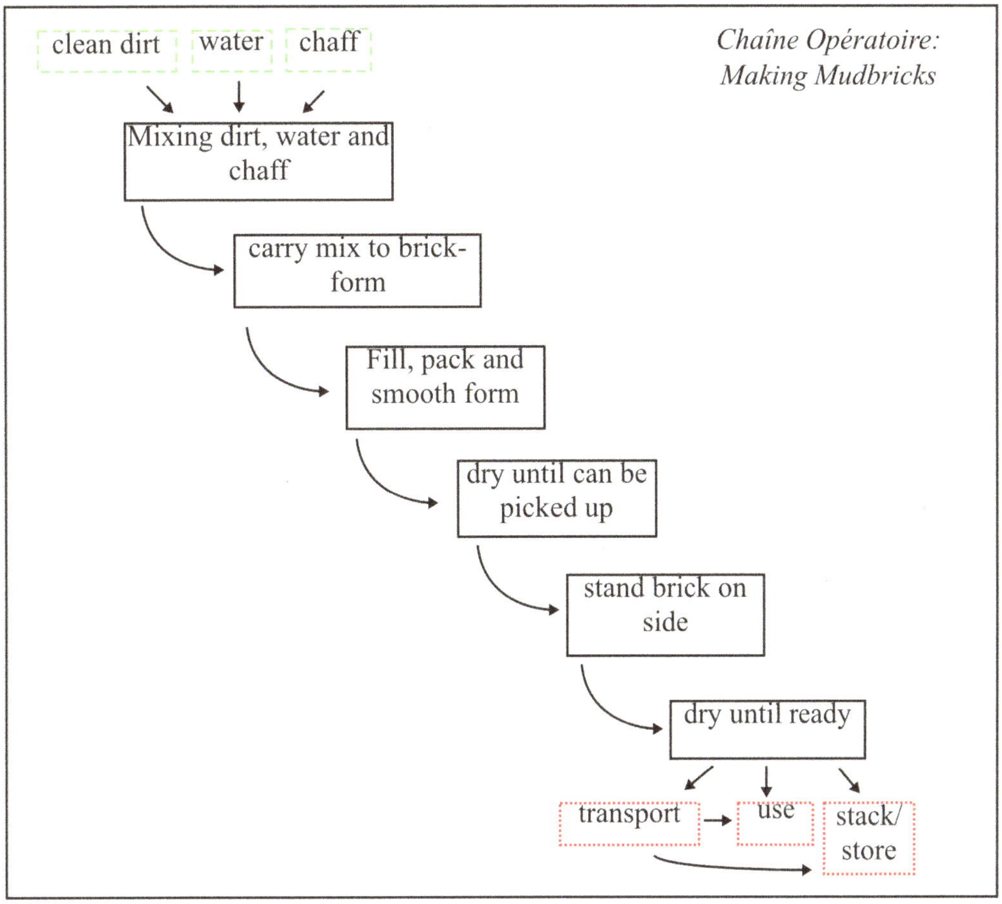

Illustration 89: Chaîne opératoire *describing the production of mudbricks. Materials needed during the various steps are indicated by boxes with a dashed line, link to further* chaîne opératoire *indicated by boxes with a dotted line.*

The *chaîne opératoire* describing the production of mudbricks is the most complex of all the processes described here. The production of mudbricks and the results of the ethnoarchaeological experiment have been described in detail above in 3.2.2 and 3.4.3.2, and thus will not be repeated here, but those results are represented in this *chaîne opératoire*.

3.5.2.3 Mud plaster and mortar

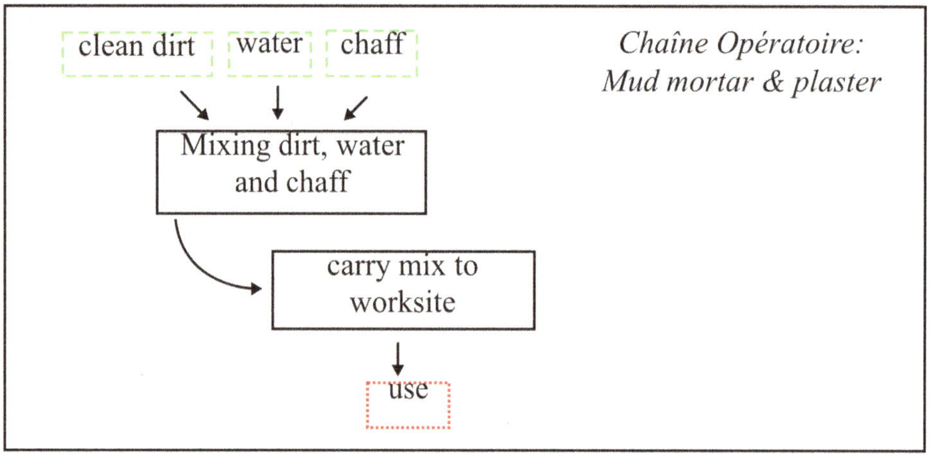

Illustration 90: Chaîne opératoire *describing the production of mud plaster and mortar. Materials needed during the various steps are indicated by boxes with a dashed line, link to further* chaîne opératoire *indicated by boxes with a dotted line.*

The production of mud plaster and mortar has also been described above in 3.2.4 and 3.4.3.4, but it is worth noting that the *chaîne opératoire* is much shorter than for mudbrick. This is due to the fact that no drying is required (quite the opposite) and that much smaller quantities are needed (as compared to mudbricks). Heimpel notes that 1/6 the volume of the bricks was added as mortar when constructing a wall.[112]

3.5.2.4 Gypsum and Lime

The production of gypsum and lime has also been described above in 3.2.5 and 3.4.3.4. The difference with regard to the *chaîne opératoire* between the two lies primarily in the temperature needed to fire lime, which is much higher than what is needed for gypsum, requiring considerably more combustible material and an appropriate oven.

112 Heimpel 2009, 124 citing Robson 1996, 1999, 67–69.

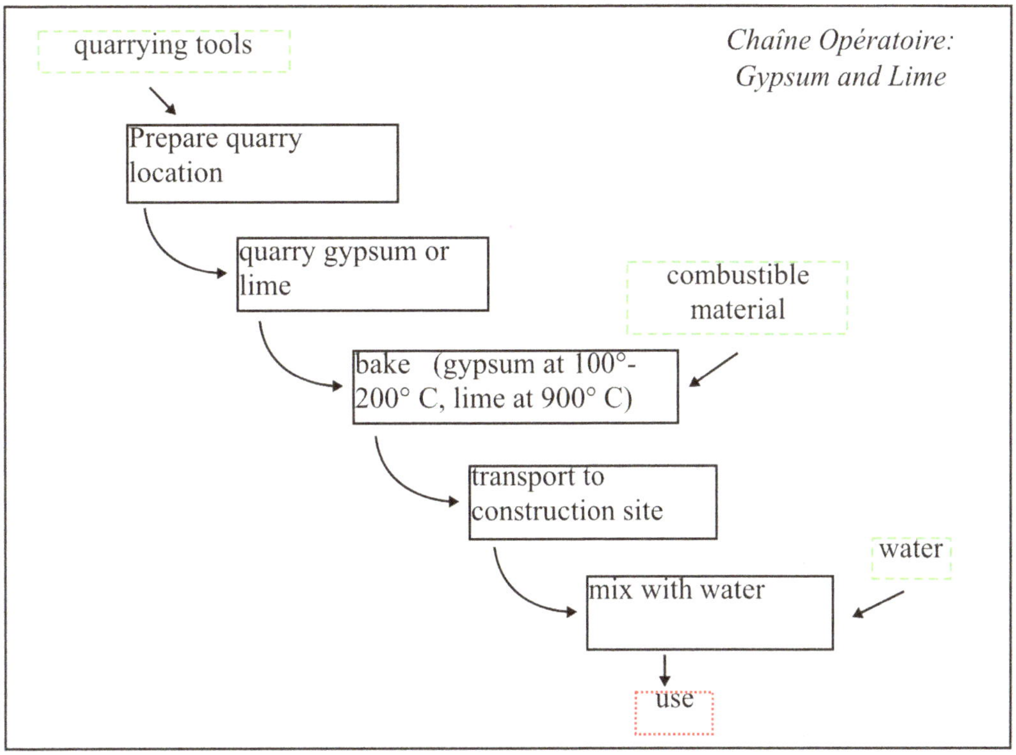

Illustration 91: Chaîne opératoire *describing the production of gypsum and lime plaster. Materials needed during the various steps are indicated by boxes with a dashed line, link to further* chaîne opératoire *indicated by boxes with a dotted line.*

3.5.2.5 *Chaff, Wood, and Reed Matting*

Chaff, wood and reed matting are all quite simple, as regards the process of collection and transportation, and thus it is not necessary to present the *chaîne opératoire* in table format.[113] It is worth repeating that the transport of wood over water would have been ideal as a carrier for other materials, such as stone.

3.5.3 Constructing the Palace: Putting Together the Pieces

Now that a *chaîne opératoire* for the materials has been discussed, one can hypothesize a *chaîne opératoire* for the construction site itself, where these disparate elements come together with the aim of producing a finished building.

113 For more information on these materials or their transportation, please see the appropriate sections under 3.2 and 3.4.3.

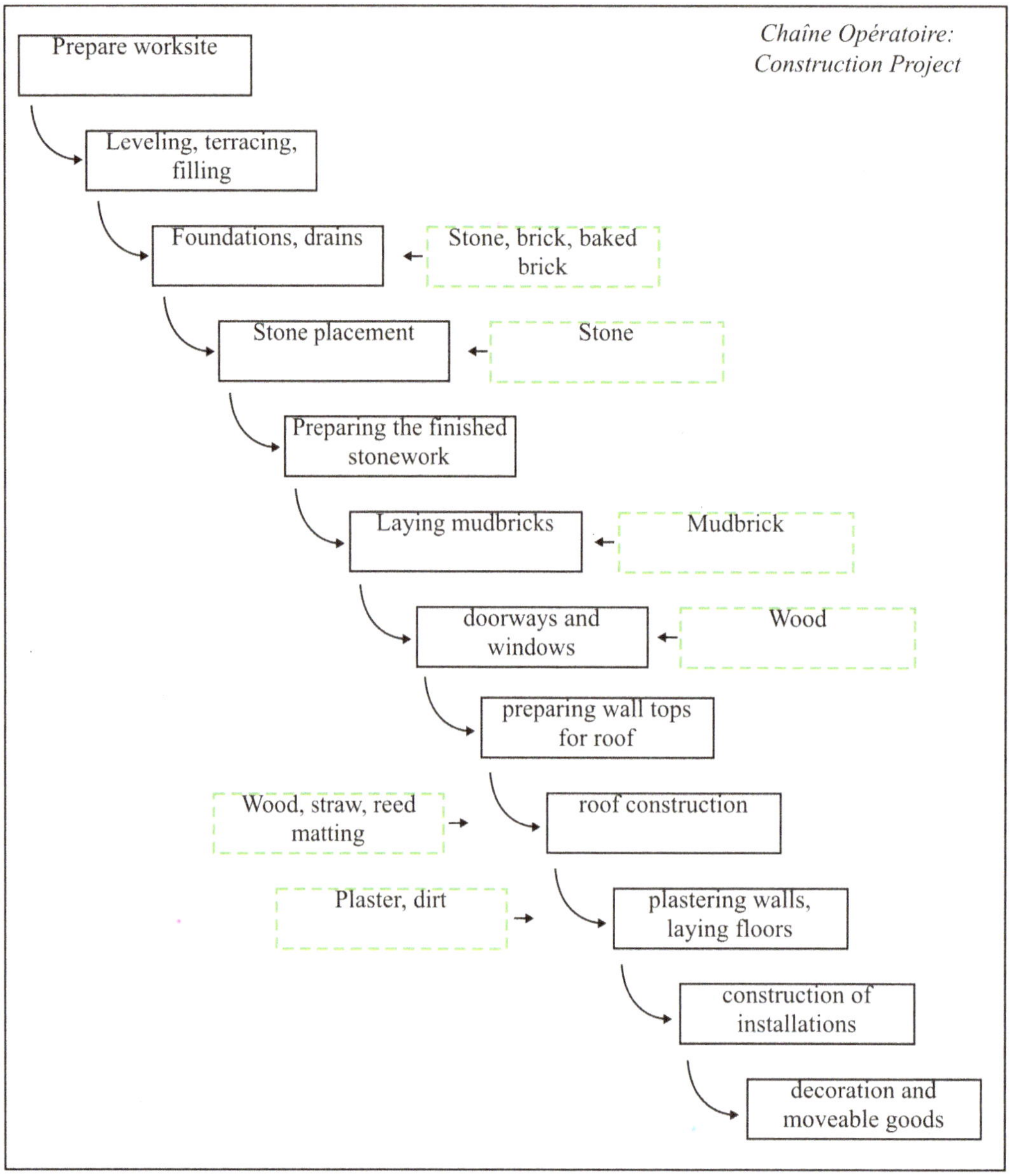

Illustration 92: Chaîne opératoire *describing the construction project. Materials needed during the various steps are indicated by boxes with a dashed line.*

One can discern thirteen different steps in the construction of a building similar to the AP Palace, beginning with the preparation of the workspace to the decoration of the architecture and the addition of moveable goods. The following sections describe each of these steps in detail. It is worth noting that the *chaîne opératoire* suggested here is not exclusive to the AP Palace, but does reflect a large public building built of stone and mudbrick, containing drains and installations. For other types of buildings the *chaîne opératoire* would have to be modified.[114] Evidence from textual sources describe the occupations involved in similar construction projects, and these occupations can also help to visualize the steps in the *chaîne opératoire* (Heimpel 2009, 221–88).

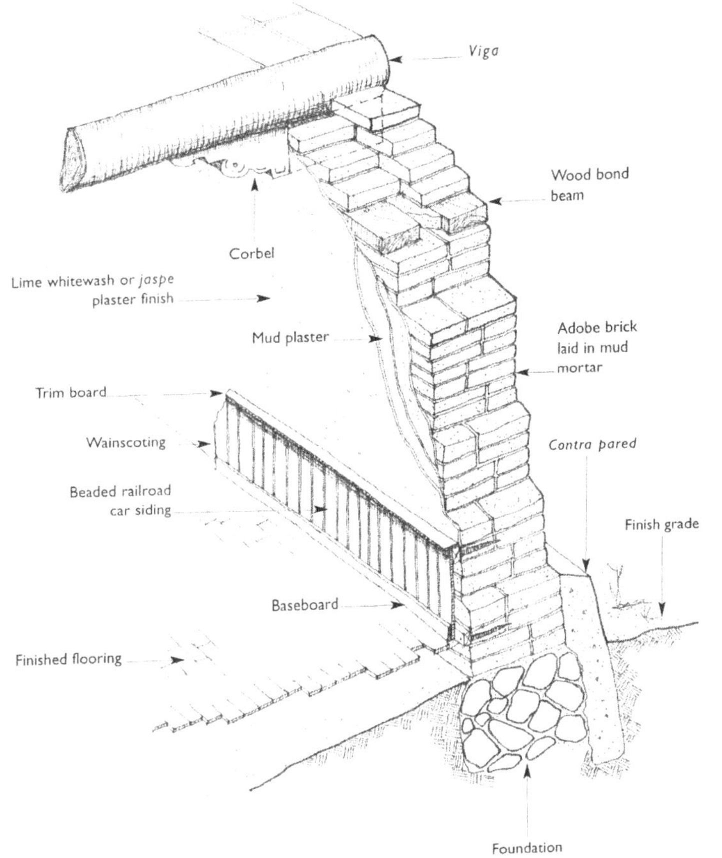

Illustration 93: Wall terminology; drawing is meant as a comparative illustration, since it comes from a different cultural context (Cornerstones Community Partnerships 2006, 31).

Illustration 93 shows the elements of construction for an adobe building from another time-period and cultural context, but is interesting as a reference showing the combination of the materials described in this analysis.

3.5.3.1 *Preparing the Worksite*

The first step in preparing the worksite is the removal of older buildings, in whole or in part. This may entail some packing or filling of the older structures so that the ground under the new construction does not settle.

114 The description of a construction project can be found in Smith 2006; the analysis of the construction of the pyramid is very detailed, see in particular pages 222-233.

The materials used in the first construction steps may have also been brought to the construction site at this point. Illustration 94 shows the reconstruction project at the southwestern corner of the AP Palace: note the presence of mudbricks, soil (for plaster) and stone, ready for use in the construction.

During the non-work hours, these construction materials presumably needed to be guarded to prevent theft. Within the Garshana archives there is even mention of the boy who guards the bricks as a job title (Heimpel 2009, 53).

Illustration 94: Overhead photo of the reconstruction project at the AP Palace. Note the mudbricks stacked in the top and right of the image, soil for plaster in the upper right, as well as the stones in the lower right (MZ V22i2240).

3.5.3.2 *Leveling, Terracing, Filling*

Once the workspace has been cleared, it may be necessary or desirable to create raised areas within the construction site. This may be necessary due to the preexisting topography, or desired by the architect. Three steps would be necessary: the leveling of the area, terracing and filling.

Leveling means the cutting into the preexisting soil, which would provide a flattened area on which to build the terracing. This is different from the removal and packing mentioned above, since this would be aimed at the terracing of an area of the construction site.

A terracing wall would then be built, which would, in all likelihood, match one of the internal walls of the structure to be built. An example of this in the AP Palace is the wall between sector C and the courtyard H3. Such walls might need packing behind them, as well as drainage (Vivian 1978, 53); there is no evidence of drainage channels in the wall between sector C and the courtyard H3, but it may be low enough to not need one, or the fact that it is a 'dry' stone wall (without mortar) may allow enough water seepage to avoid the need for specific drainage channels.[115]

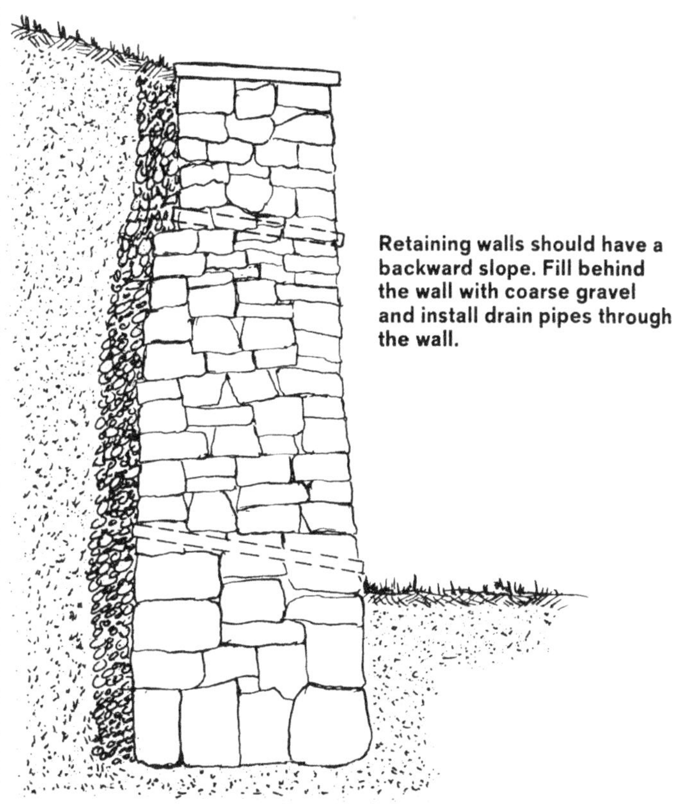

Illustration 95: High retaining wall with fill and drainage (Vivian 1978, 55).

Once this wall stands, the space would have to be further raised by filling in the area with packing material, if needed. A red packing was found in sector A of the palace, presumably to raise this sector so that the floor levels in the service wing remained at the same elevation.

115 The stone wall of the temple terrace at Mozan is a wonderful example of these problems and the solutions that ancient builders employed, see Camatta forthcoming.

3.5.3.3 Foundations, Drains

Once the construction site is ready for building activities to begin, the foundations are the first step in the construction process. Here the quarried stones are placed into trenches cut into the prepared area.[116] The foundations of the AP Palace represent a typical stone foundation, which consists of a wider stone foundation and a stone sub-structure which is somewhat wider than the brick wall placed on it (Aurenche 1977, 79). The foundations of the AP Palace are of both type III and IV according to the typology of Birschmeier and Gasche (Illustration 97) (Birschmeier and Gasche 1981, 16). The width of the foundation must be given by the architect, for this width determines the width of the brick wall above. An excellent example of this process can be found at Tell Leilan, 'The Unfinished Building' where a construction project was abandoned in the middle of laying the foundations (Weiss et al. 2012, 171). In that construction project one sees the trench, the blocks ready to be placed in the foundation, blocks in the foundation, and even the mud and sherd leveling on top for the mudbricks (see section 3.5.3.5).

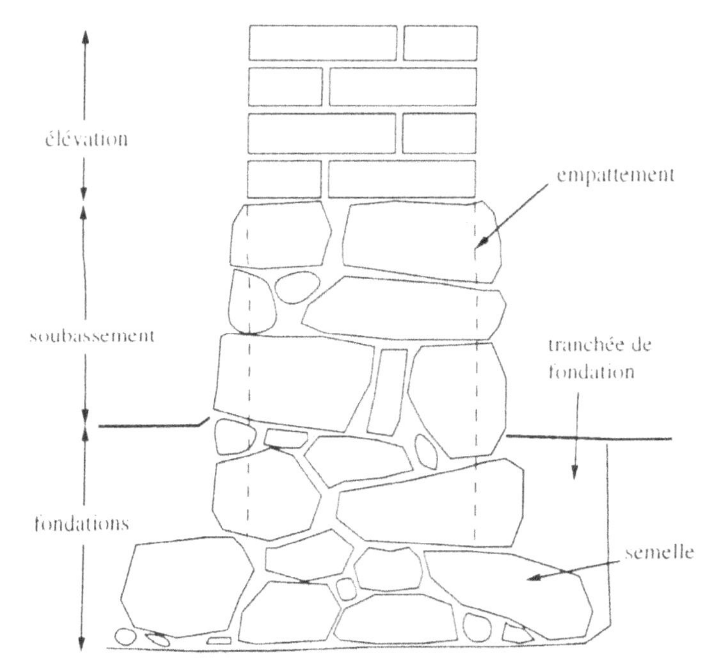

Illustration 96: Elements of a stone foundation (Aurenche 1977, 79).

During the construction of the foundations it would have also been necessary to place the drains – at least those drains that would have run under the walls. These would have been made of stone or baked brick,[117] but the

116 Logically, there would have been some overlap between these steps: for example, the soil brought out of the foundation trenches could have been used in the fill for the terraced areas, and, as mentioned above, the terrace wall would have likely been one of the walls of the structure, and would thus have needed a foundation. For more on stone placement see section 3.2.1 above.

117 Baked brick being the best material available for channeling water, see Heinrich 1934, 41.

portions that ran under or through stone foundations would likely also have been made of stone.

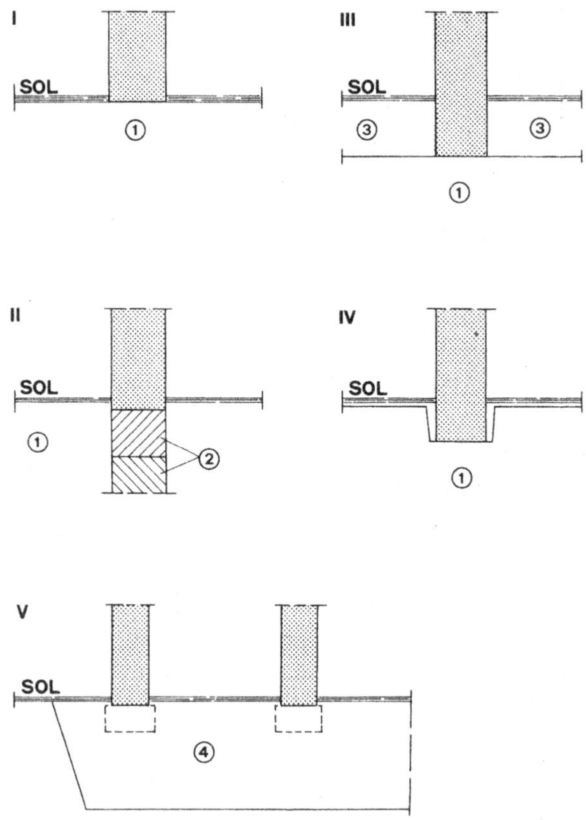

Fig. 4. — Schémas montrant les principaux types de fondations des constructions en briques crues.
Légende :
1 couches archéologiques antérieures
2 murs antérieurs
3 remblais mis en place après la construction de la base du mur
4 remblais de sable ou de gravier (p. ex. Temple Ovale de Khafadjeh et Palais achéménide de Suse)

Illustration 97: Typology of foundations (Birschmeier and Gasche 1981, 16).

3.5.3.4 Stone Placement

Section 3.2.1 above discusses the placement of stones in the rebuilding project at Mozan, and this is the best evidence for understanding the process of construction of the AP Palace walls.

The stones of the sub-structure may have been placed at the same time as the stone foundations, since the crew and materials would have been the same for both tasks. There are, however, some inconsistencies in the AP Palace between the foundations and the walls above them – in particular the doorway between A5 and A7, where the foundation runs across the doorway, indicating that the doorway was added later, or that a mistake was made. This change in plan may suggest that the foundations were constructed at a different time from the stone sub-structure.

Illustration 98 shows the section of a wall built entirely of stone:[118] note the use of larger stones as 'tie stones'. It is also interesting that the inside of the wall is plastered, but the outside, exposed to the rain, was not.

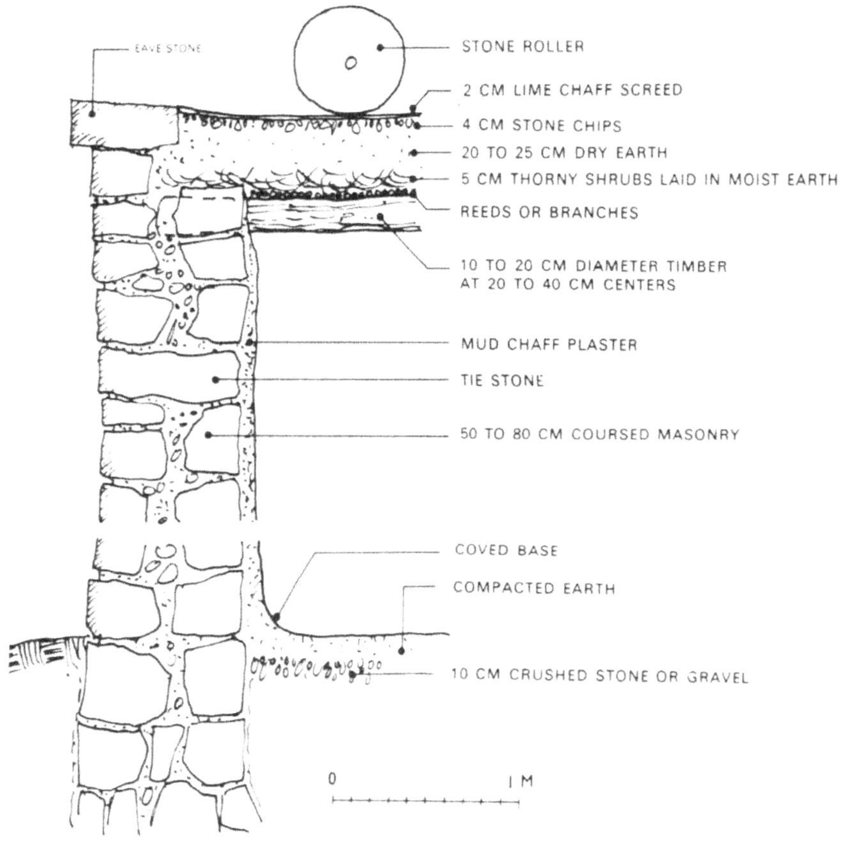

Fig. 125 - Toit plat en terre (d'après Ragette, 1974).

Illustration 98: Note here the stonework (Ragette 1974, 23).

It is also important to avoid 'vertical runs' in the stone, as this tends to weaken the wall (McRaven 1999, 19). Interestingly, the fact that masons avoid vertical runs is a further indication that when such are found (as is the case with mudbrick) it suggests that the walls were built at different points in time or by different work-crews working independently. In fact, the "only advice" given to a modern novice wall-maker was to "put one on two" so that a single stone rested above the seam between two stones on the run below (Vivian 1978, 99).

118 Aurenche 1981, 154 citing Ragette 1974, 22.

Vertical running joints will compromise the strength and durability of your wall and should be avoided at all costs.

Illustration 99: Example of a vertical run (McRaven 1999, 19).

One experiment shows that a 'waller' (a professional stone-wall maker) can build a wall 4.9-5.5 m long and 1.5 m high in a day (Garner 1984, 5). Unfortunately the hours worked are not mentioned, nor the average weight of the stones at hand.

3.5.3.5 *Preparing the Finished Stonework*

Once the stone foundations and sub-structure were finished, the top of the wall had to be flattened in order to lay the mudbricks.[119] The builders of the AP Palace used a combination of small stones, sherds and mud to level the wall.[120]

3.5.3.6 *Laying the Mudbricks*

Once the wall-top was prepared, the bricks could be laid. The wall width in the AP Palace varies between 1 ½ to 2 ½ bricks. In order to strengthen the wall, the square bricks were laid in an overlapping pattern using half-bricks to stagger the brick runs (see 3.2.2.4 above). This pattern has been described as "apparails de briques carrees" (ABC) by Sauvage (Sauvage 1998, 62–63).

119 For an interesting parallel, see Weiss et al. 2012.

120 It is within this fill that the tablet A15.231 was probably placed; see section 2.2.2.4.2.

Illustration 100: Wall construction during the reconstruction of the destroyed walls of the AP Palace. Note the workman 'splitting' a brick into two half-bricks over a pole in the foreground (MZ V22i2241).

Only one of the Garshana texts describes the size of a wall built by a worker in one day (Heimpel 2009, 288); 1.125 m^3 per male worker which corresponds to 9 cubic cubits, or about 60 bricks.[121] These workers were paid 6 lt of barley per day.

121 One 40x40x12 brick = 0.0192 m^3. 1.125 m^3 / 0.0192 m^3 = 58.59 bricks ≈ 60 bricks. The bricks used in the Garshana construction project were almost certainly of a different (smaller) dimension, but using these dimensions gives a rough estimate which can be applied to the AP Palace. It seems logical that larger bricks would mean that a worker could build a larger wall, since the number of times a brick was placed in the wall would be fewer for the same volume; thus this estimate may be low for the larger brick size.

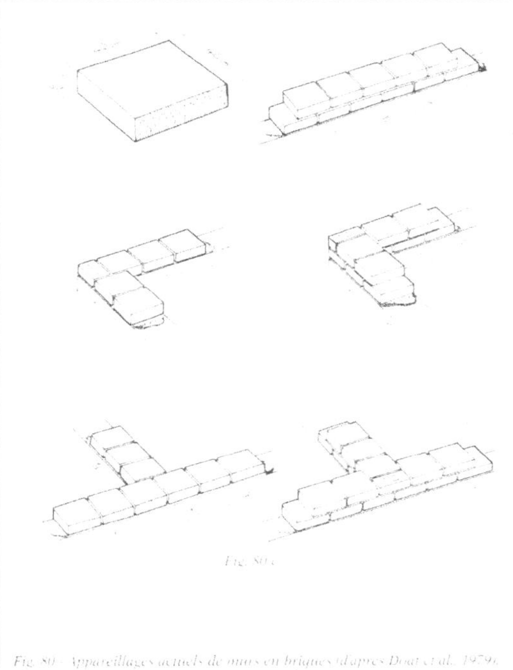

Illustration 101: Laying pattern for a wall with the width of a single brick (Ragette 1974, 23).

Illustration 102: A good example of well-laid brickwork (Aurenche 1977, 36).

3.5.3.7 *Doorways and Windows*

Doorways and windows must also be planned for in the construction, with the addition of wooden beams and matting or wooden slats as a lintel for both. Questions of access patterns are the most important consideration when placing doors, while lighting and aeration are the most important considerations when placing windows. Those few windows found in archaeological contexts tend to be quite small (Foster 2016, 233), but no windows were found in any buildings in Mozan.

One type of window would be found directly under the roof line, and may be made possible by the raising of the roof for a single room. These openings are what one might expect to find in some of the rooms in the AP Palace, especially B1 and D1, if not 'roof vents' (see 3.5.3.9 below). This type of window has been proposed for the central room in tripartite houses (Kohlmeyer 1996, 92; Akkermans and Schwartz 2002, 193; Butterlin 2006).

Illustration 103: A modern doorway with wooden lintel visible. Note the stone substructure (Aurenche 1977, 111).

Niches might have also been present, although none have been found in the excavated portions of the AP Palace. These might be present in the mudbrick portions of the walls (as, to give an example, at Tell Brak, see D. Oates 1990), the stone portions, or both. They might also have been tied to windows; niches in mudbrick walls are a common feature in modern mudbrick houses in the area around Mozan. For medieval examples of niches and niche-window combinations in very elegant stone walls, see Tronconi et al. on Italian mountain architecture (2008, 51–52).

3.5.3.8 Preparing Wall-Tops for a Roof

The last course of bricks needs to be set especially with the consideration of the roofing beams in mind. The Garshana texts suggest that the space between beams was normally 40 cm (Heimpel 2009, 135, 200) - this would vary however quite a bit based on whether reed matting or wooden slats were used, since wooden slats would be able to carry more weight than matting, allowing for a larger distance between beams. Whatever the distance, the beams would have to be set into the top of the brick wall, so that the bricks reach the top of the beam, closing the room at the top. The beams would also have to be sealed with quite a bit of mortar, since they were round.

In addition to the beams, the workers may have had to cut into the wall to make room for a gutter to drain the rainwater off the roof. This step may have been done at the end of the roof construction, but it would by necessity have to cut into or have space left for the channel, since the drain had to be lower than the level of the roof itself.

3.5.3.9 Roof Construction

To construct the roof, first the beams are laid across the standing walls, in prepared sockets or spaces in the brickwork (see previous section). Then reed mats or wooden slats are laid across, followed by a layer of straw or brush (Heimpel 2009, 173–74, 271–72). On top of this a layer of earth is laid, and compacted as much as possible. This step may be repeated, and the earth may be the same plaster as used in the next step. Finally a plaster is laid on the roof, often with a very high percentage of straw, which increases the impermeability of the plaster.

A specific type of window, 'roof vents', which were probably openings in the roof are attested at Garshana, and may be tied to a workroom environment (Heimpel 2009, 277). These are built directly into the roof itself (which is why they are found in this section of this study), and as such cannot refer to the lateral windows just under the roof mentioned above in 3.5.3.7.

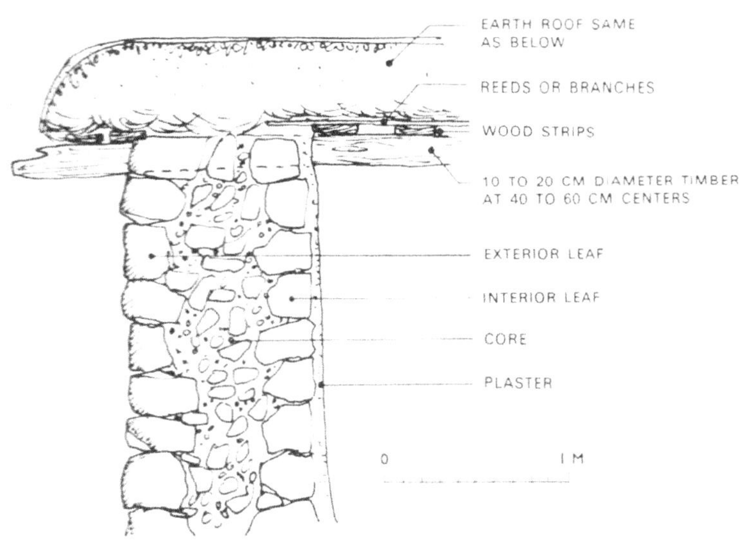

Illustration 104: Reconstruction of a roof (Ragette 1974, 23).

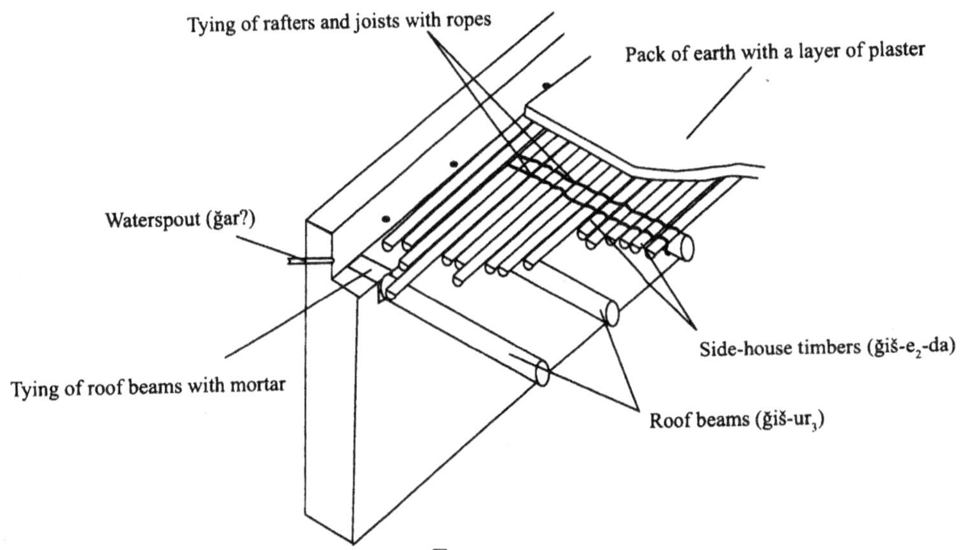

FIGURE 2

Illustration 105: Roofing elements mentioned in the Garshana texts (Heimpel 2009, 173).

Illustration 106: Various stages of the roofing process: cross-pieces, straw, matting and dirt (Cornerstones Community Partnerships 2006, 185).

If wooden beams are used to transport the stone to the worksite, as is proposed here, then they could be cut 'green' and used for transport, then set aside to 'dry' while the walls are being built, and would then be ready to be placed once the walls were all standing.[122] Green wood can take from one to three years to dry (Coles 1973, 26). It is unclear if the wood can be used in construction while still green, or if it is necessary to wait until dry. However if green wood is used, it would tend to bend under the weight of the roofing materials covering it.[123] This problem could be avoided be reusing older wooden beams or by cutting the trees early, as a first step in materials preparation, before the quarrying of the stones.

Illustration 107: Wooden beams and reed mats ready to be used in construction (Aurenche 1977, 97).

The texts from Garshana again provide an interesting source of comparative information for the use of wooden beams. Beams with 16 cm diameter could have spanned rooms of up to 3.5 m, and there were various categories of wood sizes which were used in the Garshana construction (Aurenche 1981, 154; Heimpel 2009, 198–99). Heimpel makes a calculation based on the assumption that the average span of a beam was 7 cubits, and the beams were placed an average of 24 fingers (40 cm) apart (Heimpel 2009, 135, 200). Thus 40 beams would be needed for a house of 229.6 cubits^2, or 57.4 m^2 (naturally excluding open areas) (Heimpel 2009, 135). It is important that the beam rest completely on the top of the wall, ideally with the end of the beam jutting out over the outer edge of the wall. This helps the beam from damaging the wall top were it to push out, eroding the inside edge of the wall ('Kantenpressung' – a known problem to German architects) (Heinrich and Seidl 1968, 9).

122 See for example Hammurapi ABB 2 56:22-23 iṣam warkam-ma likkisū "let them cut green wood."

123 Heimpel cites a text which says "It was not a good sign when 'the roof beams in the houses in the city of Daban [grew] branches." This suggests that the practice of using green wood was known, but was not looked on positively (Heimpel 2009, 198).

3.5.3.9.1 Rooftop Use and Access

While the archaeological record rarely shows the presence or function of second stories or rooftop areas, these were certainly used as part of the working space of ancient buildings. Modern ethnographic examples show three main types: built second stories, light constructions on top of roof, and an unbuilt working space.

Built second stories require more solid walls on the ground level to support the weight of the additional bricks. While the rooms above do not need to reflect all those below, for reasons of stability it would not be possible to place mudbrick walls on upper floors without resting them directly on first-floor walls. Thus the layout above must mirror, at least in part, the rooms below. An example of this can be found in a Sheik's house in Bahrain, built in 1830 (Nippa 1991, 190–91).

Illustration 108: House with second story in mudbrick (Aurenche 1977, 145).

The second type of upper-story use consists in the placement of light constructions to define spaces. Reed matting, brush walls, wattle-and-daub or textiles could all be used. Because of the lightness of the material, they can be placed anywhere on the roof, and do not need to reflect the room-patterns below. The disadvantage of these materials is the relative lack of protection from the elements that they afford.

Illustration 109: A second-story construction made of reeds (Aurenche 1977, 122).

Illustration 110: A flat roof accessed by means of a ladder (Aurenche 1981, 205).

The third type is probably the most common. Here no structures are built on the roof of the lower floor, but the space is accessible and often used. This can be seen very often in local modern villages, where roofs are used as a space for drying, sorting, and/or storing and for sleeping. The advantage is that this space is harder to reach, as opposed to the courtyard, so animals, children and visitors would be less likely to access this space. Also, if a ladder is used to access the roof, it can be removed, thus completely limiting access to this area. A flat roof makes access and use much easier, but some tasks can also be carried out on a (slightly) pitched roof, as is the case with drying seeds or olives.

3.5.3.10 Plastering Walls, Laying Floors

Once the roof is finished, plastering begins; both inside and outside walls can be plastered, with either a mud-only coating or a mud-coating with a second layer of gypsum applied. More on plasters can be found in section 3.2.4 above. The gypsum gives the wall a white color, which can be further decorated. Mud-plaster adheres to both mudbrick and stone construction elements, and has been used on both kinds of material.

Illustration 111: The plastered outer wall of a house; note the roof beams (Aurenche 1981, 135).

Illustration 112: Plaster can also be applied to stone (Aurenche 1981, 135).

3.5.3.11 Construction of Installations

At this stage installations can be placed in the structure, as well as the smaller superficial channels that lead to the drains. For a list of the installations, see section 2.2.2 above. One should keep in mind that many installations or elements of installations would have been made of perishable material, such as shelving in a niche, which leave little or no evidence behind.

3.5.3.12 Decoration and Movable Goods within the Building

Little is left of the decoration and the movable goods from within the buildings found within an archaeological context. Transportable objects were taken when the building was abandoned, its function changed, through looting or was destroyed in fire or collapse, and so little of what was present when the building was used can be found in the archaeological record. Ethnological accounts give a glimpse into what might have been present in the rooms; the account of an Englishwoman who visits the palace in Muskat in the early 1820s describes the harem as containing Persian rugs, porcelain vessels, wooden boxes containing clothes and jewelry, costly leather sandals, mirrors, bottles of perfume and jars of cosmetics.[124] The vast majority of these objects would not have survived in the archaeological record had they been present in the AP Palace.

3.6 Beyond the Chaîne Opératoire

3.6.1 Applying Algorithms to a Specific Structure

Where available, specific numbers or formula were given in the appropriate sections above. They are derived from ethnographic data, ethnoarchaeological experiments, textual evidence and/or planning experience.[125] As algorithms, they can be applied to a specific project, such as the AP Palace itself, in order to better understand the time, resources and energy invested. They are repeated here in list form, with reference to the appropriate section of this study, where an explanation and the references were given.

- Quarrying and shaping of stone using stone tools rather than steel takes 50% more time (3.2.1.3)
- A quarryman can produce 1 m^3 of finished stone in 11.6 days; 55% of original material remains as finished material (3.2.1.4)
- A quarryman can produce 1 m^3 of rough hewn cobbles in 1.6 days (3.2.1.4)
- A 'waller' (a professional stone-wall maker) can build a wall 4.9-5.5 m long and 1.5 m high in a day (3.5.3.4)
- 40 cm thick mudbrick wall holds a thermic difference for 12 hours (3.2.2.1)
- *Pisé* construction needs long drying times: 3 m high wall needs 18-50 days (3.2.2.1)
- 1/6 the volume of the bricks was added as mortar in construction (3.5.2.3)

124 Nippa 1991, 181–82 citing Fraser 1826

125 For an overlap between the three sources, see section 3.4.3.4 above.

- 2.6 m^3 of dirt excavated in 5 hours (3.2.2.2)
- 40x40x12 cm brick weighs 22 kg (3.2.2.2)
- 240-350 bricks can be made per person per day (3.2.2.8)
- Gypsum oven heated to 100-200 C; lime needs 900 C for 36 hours (3.2.5)
- Chaff 2.5-4 cm length for bricks, shorter for mortar, longer for plaster (3.2.6)
- 1 ½ bags of chaff (approx. 60 kg) needed for 131 bricks; approximate yield of 1/8 of a hectare of barley field (3.2.6)
- 1 hectar of grain produces 12 bags of chaff = 480 kg (3.2.6)
- Workday: 8 hours of 'normal' work; 5 hours 'strenuous' work (3.4.1.6)
- 45 kg max load per person over a day; 25-30 kg average (3.4.3 and 3.4.3.6)
- sled needs 16 persons pulling per ton of stone (3.4.3.1)
- almost 2 tons of stone over 3 canoes needed crew of 4 and drew 23 cm of water (3.4.3.1)
- mudbrick porters carried median of 150 bricks over a 432 m distance per day (3.4.3.2)
- 1.8 m^3 of dirt carried 180 m by one person in 8 hours (3.4.3.4)
- 4 wheeled wagon can carry 1350 kg; a donkey can carry 75 kg for 25 km per day (3.4.3.4)
- 4 people in 12 hours (over 3 days) produced 1000 mudbricks (40x40x10 cm) with a volume of 19.2 m^3 (3.2.2.9)
- Thus: approximately 2.5 man-hours are needed to produce 1 m^3 of mudbrick (3.2.2.9)
- 4 people in 7.5 hours carried 42 stones weighing 5.1 tons, with a volume of approximately 3 m^3 (3.2.1.6)
- Thus: approximately 10 man-hours are needed to place 1 m^3 of stone (3.2.1.6)
- 16 cm diameter roof beam could have spanned rooms of up to 3.5 m, and the beams were placed an average of 24 fingers (40 cm) apart (3.5.3.9).

It is important to note that these figures come from a variety of sources, and are really meant as a rule of thumb to have a general idea, rather than fixed algorithms. Also, they cannot be multiplied: while one person can carry 1.8m^3 of dirt over 180m in 8 hours, this does not necessarily mean that 2 people can carry the same amount over double the distance (however 2 people can carry double the amount over the same distance in the same time).

The Garshana archives have also given a clear picture as to the quantities of barley given to different workers. These numbers can also be useful as a rule-of-thumb when considering the resources needed in a construction project (from sections 3.2.2.8 and 3.4.1.6):

- men's standard wage: 5-6 lt of barley average (max 8)
- women's standard wage: 3 lt of barley
- brick maker's wage: 5 lt of barley
- slave's monthly wage: 60 lt of barley
- scribe's monthly wage 90 lt of barley

3.6.2 Construction and Ritual

While this chapter describes the process of construction from a practical, functional viewpoint, it is worth noting that there is a large corpus of ancient texts and scholarly research that discusses ritual practices associated with construction projects. The presence of foundation boxes within buildings (even if none has been found so far for the AP Palace) is a part of this aspect. These rituals played a fundamental role in the social perception and traditions associated with construction; while an analysis of these texts and their connection to the procedural analysis outlined here would be quite interesting, such an analysis lies outside the scope of this study.[126]

3.6.3 The 'Who' of Construction

This chapter has focused a great deal on the 'how' of construction, but has said relatively little as to the 'who'. Considerations of the amount of effort needed gives a glimpse into what each person 'invested' in the project, and the textual evidence gives a sense of the dynamics of interaction between the various players. Yet a sense of the actors themselves does not come across in this section. In part it is because of the paucity of information that one has from the archaeological record, and in part due to the fact that the aim here was to understand and quantify, as much as possible, the process of construction on an almost abstract level.

Such a 'structuralist' approach is necessary in understanding the process on a wider level, but such an approach can only be enriched by further consideration of some of the actors involved. An equally in-depth hermeneutic look at the structure is beyond the scope of this study, and would probably not

126 For a first important attempt to collect the royal description of construction procedures and building materials, see Lackenbacher 1982 and 1990. Focused on the building rituals is the vast research conducted by C. Ambos. See Ambos 2004 and 2010 with further extensive literature on the topic, and in Ambos 2010, 447-477 a synthetic useful appendix of the textual sources. For a consideration of the cosmological, theological and ideological dimensions see Hilgert 2014. For an examination of the construction of temples see the volume edited by Boda and Novotny (2010).

be possible due to the aforementioned paucity of evidence, but the strength of combining a distanced view of process with the richness of the human experience should not be undervalued.[127] The chapters dealing with theoretical approaches and the 3D model will, each in their own way, attempt to bring out some specifics with regard to the people behind this process.

127 I realize that I open here a small window on an immense debate in our field and in the humanities and social sciences as a whole. I bring it up only in order to give the reader a glimpse down a further avenue which can be explored vis-à-vis the architecture of the past. Perhaps the author who has most inspired me to consider the richness of this combination of structure and person is P. Ricoeur (Ricoeur 1976, 1981; Moore 1990).

"... plus que tout autre témoin archéologique, l'architecture permettra non seulment l'identification, mais aussi une meilleure compréhension du comportement des groupes humains dont elle est le reflet." - O. Aurenche[128]

4 Theoretical Underpinnings of Architectural Analysis

So far this study has focused on the AP Palace as a structure, looking at the architecture from an analytic point of view. It also has looked at the elements used in the construction: what one knows about how these elements were produced from an ethnographic perspective, the understanding of the process of construction from philological texts, a reconstruction of the work sequence on the basis of a *chaîne opératoire* analysis, and the formulation of algorithms based on relationships between materials and manpower.

While the previous sections have concentrated on the analytical and material/operational aspects of the AP Palace, these considerations have, either as their foundation or as a direct consequence of their results, a tie to theory. A detailed discussion of these theoretical aspects is beyond the scope of this study, but it is important to indicate some of these aspects in as far as they influence the path this study has taken, or highlight those theoretical discussions which might benefit from the results here presented. These theoretical reflections are not meant to be an exhaustive discussion of the aspects presented, nor do these aspects pretend to encompass all of the possible theoretical discussions that this study might bring forth. However, theoretical treatises are often criticized for their abstract nature and lack of primary data: thus in a practical study such as this, it seems appropriate to open the door to some of the possible considerations, in order to suggest how this work might lend itself as a foundation for a more exhaustive theoretical reflection.

128 "... more than any other archaeological evidence, architecture will allow not only for the identification, but also for a deeper understanding, of the interactions of those groups of people of whom it is an echo." Translation mine. (Aurenche 1981, 4).

The first theoretical aspect focuses on the two postulates on which this study is based. First, the 'ethnoarchaeological link' as the assumption that, on at least a very basic level, the actions of someone performing a task today (with the same tools) are a close approximation of the actions of someone producing the same results in antiquity. Second, that there is a 'continuity of experience' – that on a very basic level, people modern and ancient perceive their surroundings (architecture, in this case) in the same way.

The second theoretical aspect looks at context: not in the sense of comparative material or urban space, but with regard to the influences and variables present in architectural design. By context the relationship between a building and the urban environment is also meant, not in a spatial, topographic sense, but rather as an embodiment of a layer of social dynamics. Finally, the cyclical and linear nature of time with regard to architecture speaks to the chronological context.

While the archaeological record presents the material nature of architecture, the people involved in the planning, construction, and use of the building can be seen, even if only in part, through this materiality. Chapter 3 focused on the elements of construction, gave examples of the actions taken by the people involved and some parallels from philological sources; how much these various actors are really reflected in the archaeological record remains a question to be explored. While this study examines the architecture from various directions, there remains a question which comes before the planning and the building: why is a new palace needed? Finally, the actor who leaves the strongest impression in the archaeological record is the architect: is what one finds an active expression of this artist, or is it an organic fitting-together of parts?

The last theoretical aspect deals with the meaning that architecture conveys on a variety of levels. Style and function are primary vehicles for analyzing meaning, when looking at the architecture as a whole. To incorporate the analysis of the elements of construction, however, it is also useful to consider the energy needed to construct the building, as if the 'energy' was a cost-index to the elements which make up the building. These ways of describing meaning are a small part of a larger question: what is the value of architecture? Finally, the 'usefulness' of a 3D model is to be found, in part, in its potential as a heuristic vehicle: an external device which can help formulate new questions vis-à-vis the architecture and the archaeological record.

4.1 Postulates

4.1.1 *Postulate 1: The Ethnoarchaeological link*

"[T]his surely is one of the achievements of experimental archaeology, that it can yield not only answers to questions asked, but answers to questions unasked" (Coles 1973, 64–65). There is little question as to the usefulness of experimentation for archaeology, be it on an active level, such as the understanding of stone-working, or on a passive level, where archaeologists observe tools being used in modern contexts and understand thus the function of ancient tools – *tannurs* being an excellent example. Such analogies can be taken too far, particularly when they are used to define meaning or intention, as is the case when current traditions are assumed to have been operative in ancient times as well. These traditions are often heavily modified over time, especially in the modern era, when such traditions become a part of a performance.[129] A very interesting discussion of the value of ethnographic analogies can be found in a dialogue between Gould, Watson and Wylie (Watson and Gould 1982; Wylie 1982).

The parallel drawn between the present and the past is not only useful for understanding the unexplained in the archaeological record, but it is also a way to test the feasibility of our hypothetical reconstructions made vis-à-vis that material culture: "The ethnographic present serves as a baseline against which information on pottery making in prehistoric times is customarily interpreted, a procedure anthropologists and archaeologists call ethnographic analogy" (Rice 1987, 114). Thus the parallel between ancient and modern can aid in the understanding of the feasibility of ancient practices, as in the case of pottery. Experimental archaeology can also lead one to understand better the conditions generated during a process, such as the temperature generated in a burning building (Aurenche 1981, 75). And even if the exact structures cannot be duplicated because of the high costs in terms of energy and materials (eg. a pyramid), a logical continuum can be postulated on the basis of the smaller projects which can be undertaken under the rubric of experimental archaeology (Abrams 1994, 62). The danger is to consider this ethnographic material as a source – it is not. Instead, as an analogy, it is an external aid to understanding, but, as it is not part of the archaeological record, it should not be given the same importance.

These parallels need not be from the same region, either. One of the most striking examples of similarity in material culture and usefulness as an ethnographic analogy, is a many-roomed structure (called a 'burg' by the

129 See for example Tilley 1999, 239–59; Comaroff and Comaroff 2009.

authors) which is still in use in Burkina Faso (Schneider 1991).[130] This structure houses many nuclear family units, and does not have the same representative needs as a palace, but can still provide an ethnographic parallel, providing the link between inhabitants and the functional use of the rooms. Especially the use of roof space in the *Elefantanjaegerburg* is of interest in investigating the use of architecture in the ancient Near East. Thus even for parallels from other cultural contexts "[t]he utility of Ethnoarchaeology is primarily seen in how it puts into question the multiplicity of functional interpretations of the archaeological record" (Andraschko 1995, 26).[131]

There are few tools for the archaeologist to 'prove' or 'disprove' the validity of such ethnographic analogies. Perhaps the most telling correlation between the past and the present can be found in the ancient texts. The 'index of terms' which was given in table 8 (section 3.2.3.2) lists the worker tasks, tool names and brick terms in Akkadian. The correlation between the terms used in ancient texts describing construction and the actual process of construction as observed in modern times lends validity to the analogy, but cannot, still, definitively 'prove' the analogy as correct.[132] Of course, an analogy does not aim to be 'proven' as a logical proposition would, because an analogy is always internally valid: what is necessary is to show that the inference one draws from the analogy regarding the ancient world is a valid one.

4.1.2 Postulate 2: Continuity of Experience

The second broad postulate is that of the continuity of the human experience. This is also the greatest source of possible error in such a study, particularly of assumptions regarding elements that are otherwise unknown but which influenced the physical record as found; this might be the case especially for social elements. There is a concept in geology, uniformitarianism, which is referred to as the "uniformity of process across time and space" (Gould 1987). This concept comes from the tradition of New Geology, and its application to human experience and (on a very basic level) cultural processes are what is postulated here. The reference to New Geology is not as out of place as might seem at first glance: the inspiration for the New Archaeology movement of the 60s and 70s came from the New Geology

130 On this structure see also F. Buccellati 2014.

131 "Die Bedeutung der Ethnoarchaeologie ist vor allem in ihrer Problematizierung der multifunktionalen Deutung des archaeologischen Befundes zu sehen."

132 One should also be aware of the danger that this correlation might be circular: it is possible that the Akkadian terms are translated as given in the table because of our 'modern' understanding of the process of construction, and thus do not reflect precisely what the ancient speakers meant when using these terms.

movement.

While the understanding of ancient material culture wholly through the lens of modern cultural norms would not lead anywhere (and would be scientifically unsound, to say the least) there is a level at which this uniformity does link modernity with the past, even the distant past. In his book on Maya architecture, Abrams expresses this uniformity in terms of the impression that architecture imparts: "One intriguing and perhaps dominant aspect of architecture at any large archaeological site is that the scale and quality of these structures have a profound impression on the observer. Archaeologists, from the moment they enter a site until the final analyses of data, are ultimately observers and interpreters of those observations. The leitmotiv of this volume is that the initial observation of large architectural accomplishments has a tremendous impact on our impressions and interpretations, just as the elite who commissioned such projects had originally intended" (Abrams 1994, xii). An examination of this 'timeless' aspect in architecture can be found in the writings of R. Arnheim (Arnheim 1977), where he deals explicitly with the effect that architecture has on a human visitor – and his implicit claim is that these effects are not culturally specific, but are true on a universal level.[133] The difficulty is in determining the point at which our cultural norms influence the archaeologist's understanding of the cultural material under study – and since there is no litmus test for this, the question must be repeatedly asked as that understanding grows. Two aphorisms of Wittgenstein underline architecture's (timeless) ability to elicit a response from a visitor:

"Remember the impression one gets from good architecture, that it expresses a thought. It makes one want to respond with a gesture" (Wittgenstein [1977] 1980, 22e).

"Architecture is a *gesture*. Not every purposive movement of the human body is a gesture. And no more is every building designed for a purpose architecture" (Wittgenstein [1977] 1980, 42e).

4.2 Context

The context of architecture on a theoretical level needs to explore the variables that affect, in a general sense, how a building 'looks'. The compendium of private buildings already present in the city can serve as a basis for the layout of a palace. The urban context both affects and is affected by a monumental construction, and one can ask if there are relationships

133 Such reasoning is not limited to Arnheim or to proponents of Gestalt psychology – both Ankerl (sociology), Abrams and Unwin (architecture) also seem to argue along these lines (Ankerl 1981; Abrams 1994, 7; Unwin 2003).

between buildings, places, cities and people which can be explored for any urban context, regardless of the time period. This timelessness also comes to the fore when considering the relationship between architecture and both cyclical and linear chronological change.

4.2.1 Variables of Design

Design in architecture is conditioned by certain forces: standardization, technological changes, tradition, innovation.[134] Each of these has an impact on the final product of an architectural enterprise, and as such can be of use when describing a building even when so little is known of the architect or the urban setting.

An example of standardization is the change from *pisé* architecture to the use of mudbricks which were made in standardized forms. The use of mudbricks means that there is more of a tendency to build buildings with right angles, as opposed to round buildings. Change is brought often by new technological forms, such as the use of lime as plaster. Tradition plays a role particularly since the knowledge needed for such construction projects was passed on most likely through an apprenticeship type model (Wendrich 2012). Thus, along with the technical aspects of construction, a compendium of forms (how a house 'should' look) is transmitted to the apprentice. The last conditioning force in architectural design is innovation: change in the ancient Near East comes often as an influence from another cultural sphere, brought in through a variety of possible mechanisms of contact.

In addition to the forces influencing design, the local conditions as to where the building must be constructed plays a large factor in determining the layout of the final constructed building. The most basic level is the availability of materials for construction: "Since architecture is ultimately a collection of modified and unmodified raw materials, the key resources necessary for construction within the Copan Valley must be described" (Abrams 1994, 16). The place within the topography of the city as well as other urban conditions affect the final 'product' of the architect.

4.2.2 The Influence of Vernacular on Planned Architecture

Eliade, in his discussion of myths and time, ties monumental architecture to archetypes, and distinguishes between the 'profane' and the 'mythical' (Eliade 1974, 6, 35). Such an approach fundamentally separates, then, monumental and vernacular architecture, but this differentiation does not seem applicable to the architecture of the ancient Near East, in particular palatial architecture, which by definition is also a residence and as such often

134 For an excellent study of these forces of design, see Zevi's *Architettura in Nuce* (1972).

shares many elements with private houses. Semiotics offers another approach to monumental architecture from a non-architectural point of view (Petrosino 2011). Here what is especially in view is the relationship between the structure as an edifice and what it means for the 'concept' of inhabiting, even harking back to the philosophical domain with reference to the famous "Bauen, Wohnen, Denken" essay of Heidegger (1954).

But of more direct interest is not only the structural link in building typology, but also the implications in terms of how the experience in planning may have developed. One knows next to nothing about individual architects in Bronze Age Mesopotamia (for more on architects see 4.3.3), but one does know that there were specialized house builders who would have developed their skills in the vernacular sphere, and then applied them on a larger scale on larger construction projects such as palaces. The tablet found in the AP Palace in sector H, A15.231, gives evidence of how sophisticated this approach might have become, but the basic steps followed in the actual construction, including the surveyor's techniques, would presumably have been borrowed from the vernacular sphere.

Architecture can also give evidence as to changing social patterns or needs, both within the structure itself and its role within the urban framework. There are many studies of this for vernacular, private structures (Duering 2009), but similar questions regarding functional and symbolic change in use-patterns can also be asked of planned, public buildings. The interaction between these two kinds of structures is also of interest, both in terms of difference and in terms of similarity. To what extent can the differences in construction and use between private and public be seen as a real break, conditioned by the birth of new institutions, the need for which arose from the 'urban revolution'? On the other hand, to what extent does the similarity between public and private architecture reflect a logical expansion from the private to the public, thus building a continuity with the power structures established within household and familial structures (Lévi-Strauss 1988)?

4.2.3 The Role of Architecture in Creating an Urban Environment

There is an interplay between a building and the urban environment in which it rests; this interplay can be intended or incidental, and works in both directions – the building affects the environment as much as the environment affects the building (G. Buccellati 2010; F. Buccellati 2010).

The exhibit on Shrinking Cities in Frankfurt ("ShrinkingCities - Frankfurt" 2016) discussed the modern problem of diminishing demographics in today's first-world cities. The exhibit was structured in five chapters:

Negotiating Inequality, Self-Governance, Creating Images, Organizing Retreat and Occupying Space. The focus was primarily on the city as a whole, with the buildings within constituting the parts. The questions raised in the exhibit were specific to a certain type of city, but these five themes seem applicable, at least in part, to the urban environments of the past as well. To what extent does a palace or a temple reinforce inequality through marked differences with other buildings around it, through elements emphasizing monumentality and prestige? Can architectural elements aid in understanding mid- and low-level hierarchy within the city, perhaps through the construction of a city wall in identifiable sections?[135] Does the position of a building like the AP Palace – on the JP Plaza and replacing a portion of the inner city wall – represent a conscious effort to 'frame' the building as if an image? Or is it a political statement, declaring that the power of the city was such that a second line of defense was unnecessary? Does the AP Palace frame the *abi* in such a way as to limit access, making it more distant and more prominent at the same time? Does the visibility of the AP Palace tend to reflect its actual size, and does it use that visibility to project its own monumentality over a large portion of the urban environment?

Such questions are beyond the scope of a study focused on the AP Palace as such, and more excavations in the area around the Palace would be needed. However, the understanding gained from the research presented here is the first step towards answering such questions. While they cannot be answered, just positing them and considering the Palace within the framework of the wider urban environment adds to that understanding.

4.2.4 Architecture and History

The question about the reasons for changes in the architectural representation of the palace can be placed in the wider framework of history as a whole, and of architectural history in particular.

Stephen Gould's seminal monograph on time, *Time's Arrow, Time's Cycle*, draws on geological histories of the earth to explore the essential dichotomy between cyclical and linear events in history (Gould 1987). The question that this essay raises for archaeology is the presence or absence of a clear understanding of these two concepts and how they affect our specific research. The 'arrow' of time is the metaphor used to describe history as "an irreversible sequence of unrepeatable events" (Gould 1987, 10). This model of the historical process is often used to explain progress, a series of steps leading towards 'modernity'. The development of writing is often couched in these terms, each change a movement towards a simpler, more efficient way of

135 For an interesting example of this, see Helms and Meyer 2016.

communicating.

The 'cycle' of time, instead, reflects a vision of history where "apparent motions are parts of repeating cycles, and differences of the past will be realities of the future" (Gould 1987, 11). Here historical processes are seen as repeating elements which punctuate the human experience. An example of this would be the interaction between religious and political power within society.

These approaches both contain large flaws. Studying historical processes as a direct series of steps (the 'arrow') means that the goal of this process is defined through the hindsight of the researcher; each event is seen as a vector pushing towards or away from an objective. This excludes the secondary ramifications of development, and can easily fall into the trap of an 'apologist' description of history along a single line of development.[136] Cyclical development, on the other hand, actually contains two very different concepts: immanent structures and precisely repeated events. Immanent structures would include such concepts as archetypes (Eliade 1974), whereas repeated events would be reflected in recurring cataclysmic events.

One should also pose the question if the 'arrow'/'cycle' dichotomy is, itself, a product of a specific cultural mindset, thereby obscuring rather than illuminating historical processes (Gould 1987, 8–9, 13). A lengthy discussion of this problem is beyond this study, and one may question whether the discussion resulting from such a division is fruitful.

This division is of relevance, however, to our consideration of the palace because of the role that both the AP Palace and the methodology here described can play in analyzing Near Eastern society and its wider context. The Palace can be seen as a step in the continuum of development (arrow) in architecture, monumentality and social space. The methodology can be employed to compare various architectural aspects of buildings from disparate time periods in order to identify common patterns, whether immanent structures or repeating modes (cycle).

Zevi expresses an interesting point of view where he says that all history is contemporary, but architecture is the most historical of disciplines (Zevi 1994, 13). In light of Gould's remarks, one could say that the study of an architectural monument is at the same time linear and cyclical. It is linear (hence historical in Zevi's sense) because one can trace its development through time, on the basis of external events that are tied to it – through documents that relate to it or through the evidence of the stratigraphic history that the archaeologist can deduce from the accumulations that built up within it. But it is also cyclical (contemporary, in Zevi's sense) because it carries

136 Gould's example is that of 'Whiggish History' where English historians define historical (primarily political) development as a series of steps culminating in the political theories espoused by the Whig party of their time (Gould 1987, 4–5).

within itself the mark of its own accretions, through its own developmental history (e. g., through studies such as those carried out in the field of *Bauforschung*). Thus architectural history is particularly rich, and its archaeological dimension all the more complex.

4.3 Actors

One may think of architecture in an archaeological context as the converse of architecture in a modern context. In the first case, the product is present and one must look for the designer and behind him for the client, in the second the search is for a designer who can interpret a client's wishes and bring about the product. Thus a study of architectural works is a study of works 'in search of an author,' as it were, and the difficult task for the archaeologist lies in the need to discover the architect behind the architecture. To help in this task, archaeology should engage in a study of the theoretical dimension of architectural analysis: this will allow one to articulate insights into both the nature of the product, i. e., a building, and the behavioral environment that made its execution possible.

4.3.1 The Human Background

Every building 'represents' certain people, most likely all or at least most of the following: client, architect, surveyor, workers and users. But how much of their influence remains in the archaeological record?

In a generic way, the nature, if not the person, of the client can be deduced from the type and complexity of the building. Foundation deposits or other written documents found within a building can actually give information about the very person who commissioned it. Thus it is clear that Naram-Sin was responsible for the construction of a large public structure at Tell Brak: from which one can infer not that he would have personally intervened in the design or even the commission of the building, but that his concerns with regard to the political and military expansion would be reflected here, and represented by whatever official of his court or army would have undertaken to carry out the king's policies. For the AP Palace, the accumulations above the first floors of the building show that a king by the name of Tupkish, and members of his court, used the Palace when first built: from this one can assume that he had commissioned its construction or that it was commissioned for him, and that he was also involved on some level with some of the choices inherent in the construction process.

Of individual architects instead next to nothing is known, and while for certain aspects of art history one relies on stylistic criteria for establishing connections among individual works of art, attributing them to individual 'masters,' the same is not true for architects. One must, however, assume that indeed there were skilled specialized individuals, not only because of the complexity of some of the buildings, but also because of the careful planning that went into it, as was seen in chapter 3. Textual evidence is, in fact, available from later periods that relate in detail the responsibilities (also legal) of a person that has been described as being in between an architect and a mason (*itinnum*).[137]

Another person who would have been of critical importance was the surveyor.[138] Known in Akkadian as *abi ašlim*,[139] "the father of the rope," the surveyor was responsible not only for locating the footprint of the building within an urban environment, but also for laying out the footprint of any given building, in particular the corners of the walls.

As for the way in which a building was utilized by those who lived or worked in it, i. e., its function, there are clues from a number of installations and especially from objects found either in situ or strewn in the accumulations above the floors. It is next to impossible to gauge the number of people who would have worked in it, except where written texts give ledgers with lists of individuals and their tasks.

4.3.2 Palace Architecture: Motivations for Change

Perhaps the 'first question', the one which launches a construction project of the kind discussed in this study, is this: *is a new palace needed?* The commissioning person makes an active decision to begin the project, and there are cases where a new ruler does not construct a new building, or other cases where tradition or the political and/or social configuration is such whereby a new structure is not wanted. The premise of this study is that the question is answered with 'yes' for the AP Palace at Tell Mozan, so it is important to look at some of the possible reasons behind this response,[140] as well as a note on why the answer might be 'no' in other cases.

137 "The OB passages show the *itinnu* as a craftsman directing the building of houses with the help of hired men who make and deliver the necessary bricks. Neither the translation 'architect' nor 'mason' quite fits. The OB references indicate furthermore that the *itinnu*'s were organized in guilds, under an overseer (*aklu*...) and were connected with the palace which granted them holdings for their support" (CAD I and J 297b).

138 On this see the Ph.D. dissertation by S. Hughey (1997).

139 See CAD A2 448a.

140 Oppenheim, in his discussion of *The Great Organizations*, speaks of the "desire of every powerful ruler to build a new palace" without further discussing the reasons behind this desire (Oppenheim 1977, 97). A detailed explanation of the ideological background of the royal building activity is outside the scope of this work, but for pertinent bibliography see Lackenbacher 1982, 174–75 and Matthiae 1994, 36–37. For textual sources, and connected interpretation, see note 126 above.

There are three primary causes for answering 'yes' to the question of whether a new palace is even needed: the need to distance oneself from the previous ruler, to change or remove the semiotic message and/or psychological impact of an existing palace, or to affect the urban texture. These causes also are tied to the creation and reaffirmation of elite status, which is a further consideration tied to the decision to construct a new palace.

4.3.2.1 Architecture as a Statement of Disassociation

Probably the most common reason for constructing a new palace is the need or desire to disassociate the new ruler from the previous ruler. Here there are several aspects which contrast with each other: on the one hand, there is the desire to demonstrate legitimacy, and one element supporting legitimacy is lineage, thus taking over the palace of the previous ruler would be a way to underline this claim of dynastic coherence. On the other hand there is a need or desire to distance the new ruler from a previous one, and one of the most effective ways of doing that is to move spatially to another palace which becomes a new symbol for a new king. A new building then links aspects of 'newness', of 'distance' and of 'durability' to the new king.

The 'newness' of a newly constructed palace might draw an analogy[141] between the new king and a son who starts a family and requires a dwelling of his own: a son leaves the family, where he is not at the top of the hierarchy,[142] and creates his own space in which a new family is created with him at its head.[143]

The potential 'distance' of the new palace from the old is a further consideration: it is very unlikely that a new king would raze the old palace and construct his new palace on top, and in the case of the AP Palace at Tell Mozan it can be demonstrated that the palace, after the reign of Tupkish, was no longer used as a palace but still functioned in some administrative capacity during the reign of Tupkish's successor (see section 2.1.3). Thus the distance that the palace has from the old seat of power[144] also reflects a shift from an

---

141 Another reason for building a new palace might be to stimulate the local economy by providing a large public-works project as soon as instated as king. This economic aspect, however, would be best studied concomitantly with texts dealing with the freeing of debt upon taking power, which would lead too far from the goals of this study.

142 On the other hand kings also stress filiation as the reason for legitimacy, so the issue is clearly a complex one.

143 Here too it would be interesting to link this phenomenon to the relationship between changes in the social hierarchy within extended families and changes in space – for example the move to a new tent by one of the sons within a nomadic group. However this line of questioning also falls outside the scope of this study.

144 See Winter 1993. It is interesting how the language used to describe power is so infused with

old to a new king.[145]

The 'durability' of a building is not only a practical consideration: this durability reflects, on the level of memory, on the (perceived) durability of the social institution that it houses (Ankerl 1981, 30–31). As such, the new king would want a new palace to 'immortalize' his reign, as it were.[146]

4.3.2.2 *Using Architecture to Change the Message*

A new palace can also be used as a method of communication beyond the disassociation: it can be used to showcase some achievement or new political message, expressed in the form, material or decoration of the new building.

The form of the building[147] can express a new function within the palatial household, such as workspace for a new kind of artisan or areas such as a scribal school. Including these activities within the walls of the palace would be a clear statement as to the direct control the king has over a specific activity. Two examples come to mind: the Zimri-lim palace and the Akkadian seal cutters. The palace of Zimri-lim at Mari seems rather unique in that a number of identifiable aspects of administration are physically present within the walls of the palace (Dalley 2002, 50–69). The second example is not present in architecture, but shows the level of control being discussed: the Akkadian control over the iconography present on seal impressions. Only members of the royal household or high functionaries were allowed specific scenes on their seals (G. Buccellati and Kelly-Buccellati 2002, 15–17; Rakic 2003). Such a 'monopoly' shows a clear understanding of the power of images, and one would expect that specific seal cutters would be allowed to cut such seals, and they would be within the direct employ of the palace and perhaps

spatial metaphors: 'seat of power' or 'royal court'. A further research question which also lies outside of the goals of this study could investigate the use of similar metaphors in Akkadian and Sumerian as tied to the architectural evidence gleaned from archaeological contexts.

145 Such attempts to create distance need not be limited to architecture: in Urkesh the ED III seal impressions excavated are closer to southern models and those from nearby sites than the Akkadian seal impressions of the Tupkish period. In fact the Tupkish seals have a completely new iconography – perhaps seal iconography is another vehicle used to distance a ruler from his predecessor.

146 An interesting question, following this line of reasoning, revolves on the interpretation of the concept of 'institution' – it seems that the desire for a new palace is meant to immortalize an individual king, instead of immortalizing the institution of a particular city's monarchy or dynastic line. Again, however, this question leads too far from the central questions of this study, and would need a detailed study of textual records as well as a study of a series of palaces located in the same city, built by a succession of rulers.

147 Of course, the form of a building is always an expression of some sort, as discussed in other parts of this study. What is brought into focus here is the need to build a new palace as a way to incorporate something into the new form that an old palace could not accommodate.

even working within the palace walls. Of course other, private, seal cutters might have been capable of cutting such seals, but it seems probable that a bureaucracy which guarded the use of images would also take great care in controlling the people allowed to produce the images. It is also possible that the technical skill and artistic sensitivity were only developed within schools or workshops controlled by the administration, and through this relationship specific elements of iconography were kept within the control of the state.

This could have also been the case in Urkesh also where the numerous seals cut for Uqnitum's administrators were controlled as to their iconography and seal inscriptions (F. Buccellati 2014a). In the south, seals of royal servants contained the name of the servant as well as the name of the royal patron (Frayne 1993). Also in the south the seals of royal servants had a distinctive iconography, only connected with that servant.

The materials used in the construction of a palace can also be a way of communicating something new, and thus their availability could be the reason for building a new palace. One example of this might be access to a new source of wood, which is stronger and the available trunks longer than what was available in the past. Such logs would make the construction of wider rooms possible; this might be particularly appealing since the throne room of many palaces is one of the longest and widest rooms in the building, thus a new, wider throne room would reflect directly on the importance of the king. Also, longer logs would mean that the *iwans*[148] in the structure could have wider openings towards courtyards, and thus would give more working-space within the *iwan*.

Finally, and perhaps most important, the chance to use a new palace to commission new statues, new furniture or new orthostats to place in the structure would have been a compelling reason. There is archaeological evidence of such decoration primarily from Assyrian contexts in later times, but such elements would most likely have been present in earlier palaces. One of the best examples of such treasures tied to the king are the finds from Ebla (Matthiae 1977, 1985, 2010b).

4.3.2.3 *Affecting the Urban Texture*

A new palace might also have been built, in part, in order to affect the urban texture of the city or to emphasize relationships between institutions by tying their institutional 'homes' together in some way within the urban setting.

A new palace, as long as it is placed within the city, changes the urban landscape, be it through destruction, creation and/or modification of parts of the urban texture of the city. In some cases this may be used actively in an

148 For more on the use of the term *iwan* see section 2.4.3.

attempt to use change in the urban texture as a means of communication. The AP Palace, for example, destroys a part of the inner city wall; this may be an expression of confidence and security, a statement conveying the fact that the outer city wall is enough to defend the city, that the army is large enough to man the longer wall, and that the lower town is important enough that it would not be given up by the defenders.

Additionally, the changes that the new palace makes in the urban landscape may be used to underline its relationship to other institutional powers, such as a temple of the city or economic centers. The AP Palace fronts on the plaza, and would have seen and been visible from the temple atop the temple terrace.

4.3.2.4 *Using Architecture to Achieve or Reaffirm Elite Status*

While the king has a palace because of his position as king, it is also true, to some extent, that the palace itself underlines and reaffirms that power. Thus the palace embodies the institution as much as the king does, and as such the palace is perhaps the most potent symbol of the royal power.[149]

Additionally, while the king is at the top of the political hierarchy of the city, he does have a 'peer group' – other kings in the region. The relationships between these kings were, presumably, ever changing, in part due to the personalities, the power of the city (be it political, economic, military or religious) or outside influences. The decision to construct a new palace may be influenced by the desire to express a change in the status of the king within his city or vis-à-vis the other kings in the region.

One of the most entertaining correspondences between kings in the Ancient Near East are the letters written between Shamshi-Adad and his sons, Yasmah-Addu and Ishme-Dagan. Each ruled a city, but what comes out in the letters is the amount of material and people being sent from one city to another. Of course, these exchanges are especially marked in this case because the three rulers are related and the cities part of a larger political whole, but there is no reason to think that such exchanges did not go on between other rulers in the same region.

149 This has been explored in the literature, in particular the nicely titled volume of the DAI *Macht der Architektur-Architektur der Macht* (The Power of Architecture-The Architecture of Power) (Schwandner and Rheidt 2004).

4.3.2.5 *Deciding not to Build a Palace*

While there are many reasons to build a palace, there must have also been cases where the decision was taken not to build a new palace. Three reasons come to mind: the lack of resources, the extent of the existing palace or an expression of continuity.

It goes without saying that a new palace requires a large amount of resources; if the new king cannot afford to build a new palace, then he may decide to continue reigning from the palace of his predecessor. Also, if he does not have enough resources to build a palace on the same scale as his predecessor, it may seem that his power has diminished (which may well be the case, since he cannot afford a similar or better palace) and thus by continuing the use of the old palace he attempts to maintain the appearance of having the same status as his predecessor.

The second possible reason for not building a new palace is that the old palace may contain so many workshops, storage areas, schools and living areas that a new palace would have to be enormous, thus 'costing' a disproportionate amount of resources and requiring the leveling of a large portion of the urban space.

Finally, the re-use of a predecessor's palace may be a way to underline the legitimacy of the new ruler (see also 4.3.2.1). This may be especially used in cases where a claim to legitimacy, most often tied to lineage, is shaky at best.

4.3.3 *The Architect as Agent*

For the periods here under consideration, the particular problem arises that one cannot identify any of the architects responsible for any of the buildings uncovered, nor is there any (ancient) theory of architecture that one can rely on. In Mejier's article on *emic* and *etic* aspects of architecture in the ancient Near East, he postulates that there was never 'a Mesopotamian Vitruvius' because the ancient Mesopotamians did not have the same drive towards abstraction present today (Meijer 2008). Thus, Meijer suggests that one cannot create a typology of 'architectural orders' in which buildings are divided into classes based on aesthetic principles, even if one can create typologies based on materials used, methods of building or division of space, as in the article of Margueron on domestic architecture in Ville I of Mari (Margueron 2008). Such architectural orders are not possible, following Meijer, not because of the lack of information retrieved by archaeologists, but due to the lack of abstraction in the ancient's concept of architectural forms.

One can argue, however, that this point of view should be reassessed. Consider how such a lack of theoretical derivation from universal abstract principles affects everything that can be said about Mesopotamian culture. What would be, for example, the justification for a work like the *Chicago Assyrian Dictionary*, given the lack of an abstract Akkadian linguistic theory that might support the choices in classification that are at work there? Rather, one might argue that an *emic* analysis is possible even in the absence of an explicit (ancient) articulation of conceptual categories by the carriers of that culture, on the basis of a careful distributional analysis that identifies real patterns in the data, behind which one is led to assume the existence of equally real patterns of classification. In this way, one is led to recognize the agent behind the work, in ways that are, in any case, fully arguable because they are based on specifically definable patterns.

4.4 The Search for Meaning in Architecture

"Architecture immortalizes and glorifies something. Hence there can be no architecture where there is nothing to glorify." (Wittgenstein [1977] 1980, 69e)

"Longfellow: In the elder days of art, Builders wrought with greatest care Each minute and unseen part, For the gods are everywhere" (Wittgenstein [1977] 1980, 34e).

The search for meaning in architecture will probably never end, as architecture continues to change as the search for meaning progresses. However, this study may constitute one step on this endless path, and it may be of use to highlight the elements of this study which bear on this question. In the archaeologists' search for meaning, one can say that the choices made by ancient architects and builders are made within the context of a web of factors, be they practical, technological or symbolic on some level. Discerning and defining these factors is difficult, since "not everything about an architectonic formation is meaningful in the same way. And yet it also becomes evident that everything is not meaningful in every way" (Preziosi 1983, 210). Thus a part of the archaeologists' task is to search for such interpretations and found these hypotheses within the context of archaeological research, even if this challenge is one which may never be completed.

In the cultural complex of Mesopotamia, structures hold special meaning, in particular temples. Temples are important examples here, because the structure itself becomes another representation of the godhead, much as a cultic statue and, at times, a priest/king also embody the deity. Each of these images of the deity are born in a religious context, where the human actors are merely fulfilling the design of an otherworldly playwright.

While these elements are specific to temples and their religious aspect, they can be transferred to a limited extent onto other types of architecture.

Private houses to some extent reflect the personality of the homeowner, despite overarching paradigms, such as the tripartite house. In particular, one can see individuality in private architecture in installations and the areas dedicated to specific work areas. Public political structures instead embody the power of the office which they house, much as the vestments of the king are a 'portable' embodiment of the office, so is the palace an immovable representation of the same.

4.4.1 *Style in Architecture*

Related to the search for meaning in architecture is a consideration of style: 'how are choices made?' is the basic underlying question. The individual agent's inclination goes hand in hand with social constraints, needs of use, availability of resources, and other limitations of this type that severely affect, in the case of architecture, the real options.

If one takes style to be the recursive choice of non mandatory traits,[150] then in the case of architecture this choice is particularly conditioned by the concrete needs that a building is intended to serve. Take the case of a courtyard: it is not only a node within the communication network of spaces (the link for access to different rooms) but also an open space where certain activities must take place that cannot be carried out indoors; it provides more space for activities that require a larger number of people than could easily be accommodated in a roofed space; it serves as a source of light for rooms that front it and that cannot have windows or other openings; it can offer a sense of perceptual intimacy by being totally enclosed by rooms without access to the outside. And so on.

Ankerl's work (1981) combining Architecture and Sociology provides great insight into the combination of space and communication. For him, architecture is a "system of multilinearly interlinked spaces", (Ankerl 1981, 171) and a proper analysis of these links and spaces can help define style and function of a building, like the AP Palace, even in the absence of the users' self-expression in this regard.[151] This absence makes his work of particular use to archaeologists, since his understanding of architecture is based on many of the same elements of material culture that are available to, and limit, archaeological research. Such a study can and should go hand-in-hand with an

150 Answers to the question 'what is style?' could fill bookcases, and a complete bibliography is outside the scope of this study. Some of the authors who have influenced this study are: Schapiro 1953; G. Buccellati 1981; Panofsky 1983, 1997; Sackett 1990.

151 Ankerl's book was not well received (Michelson 1984; Sydie 1984; Ankerl and Michelson 1985), but the criticism focuses primarily on other aspects of his book. Relevant for this study is his discussion of these "multilinearly interlinked spaces" which was not criticized by reviewers.

anthropological approach, such as the articles published in the *Der Gebaute Raum* volume, in particular those of Delitz, Hahn and Lang (Delitz 2010; Hahn 2010; Lang 2010; Trebsche, Müller-Scheeßel, and Reinhold 2010).

4.4.2 The Role of 3D Modeling as a Heuristic Vehicle

In the discussion of the need for 3D models in chapter 5, the heuristic aspects of 3D models comes to light. In this theoretical portion of this study it is worth exploring this aspect more in depth, since it is a powerful vehicle which can aid in the understanding of the 3D model as a tool for research.

A heuristic model is a tool for conducting research in an environment when a model can help filter the variables present in the description of a problem or situation. Abbott defines 'heuristics' as "a discipline that aims to facilitate invention and discovery of new facts and ideas in the sciences" (Abbott 2004).

The strength of a heuristic model is not only in the fact that it reduces the number of variables present in a certain situation, but it also becomes a vehicle which allows for the discovery of new information. This comes about in two ways: first, by reducing the number of variables the situation becomes clearer, and thus more malleable to the intuitive or imaginative aspects of how one approaches the problem. The second use of this vehicle is in the ability to quantify these reduced variables.

By means of explanation one can consider the 3D model presented in the following chapters. A 3D model aids in reducing the archaeological record, which is *per definitionem* an extremely complex matrix of data with many levels, from the stratigraphic to the interpretative. The 3D model both isolates the architectural elements by defining them as (meta-)physical[152] blocks, and further defines them by allowing one to place them on distinct layers. By keeping the relationships spatial, and using a virtual 'space' which closely matches the physical space (as opposed to using 'standardized' signs for architectural elements) the distance between the physical and the model does not become a difficult bridge to span. The ability to place the data on several layers is a further aspect of the heuristic model, allowing for the juxtaposition of several different types of data – a juxtaposition which can elicit questions exactly as a heuristic model is meant to do.

To use such a model in a research environment it is important that the model be flexible enough to evolve. And here is a fundamental difference which can be seen vis-à-vis models which are produced primarily in order to 'show' others what was found or a reconstruction thereof – these are the

152 I use here the term '(meta-)physical' in the sense of something that lies beyond the physical dimension but closely approximates it, thus in a sense that remains quite distinct from the philosophical meaning associated with the term when written as 'metaphysical.'

models used primarily for communication. Such models change in that they become more precise, or adapt to changing understandings of what the building would have looked like in antiquity, but they do not change because of the needs of the researchers themselves.

A 3D model which is used heuristically, instead, reflects not only changes in the understanding of the ancient record, but also incorporates changes vis-à-vis differences within the definition of the record as such. An example might be the material used in the foundation of a wall in relation to the wall above. The material might be the same, and the 3D model might not differentiate between the parts of the wall above and below the floor level. However, it might be of interest to the researcher to see which walls had more or less of the foundation material, so the model might be changed to separate the wall into two segments. Such a model is flexible, meaning also that the data is primary: thus the model is subordinated to the research question and the data, rather than the other way around.

4.4.3 The Value of Architecture

"The house itself can be conceived of as embodying several values: a use value and exchange value, following Marx, as well as what could be considered a social or moral value, following Mauss" (Abrams 1994, 41)

There are three methods of measuring architectural construction: subjective, volumetric and energetic (McAdams, n.d., 5). *Subjective* measurement is an indication of the experience of the viewer, normally the archaeologist who excavates and interprets the newly uncovered building. *Volumetrics* is based on calculating the cubic volume of the construction elements as well as the floorspace. *Energetics* is a study of the way in which energy was expended in creating a particular edifice.[153] The first method is discussed to some extent in the postulates, see section 4.1. Volumetrics is a calculation of the volume of the building, and as such can be seen in the application of the 3D modeling technique to the AP Palace, as will be shown in chapter 6. The final method is that of energetics, which focuses on the calculation of the energy involved in a construction project, and is discussed with regard to value in 4.4.3.1 below.

By using energetics in such an analysis, the question arises if such an approach can lead to a better understanding of 'value' in relation to architecture. If one can discuss the differing amounts of energy needed in

153 Abrams, among others, was of particular use in the development of this monograph with regard to the question of energetics (Abrams 1994; Smith 2006; Devolder 2012; Fitzsimons 2014).

constructing different types of architecture, then it is important also to consider the reasoning behind the choices, in particular the decision involved when the chosen type of construction needs more energy than another. Sometimes the reasoning behind the decision is based on an improvement to be had on the technological level, but in some cases a social or ideological level can be posited.[154]

Value also plays a role on a higher level of analysis, that of the function of the rooms. The patterns of access as well as the types of sectors present were discussed in chapter 2. But these two factors also lend themselves to a discussion of the value of certain types of work being done in these areas of the palace, which further leads to a discussion of the 'value' of the work being done and the social 'value' of those workers or administrators.

The last layer of discussion regarding 'value' rests on the understanding of the social institution which the palace embodies. Elsewhere the dual-role of the palace as home and as seat of institutional power has been discussed (the *babānu-bitānu* relationship), but it is worth taking up again within this discussion of the concept of 'value' since architecture becomes a symbol for that institutional embodiment. The energy invested in the construction of the palace is also a way of examining the 'value' of the institution which it houses. This relationship between the social and the physical worlds is by far the most difficult to explore, meaningfully, as archaeologists, and the most difficult to tie back to the data from the record. Yet it is worthwhile despite these risks, since it is through these types of questions that the social aspect of ancient society can be discussed, and if such questions are not confronted by archaeologists, who have a unique grasp of the data from the archaeological record, then who should attempt such questions?[155]

4.4.3.1 Value and Energetics

The following quote from a research on Mayan architecture can help in understanding the value of energetics as employed in volumetric analysis: "Architecture, as a collection of raw and manufacture components, is translated into the composite cost of procuring and transporting those materials, manufacturing necessary parts, and assembling the final product" (Abrams 1994, 2). Further: "The analyses focus on the comparison and interpretation of collective measures of architectural cost rather than on the more symbolic or psychologic dimensions of the architecture, although these factors are in reality not disarticulated" (Abrams 1994, 7).

154 As to some of the problems inherent in this line of questioning, see Meijer 2008.

155 Of course, one might argue that such questions should not be asked at all; such an argument is made for religion by Oppenheim in his famous chapter "Why a 'Mesopotamian Religion' should not be written" (Oppenheim 1977, 172–82).

A practical example of the usefulness of energetics in determining value is related to how one can ascribe meaning to specific choices made in constructing a building. In the discussion of construction and the considerations of the materials chosen for the AP Palace, one sees how the use of stone in the building meant a greater expenditure of work or energy than would have been the case had the building been built entirely of mudbricks (see chapter 6). There are clearly technological benefits to stone, primarily its ability to block humidity rising from the ground into the walls thereby damaging them. However it is a further interpretative step to say that stonework is linked to the definition of the structure as a palace, be it either to say that palaces are built from stone (in part) as a symbolic necessity or to say that only the economic/energetic resources available to a ruler or his court could have constructed buildings out of stone.

What is the foundation of this interpretive step? One can identify a twofold basis for such a hypothesis. First, stonework is a commonality shared by some other palaces in the region, particularly Tell Chuera (Palace F). While it cannot be stated as fact that such a symbolism was apparent to ancient urban populations, one can show a correlation between a palace or palatial structures and the presence of stone within the corpus of comparative material from the region. It is true that stone can also be found in some private structures, but in Mozan the stone used in these cases seems to be used secondarily, since they are neither shaped to fit their position nor do the walls uniformly employ stone, even within the same structure. Second, the presence of stone in larger, representative structures is a commonality shared also in the ethnographic record. Buildings constructed and in use within the region today share the presence of stone, for example the *mukhtar*'s (village head) house in the modern village of Mozan, where it is thought that the very stones used in that construction were quarried from the tell and perhaps even the AP Palace itself in a rather fitting continuation of use.

Such considerations are also made by D. Preziosi in his study of Minoan architecture: "If the Minoan corpus resembles other architectonic systems, then it will likely be the case that certain materials may come to take on more direct signification than is evident here. It may turn out that for the Minoan, the use of certain materials may have had connotations of its own. One may imagine, for example, that such is the case with respect to contrasts in texture and finishing of stone; it is generally the case that the major (western) facades of great public structures such as the palatial compounds were composed of finely hewn and squared hard limestone (vs. many private structures). The presence of such material may thereby have perceptually cued (or enhanced the geometric perception of) certain social and functional contrasts" (Preziosi 1983, 210). The symbolic valence of materials is particularly difficult for archaeologists to determine since what is missing is not only the ability to interview the inhabitants of these buildings but also a series of other potentially symbolic elements which might have altered or enhanced the symbols available to us. An example of this is color in the form of fresco or secco wall painting (i. e. Til Barsip), which is only rarely preserved in the architectural remains in the ancient Near East,[156] but which possibly played a major role in defining the significations, connotations and usages of architectural space (Preziosi 1983, 210).

4.4.3.2 Value and Function

Value can be discussed also within the structure itself, by looking at function and room distribution. The location of specific areas, such as the kitchen or the storage of precious goods, can be tied to the practical considerations of service and safety, but these areas as well as others, such as scribal installations, may be a means to determine the value of specific tasks within the royal household. Such relational values between functional areas are of particular promise when attempting to understand the people working in the palace as opposed to a study of the architectural spaces as divorced from their users.

4.4.3.3 Value and Social Institutions

The use of energetics as a basis for discussing value is, at its most basic level, a very materialist approach, admittedly so (Abrams 1994, 7). However, on the basis of the data and analysis from such a materialist approach, a wider spectrum of questions can be asked, and the understanding gained through an analysis of energetics can aid in answering such questions. "By converting buildings into the energy and labor expended in their construction, a series of reconstructions concerning social power, labor organization, and economics can be generated" (Abrams 1994, xi).

There is a further consideration which can be made: to what extent does such architecture influence, perhaps only on an unconscious level, the patterns of the society in which it plays a role (Freitag 1992; Bradley 2000, 124; Lefebvre [1974] 1991; Bourdieu [1980] 2005)? For the technical aspects of construction do not only have a causal or practical relationship to the society in which they function, but also define one of the dimensions of that society (Castoriadis 1984; Delitz 2009, 75). As Mark Edmonds put it: "We need to understand how, under certain conditions, practical routines carried forward particular concepts of identity, community and authority" (Edmonds 1999, 9).

156 On wall decorations see Nunn 1988; Albenda 2005.

Such questions seek to embrace entire societies, and attempt to reach sweeping conclusions which are far removed from the archaeological record – a path where archaeology could easily loose touch with the material culture which is at the core of our discipline. And yet such studies are written, and perhaps archaeology can play a role in such a discussion precisely because of this focus on material, as a source for examples removed from the complexities of a highly stratified, industrial society.

"In Western thought, what is crucial is not the edifice of knowledge itself, but the will to architecture that is renewed with every crisis – a will that is nothing but an irrational choice to establish order and structure within a chaotic and manifold becoming, a will that is one choice among many" (Karatani 1995, 18). Karatani tries to link (in Western thought) the 'will to architecture' as a desire for a choice, any choice, when confronted with the chaos of change. The value in architecture for Karatani in this case is not inherent in the materiality, but is in the fact that the construction itself is both a sign and a means for creating stability. As archaeologists, one often links changes in stratigraphic horizons with moments of upheaval: thus one might try to understand the act of construction of a palace as a mechanism to overcome the chaos of change or upheaval.

"The house is a machine for living in."
- Le Corbusier[157]

5 The Construction of 3D Models: Methodological Aspects

This chapter deals with some of the methodological aspects of 3D models. The explanation and results of the application of this method to the AP Palace at Tell Mozan can be found in chapter 6, while a vademecum to the BlockGen plug-in as well as the program code can be found in the appendix, and the complete data used to complete the model can be found in the catalog.

5.1 The *UFO Problem*

3D modeling has become more and more sophisticated over the last two decades. The aim of this development has been primarily to increase the quality of the final model, both in terms of the number of polygons per surface as well as the resolution of the textures applied to these surfaces. This sophistication has as a necessary consequence that the creation of 3D models has become a complicated process, and requires special training.

Thus the common practice in archaeology is for a project director to get a professional firm or a team from a university technology department to come to the excavation and produce a model. Normally they come to the excavation for a few days or a week, collecting data; then they produce a very detailed model, using the latest software and/or hardware. The end-result of such a model, for the archaeologists, is often a collection of 2D JPEG images, and perhaps a film clip showing a walkthrough.

What value does this result have for the archaeological project? The primary value of this result is a didactic one, where the still images can be used as slides or printed out and shown at the site. An animated walkthrough can also be quite useful in a didactic setting, giving the possibility to

157 Corbusier 1970, 4.

demonstrate the impact of the reconstructed architecture on a visitor.

However, it is quite difficult for the archaeologist to interact with and adapt the 3D model itself; first, the hardware and software required can be quite expensive, and difficult to set up. While the 3D modeling team gives a copy of the model to the archaeologists, the software used is often quite expensive and runs only on high-end computer systems. The second hurdle for an archaeologist is that the software used is quite complex, and therefore opening, manipulating and exporting portions or new images of the model requires a big investment in time to learn to use the software.

Thus a good metaphor for this situation is that of a UFO 'visit': a team whose skills are nearly incomprehensible to the locals arrives, collects a lot of data and asks a lot of questions, then after few days departs, never to be heard from again, leaving a nearly magical[158] final product behind. How this product came to be is unclear to the locals, and its use is very limited vis-à-vis the functionality it would have in the hands of one of the 'aliens'.

This is of course a tongue-in-cheek analogy for what goes on, but it serves to highlight the problems: the lack of interaction between the modeling team and the archaeologists, and the lack of understanding as to how to manipulate the final product and use all of its potential within the archaeological process.

5.2 The Problem of Interaction: Archaeology and 3D Technology

This want of interaction is worth exploring more in depth, so as to better understand the solution that this study is proposing. Three main points of difference are responsible for this lack of interaction: accuracy, didactics and stratigraphy.

5.2.1 Accuracy

Computer scientists and model builders look primarily for accuracy in terms of verisimilitude in the model. This often leads to a great deal of energy invested in applying textures which most resemble the material present in the excavation. Accuracy for the archaeologist does not mean visible verisimilitude, but rather measurable precision. This means that the corners of walls, rabetting and floors must be represented as less than 90 degrees, jagged or uneven, if that is what is present in the archaeological record. All too often these uneven lines present in the excavation are often 'corrected' in a 3D model – the tops of walls, for example, which are almost always jagged, curved or

158 In the sense of Clarke's third law: "Any sufficiently advanced technology is indistinguishable from magic" (Clarke 1973, 21).

sloping, are represented as flat level surfaces, if not directly reconstructed to a 'standard' height. Concisely, the 3D modeler aims at 'visual' accuracy, while the archaeologist wants 'measurable' accuracy.

5.2.2 *Use of the Model*

The second difference in perspective between the 3D modeler and the archaeologist is the question of the use of the model. The 3D modeler often aims to represent the building as a reconstruction of what it probably looked like. The archaeologist, on the other hand, wants a model to show both the building as it was found and the specific context, either with other buildings or with the material found within the building, or might want to compare the perception of volumes between this and another building's 3D model. Thus, what the 3D modeler sees as a finished product in its 'singular perfection', the archaeologist sees as the central and original building block to which other data must be added. 3D as reconstruction is a case in point: the 3D modeler wants to know from the archaeologist 'how things were' to create a single final model, while the archaeologist is interested in using the model as a tool to see and compare different reconstruction possibilities, all of which are possible.

5.2.3 *The Fourth Dimension*

Finally, the 3D modeler sees a building with the eyes of an architect, looking at a frozen three dimensional object, executed as planned.[159] The archaeologist, however, looks at a building and sees a process of use over time, the growth of stratigraphy and the physical evidence in the building showing the changing functions of rooms and installations. The element of time can be very difficult to introduce into a model, in part because the programs used are not designed to include time as a dimension: the very definition of a CAD program is that it produces a single frozen model. One successful attempt was the 3D model of ancient Troy produced for the exhibit "TROIA – Traum und Wirklichkeit" which included a slider which allowed the user to change the model based on the chosen time period ("TROIA Traum und Wirklichkeit" 2015; "Troia VR" 2015). The project was, however, only possible through the intense collaboration between the archaeologists and the modelers.

159 Even Zevi's insistence on the four-dimensions of architecture do not really encompass what the archaeologist sees; Zevi's four-dimensions are limited to the experience of a visitor moving through a building over minutes or hours, and not the changes a building goes through over years (Zevi 1972, 47, 51).

5.3 The Need for 3D Models

In our exploration of 3D models it is important to consider their role in archaeology in a more general sense. 3D models are a part of a larger group of techniques which are used by archaeologists in their work, employed primarily in aspects of communication but also in the description of the material record.

3D models stem from the drawing tasks which were such a fundamental part of the documentation of field archaeology in its early years,[160] and which still plays a central role in the documentation carried out today. In fact, the technique in use in this study is based on a CAD program – CAD being an acronym for Computer Aided Design, and having been primarily created for architects.

There are many types of models in use today, just as there were (and to a more limited extent still are) many types of drawings used in the past. The need for different types of models arises from the different needs of the archaeologist and the different types and amounts of data available – these different models correspond then to different goals. Four general types of goals can be identified: Communication, Visual Interactivity, the Problematics of Reconstruction, and Volumetrics. These various goals behind 3D models are not mutually exclusive; on the contrary, they tend to reinforce one another, and some models try to include all of them.

5.3.1 *The 3D Model's Ancestor: Hand-drawn Illustrations*

The need for illustrations is as old as archaeology itself, arising from the need to communicate, in publications, the individual objects found, assemblages of objects, architecture, and stratigraphic relationships.[161] Doerpfeld's plan of Troy (Illustration 113) is a wonderful example of this, having been published in 1891 and showing overlapping phases of the settlement (Schliemann 1891, Taf. III). If it can be criticized, it is for the quantity of overlaying information and not the paucity of material presented.

Medri's book on archaeological illustrations has a very nice sequence of drawings of the 'domus of the mosaics' at Roselle, which show the diverse possibilities of archaeological draftsmanship from a plan showing each element of the construction materials to an orthographic view of the building.

The plan of Troy and the general plan of the Domus of the Mosaics are traditional parts of the archaeological record, and as such should not be replaced by 3D models, since they reflect a stratigraphic and a structural reality that a 3D model would have a hard time communicating.

160 See Liverani 2013, in particular pages 67-74.

161 For a seminal study on the communicative power of illustrations, see Tufte 1990; 1997.

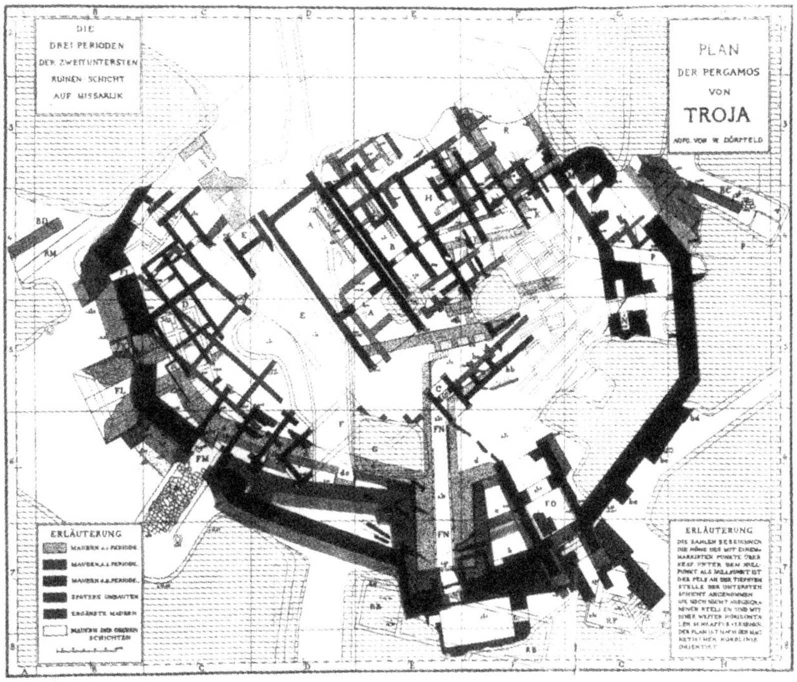

Illustration 113: Doerpfeld's illustration of Troy (Schliemann 1891, Taf. III).

The prospective drawing of the Domus, however, attempts to communicate the building as a volume through the use of recognizable shapes and shading. It is worth noting that a hand-drawn rendering of a building tends to communicate 'more with less' when compared to a digital 3D rendering: the artist chooses to emphasize (in darkness of the line or by increasing the relative size) certain elements which are more important, while a computerized 3D rendering uniformly (and thus more accurately) represents the model.

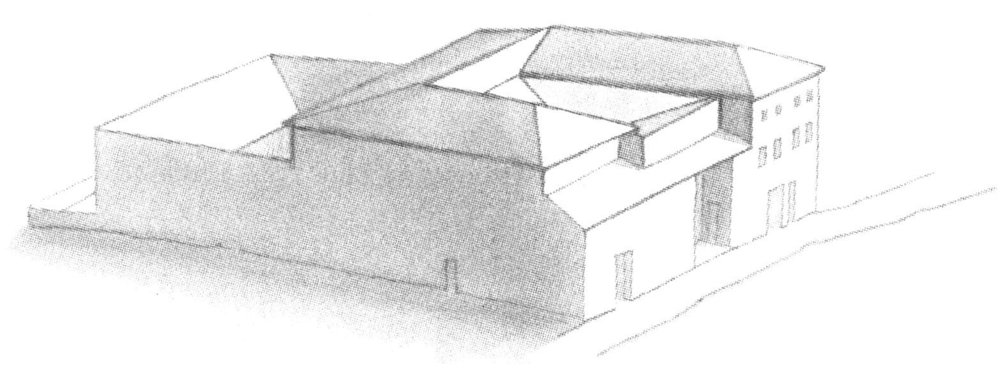

Illustration 114: Domus of the Mosaics, Roselle; prospective drawing (Medri 2003, 200).

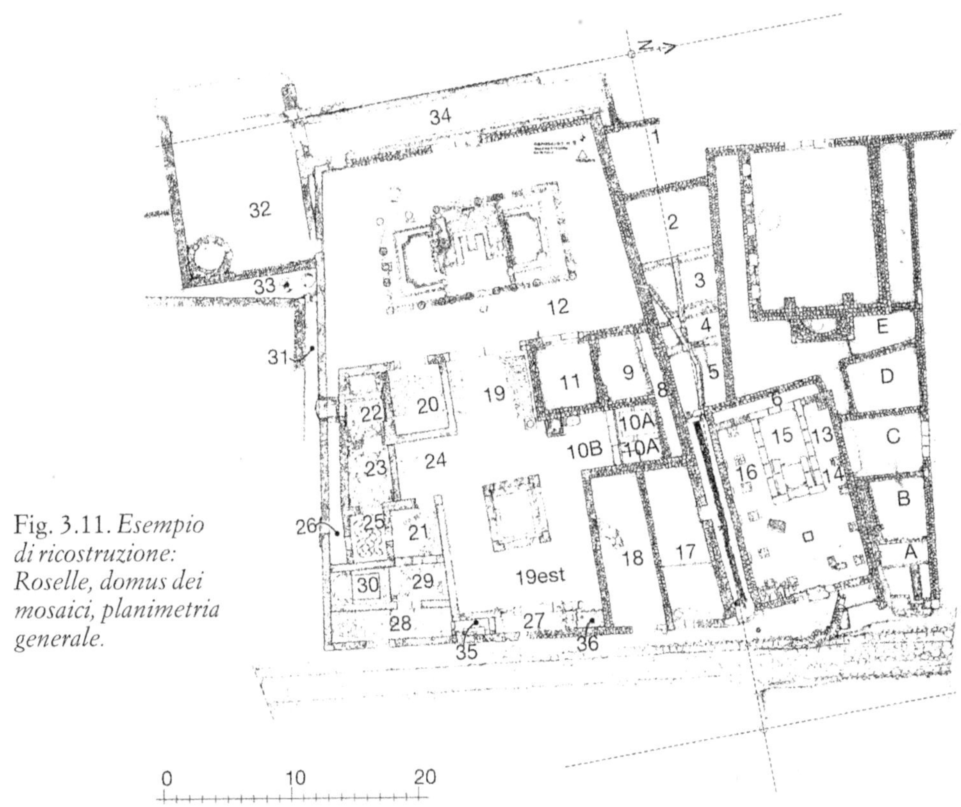

Illustration 115: Domus of the Mosaics, Roselle; general plan (Medri 2003, 194).

5.3.2 Goal for 3D Modeling: Communication

Communication is probably the most prevalent goal for 3D models, since the drawings, forerunners of 3D models, were primarily used in communication. What is being communicated can be placed in three general categories: the urban setting, monumentality and the 'daily life' of the buildings. Models which communicate the urban setting focus on putting the building in the context of a wider settlement, visualizing the place that a building occupies vis-à-vis other contemporary buildings. The 3D model aids in this visualization in that it includes the height of the various buildings as well as other built-up urban elements, such as the city wall. Such models can also be used for larger scale representations, such as the distribution of settlements within a region. On such a scale, the presence of the vertical dimension aids in communicating the relationship between these settlements and the landscape in which they are situated.

The second aspect of the goal of communication is that of monumentality. 3D Models excel at communicating the rather indefinable quality of monumentality. The proportions of the building, the visual impact from various points-of-view, the materials used, as well as the relationship between architectural and decorative elements all contribute to the monumentality of a building. Each of these can be described in text form, and individual representations can be illustrated in various ways, but the closest we can come to understanding the effect of a building on a viewer is through 3D models.

The third aspect of communication is the representation of the 'daily life' which would have played out in the building itself. Such representations almost always have the presence of human figures within the architecture, dressed in what we think the ancients would have worn and carrying out tasks we have identified from the archaeological record. Such representations give a sense of the proportions of the building, since it is filled with human figures which act as a scale, and it also gives a sense of the function of various sectors of the building or the surrounding areas.

5.3.3 Goal for 3D Modeling: Visual Interactivity

The second type of goal for 3D models is the possibility for visual interactivity. This goal has two aspects: the interaction of the various elements among themselves to create wider messages, and the experience of being within the building which such models can provide.

By constructing a model which includes various elements of the building, including architectural elements but in some cases also decorative elements, one can analyze how these elements were combined to communicate a message (Micale 2007). This message may be present in part in the individual elements, but is only complete when considered as a whole. The classic pre-digital example of this multi-element communication is the program on the orthostats present in Neo-Assyrian palaces. The images (and, to a limited extent, the texts) engraved on these stone slabs present a series of motives which are combined with their place within the architecture, which indicates both sequence and audience, but also their relationship to other orthostats.[162]

The second aspect of visual activity is the experience of being in the building, attempting to emulate, as much as possible, the effect that the building has on a visitor. Such studies can be problematic, since they postulate a similarity of experience for both the ancient and modern viewer. A further

162 See the forthcoming Ph.D. thesis of P. Serba (Goethe University, Frankfurt am Main) for an excellent example of a model exploring this aspect of communication. A seminal work in this area, but outside of Near Eastern archaeology, is the work of M. Forte on the Scrovegni chapel which uses G. Bateson's theories on cybernetics to create an 'ecology' in order to understand and communicate the wealth of information in the Scrovegni Chapel in Padua (Borra et al. 2003).

problem is that they are limited to the visual aspects of experience, excluding other senses; A. McMahon studied the palace at Khorsabad in a seminal study of architecture and sound (McMahon 2013). An approach such as this can be suggested by founding the argument of experience on the most basic conclusions of gestalt psychology; this approach has been explained more at length in another publication (F. Buccellati 2010). Another solution to this problem might be to embrace the discontinuity between ancient and modern visitor, attempting to negate the problem posed by this discontinuity by emphasizing the importance of the modern confrontation with the ancient remains, whether or not it had any overlap with what the ancients may or may not have experienced within the same environs. Such an alternative approach, however, may not further archaeology's goal of understanding the past but rather be rooted solely in the present, eschewing the hermeneutic potential which discovered elements of material culture represent.

5.3.4 Goal for 3D Modeling: Problematics of Reconstruction

The third goal in creating a 3D model is to approach questions which arise when creating a reconstruction of a building discovered in an archaeological context. What is found in the archaeological record is not a complete structure, but is a mere portion of the building; doors, windows, furniture, decoration, and roofing are just a part of what is partially or completely missing. In creating a 3D model questions relating to these missing elements arise, and as such the model becomes a heuristic vehicle for innovative research (Favro 2012). Questions regarding lighting sources (windows) and the presence of second stories must be posed and answered when building such a model.[163]

5.3.5 Goal for 3D Modeling: Volumetrics

The fourth and final goal in building a 3D model relates to volumetrics, whereby the volumes of both the constructed spaces and the open spaces can be quantified and analyzed. The first aspect, the consideration of the constructed spaces in the archaeological record, focuses on the construction materials present: the ability to measure, with great precision, the quantity of material that was incorporated into the building as a construction project. Such an analysis can be augmented when combined with a hypothetical reconstruction, which can be as simple as raising all the walls to a uniform height or as complicated as integrating missing portions of the building in either the horizontal or vertical dimensions.

163 A fundamental work regarding questions of lighting and second stories is J.C. Margueron's book on palaces (1982).

The second aspect of volumetrics is the analysis of the open spaces available in a building. One possible direction of research here would be the proportion of roofed vs. open spaces present in a building, which would lead to analyses of lighting or function of sectors. Such analyses are much more telling when based on the volume (thus expressed in m^3) rather than the floorplan (expressed in m^2) of the built environment. Another possibility would be to consider room sizes (in terms of m^2) in relation to the proportion of the wall length. Such a study would be of interest when considering room function, whereby many small square rooms might have been used for storage, long narrow rooms used as corridors, and long rooms open on the long side would have been used as working rooms due to the natural lighting available. This analysis has been done for the service sector of the AP Palace, see section 2.1.4.5.

5.3.6 Visualizing 3D in Three Dimensions

It is important to note that a digital 3D model is (almost) never visible in three dimensions. There are only two cases where a digital 3D model can be perceived in three dimensions: as a stereo image and as a 3D printed object.

It is possible to 'trick' the human brain into seeing a three-dimensional object by showing the two eyes two slightly different images. There are several techniques which have been used to achieve this effect, and the technology in this field is advancing so fast that a description of these techniques would be soon out-of-date. The general principle, however, is based on the parallax[164] between an object with volume and one's two eyes – since each eye sees a slightly different 2D image, the human brain can 'recreate' in the imagination the volume of the object in three dimensions.[165] Such stereo images have been around for much longer than digital 3D models or even computers: photography perfected this technique, and it has only been adapted for 3D models and the technological possibilities that computers have made available.

The second possibility for perceiving a 3D object in three dimensions is to have a digital model 'printed' as a physical object. The technical tools for printing 3D objects is new, and new tools, machines and success stories can be found almost weekly in the news. The ability to transform the virtual reality of a digital 3D model into physical reality gives one the chance to show a wide audience the architectural model, and will have wide reaching consequences,

164 Parallax is defined as the "difference or change in the apparent position or direction of an object as seen from two different points" ("Parallax" 2005).

165 This is, of course, oversimplified in the extreme, and does not take into account the philosophical and neurological aspects that this problem entails. A more detailed exploration of the problem would go beyond the scope of this study, however.

such as in relating context to museum visitors.

There is a 'hidden' third possibility for perceiving a 3D object, which is linked to the first, stereo photography. While stereo photography 'tricks' the brain by showing two different images to ones two eyes (parallax) there is the possibility to use a similar technique by showing a series of images (to both eyes) over a period of time. Or, more concisely, an animated video of the 3D model. In this way the brain has a series of images which it collects over time, and by comparing these images an object with volume can be imagined (F. Buccellati 1998).

5.3.7 The Power of 3D Models

One of the attractions of 3D models for archaeologists is that they communicate the essence of a building much more succinctly than a long text would: the saying 'a picture is worth a thousand words' is still very much at work in the digital age. Such models are, at the same time, quite a responsibility for the author, since 2D plans or 3D models are often the primary (if not the only) source used by others to compare buildings and to refute or defend more general theses on architectural development. What Maura Medri says regarding drawn reconstructions is just as true of 3D models: "... the more complex theme and the primary subject of a reconstructive drawing is architecture: to suggest the reconstruction of a building implies a precise scientific responsibility because this type of graphic image ends up gaining a kind of autonomous life, being distributed more than any other type of illustration; it almost includes its own accreditation, remaining fixed in the scientific and popular literature, without anyone trying to understand if it is correct, arbitrary or even well thought out – thus contributing to a theoretical framework and becoming a fixed point of comparison for other reconstructions" (Medri 2003, 186).[166]

At the moment, the most common procedure for producing a 3D model for an archaeological excavation is to get help from outside of the archaeological team, most likely from someone who is not even associated with archaeology. This lack of control over the final product is a real problem, and the methodology proposed here is, in part, an attempt to find a solution to this problem.

5.4 Current 3D Modeling Practices

An overview of current 3D models is useful as a measure for the 'state of the art' at the point in which this discussion is being written. However, since changes in hardware and software make each model 'dated' within just a few

166 Translation mine.

years, a comprehensive overview of the models currently in use would be of very limited use to most readers. The overview presented here will be limited to a discussion of four broad categories: extrude models, complex models, photo-generated models and 3D scans.

5.4.1 *Extrude 3D from 2D*

The simplest method for producing a 3D model is to begin with a 2D outline of the walls present in a building, and to extrude these outlines in the third dimension, so as to create a volume of each wall.

This method produces the fastest results, since one can easily digitize existing ground-plans, if the data is not already available within a 2D coordinate system. The extrude tool is by now ubiquitous in CAD and 3D-creation programs, and is quite easy to use. This method is also of great use when attempting to create 3D models from published plans, without access to the actual excavation.

The disadvantages of an extruded model are the fact that the model's third dimension is really a rough estimate: the bottom of the walls are normally fixed at a single elevation, and the extruded walls are almost always raised to an even height. Thus the addition of the third dimension is meant to give volume to the walls, but almost never reflects the volumes of the walls as discovered in the archaeological record.

5.4.2 *Complex Models*

Complex models, on the other hand, are much more difficult to produce, and require special training if not a dedicated technician. Often, these models are produced with a specific viewing-technology in mind, and the model is constructed on the basis of the possibilities of this hardware.[167] Such models are most often created directly in a modeling program, using the programming complexities that the individual program provides in order to make a model with a high level of detail. Some of the programs currently in use are AutoCAD Architecture, 3D Max, Blender or Maya.

The disadvantage of such a model is that the complexity requires someone on staff (typically not an archaeologist) who is able to create and manipulate such models, and that they are very difficult to alter or adapt to a changing understanding of the building being modeled.

5.4.3 *Photo-modeling*

Photo modeling is the use of a large number of 2D digital photographs

167 For examples see G. Lock's book on the use of computers in archaeology (Lock 2003, 152–53).

and a rendering program which is able to extrapolate the geometry of an object by the differences between the different photos. This technology has developed a great deal over the last ten years; one example is the off-site rendering server at the University of Leuven (http://www.arc3d.be/ last accessed December 2016). This technology has been developed for and used primarily with movable objects, and in only a few cases has architecture been modeled.[168] Recently, attempts have been made to use the same technology with video (as opposed to still images), but these programs are still in developmental stages (two such projects are ProFORMA and 3-Sweep). The main disadvantage is accuracy, especially with architecture: the models produced seldom reflect the right-angle geometry of architecture, producing often rounded edges or concave/convex wall faces.

5.4.4 3D Scans

The last category of 3D models are those based on 3D scanning technology. This technique uses a 3D scanner, which measures the geometry of an object directly; there are many technologies available, employing lasers and/or digital images, and new technologies are being developed and refined constantly.

The disadvantages are two: the 3D scanning machine itself is so expensive that it is difficult for one team to have access to it over a longer period of time, and the data produced by such a machine (point-clouds) are so complex that many hours are needed in refining the data before a usable model is produced.

5.5 Embracing Simplicity: BlockGen

In part because of the disadvantages outlined above, for the present analysis of the AP Palace at Tell Mozan a new modeling technique was developed. This technique is based on a plug-in[169] for AutoCAD[170] called BlockGen, which was developed solely for this model, and which will be made available as an open-source download.[171] The key point is that what is being proposed is not a way of creating a model to 'look at' extrinsically but

168 One such project was carried out at Mozan, see F. Buccellati, Dell'Unto, and Forte 2005.

169 A plug-in is a program which cannot function by itself, but depends on and augments another program.

170 By *AutoCAD* the specific program produced by Autodesk is meant – the general term for these types of programs is CAD software. CAD is an abbreviation for Computer Aided Design.

171 For download links to the latest version of the DLL, see the publisher's website (www.undena.com) or the pages dedicated to the AP Palace on the Mozan / Urkesh Project website (www.urkesh.com). A GitHub project page is also in development.

instead a model which is a real tool for archaeological research in the field.

5.5.1 *Desiderata*

In order to clarify the need for a new technique, it may be of use to explain the desiderata from the perspective of an archaeologist - desiderata which could not be filled by the techniques outlined above. The following seven desiderata cover,[172] on a general level, what a field project needs from a 3D model, and for each point the advantage of the BlockGen plug-in is briefly discussed. As the explanation of the BlockGen plug-in develops over this chapter, how this tool specifically responds to these desiderata will become apparent.

5.5.1.1 *Precision in Reflecting the Actual Archaeological Record*

The 3D model must reflect the actual archaeological record – the structure as found. This means that each XYZ coordinate must be set independently, in order to allow the modeler to construct any linear shape. BlockGen allows for series of points to be entered with little constraint as to the variation from point to point, each of which are defined by their independent XYZ coordinates.

5.5.1.2 *Use, As much as Possible, Data Already Collected in the Field*

In order to minimize the time needed in the field to collect data, and in order to favor the interface with the excavation strategy as it develops, it is important to use the data which is already being collected during the normal course of excavations. Thus an excavation which measures the wall corners in a single local grid system, and measures the elevations of wall-tops and floor levels, already has almost all of the data needed to create a model with the BlockGen plug-in.

5.5.1.3 *Have the Results Available in a Lasting Format*

To insure the durability of the data, it is important that what is collected in the field be conserved in a format which will be legible and useful to archaeologists and modelers long after the programs we use today have gone out of use. The script files which give BlockGen the data are ASCII-based files, which are the most standard text file format available.

5.5.1.4 *Allow for the Integration of Stratigraphy as well as Architecture*

The model produced should not be limited to the building of architecture, but should also allow for the possibility that the user would want

172 On these *desiderata* see also F. Buccellati 2015.

to reflect stratigraphic relationships. BlockGen creates volumes, which can define architectural elements but can also define stratigraphic volumes just as well.

5.5.1.5 *Allow for the Inclusion of Objects*

The model should allow for the inclusion of objects as well as stratigraphic elements, so that studies such as distribution analyses can be carried out hand-in-hand with a model which reflects the architectural/stratigraphic situation. Since BlockGen is an AutoCAD plug-in, the many features of AutoCAD are available for the inclusion of objects, and can interact with the solids created using BlockGen.

5.5.1.6 *Allow for Change and Expansion of the Data*

The model should be easily manipulated, allowing for incremental growth in the model as the understanding of the archaeological record changes or is added to in further excavations. BlockGen's script files can be easily modified, and the running of the individual scripts is simple enough that the whole model can be re-created on the basis of modified data within minutes – such a rebuild of the model of the AP Palace takes approximately 5 min, and is a very complex model.

5.5.1.7 *Allow for the Inclusion of the Model in Other Programs*

Finally, the model should be available in a format which can be imported into other programs. While the model can be manipulated in a variety of ways within standard CAD programs, no program can do everything. GIS, animation and interaction are three areas where the use of the generated 3D model could be used to understand and communicate the archaeological record (see also 5.6.2 below).

5.5.2 Data Collecting in the Field: Planning and Methods

As discussed in the first two points of the desiderata, both precision and the use of data already collected in the field (5.5.1.1 and 5.5.1.2) are important when planning to create a 3D model. Three methods can be used to achieve a high enough accuracy without taking too much extra time for data collection in the field. There may be other methods, but these three have been used in the field in the past, and the data collected are sufficiently accurate for a 3D model using the BlockGen plug-in.

5.5.2.1 *Method 1: Surveying*

The first method is to survey each corner of each wall (or volume) as a

XYZ coordinate, and additionally measure variations in the Z coordinate to determine wall height and different construction materials if present. These coordinates are often taken in any case by a surveyor using an EDM or a Total Station in order to produce plans of the excavation areas, and in such cases the only additional data needed for the 3D model is the taking of multiple Z coordinates, which however can also be done after the surveying using an elevation rod and a level.

These coordinates can also be taken with a very accurate GPS system (such as dGPS) but the accuracy is almost always too low to create an accurate model. This is especially true for the Z dimension – GPS devices have much lower accuracy in the vertical dimension than is true for the XY plane.

5.5.2.2 *Method 2: Photogrammetry and Elevation Measurements*

The second method is the use of photogrammetry supplemented by elevation measurements. The most likely scenario here would be the availability of a sequence of kite photographs augmented by a series of elevations from plans or taken with a level.

The kite photographs cannot be used directly, but need to be orthorectified in order to compensate for the distortion of the camera lens. Also, if there are large jumps in elevation within the photographed area, the rectified images will remain distorted, and diminish the accuracy of the model. These orthorectified images provide the X and Y coordinates for the model, to which the elevations taken provide the Z coordinate.

5.5.2.3 *Method 3: Extrapolation from Publications*

The final method is the extrapolation from publications, which can be extremely useful for creating models for buildings which are no longer accessible. Most publications include a detailed plan, from which the X and Y coordinates can be derived. The elevations are more problematic – if they are present on the plan or in the documentation, then they can be adapted for use with the BlockGen plug-in. If, however, only a few elevations are given, then the best method may be to create an extrude model, which is faster albeit with very limited accuracy in the Z dimension.

5.5.3 *Using Scripts*

BlockGen is a Plug-in for AutoCAD, and is primarily used within script files. The practical use of scripts and BlockGen will be discussed in the appendix dealing with the technical aspects of this program, but the use of AutoCAD and the creation of BlockGen as a plug-in is not casual, and bears discussion.

AutoCAD[173] is a program with a multitude of functions, and is in use in many archaeological field and documentation projects. Unfortunately the program does not provide a function to define each corner of a volume, but only four of eight (with a simple box). This allows for the creation of extrude models (see 5.4.1), but does not give the accuracy or flexibility desired (see 5.2.1 and 5.5.1.1).

Thus the use of a plug-in allows one to continue to use the functionality of AutoCAD, alleviates the need to learn a new program for those projects where AutoCAD is already in use, but adds the ability to define a solid by defining XYZ coordinates for each corner.

While the plug-in can be used directly through the AutoCAD interface, it is primarily of use in script files. Script files are lists of commands in a simple ASCII text file; ASCII is perhaps the most long-lived file format in existence, which ensures the durability of the data (see 5.5.1.3). By using script files, one can write and change the file, and then run the file as many times as desired in AutoCAD. Thus the coordinates for a wall can be entered once or copied from another source (surveyor's logs, for example), and the script generating the wall can be run in AutoCAD as many times as needed, for example when the model changes or an error is detected in the coordinates.

These script files are not limited to BlockGen commands, since the script files are a standard part of AutoCAD itself, and they merely call on BlockGen as any other AutoCAD command. This allows for the generation of very detailed models: different sectors or materials can be placed on different layers, colors can be employed to discern elements, and the gamut of AutoCAD functionality can be used to define and display the model.

5.6 Beyond the Architectural Model: Software

Once the scripts have been run and the model generated, the model as derived from the coordinates is complete, but further work may be done to improve the model, and the functions of AutoCAD or other programs may be used as tools for analysis (the transportability of the model into other programs is one of the *desiderata* mentioned above; see 5.5.1.7). This section focuses on using the model in AutoCAD and other software environments, while the next section considers conceptual areas of expansion.

173 AutoCAD 2012 was used for this study. BlockGen should work with AutoCAD versions after 2010, but does not work with any of the 'lite' versions of the software because of limited 3D functionality.

5.6.1 AutoCAD

5.6.1.1 Adding to the Model

In order to better reflect the archaeological record, one may want to add some elements to the model which cannot be created with the BlockGen plug-in. Examples of this may be curved walls, installations, pits or pathways. Additionally, one might want to add textures to some of the architectural elements, to better reflect the materials from which they are constructed.

Elements with curves are not possible with the BlockGen program, but AutoCAD provides several tools with which to create arcs and circles. These can be placed in a script file as the BlockGen commands are, or they can be created directly in AutoCAD and then inserted into the finished model. The advantage with a script file is the durability of the data and the ease with which it can be changed, but for complicated elements the creation directly in AutoCAD is often the only possibility.

Additionally, one may want to apply textures in order to make certain architectural elements or groups of elements appear more similar to the material from which they were made. There are three possibilities, with varying degrees of complexity: color, pattern and image.

The application of a color to a volume or a set of volumes is quite easy, so that one can apply a light tan color to a set of walls which were constructed in limestone. This can be done at the level of a layer, and as such can be a part of the script files containing the BlockGen commands.

To apply a specific texture to a volume takes more time, but the pattern can be chosen to reflect the material – an example might be a brick pattern for a mudbrick wall. This would not reflect the actual brick pattern as found in the archaeological record, but the appearance would reflect that material.

Finally, an actual image of the archaeological record can be applied to a specific volume, and can be placed in such a way as to reflect exactly what is present. This requires considerably more time, as well as quite a bit of experience in AutoCAD, but the results combine the volumes as well as the visible portions of the material used in the construction, which can be a very valuable tool.

5.6.1.2 Using the Model

AutoCAD contains a series of functions with which one can measure and manipulate the 3D model produced with the BlockGen plug-in. The availability of such functions is one of the advantages of using a plug-in for a pre-existing program. Two of these commands are of particular use as a tool for archaeologists: the functions for measuring and the ability to render the model.

With the precision available in the model as produced through the BlockGen plug-in, measurements in the model give an accurate count of distance, area and volume within the construction elements and the open spaces within the structure being examined. Each of these functions can be employed in a myriad of ways to better understand the structure and the ancients' use – here only one example of each is given, in order to give a sense of the use of these tools.

The measurement of distance can give an accurate measure of the distance traversed by a person when going from the entrance of a sector to a specific room. This can then be compared to the distance traversed to reach other rooms, or this path can be compared to the direct distance ('as the crow flies') between these two rooms. This helps quantify the ease of access within specific sectors of a building.

The measurement of area can also be a tool for research, for example in determining the area of roofed rooms vs. courtyards in a building, or the proportion between perimeter and area for all the rooms in a building as a way to examine room typologies (corridor, room, courtyard). For a more detailed explanation and the application of this method to the AP Palace, see chapter 2.

Finally, the measurement of volume is a powerful tool for research, in particular when combined with the ethnographic data, represented as algorithms, as detailed in chapter 3. A precise quantification of the amount of stone, mudbrick and wooden beams used in a specific structure in combination with an understanding of the energy (manpower) and skills needed allows for a detailed analysis of the 'cost' (in terms of energy and resources) of a structure. For an application of ethnographic data ('algorithms') to the AP Palace, see chapter 3. Additionally, the choices made in terms of material, size and location are all conditioned by the availability of resources and energy, and are thus, for certain types of buildings in certain cultural milieus, an expression of prestige and/or power.

The second function of AutoCAD that can be used as a tool with a 3D model derived from archaeological data is the ability to 'render' a certain viewpoint. This entails creating a high-quality 2D image of one specific view of the model. This tool is often tied to the communication aspect of 3D models, but a case can also be made for its use a tool for research. These rendered images give the archaeologist the ability to 'see' through the eyes of the ancients in a way that is not possible on the archaeological excavation. One example is an analysis of the line-of-sight within the building itself, as with the two control rooms in the AP Palace (see chapter 2). Another example is to analyze the relationship between the structure and the landscape or urban setting: the areas which someone in (or on the roof of) the structure and the area in which the structure can be seen (F. Buccellati 2010). Such an analysis of the viewshed of a building can aid in the analysis of control areas and prestige.

5.6.1.3 *Exporting to other Programs*

Since AutoCAD is a common program, the file formats that can be produced are often readable by other programs, in either DWG or DXF formats.[174] The readability of the files is an important consideration, since, as the next sections show, additional programs provide a series of functions which are not currently available in AutoCAD.

5.6.2 *GIS Programs*

In addition to working with the 3D model in AutoCAD, the model can be included in a GIS program. GIS stands for Graphic Information System, and is primarily used for site topography and landscape studies.[175] The ability to link databases to graphic portions of the data allows the user to display and query a wide variety of information.

5.6.2.1 *Integrating the 3D Model with Other Data Sources*

The power of GIS is the ability to include a wide variety of data sources in the same visual space. These vary from the 3D models discussed in this study, to topographic models, satellite or kite imagery, or the findspots of objects.

The 3D models presented in this study can be inserted into a GIS framework as a layer, and the various elements can be analyzed as blocks or in relation to the other data layers included in the GIS framework. A similar type of data are topographic models, derived from GPS data, a survey or DTM[176] data.

Raster images such as TIFF or JPG can also be added, so that the imagery from satellites or overhead photos can also be added. Satellite images are particularly useful when comparing landscape features over time or in various seasons.[177] Overhead images, such as those taken with a kite, balloon or airplane, are also of great use within a GIS framework. Consider that these

174 These two file formats are quite common, and have been constantly in use by AutoDesk, the makers of AutoCAD and 3D Studio Max, and the current owners of Maya.

175 For more on using GIS see M. Forte's book on GIS in archaeology (2002) and the volume edited by Okabe on GIS and Digital Humanities (2006).

176 DTM stands for Digital Terrain Model, and is the format commonly used for the graphic representation of three dimensional data as measured from satellites or LIDAR.

177 For an interesting comparison of various CORONA images, see Ur 2013a; 2013b.

images need to be orthorectified in order to 'fit' into the coordinate system of the GIS (the problem of orthorectification was discussed in section 5.5.2.2 above).

Clusters of points can also be added, together with links to an external database. This is particularly useful when including objects in the GIS, in order to analyze the distribution of a class of objects within a building, for example. Here the 3D model and the positions of the objects in three dimensions can interact, so that one can see the position of each object and refer to it specifically through the linked database.

The disadvantage of a GIS system is, in fact, that it is limited to representations in 'visible' space. While the comparison of such data is of great use, no narrative or argument can be communicated or even constructed in a GIS platform – it can only serve to show spatial relationships between these diverse data sets. Any argument or narrative needs be built outside of the GIS, and can only refer to the information gleaned from the GIS as a 'snapshot' of these graphical representations. As such, it is an excellent analytic tool, and has a great potential as a heuristic device, but it is intrinsically incapable of a synthetic or narrative approach.

5.6.3 Animation Programs

Animation programs are a further type of software with which the archaeologist can manipulate the model to include specific lighting, and to design camera paths through the building, to re-produce specific images with specific camera settings, or to insert figures or rendered objects. While some of these functions are also available in AutoCAD, external programs such as 3D Studio Max, Maya or Blender tend to accomplish these tasks much better.

5.6.3.1 Specific Lighting

Animation programs often allow the user to insert specific lighting, particularly the sun position for a specific date at a specific point in the world. This can be very useful for research aimed at determining the position of shadows at certain times of year (eg. summer/winter solstice) or the amount of light that would fall into a room during summer or winter (eg. The light from an iwan that carries into the neighboring rooms). The presence or absence of windows, either in the walls or along the roof-line, would also affect lighting conditions within the rooms (Butterlin 2006; Micale 2005, 2007).

5.6.3.2 Walkthrough

An animated walkthrough of the 3D model allows the viewer to perceive the model as a three-dimensional object through motion (F.

Buccellati 1998) (see also 5.3.6). This can be an aid to research designed to convey the differences between haptic and ocular space (see chapter 2). Such images can help visualize the differences in perception between large rooms, such as the stone courtyard in the AP Palace) – where a wide area can be seen but there is little room for haptic interaction with stored objects – and a small room, such as the rooms in the service wing – where one cannot see much farther than the storage space one can interact with.

5.6.3.3 *Reproduce Camera Images*

Animation programs can also reproduce the exact camera lens, position and direction of a picture taken in the field (see also the discussion of viewpoint under 5.6.1.2 above). This can be of great use in visualizing the ancient structure's impact on the urban landscape as represented in the tell topography, such as the relationship between a public building and a plaza or city gate. It can also help in deciding excavation strategy, in that the reconstructed portions of the model can help determine the position of new excavation areas designed to prove or disprove that reconstruction hypothesis.

5.6.3.4 *Avatars and Activities*

Animation programs also contain complex tools used to create 'avatars' or virtual manikins. These human forms allow the viewer to have a sense of scale; for example, a series of doorways may be seen as particularly narrow or wide when a human form passes through them. These figures can also be involved in specific tasks, so that someone viewing the animation can 'experience' the function of some of the rooms on the basis of simulated activities.

5.6.4 *First-Person Interactive Environments*

Lastly, and most complicated on the level of programming, are first-person interactive environments. These programs provide a level of detail similar to those of the animation programs, but allow the user to interact with the model in real time, and potentially with other users within the virtual environment. This study is not the place for a more detailed description of the functionality of these programs, but their use in the communication as tied to the 3D model created should be mentioned. One specific program designed for (Egyptian) archaeology, Cave UT, is a good example of the use of a 3D model within a First-Person Interactive Environment. Finally, 3D models can also be used in online environments, such as Google Earth and Second Life.

5.6.4.1 *Interaction as Communication*

While First-Person Interactive Environments were originally designed as games - *First Person Shooters* and, more recently, *Open World Environments* - their potential to allow a user to interact with a virtual environment, the ability to program trigger events and the addition of audio interaction between the program's users were seen as a potential tool for communication and teaching.

The interactivity of the program means that a user can wander through a model, deciding on their own the direction to travel. This is accomplished by using a standard mouse, or more specialized 3D user input devices. The user then actively explores the environment, as opposed to animation sequences, which are by nature passive explorations.

Additionally, these programs allow the programmer to trigger events, so that when a user enters a specific space an action is carried out. An example might be an explanatory audio file which can be 'triggered' when a user enters a specific room.

Finally, users interacting in the same environment can also communicate with each other over a shared audio channel. Thus an archaeologist or an educator can guide a group through a model, asking and answering questions along the way. Through this technology, none of these people need to be in the same room or even on the same continent for this tour to take place.

5.6.4.2 *Programming Example: Cave UT*

One example of the use of a 3D model within a first-person interactive environment is the project of J. Jakobson, called Cave UT.[178] While Cave UT is rather dated (updated last in 2005), it has the advantage of having a clear and relatively simple explanation of how to go about inserting a 3D model into a graphics engine. The program also explains how to link several computers and digital projectors in order to enhance the tri-dimensionality of the object, as well as use the software in dome environments.

5.6.4.3 *Online Environments*

Finally, the 3D model can be inserted into larger online environments, such as Google Earth or Second Life. Both of these environments allow users to interact with the model, but have the advantage that once set up, they are always available to the widest possible audience.

---

178 See http://www.publicvr.com and http://publicvr.org/ut/CaveUT.html (last accessed December 2016).

5.7 Beyond the Architectural Model: Concepts

The capabilities and results of computer applications are so sophisticated that they can, at times, obscure the research questions for which they are being employed. In such cases, the technique becomes an end in itself.[179] A goal of this study is to show, instead, how technique must remain tightly integrated with the substantive issues of the research in two major ways. On the one hand, the technique must be flexible enough not to pose demands on the original intent, while on the other hand there must be a clear subordination of technique to method. Furthermore, 3D graphic rendering has an unparalleled impact on the apprehension of the concrete reality of the spatial volumes present within an excavation, and this impact needs to be reviewed and assessed as well.

A close interrelationship of technique and method means that the tool (in our case, 3D representation) must not be a closed box that must be faced as a completed entity in itself. This point was discussed above, tongue in cheek, as 'the UFO problem': an Unidentified Flying Object is taken as a metaphor for an extrinsic point of reference, which takes in data, processes it in 'alien' thought processes, and returns a finished product. In the case of a 3D model, the final product is derived from the archaeological data, but the final product is generally seen as a packaged result, and the archaeologist typically no longer interacts with the original data with the aim of refining that result. That result, then, represents a frozen, static moment of research – however rich in detail this might be. In contrast with the UFO image, this study proposes a 3D tool that interacts dynamically with the definition of the research question itself as it unfolds, particularly as a result of the ever varying perspectives of the excavation (this aspect is dealt with especially in sections 5.7.1 and 5.7.2 below). The method is here, in the first place, the way in which volumetric correlations are perceived and projected, and the technique is the tool through which the representation actually takes form.

Secondly, one should not condition the analysis of the data on the basis of the requirements of the tool, but rather the tool should adapt to fit the question being asked. This ties in to the point just made, namely that the tool is not a closed box, but rather should be embedded within the research context. This tool represents a set of analytical components that together link, in a new way, the primary documentation with a system of meaning. The tool takes its starting point from data recorded in the field, and offers in the first place a check on their validity; it accommodates diverse and alternative interpretive proposals, rendered graphically in ways that reflect and assist the perception of

179 For more on the difference between 3D technology as the end or as the means for research, see F. Buccellati 2016.

the excavator (see section 5.7.3 below).

3D representations have a privileged status in communication, because they render spatial relationships not only statically (from a fixed point of view), but also dynamically (from any possible point of view, through a rotation of the image and varying distances). This has an important impact on how understanding is communicated. It works in the first place at the moment of the excavation and interpretation when individual excavators can express their understanding of the situation graphically. But it works also at the level of the communication on a larger scale, with regard to both the scholarly argument and a more didactic narrative. The general issue of communication is dealt with in section 5.7.4, and the specific aspect of interactivity in section 5.7.4.3 below.

5.7.1 Architecture and Stratigraphy

One of the key concepts, or moments of understanding, in field archaeology is that of deposition (G. Buccellati 2006). Deposition is the study of how things have come to be where they are (emplacement) in an excavation. Thus a series of similar sherds are found strewn on a compact surface (emplacement) and the conclusion is that a pot collapsed onto a floor and shattered (deposition). This is then followed by reconstruction, which is an understanding of the way things were in a fixed – 'ideal' – moment in time: the pot standing upright, perhaps on a stool or table. Finally, interpretation represents a perception of the possible meaning between systems of objects: the style of the pot indicates a certain cultural affinity, or its association with other objects in the room indicates a household environment.

While 3D graphics and the study of volumetrics is particularly focused on the 'reconstruction' moment, as an ideal recreation of the architecture, it is also inexorably tied to the other moments. Depositional analysis, then, is the study of the effect of time on the location of material culture, and how we can reverse the process through investigation in order to posit a different, perhaps more meaningful, order (reconstruction). Depositional analysis, then, is what leads from what one finds (emplacement) to the data from which the 3D model is generated: for what is found is not a palace, but rather collapsed walls made of unbaked mudbrick, lying on top of many layers of accumulation.[180] The investigation of these elements allows for an understanding of 'what happened' over time. First the palace was constructed, then there are levels of royal use, followed by levels of remodeling for a non royal occupation, abandonment and finally structural collapse.

180 One of the few examples of the modeling of stratigraphy is the *3D-Quader methode* used in the analysis of the Rotes Haus in Sheikh Hamad (Kreppner 2012).

A 3D model can go beyond the moment of reconstruction and can include layers of accumulation, rendering changes over time as well as help visualize and understand these steps, and through the distribution of movable objects within immovable constructions we can interpret how the deposits formed. Such depositional studies are already an integral part of the work of archaeology, of course – what is innovative is the application of 3D modeling to understand patterns in the vertical dimension, which might otherwise be lost in a study involving 2D slices of a 3D space.

5.7.2 The Movable and the Stationary

3D models represent stationary structures, composed of architectural elements. Here stratigraphy, deposition and interaction can be visualized in a three-dimensional space as opposed to overlapping or perpendicular two dimensional slices. However, such models can also be very useful in analyzing the distribution of the 'movable': the objects found within these structures. Here the spatial combination of architecture and categories of objects can help consider questions of function of either the rooms or the objects themselves.

Hand in hand with deposition we must understand the interaction of the elements discovered. This is not on a temporal basis, as with deposition, but rather investigates the meaning created by complexes of contemporary elements within the architectural context. This investigation lies at the core of the moment of interpretation: if the elements discovered form a significant whole, the understanding of this whole must transcend the collected meaning of each diverse element.[181]

Thus one can insert the findspots for groups of objects within the 3D model of the architecture, and in this way visualize the distribution of the selected group. Such a paring allows one to see the relationship between objects, the architectural context through the 3D model, the stratigraphic context (as discussed in 5.7.1) as well as other groups of objects.

Two particularly telling examples of the analysis of architecture and objects come to mind: the distribution of tablets in the Puzurum archive at Terqa (G. Buccellati 1984), and the distribution of slingballs in a building at Tell Hamoukar (Reichel 2002).

---

181 This statement contains quite a bit that could be discussed at great length, such as who defines the 'significance' of the whole, whether the 'understanding' is a reflection of the past or only of the present and the idea that the whole is greater than the sum of its parts in relation to cultural studies. However, such a discussion is beyond the scope of this study, and this section is meant only to elucidate the usefulness of 3D modeling in defining, pursuing and visualizing research questions.

5.7.3 Realtime Representation

In its most concrete aspect, a flexible 3D model like the one proposed here has an immediate impact on the process of excavation in that it proposes easily definable alternative scenarios that are to be tested through the excavation itself.[182] Typically the excavator, starting from the known situation in the ground, proposes a possible reality to be uncovered which the excavation is expected to bring to light. Thus, for example, a line in the ground is interpreted as the face of a wall, hence the area on one side of the line is treated as consisting of the brickwork that makes up the wall itself, while the material on the other side is treated as the accumulation that had built up against the face of the wall. The excavation proceeds therefore on the basis of the understanding the excavator has of what existing clues may indicate, and revises them as needed in the measure in which the excavation confirms or invalidates the initial assumption. This is the mental attitude that is brought to bear on the excavation process, and which is often left undeclared and undocumented: if indeed the situation turns out to be as assumed, the end result validates itself; otherwise the wrong assumption is superseded by another and work proceeds following the new hypothesis, discarding the old understanding.

A dynamic 3D model, i. e., one that can be produced and modified at will by excavators in the field, introduces a substantially different approach, in several important ways.

By virtue of its being three-dimensional, hence closer to the volumetric reality of the projection itself, it will project the assumed scenario in a form that can much more easily be assessed and evaluated. It will, in other words, project the concrete potential of the proposed reality in ways that can be perceived much more explicitly (the wall as a volume and the accumulation as a void that has been filled).

This proposed reality will be all the more 'realistic' as its three-dimensionality will show how it would link up with other volumes and spaces directly or potentially linked with the one that is emerging, known or projected on the basis of other data. The contextual consequences of the scenario proposed will be, in other words, much more readily visible, so that the potential risks of the proposal will be more apparent and be more easily subjected to a proper evaluation.

A 3D model of the type advocated here could include multiple proposals that present alternative scenarios, and thus can be clearly evaluated when selecting the excavation strategy to be pursued. As new elements are

182 Consider this impact in light of the discussion of the heuristic power of 3D models as discussed in section 4.4.2.

uncovered, a possible needed revision of the initial strategy can be more easily implemented by calibrating against each other the alternative scenarios that had already been proposed.

The record of the proposed alternative scenarios becomes an integral part of the record and thus enhances immeasurably the documentary aspect of the strategic choices made. In the absence of this or a similar method, the excavator's intuitive insight remains implicit and generally undocumented. The record of these alternatives is critical in archaeology because the stratigraphic evidence is uncovered through the excavation process, and the potential loss of information as a result of a given strategic choice ought to emerge from the record as much as the information that has in fact been gained and eventually recorded in its completed version. By including these choices the archaeologist also includes the reasons for rejecting alternative interpretations, which are also often left out of the documentation.

It appears, therefore, that a 3D model closely correlated with realtime excavation can add a whole new dimension to the strategic aspect of the process itself. In the excavation process the goals shift in the measure in which new clues become available, and the means must be revised accordingly, on the basis of potential new connections that are brought to light. Heuristics, then, means to project as many possible alternative configurations as seem reasonable, and to proceed with one while keeping clearly in mind the alternatives.[183]

5.7.4 3D in a Didactic Context

While the aim of the 3D modeling proposed in this study is not primarily didactic, it is important to consider how such models can be used to communicate the many facets of archaeology to various audiences. At times it seems that in archaeology the research itself and the communication to a broader audience are two separate worlds requiring separate ways of thinking – from the questions posed, to the graphics chosen, and even the tone of writing. To some extent this is understandable and necessary. But by divorcing these two aspects, one tends to build a barrier where the broader public would never read a scientific paper and an archaeologist seldom puts much effort into new vehicles of mass communication. By integrating aspects of communication, even in a secondary role, into the process of archaeological research in general and the 3D models used here in particular, the archaeologist can aim to demonstrate to contemporary audiences the value of their individual work as well as their discipline as a whole. In this way archaeological research can integrate, from its inception, this responsibility to

183 See also the discussion of heuristics in chapter 4.

communicate and impact the modern world, without shifting its primary focus away from the material culture of past civilizations.

5.7.4.1 Communication of Meaning: Presenting the Value of Archaeology

Since meaning is embedded in the spatial reality of the architecture we study, the communication of this meaning should be an integral part of our communication to our audiences. While 3D models should not be constructed merely as an illustrative tool, this aim can and should be one of the secondary goals of such a model. Precisely because such a model arises out of scholarship can it be a tool with which an archaeologist communicates the archaeological, historical and cultural understanding of his or her particular research – from within that research, as it were. The kinds of 3D models discussed in this study, constructed organically, as it were, within the research project, can and should have an impact which reaches wider audiences.

5.7.4.2 The Ethical Dimension of Communication

There is more and more interest among archaeologists to find new ways to present their results directly to a wider audience; a conference was recently held in Frankfurt on the social role of archaeology (Schuecker 2012) organized by the German Archaeological Institute (DAI-RGK), and several of the Research Training Groups (Graduiertenkolleg) funded by the German Research Council (DFG) have included elements designed to reach a wider audience.[184] The reasons for this are threefold: technology, interest and funding agencies. New technologies have made it possible for archaeologists to speak to wider audiences directly, without needing to rely on a larger media organization. Take for example the YouTube phenomenon, where scholarly work and lectures can be disseminated world-wide in minutes.[185] There has always been an interest in archaeology from a wider public, but this interest is more apparent today, perhaps because the technological advances mentioned previously help quantify that interest in terms of webpage hits, YouTube views and the like. Finally, funding agencies are beginning to request that such outreach programs be included in applications; these agencies are, for the most part, funded through taxes, and thus see as an obligation the promulgation of the results of funded research.[186]

184 The "Value and Equivalence" Group (Frankfurt a.M. and Darmstadt) and the "Early Monumentality and Social Differentiation" Group (Kiel) both have developed exhibits of their research results.

185 A good example of this is the Cotsen Institute of Archaeology's YouTube channel: http://tinyurl.com/l2jbjk4 (last accessed December 2016).

186 It is interesting that publishing is undergoing similar pressures, with technology making

There is a danger in communication, however. Technology in general and, in particular, 3D graphics are wonderful tools for reaching a larger audience, and to recreate the experience of being at a site, almost to the point of replacing an actual visit. While this is a wonderful development for communication and learning, it can also have the negative effect of alienating the local 'stakeholders' from their cultural heritage (Micale 2012). The danger is that technology allows for less research to be done at the actual site, since so much information can be collected and then studied elsewhere. In addition, while a wider audience may come to appreciate a site, they also have the sense of having been there, and might thus be less inclined to visit the site.

In fact, a part of this study was meant to include the installation of a poster and computer with the results of this study at the local museum in Hassake, Syria, where the finds from Tell Mozan are to be displayed. Unfortunately, the terrible upheaval taking place in Syria at the moment has put these plans on hold, but the hope of communicating the results of this study to local, national and international audiences remains.

5.7.4.3 Interactivity

While a film-clip is a passive way to visualize the model, there is also the possibility to insert the model into an interactive environment, so that the user is actively engaged with the space. These first-person interactive environments allow the user a totally different experience, and the software behind such environments offer a range of tools which can be used to engage the user. This aspect was mentioned already in section 5.6.4, but it is worth considering here because of the impact that this technology can have on learning. Current programs allow for users to 'move' within the virtual space, exploring the architecture and elements placed within it. Audio or movie segments can be tied to specific locations, so that, for example, a short video demonstrating an ethnoarchaeological experiment can be placed in a specific room. These tools allow the archaeologist to embed explanation within the spatial context of a building or excavation – and this modality of learning can be made available without the active participation of the archaeologist, but with the active involvement of the audience. Such a tool has great potential for communicating the results as well as the process of archaeology to a vast audience.

---

distribution nearly free, and funding agencies looking favorably on the use of such distribution networks. For an interesting series of papers on this subject, in a book which is itself an example of free online distribution, see Archaeology 2.0 (Kansa, Whitcher Kansa, and Watrall 2011).

"Many indices point to architecture as an appropriate paradigm for all human creation... Indeed on the phenomenological level space preexists other objects which will be situated in it [...] It shares with all industrial design the characteristic of usefulness, but it transcends this aspect not only by preexisting (by its primacy), but also through its stimulating and communicative nature. As sign it is unique too[...] It is more multisensory than cinematographic art; its reading is multilinear; and we are not likely to find any other sign system which in its morphology and syntax provides a better opportunity for a structural analysis than that composed from spaces." - G. Ankerl[187]

"Voll Verdienst, doch dichterisch,
wohnet der Mensch auf dieser Erde."
- from F. Hölderlin's "In lieblicher Bläue" [188]

6 Application to the Tupkish Palace at Urkesh

The last section of this study returns to the AP Palace of Mozan, this time examining the building through the 3D model. Chapter 3 looked at the elements of construction, culminating in an understanding of process as expressed in a sequence of linked *chaîne opératoire* and a series of algorithms which, hand in hand with the 3D model, allows one to calculate the energetic cost of the construction of the palace. In Chapter 5 the methodology used here was discussed and placed within the context of other 3D methods and software capabilities. Here these elements will be applied to the Tupkish Palace at Urkesh.

187 Ankerl 1981, 159.

188 This phrase from a poem of Friedrich Hölderlin was the inspiration for one of Heidegger's most influential essays on architecture: "Poetically man dwells..." Heidegger makes the point that technical ability is not enough to create a dwelling, but that the poetical nature of man is just as essential (Leach 1997, 109–19).

6.1 Exploring the 3D Model

As described in chapter 5 and in the appendix and catalog, the model of the AP Palace is built in several layers in order to separate the different construction materials as well as the portions of the building which are no longer in the archaeological record but can be reconstructed on the basis of indirect evidence. The layers present reflect the stone sub-walls, the mudbrick superstructure as well as the concomitant reconstructed portions of each. A further layer includes the installations present in the palace.

6.1.1 *The Data*

The data used for the model is presented in detail in the catalog at the end of this study, but how the data were collected and extrapolated should be discussed. The data collection was organized, supervised, checked and corrected by the author; a number of people assisted in this process, and this is the place to acknowledge their generous help and skill. The majority of the data were taken during a survey of the palace done by the author together with Barbara Pritzkat and Laura Ramos. Here the wall corners were measured using an EDM, and the X, Y and Z coordinates were measured. During the 2010 season, further measurements were taken together with Hans Barnard and Stefania Ermidoro within the framework of a graphic documentation project focused on the conservation of the AP Palace. Measurements and documentation were also carried out together with Elena Asero and Yasmine Mahmood. The photographic documentation was taken by the author and Diadin Mustafa. The coordinates taken in these various steps have an accuracy of between 2 cm and 8 cm, depending on the accessibility of the point and the way in which the measurement was taken.

The basis of the model is thus a very precise series of 3D solids representing the walls as found in the archaeological record, and divided by material (stone and brick). However, to be of use as a tool for calculating the volumetrics of the building, it is necessary to reconstruct the portions which were damaged or eroded. The reconstructed volumes are, by necessity, estimates; these estimates, however, are based on an understanding of the palace. The height of the reconstructed brick walls are based on the extant height of the brick walls in sector C, including the difference in elevation between sector C and sector H.

The coordinates which define the volumes used in the model can be found in the catalog at the end of this study, in the appendix.

6.1.2 *Layers: Stone*

The initial layer present in the model are the extant stone walls of the palace. Several walls are missing, particularly those in sector A, which had been mined in recent times (see chapter 2). In illustrations 116-118 one sees the extant stone walls with the addition of the reconstructed stone walls.

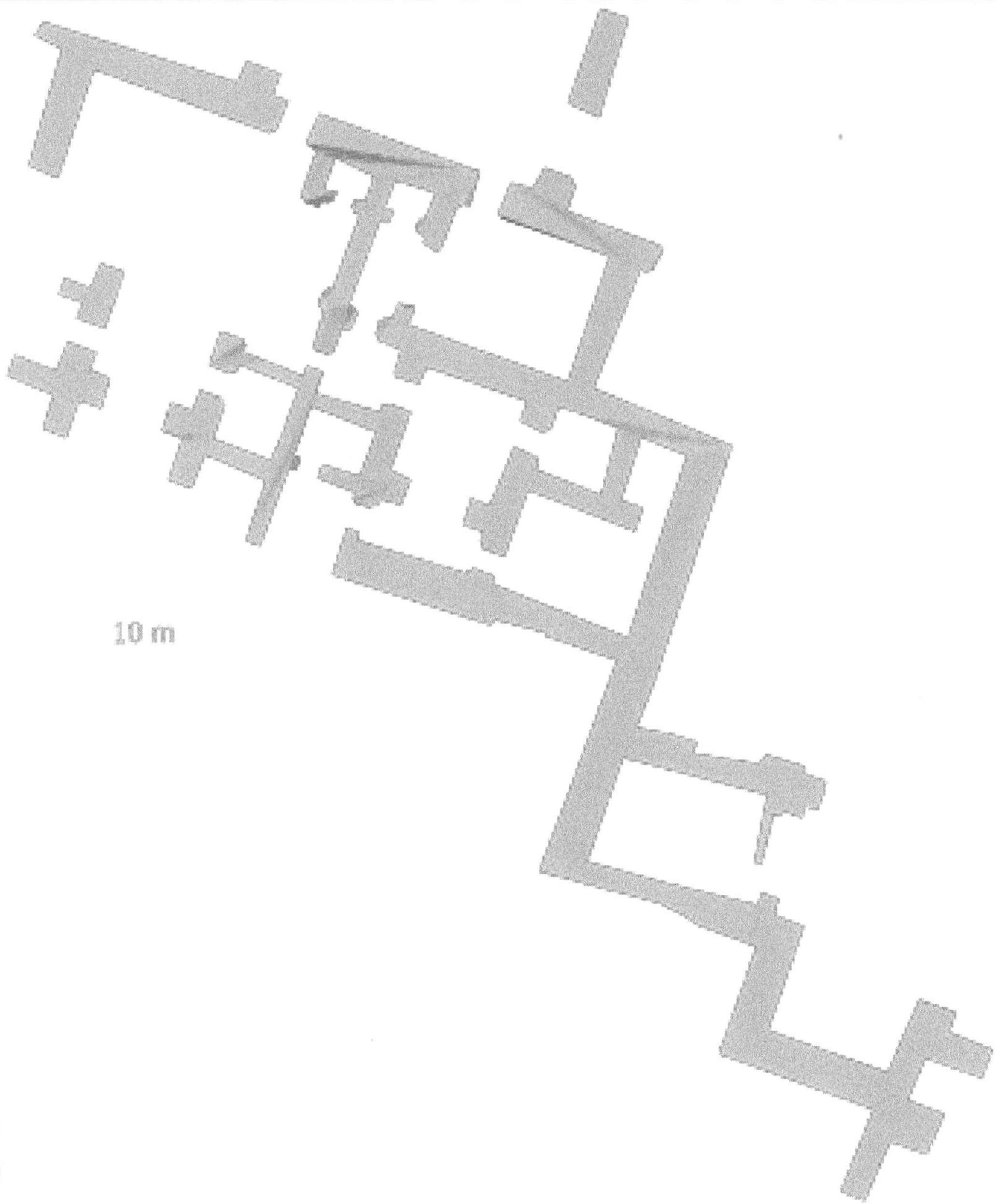

Illustration 116: 3D Model of AP Palace showing existing stone walls - overhead view.

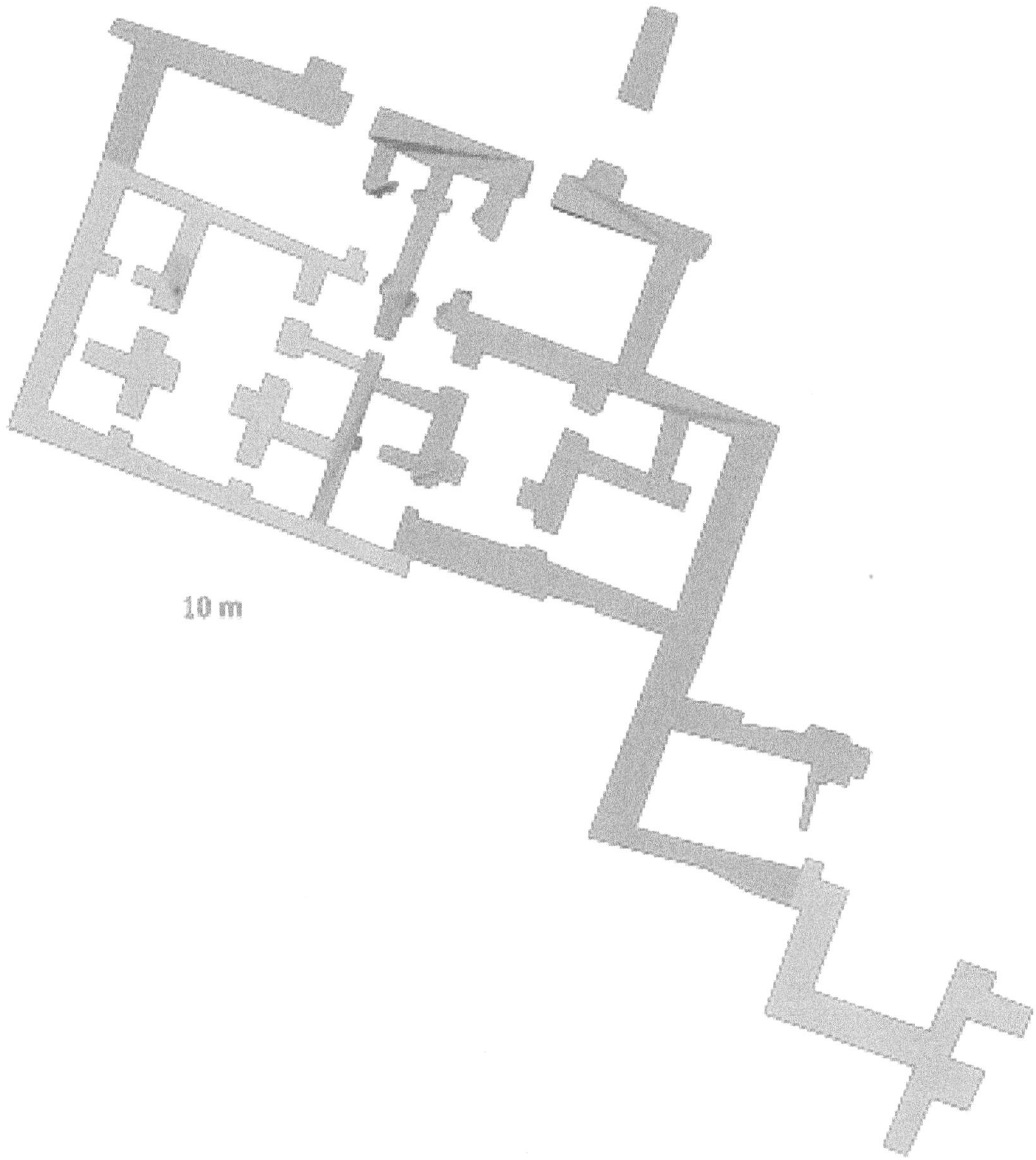

Illustration 117: 3D Model of AP Palace showing existing and reconstructed stone walls - overhead view.

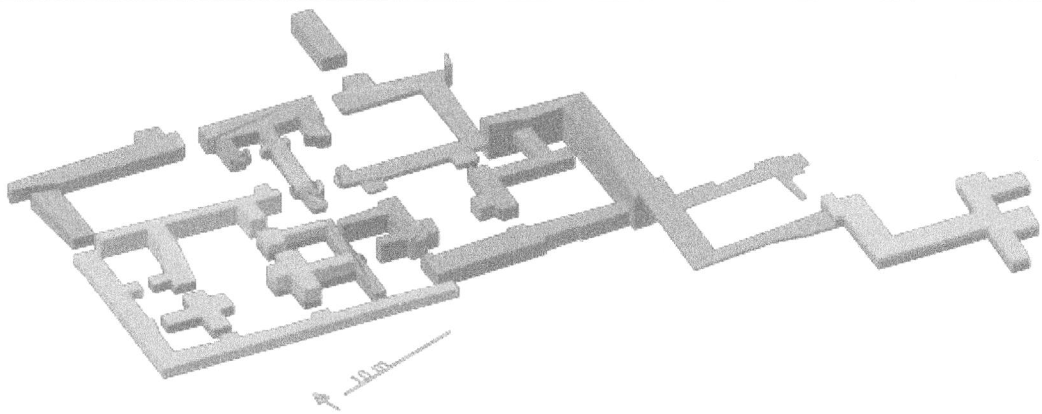

Illustration 118: 3D Model of AP Palace showing existing and reconstructed stone walls - view to NE.

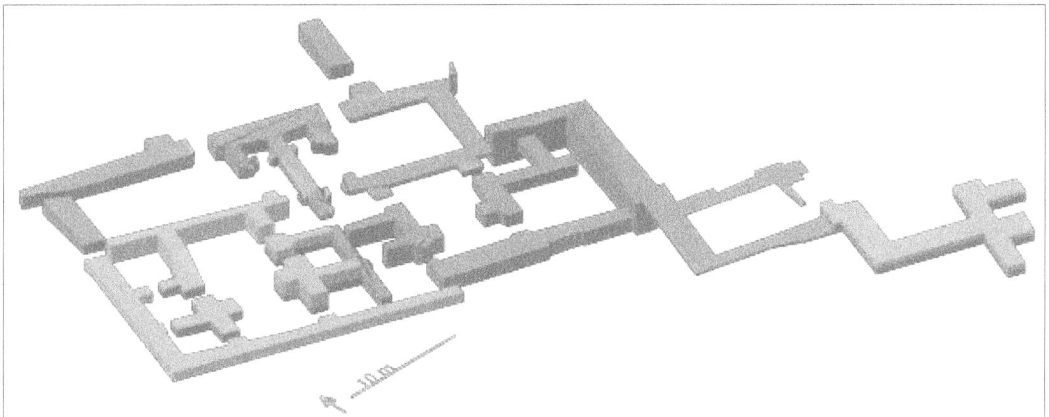

Illustration 119: 3D Model of AP Palace showing existing and reconstructed stone walls - overhead view.

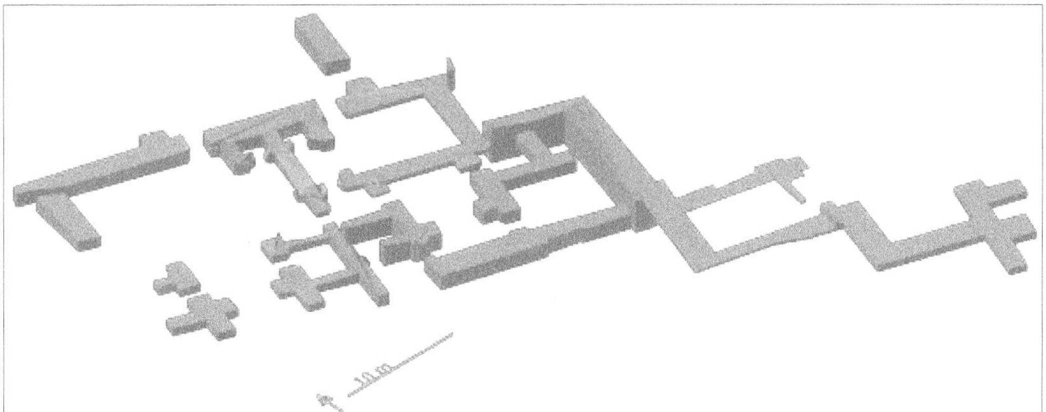

Illustration 120: 3D Model of AP Palace showing existing stone walls - view to NE.

6.1.3 Layers: Brick

The second layer represents the mudbrick present in the archaeological record, as well as the reconstructed mudbrick portions of the walls.

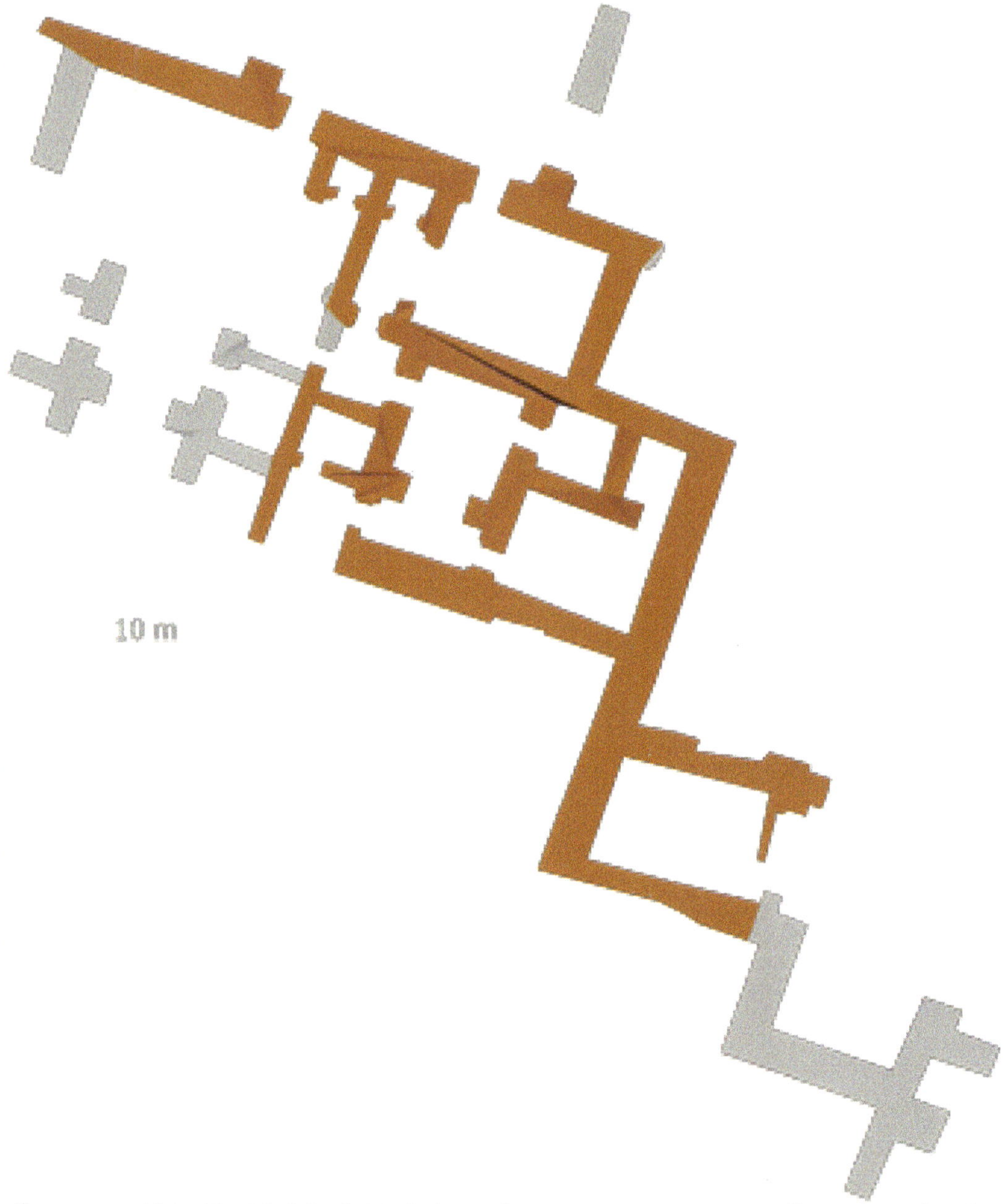

Illustration 121: 3D Model of AP Palace showing existing stone walls and mudbrick - overhead view.

The reconstructed mudbrick portions of the walls represent the walls as raised to the presumed height of the roof. The elevation of the roof in the service wing is estimated to be 2.9 m above the floor level. This is based on the elevation of the extant walls in sector C, particularly the walls in C1, C4 and C8. The reconstructed roof level in the formal wing is estimated 2 m higher than the level in the service wing due to the 2 m high difference between the floor level of the two wings.

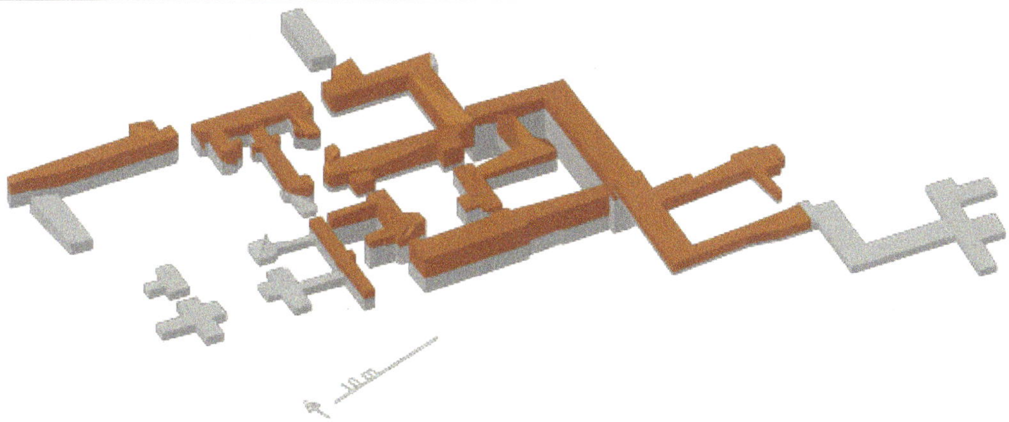

Illustration 122: 3D Model of AP Palace showing existing stone walls and mudbrick - view to NE.

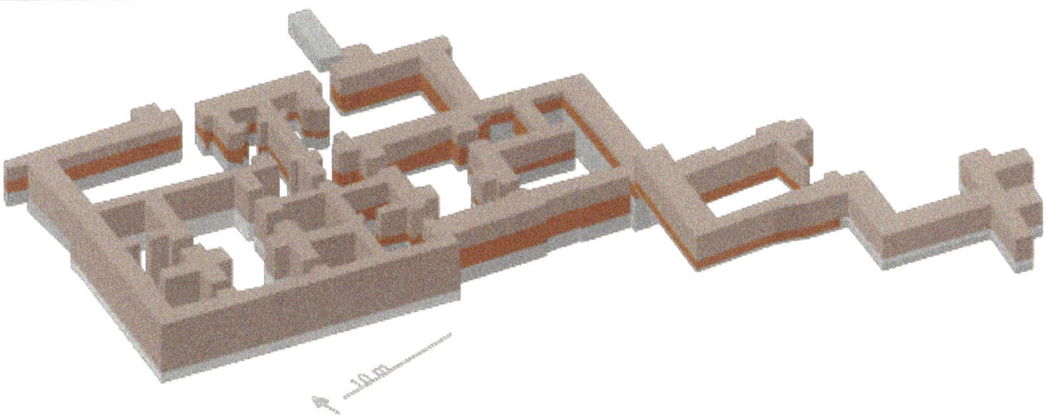

Illustration 123: 3D Model of AP Palace showing existing as well as reconstructed stone walls and mudbrick - view to NE.

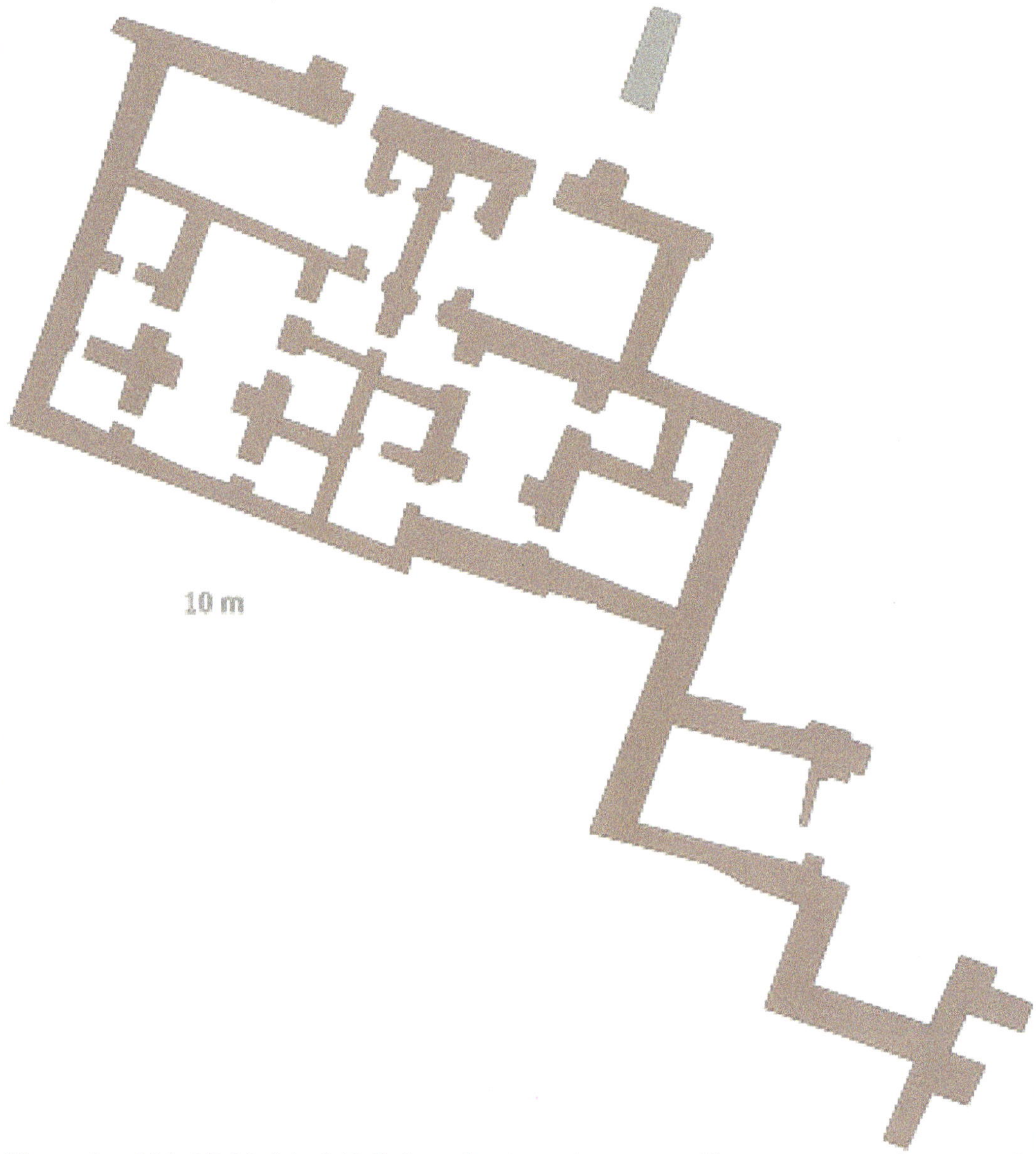

Illustration 124: 3D Model of AP Palace showing existing as well as reconstructed stone walls and mudbrick - overhead view.

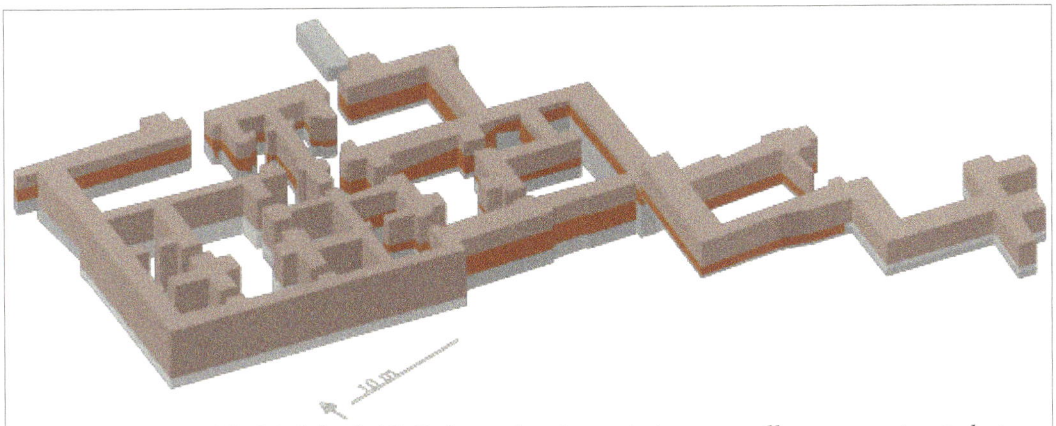

Illustration 125: 3D Model of AP Palace showing existing as well as reconstructed stone walls and mudbrick - view to NE.

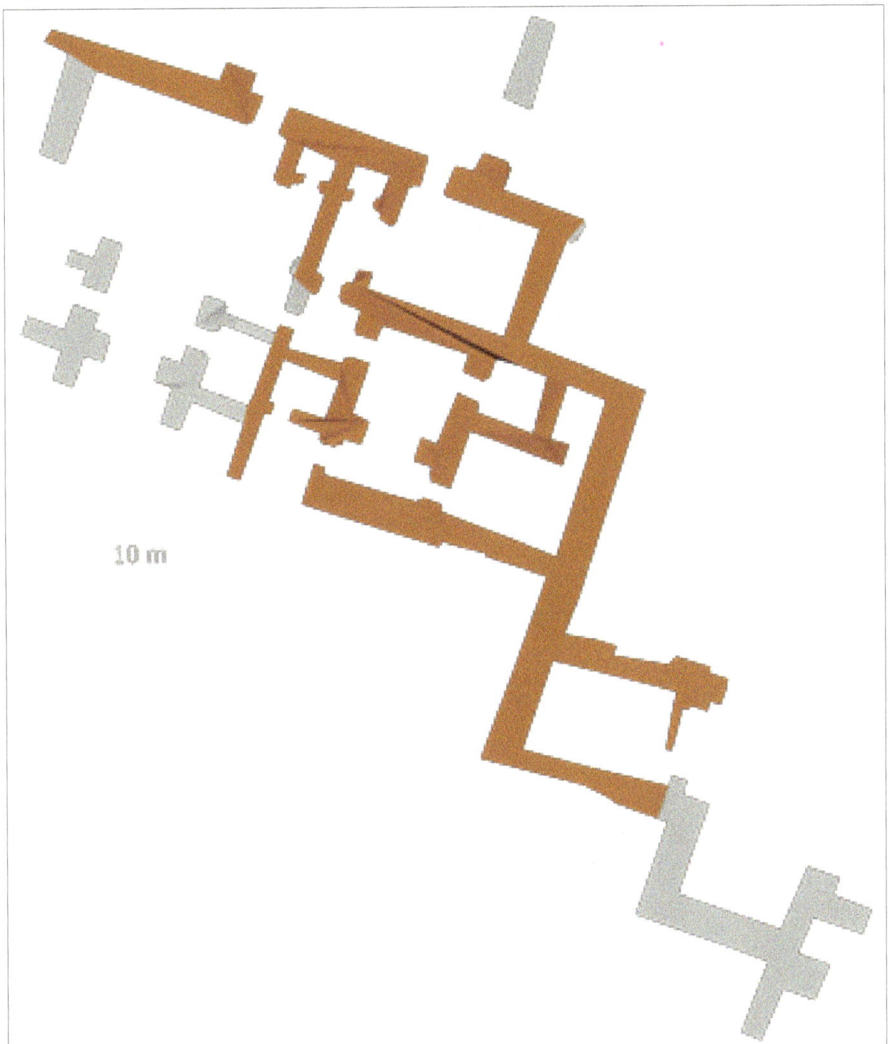

Illustration 126: 3D Model of AP Palace showing existing stone walls and mudbrick - overhead view.

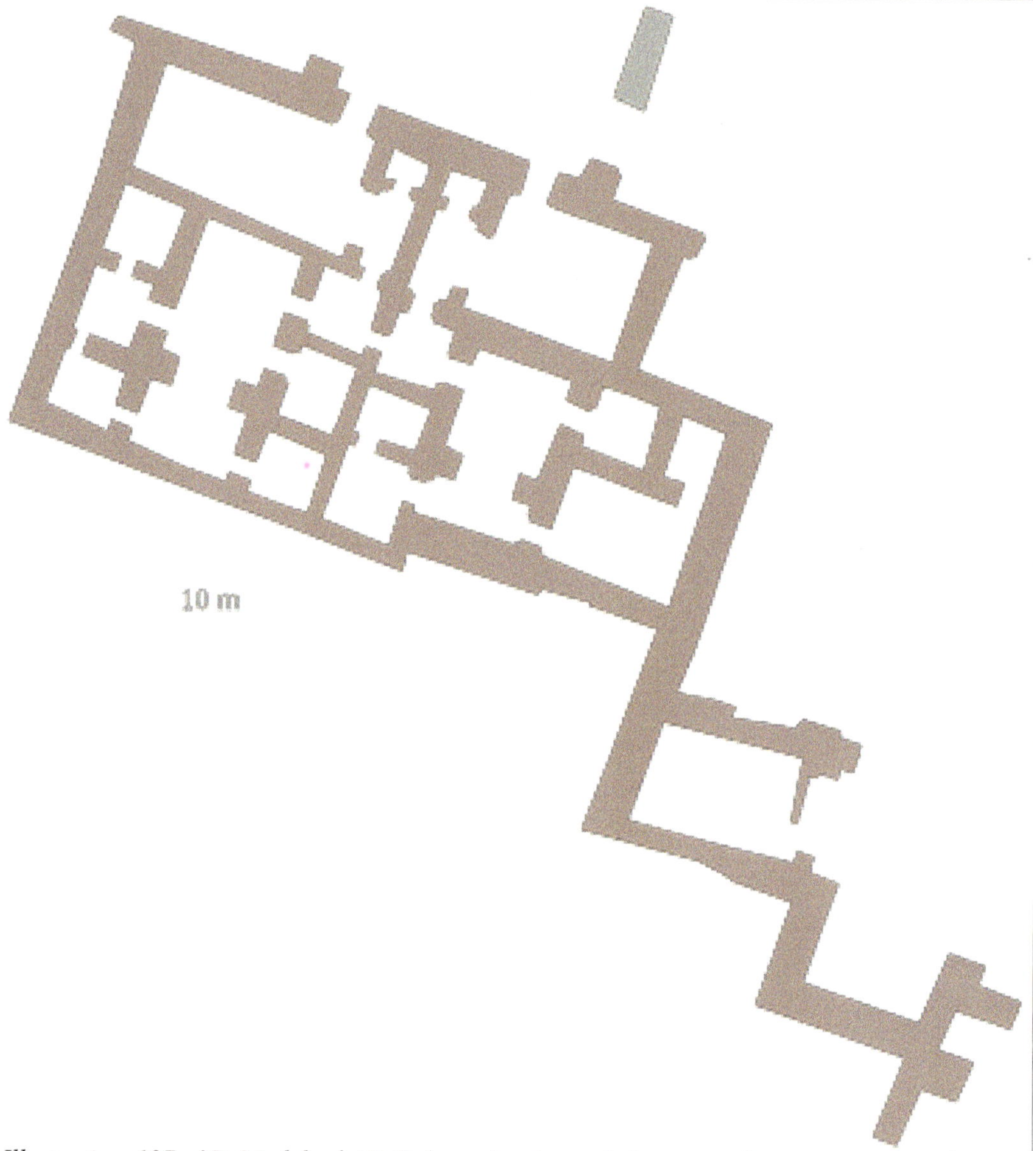

Illustration 127: 3D Model of AP Palace showing existing as well as reconstructed stone walls and mudbrick - overhead view.

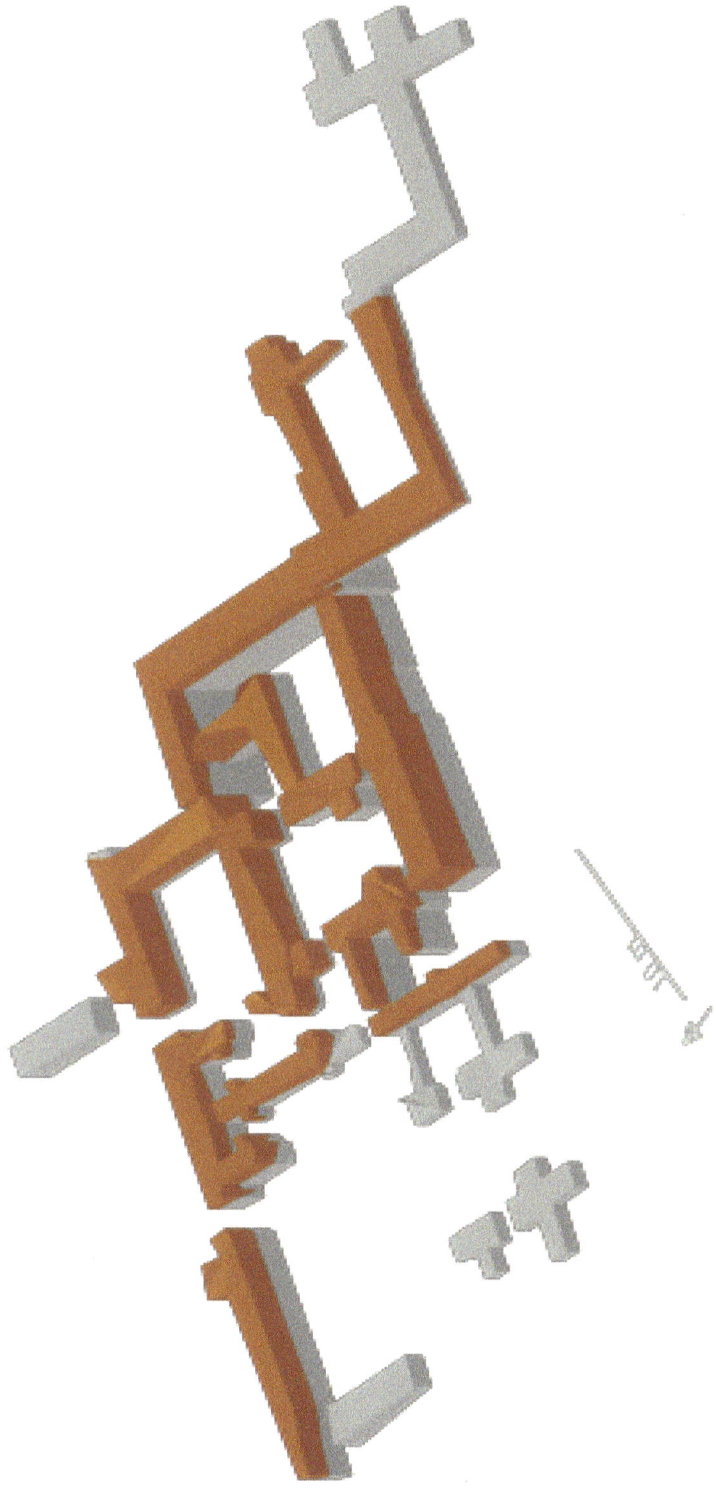

Illustration 128: 3D Model of AP Palace showing existing stone walls and mudbrick - view to NE.

6.1.4 Layers: Installations

The final layer shows all the walls, both extant and reconstructed, and includes the installations which are directly part of the architectural footprint of the building. This includes the pebble path and the baked brick platform in sector F, the platform in X, stone door sills in D1 and H4, and the stone courtyard in H3.

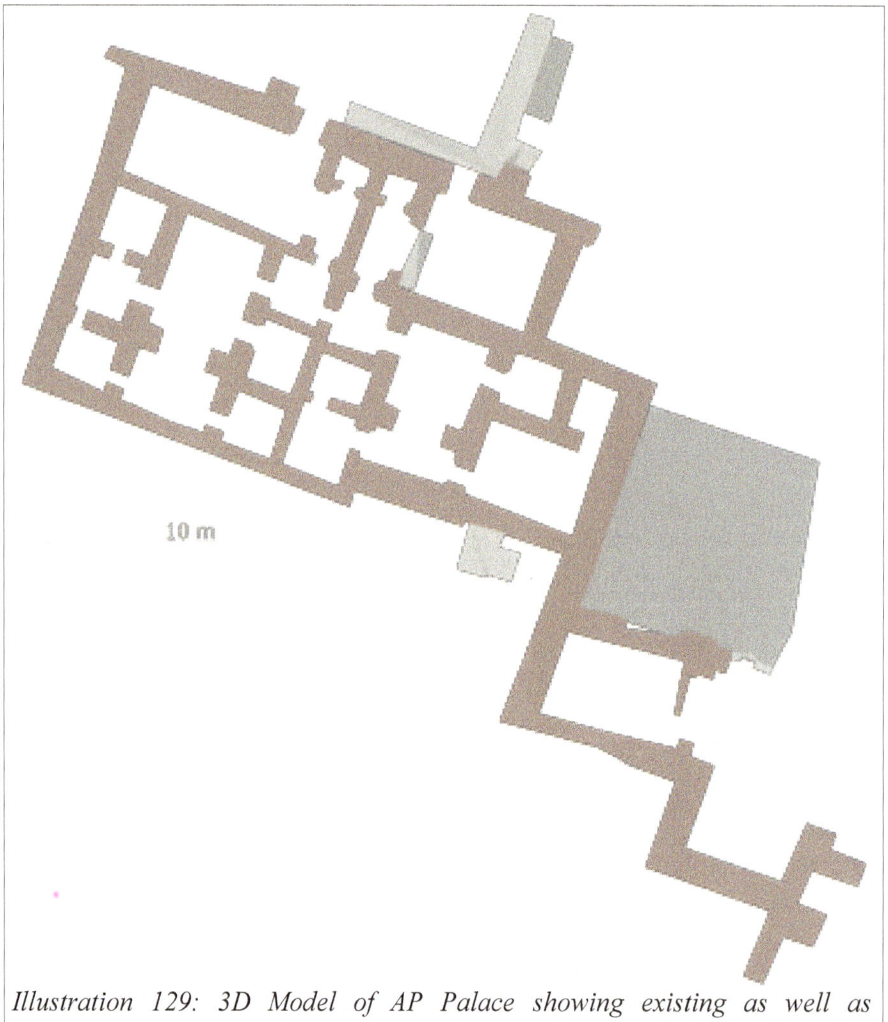

Illustration 129: 3D Model of AP Palace showing existing as well as reconstructed stone walls and mudbrick, including installations - overhead view.

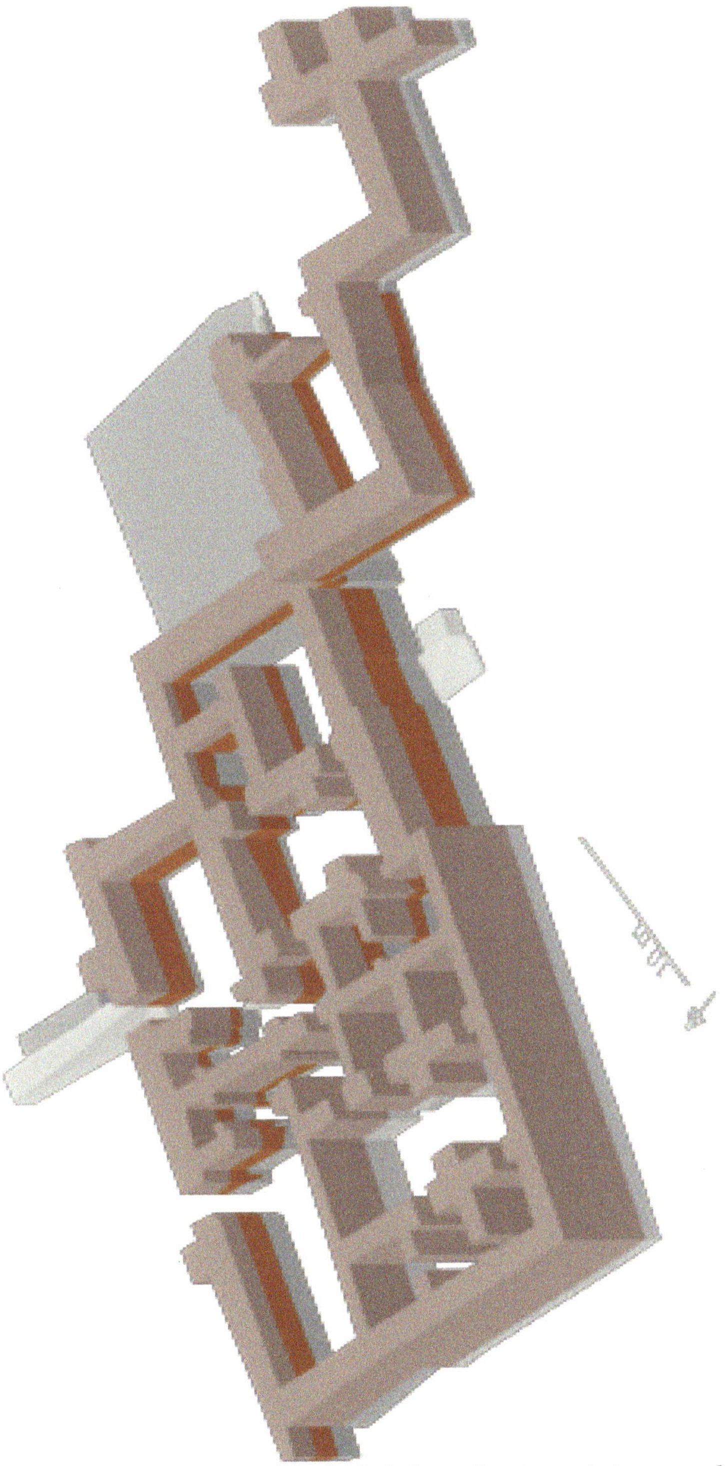

Illustration 130: 3D Model of AP Palace showing existing as well as reconstructed stone walls and mudbrick, including installations - view to NE.

6.1.5 The Precision of the 3D Model

As explained in chapter 5 (5.5), the data used with the BlockGen plug-in are derived from the coordinates taken in the field. One of the *desiderata* of

CORRECT SCRIPT

```
;088 - F1 E
;
clayer Text
filedia 0
text 36148,44193,8292 7 -90 AP 805
text 35981,43737,8319 7 -90 AP 802
text 36144,43668,8300 7 -90 AP 803
text 36290,44145,8287 7 -90 AP 821=Y1r15
text 36148,44193,8296 7 -90 AP 805
filedia 1
;
clayer 3DPolylines
3dpoly
36148,44193,8200
35981,43737,8200
36144,43668,8200
36290,44145,8200
36148,44193,8200

;
clayer Stone
WallGen
36148,44193,8200
35981,43737,8200
36144,43668,8200
36290,44145,8200
36148,44193,8200
;
36148,44193,8343
35981,43737,8305
36144,43668,8298
36290,44145,8343
36148,44193,8343

;
```

ERRONEOUS SCRIPT

```
;088 - F1 E
;
clayer Text
filedia 0
text 36148,44193,8292 7 -90 AP 805
text 35981,43737,8319 7 -90 AP 802
text 36144,43668,8300 7 -90 AP 803
text 36290,44145,8287 7 -90 AP 821=Y1r15
text 36148,44193,8296 7 -90 AP 805
filedia 1
;
clayer 3DPolylines
3dpoly
36148,44193,8200
35981,43737,8200
36144,43668,8200
36290,44145,8200
36148,44193,8200

;
clayer Stone
WallGen
36148,44193,8200
35981,43737,8200
36144,43668,8200
36290,44145,8200
36148,44193,8200
;
36148,44193,8343
35981,43737,8305
36244,43668,8298
36290,44145,8343
36148,44193,8343

;
```

the methodology presented here is the ability to quickly change the model to reflect the changing perception of the archaeological record. As a practical example of this functionality of the BlockGen plug-in, the script file for block 088-F1 has been altered.

The two script files shown above differ in one X value in one of the coordinates which generates this 3D block. By changing the value of this single coordinate, the volume produced by the BlockGen plug-in is also altered, as seen in the difference between Illustration 132 and Illustration 131: the changed point is in the lower right of the two images.

This example demonstrates the flexibility which the use of this plug-in gives the user: should the understanding of the archaeological record change,

Illustration 131: Block 088-F1 E generated with the erroneous script file.

Illustration 132: Block 088-F1 E generated with the correct script file.

the script files can quickly be changed with new data. The old block can be deleted singly and replaced with the new block, or else a complete new model can be generated. The idea of completely replacing the model is unheard of when using a method which is not based on script files: and yet, to regenerate the *complete* AP Palace using all of the script files given in the catalog takes less than five minutes using a normal desktop computer.

6.1.6 Calculating Volumes

The 3D model is in first place a visual representation of the volumes present in the palace, but as has been highlighted in chapter 5, this is merely one use of the model in the context of a research project. Just as important is the ability to calculate, with great precision (as precise as the data used to generate the model), the volume for each of the solids comprising the model. Thus one can give a total for the volume of stonework and brickwork[189] present in the palace. The following table gives the total amount of stonework and brickwork, both extant and reconstructed, for the AP Palace.

Thus the total amount of extant and reconstructed stonework in the excavated portion of the Palace is 429.84 m^3, and the total amount of extant and reconstructed brickwork in the excavated Palace is 991.38 m^3. Note that the excavated portion of the Palace probably had more stone than is reflected in the numbers here: when reconstructing missing portions of walls where no mudbrick was present, it was assumed that no stone was to be reconstructed (unless nearby walls gave enough evidence to reconstruct the height of stone). Also, the reconstruction is limited to the walls which are present in the architectural record: no reconstruction was made for the estimated footprint as given in section 2.3 because of the lack of data.

6.2 Using the 3D Model of the AP Palace as a Tool

The primary goal of the model, as has been stated many times in this study, is not to furnish an aesthetically pleasing model to be used (primarily) in communication, but rather as a tool to aid in answering research questions and in helping to formulate new questions (see in particular section 4.4.2). Four examples of this use of a 3D model are given here: the use of the volumetric measurements of the AP Palace together with the 'algorithms' presented at the end of chapter 3, questions of visibility, linking the volumes to the question of manpower and finally the 'cost' difference in materials as an aid to discussing perception, monumentality and prestige.

189 The terms 'stonework' and 'brickwork' are used rather than stone and brick since the volumes calculated by necessity include mortar.

6.2.1 Combining the 3D Model with the Algorithms

3D Block Name	Stonework (in m³)	Reconstructed Stonew. (in m³)	Mud brick (in m³)	Reconstructed Mud Brick (in m³)	Installation (in m³)
001- F E-SE	1.59		2.30	3.50	
002- F S	5.05		13.37	17.04	
003- F S_Corner	0.81			0.61	
004- D1 E	3.19		14.04	11.30	
005- D1 S	5.78		22.28	20.49	
006- D1 S-SW	0.25		1.23	0.78	
007- D1 W	2.80		1.26	5.52	
008- D2 SW	0.30		0.38	0.94	
009- D3 SW	0.24		0.13	0.52	
010- D3 W	1.26		0.31	2.78	
011- D2 NW	0.58		0.20	1.37	
012- D2 W	2.95		1.83	8.44	
013- D2 SW	0.69		0.67	2.42	
014- C7 W	0.91			4.83	
015- D3 N	15.60		8.94	22.86	
016- B3 W	2.65		2.65	3.58	
017- B3 SE	0.22		0.14	0.63	
018- B2 SE	0.14		0.00	0.93	
019- B1 N	21.76		19.37	21.83	
020- B1 W	9.22			24.08	
021- A3 N	5.40	11.09		26.91	
022- A6 N	2.37	3.09		12.28	
023a- A4 EN	2.29	2.35		17.25	
023b- A4 ES	6.49	1.14		40.80	
024- A4 W	31.71			171.24	
025- A3 E	6.97		4.46	22.37	
026- C7 NE	0.31		1.41	2.82	
027- C4 NW	0.76		2.51	2.20	
028- C4 ES	17.09		11.53	28.91	
029- C8 NE	80.06		29.83	14.70	
030- C1-2 S	28.44		38.60	36.06	
031- C2 ESE	0.54		0.73	0.68	
032- C6 E	17.51		9.86	23.22	
033- B1 S	22.10			22.10	
034- R1 N	0.66		13.27	31.94	
035- R1 SW	6.48		21.06	63.17	
036- R1 E	0.28		0.88	2.71	
080- R2 N1 Door	0.01				
081- R2 N2 Door	0.04				
082- R2 N3 Door	0.02				
083- Platform 1					3.11
084- Platform 2					2.08
085- F ColorSteps					
086- F ColorPlatform					0.76
087- PebblePath					24.21
088- F1 E	9.73				
089- D1 W Door					3.89
130- I	25.52	17.82		94.34	
Total	**340.75**	**35.48**	**223.22**	**768.15**	
131- H3 (Stone courtyard)	53.61				
Total	**394.36**				
Total Stonework	**429.84**				
Total Bricks	**991.38**				

Table 11: List of volumes of materials present (or reconstructed) for each wall portion.

One of the results of the comparison between the archaeological record, textual evidence and the ethnographic data in chapter 3 was a series of algorithms or general formulae (section 3.6) with which one could use volumetric measurements to explore the value, in terms of labor or energy, of the choices made in construction. With the 3D model now in hand, these algorithms can be applied as a case study to the AP Palace. In the following sections, the algorithms are reproduced from chapter 3 and applied to the 3D model. This is by no means an exhaustive case study: presented here are only some of the possible combinations of these two data sets.

6.2.1.1 *Algorithms: Quarry*

- A quarryman can produce 1 m^3 of rough hewn cobbles in 1.6 days
- Quarrying and shaping of stone using stone tools rather than steel takes 50% more time.
- A quarryman can produce 1 m^3 of finished stone in 11.6 days; 55% of original material remains as finished material

The 429.84 m^3 of stonework in the excavated portion of the AP Palace were probably hewn at the quarry site, which was presumably in the nearby mountains (see sections 3.2.1 and 3.4.3.1). There is then the question of the mortar placed within the stone wall: as with mudbrick walls, a certain amount of space was filled in between the stones. However, the stones rested directly on one another, thus the amount of mortar would seem to be less in a stone wall as compared to one made of mudbrick. For the purpose of this study it is assumed that 1/10 of a stone wall was composed of mortar (as opposed to 1/6 of a mudbrick wall, see below). The total amount of stone present is then 386.86 m^3.

Since the stones used were not finished blocks, but were shaped as rectangles, and stone tools were used, it seems reasonable to estimate between 2.5 and 3 days for a quarryman to produce 1m^3 of rough hewn building blocks. Thus the 386.86 m^3 would have required between 967.15 and 1160.58 man-days, or (using the 8-hour workday given in 3.6.1) between 7737.2 and 9284.64 man-hours.

6.2.1.2 *Algorithms: Stone*

- 4 People in 7.5 hours carried 42 stones weighing 5.1 tons, with a volume of approximately 3 m^3
- approximately 10 man-hours are needed to place 1 m^3 of stone
- A 'waller' (a professional stone-wall maker) can build a wall 4.9-5.5 m long and 1.5 m high in a day

To carry 386.86 m^3 it would have taken approximately 3868.6 man-hours,[190] or 483.58 8-hour man-days.[191] Assuming a crew of 4 carrying stone (reasonable, since more would just get in the way and the weight is too much for less) 120.89 crew-days were needed. 386.86 m^3 would have weighed about 657.66 tons.[192]

The placing of 386.86 m^3 of stone in the walls would have taken approximately 3868.6 man-hours or 483.58 8-hour man-days.

6.2.1.3 *Algorithms: Mudbrick Production*

- 4 People in 12 hours (over 3 days) produced 1000 mudbricks (40x40x10 cm) with a volume of 19.2 m^3
- Thus: approximately 2.5 man-hours are needed to produce 1 m^3 of mudbrick
- Chaff 2.5-4 cm length for bricks, shorter for mortar, longer for plaster
- 1 ½ bags of chaff (approx. 60 kg) needed for 131 bricks; approximate yield of 1/8 of a hectar of barley field
- 1 hectar of grain produces 12 bags of chaff = 480kg
- 2.6m^3 of dirt excavated in 5 hours
- 40x40x12 cm brick weighs 22 kg
- 240-350 bricks can be made per person per day
- mudbrick porters carried median of 150 bricks over a 432 m distance per day
- 1.8m^3 of dirt carried 180m by one person in 8 hours
- 1/6 of a mudbrick wall is composed of mortar

991.38 m^3 of mudbrick construction reflects the volume of the walls produced, but not the volume of the total mudbricks used, since a portion of that was mortar. Using the calculation of 1/6 of a mudbrick wall being composed of mortar, one gets 826.15 m^3 of mudbricks used in the construction and 165.23 m^3 of mortar. The time required to excavate the dirt needed for 826.15m^3 would have been about 1588.75 hours.

826.15 m^3 of mudbrick would have required 2065.37 man-hours to produce, or 516.34 crew-hours (assuming a crew size of 4). Because of drying

190 The formula used here is: 3/4 (what one person can carry in 7.5 hours)=0.75 – 386.86/0.75 (7.5 hour days needed to carry 386.86 m^3 of stone)=515.81 – 515.81*7.5 (hours needed to carry 386.86 m^3 of stone)= 3868.6 hours.

191 This figure is really a rough estimate: it assumes a standard stone weight, and the experiment did not state the distance over which the stone was carried. Nevertheless it remains a plausible index for calculating the time it took to carry stone to the work site from the place where it was deposited.

192 5.1 t / 3 m^3 = 1.7 t – 386.86 m^3 * 1.7 t = 730.7 tons.

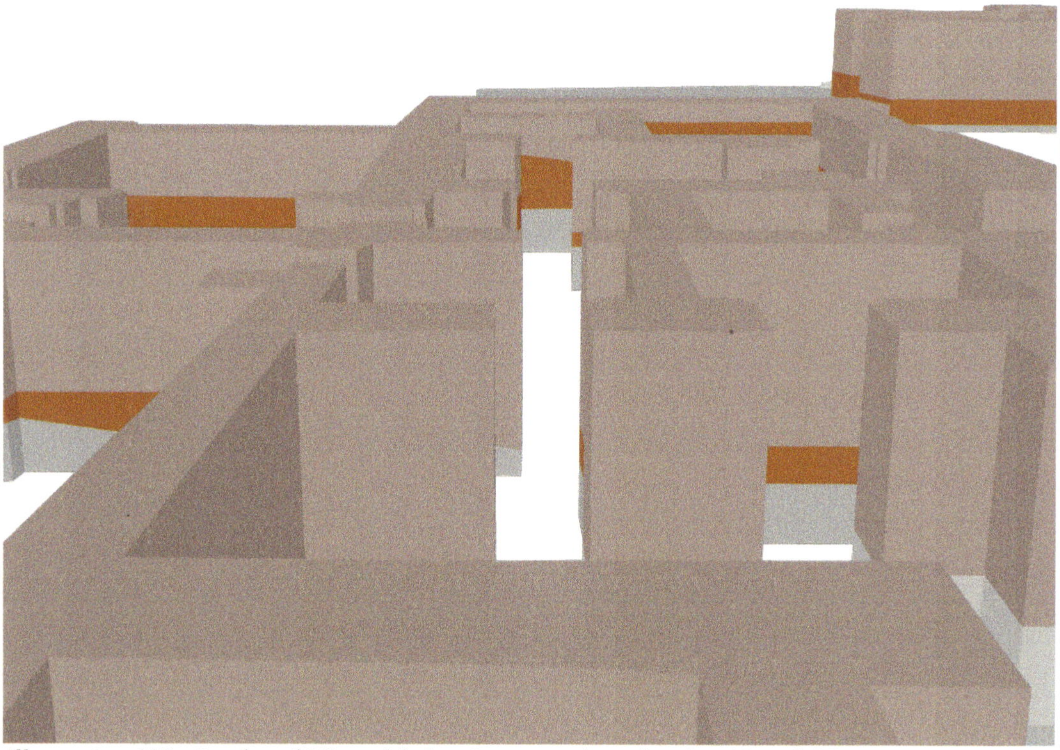

Illustration 133: Render of 3D model showing centrality of nodes A7 and C7.

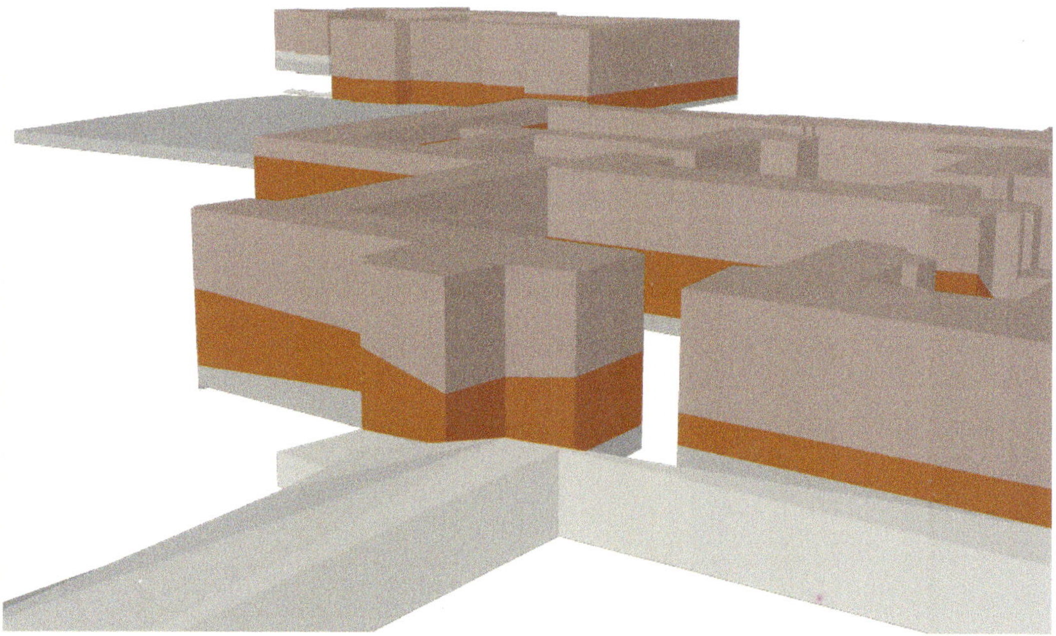

Illustration 134: A render of the AP Palace 3D Model showing differences in elevation between formal and service wings.

time, however, it is probable that several crews working in rotation in different areas (thereby working 8 hour days, instead of an average of 4 as above) could have produced more bricks in the same amount of time.

826.15 m^3 of mudbrick corresponds to 51,634 bricks (size: 40x40x10 cm). These bricks would need 23,649 kg of chaff,[193] or the chaff production of 49.2 hectars (0.492 km^2) of land.

6.2.2 *Looking at Visibility*

The second use of the 3D model as a tool for research presented here is based on being able to project visibility on the basis of the reconstructed model. Two examples elucidate this point: the rooms A7 and C7 which alone control access to the 16 rooms in sectors A and C, and the difference in elevation between the service and formal wings of the AP Palace.

As mentioned in section 2.2.1.1, the rooms A7 and C7 completely control access to sectors A and C. Illustration 133 uses the 3D model to show how the line of sight is clear from A5 through to C4: by far the longest line of sight in the service wing. In the render one sees the courtyard A5 in the lower portion of the image, followed by the rooms A7, C7, C5 and finally C4.

The second example given here to show how questions of visibility can be explored through the 3D model relates to the difference in elevation between the service and formal wings of the Palace. In section 2.1.2 the difference in elevation between these two areas of the palace was described. How would this have affected the perception and use of the architecture? This question has already been posed in this study, see section 2.1.6.6. The rendering shown here (Illustration 134) shows how the level of the stone courtyard would still have been below the roof level of the service wing, but would still have allowed access to the roof above the service wing from the formal wing. Furthermore, it would have been possible to see the plain level even standing on the stone courtyard (assuming that the reconstructed elevation of the roof level is correct).

These two case studies are meant as examples; questions relating to visibility increase as more buildings are added. By adding a similar model of the temple terrace, one could examine the line of sight between these two monuments, or by adding geophysical data such as magnetometry readings, the visibility between the Palace and the rural area could be studied.[194]

193 51,634 bricks / 131 bricks = 394.15 * 60 kg = 23,649 kg.

194 Some of these questions were posed in F. Buccellati 2010.

6.2.3 Time, Work crews and Volume

The interpretation of the tablet A15.231 found in the AP Palace, which contains the architectural plan discussed in chapter 2, may help us estimate the amount of time that it would have taken for the erection of the walls, which is perhaps the most time consuming construction moment. The basic assumption is that many different crews were working concurrently on the project, which implied a very careful assessment of the work flow and coordination. Procurement and transport would have taken even longer, but could have been planned equally carefully, with concurrent shipment, thus also reducing the total amount of time.

Based on the 3D model, the volume of the excavated portions of sector I are:

Piece	Stone (in m^3)	RecStone (in m^3)	RecBrick (in m^3)
130- I	25.52	17.82	94.34

Thus the (reconstructed) amount of stone in the excavated portion of sector I is 43.34 m^3 and the reconstructed amount of mudbrick is 94.34 m^3. Based on the tablet, the excavated area reflects 35% of the estimated total linear wall distance for sector I. Thus the crew to whom tablet A15.231 (always assuming that the sketch on the tablet reflects sector I) was given was responsible for building 123.82 m^3 of stone wall and 269.54 m^3 of mudbrick wall.

Extrapolating from this, and based purely on wall volume, the amount of stone wall built by this crew was 27%[195] of the total excavated for the AP Palace, while the amount of mudbrick wall built by this crew was 28.8%[196] of the total excavated are of the AP Palace. This calculation is, admittedly, skewed or even misleading: what is compared here is the total estimated size of sector I with only the excavated portion of the AP Palace as opposed to the total estimated size of the Palace. But the total estimated size of the wall volumes of the unexcavated portion of the palace would be a pure guess, since there are no parameters one could use to formulate a hypothesis as to unexcavated wall volumes for wings of the palace of which we have no information.

6.2.4 The Cost of Monumentality

The last example of using the 3D model as a tool for research is a comparison of the energy invested in the stone courtyard in sector H. The excavated portion of the stone courtyard has a volume of 53.61 m^3. Note that

195 269.54 m^3 /991.38 m^3.

196 123.82 m^3 /429.84 m^3.

the damage to the stone courtyard from pits is not removed from this estimate, since there is clear evidence that the stones were present at the time of the use of the palace, but were removed during the Khabur period when the pits were dug.

A conservative estimate of the total size of the stone courtyard puts the excavated portion at 40% of the total surface, but the courtyard may have been bigger, reducing the excavated portion to 25% of the total surface area (see section 2.3.2). This would mean that the total stone courtyard would have a volume of between 134 m^3 and 214.4 m^3.

Using the algorithms above, it becomes clear that the production of that volume of stone requires approximately eight times more energy than the same volume of brick. 134 m^3 of stone takes a quarryman a minimum of 2680 man-hours[197] (see 6.2.1.1) while 134 m^3 of unbaked mudbrick would have required 335 man-hours (see 6.2.1.3).

Since the use of stone was much more costly in terms of energy (8 times more costly in terms of production!), one is left asking why. A functional explanation might propose that a stone courtyard was easier to maintain: but then why only the one courtyard in this wing of the Palace, and not the other courtyards? It seems that a decision was made to invest in the courtyard for reasons linked to social considerations more than technological ones. One can hypothesize that the courtyard was paved with stone in order to emphasize the status of the royal court through the linked concepts of perception, monumentality and prestige. Some of these concepts are explored in chapter 4 of this study, but a complete analysis of this question would require more data, comparative material and, ideally, textual evidence. What the use of the algorithms in combination here provides is a way to quantify the cost of the decision to use stone rather than beaten earth or mudbricks to pave the courtyard, and it is this cost which gives one the empirical data on which to base a comparison and discussion of questions of perception, monumentality and prestige.

197 2.5 days to produce 1m^3 of stone = 20 hours assuming an 8 hour day.

"Die Architektur ist – die Vielfalt der Ansätze zeigt es – eine komplexe Angelegenheit: Sie ist Kunst, Wissenschaft, Technik, Sozialtechnik, Artefakt; sie hat einen ökonomischen, juridischen, hygienischen, technologischen, einen Klassen-, Geschlechts- und Generationen-Aspekt, kurz: sie ist (wie Marcel Mauss sagen würde) ein 'totales' soziales Phänomen." - H. Delitz[198]

7 Impact and Directions for Future Research

7.1 Impact

Ideally, this study will have an impact in the field in five areas:

(1) The architectural analysis of the AP Palace at Tell Mozan, as evidenced in chapters 2 and 6, is a major contribution to our understanding of the public buildings of ancient Urkesh, and of palaces from this region and time period. As a part of this analysis the proportion of perimeter to area was used to support typological definitions of rooms (2.1.4.5) and an access analysis (2.2.2.1) were used. These methods are seldom (if ever) used in the field, but show promise within the framework of architectural analysis.

(2) The detailed combination of data from the archaeological record, ethnographic parallels and textual evidence in chapter 3 gives a deep understanding of the process of construction in general, as well as giving a series of algorithms by which one can quantify the energy invested in the construction project. These algorithms are applicable in general to structures in stone and mudbrick, and as such can be used to define and compare the cost and value of such structures in a meaningful way.

(3) The theoretical considerations brought up in chapter 4, while not offering a detailed discussion of the issues raised, introduce aspects of theory

198 "Architecture is – as the large number of approaches demonstrates – a complex matter: it is Art, Science, Techne, Social Engineering, an Artifact; it has economic, juridic, hygenic, technological, class, gender, and generational aspects, in short, it is (as Marcel Mauss would say) a 'total' social phenomenon." Translation mine. (Delitz 2009, 74).

which can be tied to the data presented in this study. Such a link between theory and data is fundamental, and strengthens the understanding of both.

(4) The methodological approach to architectural analysis done hand in hand with ethnographic data and using 3D modeling techniques gives a concrete example of the potential results and the inherent value of 3D models. Such a model, done 'for archaeologists, by archaeologists', is a much more versatile tool for archaeology, and has real benefit in both formulating and answering research questions. The 3D model of the AP Palace at Mozan is a telling example of how such a model can contribute to reaching the research goals.

(5) As a vademecum, the study shows how an archaeological project should seek to understand the various steps involved in the creation of a model, so as to understand the time, equipment and expertise required in embarking on such a project. Also, it would give the staff not directly working on the project an idea and a basic understanding of the process and the results, so as to better interface with the model's creation and benefit from its potential as a tool.

7.2 Future Research

While this study presents a closed argument, from architectural analysis to an exploration of the building through a 3D model, many avenues of research are left open. Some of these, but by no means all, are:

(1) The use of a 3D model of the AP Palace as a tool for research allows for a new level of comparison with other palaces in region. Such models could lead to show the relative energy employed in their construction, explore materials available and examine the potential for expression of prestige and monumentality. In this way a study of the energetics of the construction of a group of buildings could bring a much deeper understanding of the commonalities and differences within this (and other) typological categories of architecture, something which is lacking in the current state of research.

(2) The ethnographic analogy and ethnoarchaeological experiment used in this study, primarily in chapter 3, might be further explored, and especially expanded. There are regional and chronological differences to many aspects presented here, and the wider the base on which the ethnographic analogy rests, the better the comparison. Also, the analogy used here is drawn from many sources, at times widely distributed across time and space. While the case has been made that such examples are functional, and as such are valid across cultures, it would be good to further test these parallels with more cross cultural data.

(3) Much the same can be said for the textual evidence, which is drawn primarily from a context (Ur III) later than the AP Palace. Again, this study makes the case that the data drawn from this textual evidence is primarily functional, and as such has a wider validity, but this hypothesis can and should be further tested through a wider range of textual data, and preferably from a wider chronological spectrum.

(4) The BlockGen plug-in developed for this study should also be improved on, in terms of flexibility and ease of use. It might also be expanded in order to include more complex shapes, such as vaults; such shapes are not common in Near Eastern archaeology, but may be needed if the plug-in were to be used in other cultural contexts. In terms of use and durability, it should at some point be adapted as a plug-in for an open source CAD program, so that the models are not dependent on a for-profit platform. A reliable and feature-rich open source CAD program is not available at the moment, but when such a program is developed then a plug-in of BlockGen would certainly be welcome.

(5) Finally, the theoretical aspects discussed in chapter 4 provide a number of directions for future research, especially in combination with data such as is presented here. A more detailed comparison of the viewpoints of psychology, sociology and architectural studies on the buildings found in the archaeological record would be of benefit to the quest to understand the perception of architecture on the ancient visitors. Perhaps the widest reaching question is that relating to value: can a study such as this one lead modern archaeologists to answers relating to questions of value in architecture? While this study has presented a concrete way for archaeologists to quantify architectural evidence in terms of energetics, and from that point of departure to strive to base an understanding of concepts such as monumentality and prestige in terms of that data, a great deal of work has still to be done to further validate this approach and to widen its scope.

Bibliography

Note that in the following bibliography the abbreviations used in the most recent volume of the *Chicago Assyrian Dictionary* (Volume 20 *U and W* from 2010) have been followed.

Aaberg, S., and J. Bonsignore. 1975. "A Consideration of Time and Labor Expenditure in the Construction Process at the Teotihuacan Pyramid of the Sun and the Poverty Point Mound." In *Three Papers on Mesoamerican Archaeology*, edited by S. Aaberg, 40–78. Contributions of the University of California Archaeological Research Facility 24. Berkeley: University of California Dept. of Anthropology.

Abbott, A. 2004. *Methods of Discovery: Heuristics for the Social Sciences*. New York, NY: W W Norton & Co.

Abrams, E. 1994. *How the Maya Built Their World: Energetics and Ancient Architecture*. Austin, TX: University of Texas Press.

Akkermans, P., and G. Schwartz. 2002. *The Archaeology of Syria: From Complex Hunter-Gatherers to Early Urban Societies (c. 16,000-300 BC)*. Cambridge; New York, NY: Cambridge UP.

Albenda, P. 2005. *Ornamental Wall Painting in the Art of the Assyrian Empire*. Leiden; Boston: Brill; Styx.

Algaze, G. 2008. *Ancient Mesopotamia at the Dawn of Civilization: The Evolution of an Urban Landscape*. Chicago, IL: University of Chicago Press.

Ambos, C. 2004. *Mesopotamische Baurituale aus dem 1. Jahrtausend v. Chr.* Dresden: ISLET.

———. 2010. "Building Rituals from the First Millennium BC. The Evidence from the Ritual Texts." In *From the Foundations to the Crenellations: Essays on Temple Building in the Ancient Near East and Hebrew Bible*, edited by M. Boda and J. Novotny, 221–37. AOAT 366. Münster: Ugarit-Verlag.

Andraschko, F. 1995. *Studien zur funktionalen Deutung archäologischer Siedlungsbefunde in Rekonstruktion und Experiment*. Duderstadt: Mecke.

Ankerl, G. 1981. *Experimental Sociology of Architecture: A Guide to Theory, Research and Literature*. New Babylon: Studies in the Social Sciences 36. The Hague, Paris, New York: Mouton.

Ankerl, G., and W. Michelson. 1985. "Comment on Review of Experimental Sociology of Architecture - How Do Critics Skim a Book? & Reply" 14 (2): 150–52.

Archi, A. 1987. "The 'Sign-List' from Ebla." In *Eblaitica: Essays on the Ebla Archives and Eblaite Language*, edited by C.H. Gordon, 1:91–113. Winona Lake: Eisenbrauns.

Arnheim, R. 1977. *The Dynamics of Architectural Form*. Berkeley: University of California Press.

Aurenche, O. 1977. *Dictionnaire illustré multilingue de l'architecture du Proche Orient ancien*. CMO - Collection de la Maison de l'Orient et de la Méditerranée 3. Lyon; Paris: Maison de l'Orient; Diffusion de Boccard.

———. 1981. *La maison orientale : l'architecture du Proche Orient ancien des origines au milieu du quatrième millénaire*. Paris: P. Geuthner.

———. 1993. "L'origine de la brique dans le Proche Orient ancien." In *Between the Rivers and over the Mountains. Archaeologia Anatolica et Mesopotamica Alba Palmieri dedicata*, edited by M. Frangipane, 71–85. Roma: Dipartimento di Scienze Storiche Archeologiche e Antropologiche dell'Antichità Università di Roma "La Sapienza."

Badawy, A. 1978. *Architecture in Ancient Egypt and the Near East*. Cambridge, Mass.: M.I.T. Press.

Bartash, V. 2013. *Miscellaneous Early Dynastic and Sargonic Texts in the Cornell University Collections*. Cornell University Studies in Assyriology and Sumerology 23. CDL Press.

Bar-Yosef, O., and P. Van Peer. 2009. "The Chaîne Opératoire Approach in Middle Paleolithic Archaeology." *Current Anthropology* 50 (1): 103–31.

Bar-Yosef, O., B. Vandermeersch, B. Arensburg, A. Belfer-Cohen, P. Goldberg, H. Laville, L. Meignen, et al. 1992. "The Excavations in Kebara Cave, Mt. Carmel [and Comments and Replies]." *Current Anthropology* 33 (5): 497–550.

Bianchi, A. 2012. *Comparative Studies on the Pottery of Sector AK of the Royal Building in Tell Mozan/Urkesh*. Wiesbaden: Harrassowitz.

Birschmeier, W., and H. Gasche. 1981. "Contribution à l'étude de la voûte en briques crues." *Akkadica* 24: 1–16.

Bleed, P. 2001. "Trees or Chains, Links or Branches: Conceptual Alternatives for Consideration of Stone Tool Production and Other Sequential Activities." *Journal of Archaeological Method and Theory* 8 (1): 101–27.

Boda, M., and J. Novotny, eds. 2010. *From the Foundations to the Crenellations: Essays on Temple Building in the Ancient Near East and Hebrew Bible*. AOAT 366. Münster: Ugarit-Verlag.

Borra, D., M. Forte, E. Pietroni, and C. Rufa. 2003. "The Virtual Reality Project of the Scrovegni Chapel of Padua." In *The International Ar-*

chives of the Photogrammetry, Remote Sensing and Spatial Information Sciences, XXXIV 5/W12:83.

Bourdieu, P. (1980) 2005. *The Logic of Practice*. Translated by R. Nice. Cambridge: Polity Press.

Bradley, R. 1997. *Rock Art and the Prehistory of Atlantic Europe: Signing the Land*. New York: Routledge.

———. 2000. *The Good Stones: A New Investigation of the Clava Cairns*. Edinburgh: Society of Antiquaries of Scotland.

Broughton, J., and J. O'Connell. 1999. "On Evolutionary Ecology, Selectionist Archaeology, and Behavioral Archaeology." *American Antiquity* 64 (1): 153–65.

Buccellati, F. 1998. "3-D Rendering and Animation at Tell Mozan/Urkesh." In *Urkesh and the Hurrians: Studies in Honor of Lloyd Cotsen*, edited by G. Buccellati, 53–64. Bibliotheca Mesopotamica 26. Malibu, CA: Undena Publications.

———. 2010. "The Monumental Temple Terrace at Urkesh and its Setting." In *Kulturlandschaft Syrien: Zentrum und Peripherie Festschrift für Jan-Waalke Meyer*, edited by J. Becker, R. Hempelmann, and E. Rehm, 71–86. AOAT 371. Münster: Ugarit-Verlag.

———. 2014a. "Diachronic Developments at the Central Monumental Complex of Ancient Urkesh (Tell Mozan)." In *Proceedings of the 8th International Congress on the Archaeology of the Ancient Near East: 10 April-4 May, 2012 University of Warsaw*, 313–22. Wiesbaden: Harassowitz.

———. 2014b. "Understanding Households – a Few Thoughts." In *House and Household Economies in 3rd Millennium B.C.E. Syro-Mesopotamia*, edited by F. Buccellati, T. Helms, and A. Tamm, 35–42. BAR International Series 2682. Oxford, England: BAR International Series.

———. 2015. "What Might a Field Archaeologist Want from an Architectural 3D Model?" In *How Do We Want the Past to Be? On Methods and Instruments of Visualizing Ancient Reality*, edited by M.G. Micale and D. Nadali, 157–69. Piscataway, NJ: Gorgias Press.

———. 2016. "3D Models as Vehicles for Archaeological Research: Stratigraphy, Emplacement and Construction." *Studia Eblaitica* 2: 15–22.

Buccellati, F., N. Dell'Unto, and M. Forte. 2005. "The Mozan/Urkesh Archaeological Project: An Integrated Approach of Spatial Technologies." In *The Reconstruction of Archaeological Landscapes through Digital Technologies: Proceedings of the 2nd Italy-United States Workshop, Rome, Italy, November 3-5, 2003, Berkeley, USA, May 2005*, edited by

M. Forte, 171–83. Oxford, UK: Archaeopress.

Buccellati, F., and E. Kansa. 2016. "The Value of Energetic Analysis in Architecture as an Example for Data Sharing." *Digital Applications in Archaeology and Cultural Heritage* 3: 91–97.

Buccellati, G. 1981. "Principles of Stylistic Analysis." In *Bono homini donum essays in historical linguistics in memory of J. Alexander Kerns*, edited by Y. Arbeitman and A. Bomhard. Amsterdam: J. Benjamins.

———. 1984. "Introduction." In *L'archive de Puzurum*, by O. Rouault, vii–xviii. Terqa Finds Reports 1. Malibu, CA: Undena Publications.

———. 2005. "The Monumental Urban Complex at Urkesh: Report on the 16th Season of Excavations, July-September 2003." In *Studies on the Civilization and Culture of Nuzi and the Hurrians*, edited by D. Owen and G. Wilhelm, 3–28. Studies on the Civilization and Culture of the Nuzi and the Hurrians 15. Cornell, MD: CDL Press.

———. 2006. "A Browser Edition of the Royal Palace of Urkesh: Principles and Presuppositions." In *Les espaces syro-mésopotamiens : Dimensions de l'expérience humaine au Proche-Orient ancien: Volume d'hommage offert à Jean-Claude Margueron*, by P. Butterlin, M. Lebeau, J.-Y. Monchambert, J. L. Montero Fenollós, and B. Muller, 49–56. Subartu 17. Turnhout: Brepols.

———. 2009a. "An Architectural 'Logogram' at Urkesh?" In *Dallo Stirone al Tigri - Dal Tevere all'Eufrate - Studi in onore di Claudio Saporetti*, edited by P. Negri Scafa and S. Viaggio, 23–29. Roma: Aracne.

———. 2009b. "The Semiotics of Ethnicity: The Case of Hurrian Urkesh." In *Festschrift für Gernot Wilhelm anläßlich seines 65. Geburtstages am 28. Januar 2010*, edited by J. Fincke, 79–90. Dresden: Islet.

———. 2010. "The Urkesh Temple Terrace: Perception and Function." In *Kulturlandschaft Syrien: Zentrum und Peripherie Festschrift für Jan-Waalke Meyer*, edited by J. Becker, R. Hempelmann, and E. Rehm, 87–121. AOAT 371. Münster: Ugarit-Verlag.

Buccellati, G., and M. Kelly-Buccellati. 1995. "The Royal Storehouse of Urkesh: The Glyptic Evidence from the Southwestern Wing." *Archiv für Orientforschung* 42–43: 1–32.

———. 1996. "The Seals of the King of Urkesh: Evidence from the Western Wing of the Royal Storehouse AK." *Wiener Zeitschrift für die Kunde des Morgenlandes* 86: 65–100.

———. 1997. "Urkesh: The First Hurrian Capital." *Biblical Archaeologist* 60 (2): 77–96.

———. 1998. "The Courtiers of the Queen of Urkesh: Glyptic Evidence from the Western Wing of the Royal Storehouse AK." In *About Subartu:*

Studies Devoted to Upper Mesopotamia, edited by M. Lebeau, 195–216. Subartu 4.

———. 2000. "The royal palace of Urkesh report on the 12th season at Tell Mozan/Urkesh: Excavations in Area AA, June-October 1999." *Mitteilungen der Deutschen Orient-Gesellschaft zu Berlin*, no. 132: 133–183.

———. 2002. "Tar'am-Agade, Daughter of Naram-Sin, at Urkesh." In *Of Pots and Plans. Papers on the Archaeology and History of Mesopotamia and Syria Presented to David Oates in Honour of His 75th Birthday*, edited by L. al-Gailani Werr, J. Curtis, H. Martin, A. McMahon, J. Oates, and J. Reade, 11–31. London: Nabu.

———. 2004. "Der monumentale Palasthof von Tall Mozan/Urkes und die stratigraphische Geschichte des Abi: Bericht über die 15. kampagne 2002." *Mitteilungen der Deutschen Orient-Gesellschaft* 136: 13–39.

Burke, A. 2008. *"Walled up to Heaven" the Evolution of Middle Bronze Age Fortification Strategies in the Levant*. Studies in the Archaeology and History of the Levant 4. Winona Lake, Ind.: Eisenbrauns.

Burnet, T. 1965. *The Sacred Theory of the Earth*. London: Centaur Press.

Burrows, E. 1935. *Ur Excavations Texts: II Archaic Texts*. London: Harrison.

Butterlin, P. 2002. "Réflexions Sur Les Problèmes de Continuite Stratigraphique et Culturelle à Tepe Gawra." *Syria* 79: 7–49.

———. 2003. *Les Proto-Urbain de Mésopotamie, Contacts et acculturation à l'époque d'Uruk au Moyen-Orient*. Paris: CNRS Editions.

———. 2006. "Où sont les fenêtres? Lumière et architecture tripartite proto-urbaine de Haute Mésopotamie." In *Les espaces syro-mésopotamiens : Dimensions de l'expérience humaine au Proche-Orient ancien: Volume d'hommage offert à Jean-Claude Margueron*, edited by P. Butterlin, M. Lebeau, J.-Y. Monchambert, J. L. Montero Fenollós, and B. Muller, 41–48. Subartu 17. Turnhout: Brepols.

———. , ed. 2009. *A propos de Tepe Gawra: le monde proto-urbain de Mésopotamie*. Turnhout: Brepols.

———. 2010. "D'Uruk à Mari." *Histoire urbaine*, no. 3: 133–159.

Butterlin, P., M. Lebeau, J.-Y. Monchambert, J. L. Montero-Fenollos, and B. Muller, eds. 2006. *Les espaces syro-mésopotamiens : Dimensions de l'expérience humaine au Proche-Orient ancien : Volume d'hommage offert à Jean-Claude Margueron*. Subartu 17. Turnhout: Brepols.

Camatta, P. forthcoming. *The Temple Terrace of Tell Mozan/Urkesh (Syria): Architecture, Typology, and Comparative Analysis of Mesopotamian High Temples*. Bibliotheca Mesopotamica 31. Malibu, CA: Undena Publications.

Canby, J.V. 2001. *The "Ur-Nammu" Stela*. University Museum Monographs 110. Philadelphia, PA: University of Pennsylvania Museum of Archaeology and Anthropology.

Castoriadis, C. 1984. *Crossroads in the Labyrinth*. Cambridge, MA: MIT Press.

Chaves Yates, C. 2014. "Beyond the Mound: Locating Complexity in Northern Mesopotamia during the 'Second Urban Revolution.'" Ph.D. Thesis, Boston University.

Civil, M. 2008. *The Early Dynastic Practical Vocabulary A*. ARES 4. Roma: Missione Archeologica Italiana in Siria.

Clark, D. 2003. "Bricks, Sweat and Tears: The Human Investment in Constructing a 'Four-Room' House." *Near Eastern Archaeology* 66 (1/2): 34–43.

Clarke, A.C. 1973. "Hazards of Prophecy: The Failure of Imagination." In *Profiles of the Future: An Inquiry into the Limits of the Possible*, 12–21. New York: Harper & Row.

Coles, J. 1973. *Archaeology by Experiment*. London: Hutchinson.

Comaroff, J. L., and J. Comaroff. 2009. *Ethnicity, Inc.* Chicago: University of Chicago Press.

Cornerstones Community Partnerships Staff. 2006. *Adobe Conservation: A Preservation Handbook*. Santa Fe, NM: Sunstone Press.

Culbertson, L. 2011. "A Life-Course Approach to Household Slaves in the Late Third Millennium BC." In *Slaves and Households in the Near East*, edited by L. Culbertson, 33–48. Chicago, IL: Chicago UP.

Daimel, A. 1922. *Die Inschriften von Fara I: Liste archaischen Keilschriftzeichen*. Leipzig: J.C. Hinrichs'sche Buchhandlung.

Dalley, S. 2002. *Mari and Karana: Two Old Babylonian Cities*. Piscataway, NJ: Gorgias Press.

Deblauwe, F. 1992. "A Study of Accessibility and Circulation Patterns in the Sin Temple of Hafagi from the Third Millennium B.C." *Mesopotamia* 27: 89–118.

———. 1994. "Spacings and Statistics, or a Different Method to Analyze Buildings. A Test with Mesopotamian Houses from the Late Bronze and Iron Ages." *Akkadica* 89–90: 1–8.

———. 1997a. "A Test Study of Circulation and Access Patterns in Assyrian Architecture." In *Assyiren Im Wandel Der Zeiten*, edited by H. Waetzoldt and H. Hauptmann, 239–46. Heidelberger Studien Zum Alten Orient 6. Heidelberg: Heidelberger Orientverlag.

———. 1997b. "Discriminant Analysis of Selected Spatial Variables Derived from Mesopotamian Buildings of the Late Bronze Age till the Parthian

Period." *Mesopotamia* 32: 271–88.

Deckers, K. 2010. "Anthracological Research at the Early to Middle Bronze Age Settlement of Tell Mozan." In *Development of the Environment, Subsistence and Settlement of the City of Urkesh and Its Region*, by K. Deckers, M. Doll, P. Pfälzner, and S. Riehl, 361–78. SUN A 3. Wiesbaden: Harrassowitz.

Delitz, H. 2009. *Architektursoziologie*. Einsichten. Themen Der Soziologie. Bielefeld: Transcript Verlag.

———. 2010. "»Die zweite Haut des Nomaden«. Zur sozialen Effektivität nicht-moderner Architekturen." In *Der gebaute Raum - Bausteine einer Architektursoziologie vormoderner Gesellschaften*, edited by P. Trebsche, N. Müller-Scheessel, and S. Reinhold. Tuebinger Archaeologische Taschenbuecher 7. Münster; New York, NY; München; Berlin: Waxmann.

Dercksen, J.G. 2004. *Old Assyrian Institutions*. Leiden: Nederlands Instituut voor het Nabije Oosten.

Devolder, M. 2012. "Labour Costs and Neopalatial Architecture: A Study of the Buildings at Klimataria-Manares and Achladia and the Palace at Gournia." In *Minoan Realities: Theory-Based Approaches to Images and Built Spaces as Indicators of Minoan Social Structures*, edited by D. Panagiotopoulos and U. Gükel-Maschek, 165–80.

Diakonoff, I. 1972. "Socio-Economic Classes in Babylonia and the Babylonian Concept of Social Stratification." In *Gesellschaftsklassen im alten Zweistromland und in den angrenzenden Gebieten*, edited by D.O. Edzard, 41–52. Munich: Beck.

———. 1976. "Slaves, Helots and Serfs in Early Antiquity." In *Wirtschaft und Gesellschaft im alten Vorderasien*, edited by J. Harmatta and G. Komoroczy, 45–78. Budapest: Akademiai Kiado.

Doat, P., A. Hays, H. Houben, S. Matuk, and F. Vitoux. 1979. *Construire en terre*. Paris: Editions Alternatives.

Duering, B. 2009. "Exploring Building Continuity in the Anatolian Neolithic: Functional and Symbolic Aspects." In *Bautechnik im antiken und vorantiken Kleinasien*. Byzas 9. Istanbul: Ege Yayinlari.

Edmonds, M. 1999. *Ancestral Geographies of the Neolithic: Landscapes, Monuments and Memory*. London: Routledge.

Eichmann, R. 2007. *Uruk Architektur I*. AUWE 14. Mainz: Philipp von Zabern.

Eliade, M. 1974. *The Myth of the Eternal Return: Cosmos and History*. Princeton, NJ: Princeton UP.

Erasmus, C. 1965. "Monument Building: Some Field Experiments." *South-*

western Journal of Anthropology 21 (4): 277–301.

Ess, M. van. 2001. *Uruk Architektur II*. Vol. 1. AUWE 15. Mainz: Philipp von Zabern.

Favro, D. 2012. "Se Non è Vero, è Ben Trovato (If Not True, It Is Well Conceived): Digital Immersive Reconstructions of Historical Environments." *Journal of the Society of Architectural Historians* 71 (3): 273–77.

Fitzsimons, R. 2014. "An Energetic(s) Approach to Late Helladic Tomb Construction: Funerary Architecture and State Formation at Bronze Age Mycenae." In *Meditations on the Diversity of the Built Environment in the Aegean Basin and Beyond*, 83–120. Athens: The Canadian Institute in Greece.

Forte, M. 2002. *I sistemi informativi geografici in archeologia*. Roma: MondoGIS.

Foster, B. 2016. *The Age of Agade: Inventing Empire in Ancient Mesopotamia*. London; New York: Routledge.

Fraser, J.B. 1826. "Narrative Journey into Khorastan, in the Years 1821 and 1822." *The Westminster Review* V (IX): 436–548.

Frayne, D. 1993. *Sargonic and Gutian Periods, 2334-2113 BC*. RIME 2. Toronto; Buffalo, NY: University of Toronto Press.

Freitag, Michel. 1992. *Architecture et société*. Montréal; Bruxelles: Éd. Saint-Martin; la Lettre Volée.

Gamble, C. 1998. "Palaeolithic Society and the Release from Proximity: A Network Approach to Intimate Relations." *World Archaeology* 29 (3): 426–49.

Garner, L. 1984. *Dry Tone Walls*. Princes Risborough: Shire.

Gelb, J. 1965. "The Ancient Mesopotamian Ration System." *Journal of Near Eastern Studies* 24 (3): 230–43.

———. 1979. "Household and Family in Early Mesopotamia." In *State and Temple Economy in the Ancient Near East*, edited by E. Lipiński, 1–97. OLA 5. Leuven: Departement Oriëntalistiek.

Gelb, J., M. Civil, B. Landsberger, A.L. Oppenheim, and E. Reiner. 1956. *The Assyrian Dictionary of the Oriental Institute of the University of Chicago*. Vol. A2. Chicago, IL.

———. 1960. *The Assyrian Dictionary of the Oriental Institute of the University of Chicago*. Vol. I and J. Chicago, IL.

Gould, S.J. 1987. *Time's Arrow, Time's Cycle: Myth and Metaphor in the Discovery of Geological Time*. Cambridge, MA: Harvard UP.

Gourdin, W.H., and W.D. Kingery. 1975. "The Beginnings of Pyrotechnology: Neolithic and Egyptian Lime Plaster." *Journal of Field Archaeology* 2

(1/2): 133–50.

Green, M.W., and H. Nissen. 1987. *Zeichenliste der archaischen Texte aus Uruk*. Vol. 2. Archaische Texte aus Uruk. Berlin: Gebr. Mann.

Hahn, H.P. 2010. "Gibt es eine »soziale Logik des Raumes«? Zur kritischen Revision eines Strukturparadigma." In *Der gebaute Raum: Bausteine einer Architektursoziologie vormoderner Gesellschaften*, edited by P. Trebsche, N. Müller-Scheeßel, and S. Reinhold. Muenster; New York, NY; Munich; Berlin: Waxmann.

Harrell, J. 2008. "Tools Used in Ancient Egyptian Construction." Edited by H. Selin. *Encyclopaedia of the History of Science, Technology, and Medicine in Non-Western Cultures*. Berlin, New York: Springer.

Hauser, R. 2006. *Reading Figurines: Animal Representations in Terra Cotta from Royal Building AK at Urkesh (Tell Mozan)*. Malibu: Undena Publications.

Heidegger, M. 1954. "Bauen, Wohnen, Denken." In *Vorträge und Aufsätze*, 145–62. Pfullingen: G. Neske.

Heimpel, W. 2009. *Workers and Construction Work at Garshana*. CUSAS 5. Bethesda, MD: CDL Press.

Heinrich, E. 1934. *Schilf und Lehm: Ein Beitrag zur Baugeschichte der Sumerer*. Berlin: Verlag für Kunstwissenschaft.

———. 1984. *Die Paläste im alten Mesopotamien*. Berlin: Walter de Gruyter.

Heinrich, E., and U. Seidl. 1968. "Maß und Übermaß in der Dimensionierung von Bauwerken im alten Zweistromland." *Mitteilungen der Deutschen Orient-Gesellschaft* 99: 5–54.

Helck, W., E. Otto, and W. Westendorf. 1982. *Lexicon der Ägyptologie*. Wiesbaden: Harrassowitz.

Helms, T. 2013. "Steingeräteindustrien in frühurbanem Kontext: Eine wirtschaftsarchäologische Analyse der lithischen Funde aus Tell Chuera und Kharab Sayyar (Nordsyrien)." Frankfurt am Main, Germany: Goethe University.

Helms, T., and J.-W. Meyer. 2016. "Fortifying a Major Early Bronze Age Center – The Construction and Maintenance of Tell Chuera's (Northern Syria) Outer Defence Works." In *Focus on Fortifications: New Research on Fortifications in the Ancient Mediterranean and the Near East*, edited by R. Frederiksen, M. Schnelle, S. Muth, and P. Schneider, 142–58. Fokus Fortifikation Studies 2. Oxford: Oxbow Books.

Hilgert, M. 2014. "Fokus: Keilschriftliche Quellen zu Architektur und Bauwesen." In *Wissensgeschichte der Architektur*, edited by J. Renn, W. Osthues, and H. Schlimme, 281–96. Berlin: Edition Open Access.

Hillier, B. 1988. *The Social Logic of Space*. Cambridge: Cambridge UP.

Hole, F. 1977. *Studies in the Archaeological History of the Deh Luran Plain: The Excavation of Changa Sefid*. Ann Arbor: University of Michigan.

Hughey, S. 1997. "KI: A Mesopotamian View of the Place of Positioning: Ancient Surveying, Mapping and Field Engineering for Floodplain Waterworks and Architecture." Ph.D. Thesis, Los Angeles, CA: UCLA.

Hult, G. 1983. *Bronze Age Ashlar Masonry in the Eastern Mediterranean: Cyprus, Ugarit, and Neighbouring Regions*. Göteborg: Åström.

Izzet, V. 2007. *The Archaeology of Etruscan Society*. Cambridge, MA; New York: Cambridge UP.

Jirgens, P. 2009. "About Make It Mudbricks." *Make It Mudbricks: Manufacture*. http://www.makeitmudbricks.com.au/manufacture.html.

Johns, C.H.W. 1904. *Babylonian and Assyrian Laws, Contracts and Letters*. New York: C. Scribner's Sons.

Julien, M., and C. Karlin. 1994. "Prehistoric Technology: A Cognitive Science?" In *The Ancient Mind: Elements of Cognitive Archaeology*, edited by C. Renfrew and E. Zubrow, 152–64. Cambridge; New York: Cambridge UP.

Kansa, E., S. Whitcher Kansa, and E. Watrall, eds. 2011. *Archaeology 2.0: New Approaches for Communication and Collaboration*. Los Angeles: Cotsen Institute of Archaeology Press.

Karatani, K. 1995. *Architecture as Metaphor: Language, Number, Money*. Cambridge, MA: MIT Press.

Kelly-Buccellati, M. 2002. "Ein hurritischer Gang in die Unterwelt." *Mitteilungen der Deutschen Orient-Gesellschaft zu Berlin*, no. 134: 131–48.

———. 2013. "Landscape and Spatial Organization, an Essay on Early Urban Settlement Patterns in Urkesh." In *100 Jahre Archaeologische Feldforschungen in Nordost-Syrien - eine Bilanz*, edited by D. Bonatz and L. Martin, 149–66. Schriften der Max Freiherr von Oppenheim-Stiftung 18. Wiesbaden: Harrassowitz.

Kingery, W.D., P.B. Vandiver, and M. Prickett. 1988. "The Beginnings of Pyrotechnology, Part II: Production and Use of Lime and Gypsum Plaster in the Pre-Pottery Neolithic near East." *Journal of Field Archaeology* 15 (2): 219–44.

Klein, U. 2001. *Bauaufnahme und Dokumentation*. Munich: DVA.

Klemm, R. 1993. *Stein und Steinbrüche im alten Ägypten*. Berlin; New York: Springer.

Kohlmeyer, K. 1996. "Houses in Habuba Kabira-South: Spatial Organization and Planning of Late Uruk Residential Architecture." In *Houses and Households in Ancient Mesopotamia*, edited by K Veenhof, 89–103. Istanbul: Nederlands Historisch-Archaeologisch Instituut te Istanbul.

Kreppner, F.J. 2012. "Site Formation Processes in the Lower Town II of Dur-Katlimmu. The Case of the Red House." In *Proceedings of the 7th ICAANE 12 April - 16 April 2010, British Museum and UCL, London*, edited by R. Matthews, J. Curtis, and M. Seymour, 217–28. Wiesbaden: Harrassowitz.

Kreppner, F.J., and J. Schmid. 2013. *Stratigraphie und Architektur des "Roten Hauses" von Tall Sheikh Hamad/Dur-Katlimmu*. BATSH 11. Wiesbaden: Harrassowitz.

Kurapkat, D. 2009. "Das Wissen der neolithischen Bauleute." In *Bautechnik im antiken und vorantiken Kleinasien*, edited by M. Bachmann. Byzas 9. Istanbul; Wien: Ege Yayinlari; Phoibos.

Labat, R. 1976. *Manuel d'épigraphie akkadienne: signes, syllabaire, idéogrammes*. Paris: P. Geuthner.

Lackenbacher, S. 1982. *Le roi bâtisseur : les récits de construction assyriens des origines à Teglatphalasar III*. Paris: Recherche sur les civilisations.

———. 1990. *Le palais sans rival : le récit de construction en Assyrie*. Paris: Eds. La Découverte.

Lamberg-Karlovsky, C. 2009. "Structure, Agency and Commerce in the Ancient Near East." *Iranica Antiqua* 44: 47.

Lang, F. 2010. "'Geschlossene Gesellschaften' – Architektursoziologische Überlegungen zum antiken griechischen Hofhau." In *Der gebaute Raum: Bausteine einer Architektursoziologie vormoderner Gesellschaften*, edited by P. Trebsche, N. Müller-Scheeßel, and S. Reinhold. Muenster; New York, NY; Munich; Berlin: Waxmann.

Le Corbusier. 1970. *Towards a New Architecture*. New York: Praeger.

Leach, Neil. 1997. *Rethinking Architecture: A Reader in Cultural Theory*. New York: Routledge.

Lebeau, M. 2011. "Introduction." In *ARCANE I: Jezirah*, edited by M. Lebeau. Turnhout: Brepols.

Lebeau, M., and A. Suleiman. 2003. *Tell Beydar, The 1995 to 1999 Seasons of Excavations. A Preliminary Report*. Subartu 10. Turnhout: Brepols.

Lechevallier, M. 1978. *Abou Gosh et Beisamoun : deux gisements du VII5 millénaire avant l'ère chrétienne en Israël*. Paris: Association Paléorient.

Lefebvre, H. (1974) 1991. *The Production of Space*. Translated by D. Nicholson-Smith. Oxford UK; Cambridge, MA: Wiley-Blackwell.

Leick, G. 1988. *A Dictionary of Ancient Near Eastern Architecture*. London; New York: Routledge.

Lemonnier, P. 1986. "The Study of Material Culture Today: Toward an Anthropology of Technical Systems." *Journal of Anthropological Archae-*

ology 5: 147–86.

Lévi-Strauss, C. 1988. *The Way of the Masks*. Seattle, WA: University of Washington Press.

Liverani, M. 2013. *Immaginare Babele: due secoli di studi sulla città orientale antica*. Roma: Laterza.

Lock, G. 2003. *Using Computers in Archaeology: Towards Virtual Pasts*. London; New York: Routledge.

Margueron, J.-C. 1982. *Recherches sur les palais mésopotamiens de l'Âge du bronze*. Paris: Geuthner.

———. 1983. "Notes d'archéologie et d'architecture orientales 3: du nouveau concernant le palais d'Eridu?" *Syria* 60 (3/4): 225–31.

———. 2008. "L'Architecture domestique de la Ville I de Mari." In *Proceedings of the 4th International Congress of the Archaeology of the Ancient Near East*, edited by H. Kuehne, R. Czichon, and F.J. Kreppner, 1:421–30. Wiesbaden: Harrassowitz.

———. 2009. "À propos de la Maison Ronde de Tepe Gawra: Approche méthodologique de la restitution architecturale." In *À propos de Tepe Gawra: le monde proto-urbain de Mésopotamie*, edited by P. Butterlin, 103–19. Turnhout: Brepols.

Martinón-Torres, M. 2002. "Chaîne Opératoire: The Concept and Its Applications within the Study of Technology." *Gallaecia* 21: 29–43.

Matthiae, P. 1977. *Ebla: un impero ritrovato*. Torino: Einaudi.

———. 1985. *I tesori di Ebla*. Roma: Laterza.

———. 1994. *Il sovrano e l'opera: arte e potere nella Mesopotamia antica*. Roma - Bari: Laterza.

———. 2010a. "Early Syrian Palatial Architecture: Some Thoughts About its Unity." In *Kulturlandschaft Syrien: Zentrum und Peripherie Festschrift für Jan-Waalke Meyer*, edited by J. Becker, R. Hempelmann, and E. Rehm, 349–58. AOAT 371. Münster: Ugarit-Verlag.

———. 2010b. *Ebla, la città del trono: archeologia e storia*. Torino: Einaudi.

McAdams, R. n.d. "Slavery and Freedom in the Third Dynasty of Ur: Implications of the Garshana Archives." *Cuneiform Digital Library Journal* 2010 (2).

McMahon, A. 2013. "Space, Sound, and Light: Toward a Sensory Experience of Ancient Monumental Architecture." *American Journal of Archaeology* 117 (2): 163–79.

McRaven, C. 1999. *Building Stone Walls*. North Adams, MA: Storey.

Medri, M. 2003. *Manuale di rilievo archeologico*. Roma: Laterza.

Meijer, D. 2008. "Cracking the Code? Aspect and Impact in Mesopotamian Architecture." In *Proceedings of the 4th International Congress of the*

Archaeology of the Ancient Near East, edited by H. Kuehne, R. Czichon, and F.J. Kreppner, 1:431–36. Wiesbaden: Harrassowitz.

Meyer, J.-W. 2006. "Zur Frage der Urbanisierung von Tell Chuera." In *Les espaces syro-mésopotamiens : dimensions de l'expérience humaine au Proche-Orient ancien. Volume d'hommage offert à Jean-Claude Margueron*, edited by P. Butterlin, J.-C. Margueron, M. Lebeau, J.-Y. Monchambert, J.L. Montero-Fenollos, and B. Muller, 179–90. Subartu 17. Turnhout: Brepols.

———. 2007a. "Town Planning in 3rd Millennium Tell Chuera." In *Power and Architecture: Monumental Public Architecture in the Bronze Age Near East and Aegean*, edited by J. Bretschneider, J. Driessen, and K. van Lerberghe, 129–42. Leuven; Dudley, MA: Peeters.

———. 2007b. "Veraenderungen der Grabungsstrategie in Tell Chuera (Syrien) aufgrund der Ergebnisse der geomagnetischen Prospektion." In *Geophysik und Ausgrabung: Einsatz und Auswertung zerstörungsfreier Prospektion in der Archäologie*, edited by M. Posselt, B. Zickgraf, and C. Dobiat, 223–36. Rahden/Westf.: Verlag Marie Leidorf.

———. 2010. *Ausgrabungen auf dem Tell Chuera in Nordost-Syrien. Teil II, Vorberichte zu den Grabungskampagnen 1998 bis 2005*. Wiesbaden: Harrassowitz.

Micale, M.G. 2005. "Immagini d'architettura. Struttura e forma dell'architettura mesopotamica attraverso le ricostruzioni moderne." In *Contributi e Materiali di Archeologia Orientale. Studi in onore di Paolo Matthiae*, edited by D. Nadali and A. Di Ludovico, 121–66. CMAO 10. Roma: Universita' degli Studi la Sapienza.

———. 2007. "'From Drawing to Vision'. The Use of Mesopotamian Architecture Through the Construction of its Image." In *Workshop 11. Archäologie und Computer: Kulturelles Erbe und Neue Technologien (CD-ROM)*, edited by W. Boerner and S. Uhrliz. Vienna: Magistrat der Stadt Wien.

———. 2011. *L'immagine dell'architettura nel rilievo storico neoassiro*. CMAO 14. Roma: Universita' degli Studi la Sapienza.

———. 2012. "Near-Eastern Archaeology under Siege: From Real Destruction to Virtual Reconstruction." In *Proceedings of the 7th International Congress on the Archaeology of the Ancient Near East*, edited by R. Matthews and J. Curtis. Vol. 2. Wiesbaden: Harassowitz.

Michelson, W. 1984. "Architecture and Communication: A Framework." *Contemporary Sociology* 13 (3): 264–66.

Milano, L. 1991. *Mozan 2: The Epigraphic Finds of the Sixth Season*. Malibu: Undena Publications.

Minke, G. 1994. *Lehmbau - Handbuch: Der Baustoff Lehm und seine Anwendung*. Staufen bei Freiburg: Ökobuch.

Moore, H. 1990. "Paul Ricoeur: Action, Meaning and Text." In *Reading Material Culture: Structuralism, Hermeneutics, and Post-Structuralism*, by C. Tilley, 85–120. Oxford, UK; Cambridge, MA: Blackwell.

Moran, W. 2000. *The Amarna Letters*. Baltimore, MD: Johns Hopkins UP.

Nadali, D. 2014. "Family Portraits. Some Considerations on the Iconographical Motif of the 'Woman with Child' in the Art of the Third Millennium B.C.E." In *La famille dans le Proche-Orient ancien : réalités, symbolismes, et images*, edited by L. Marti, 227–39. Winona Lake, IN: Eisenbrauns.

Nemet-Nejat, K.R. 1993. *Cuneiform Mathematical Texts as a Reflection of Everyday Life in Mesopotamia*. New Haven, CN: American Oriental Society.

Neumann, H. 1996. "Der Sumerische Baumeister (Shidim)." In *Houses and Households in Ancient Mesopotamia*, edited by K. R. Veenhof, 153–69. Istanbul: Nederlands Historisch-Archaeologisch Instituut te Istanbul.

———. 2011. "Slavery in Private Households Toward the End of the Third Millennium BC." In *Slaves and Households in the Near East*, edited by L. Culbertson, 21–32. Chicago, IL: Chicago UP.

Nippa, A. 1991. *Haus und Familie in arabischen Ländern: vom Mittelalter bis zur Gegenwart*. Munich: Beck.

Nunn, A. 1988. *Die Wandmalerei und der glasierte Wandschmuck im alten Orient*. Leiden: Brill.

Oates, D. 1990. "Innovations in Mud-Brick: Decorative and Structural Techniques in Ancient Mesopotamia." *World Archaeology* 21 (3): 388–406.

Oates, J. 1969. "Choga Mami, 1967-68: A Preliminary Report." *Iraq* 31 (2): 115–52.

Okabe, A. 2006. *GIS-Based Studies in the Humanities and Social Sciences*. Boca Raton, FL: Taylor & Francis.

Oppenheim, A.L. 1977. *Ancient Mesopotamia: Portrait of a Dead Civilization*. Chicago, IL: University of Chicago Press.

Orthmann, W., ed. 1995. *Ausgrabungen in Tell Chuera in Nordost-Syrien. Teil I, Vorbericht über die Grabungskampagnen 1986 bis 1992*. Saarbrücken: Saarbrücker Dr. und Verl.

Panofsky, E. (1955) 1983. *Meaning in the Visual Arts*. Chicago UP.

———. 1997. *Three Essays on Style*. Edited by I. Lavin. Cambridge, MA; London: MIT.

"Parallax." 2005. *Oxford English Dictionary*. http://dictionary.oed.com.

Peters, E. 1972. "Lehmziegelhaeuser in der Altinova." In *Keban Project, 1970*

Activities, 173–82. Ankara: Orta Doğu Teknik Üniversitesi.

Petrosino, S. 2011. *Monumentum: l'abitare, il politico, il sacro*. Milano: Jaca Book.

Pfälzner, P. 2011. "Architecture." In *ARCANE I: Jezirah*, edited by M. Lebeau. Turnhout: Brepols.

Postgate, J.N. 1992. *Early Mesopotamia: Society and Economy at the Dawn of History*. London; New York: Routledge.

Potts, D. 1996. *Mesopotamia: The Material Foundations*. Ithaca, NY: Continuum.

Preziosi, D. 1983. *Minoan Architectural Design: Formation and Signification*. Berlin; New York: Mouton.

Protzen, J.-P. 1985. "Inca Quarrying and Stonecutting." *Journal of the Society of Architectural Historians* 44 (2): 161–82.

———. 2008. "Stonemasonry of the Incas." Edited by H. Selin. *Encyclopaedia of the History of Science, Technology, and Medicine in Non-Western Cultures*. Berlin: Springer.

Protzen, J.-P., and S. Nair. 1997. "Who Taught the Inca Stonemasons Their Skills? A Comparison of Tiahuanaco and Inca Cut-Stone Masonry." *Journal of the Society of Architectural Historians* 56 (2): 146–67.

———. 2013. *The Stones of Tiahuanaco: A Study of Architecture and Construction*. Los Angeles, CA: Cotsen Institute of Archaeology Press, UCLA.

"Quarry." 2010. *Encyclopedia Britannica*. Encyclopedia Britannica Online. http://www.britannica.com/EBchecked/topic/486355/quarry.

Ragette, F. 1974. *Architecture in Lebanon: The Lebanese House during the 18th and 19th Centuries*. Beirut: American University of Beirut.

Rakic, Y.Z. 2003. "The Contest Scene in Akkadian Glyptic: A Study of Its Imagery and Function within the Akkadian Empire." Ph.D. Thesis, Pennsylvania: University of Pennsylvania.

Reichel, C. 2002. "Administrative Complexity in Syria during the 4th Millennium BC: The Seals and Sealings from Tell Hamoukar." *Akkadica* 123 (1): 35–56.

Renfrew, C. 2009. "Ethics in Archaeological Research: International Responses to the Illicit Trade in Antiquities." In *Quale futuro per l'archeologia? Workshop internazionale, Roma, 4-5 dicembre 2008*, edited by A.L. D'Agata and S. Alaura, 235–49. Roma: Gangemi.

Rice, P. 1987. *Pottery Analysis: A Source-Book*. Chicago, IL: Chicago UP.

Ricoeur, P. 1976. *Interpretation Theory: Discourse and the Surplus of Meaning*. Fort Worth, TX: TCU Press.

———. 1981. *Hermeneutics and the Human Sciences: Essays on Language,*

Action and Interpretation. Translated by J.B. Thompson. Cambridge, MA: Cambridge UP.

Robson, E. 1996. "Building with Bricks and Mortar: Quantity Surveying in the Ur III and Old Babylonian Periods." In *Houses and Households in Ancient Mesopotamia*, by K.R. Veenhof, 181–90. Leiden; Istanbul: Nederlands Historisch-Archaeologisch Instituut te Istanbul.

———. 1999. *Mesopotamian Mathematics, 2100-1600 BC: Technical Constants in Bureaucracy and Education*. Oxford Editions of Cuneiform Texts 14. Oxford; New York: Clarendon Press; Oxford UP.

Rosen, A. 1986. *Cities of Clay: The Geoarcheology of Tells*. Chicago, IL: Chicago UP.

Ryan, K. 2009. "The Significance of Choice in the Late Dorset Technology of Domestic Architecture." Ph.D. Thesis, Toronto: University of Toronto.

Sackett, J. 1990. "Style and Ethnicity in Archaeology: The Case for Isochrestism." In *The Uses of Style in Archaeology*, edited by M. Conkey and C. Hastorf, 32–43. Cambridge; New York, NY: Cambridge UP.

Safar, F. 1950. "Eridu 1948-1949." *Sumer* 6: 27–38.

Salonen, A. 1972. *Die Ziegeleien im alten Mesopotamien*. Helsinki: Academia Scientiarum Fennica.

Sauvage, M. 1998. *La brique et sa mise en oeuvre en Mésopotamie : des origines à l'époque Achéménide*. Paris: Éd. Recherche sur les Civilisations.

Schapiro, M. 1953. *Style*. Chicago, IL: University of Chicago Press.

Schiffer, M.B. 1975a. "Behavioral Chain Analysis: Activities, Organization, and the Use of Space." *Fieldiana. Anthropology* 65: 103–19.

———. 1975b. "Archaeology as Behavioral Science." *American Anthropologist*, New Series, 77 (4): 836–48.

———. 1999. "Behavioral Archaeology: Some Clarifications." *American Antiquity* 64 (1): 166–68.

Schlanger, N. 2005. "The Chaîne Opératoire." In *Archaeology: The Key Concepts*, edited by C. Renfrew and P. Bahn, 25–31. London; New York: Routledge.

Schliemann, Heinrich. 1891. *Bericht Über Die Ausgrabungen in Troja Im Jahre 1890*. Leipzig: Brockhaus.

Schloen, J.D. 2001. *The House of the Father as Fact and Symbol*. Studies in the Archaeology and History of the Levant 2. Winona Lake, IN: Eisenbrauns.

Schmidt, K. 2006. *Sie bauten die ersten Tempel - das rätselhafte Heiligtum der Steinzeitjäger - die archäologische Entdeckung am Göbekli Tepe*. Munich: Beck.

Schneider, K. 1991. *Die Burg des Elefantenjägers: Geschichte des "Grossen Hauses" von Bindouté Da (Lobi, Burkina Faso)*. Stuttgart: F. Steiner.

Schuecker, N., ed. 2012. *Integrating Archaeology: Science, Wish, Reality*. Frankfurt a. M.: Römisch-Germanische Kommission.

Schwandner, E.-L., and K. Rheidt, eds. 2004. *Macht der Architektur--Architektur der Macht: Bauforschungskolloquium in Berlin vom 30. Oktober bis 2. November 2002, veranstaltet vom Architektur-Referat des DAI*. Diskussionen zur archäologischen Bauforschung 8. Mainz am Rhein: P. von Zabern.

Seamon, D. 2013. "Environmental Embodiment, Merleau-Ponty, and Bill Hillier's Theory of Space Syntax: Toward a Phenomenology of People-in-Place." In *Rethinking Aesthetics: The Role of Body in Design*, edited by R. Bhatt, 204–13. New York, NY: Routledge.

"ShrinkingCities - Frankfurt." 2016. Accessed December 1. http://www.shrinkingcities.com/frankfurt.0.html?&L=1.

Sievertsen, U. 2014. "Bauwissen im Alten Orient." In *Wissensgeschichte der Architektur*, edited by J. Renn, W. Osthues, and H. Schlimme, 131–280. Berlin: Edition Open Access.

Smith, C.B. 2006. *How the Great Pyramid Was Built*. New York, NY: Harper Paperbacks.

Soden, W. von. 1965. *Akkadisches Handwoerterbuch*. Wiesbaden: Harrassowitz.

Steinkeller, P. 1987. "Review of 'Umma in the Sargonic Period' by Foster, B.R." *Wiener Zeitschrift für die Kunde des Morgenlandes* 77: 182–95.

Stone, E. 1981. "Texts, Architecture and Ethnographic Analogy: Patterns of Residence in Old Babylonian Nippur." *Iraq* 43: 19–33.

———. 1987. *Nippur Neighborhoods*. OIP 44. Chicago, IL: Oriental Institute of the University of Chicago.

Sydie, R.A. 1984. "Review of Ankerl - Experimental Sociology of Architecture." *The Canadian Journal of Sociology* 9 (4): 473–76.

Tamm, A. 2008. "Palastartige Bauten Nordsyriens im 3. Jahrtausend vor Christus." Magister Thesis, Frankfurt (M): Goethe University, Frankfurt (Main).

Tilley, C. 1999. *Metaphor and Material Culture*. Oxford, UK; Malden, MA: Blackwell.

Trebsche, P., N. Müller-Scheeßel, and S. Reinhold, eds. 2010. *Der gebaute Raum: Bausteine einer Architektursoziologie vormoderner Gesellschaften*. Muenster; New York, NY; Munich; Berlin: Waxmann.

"TROIA Traum und Wirklichkeit." 2015. Accessed April 30. http://www.troia.de/pages/portal.php.

"Troia VR." 2015. Accessed April 30. http://www.uni-tuebingen.de/troia/vr/index.html.

Tronconi, O., M. Pugnetti, C. Pessina, and V. Puglisi. 2008. *L'architettura montana: tecnologie, valori ambientali e sociali di un patrimonio storico-architettonico vivo ed attuale*. Santarcangelo di Romagna (Rimini): Maggioli.

Tufte, E. 1990. *Envisioning Information*. Cheshire, CT: Graphics Press.

———. 1997. *Visual Explanations: Images and Quantities, Evidence and Narrative*. Cheshire, CT: Graphics Press.

Udy, S. 1959. *Organization of Work: A Comparative Analysis of Production among Nonindustrial Peoples*. New Haven, CT: Human Relations Area Files Press.

Unwin, S. 2003. *Analysing Architecture*. London; New York: Routledge.

Ur, J.A. 2013a. "CORONA Satellite Imagery and Ancient Near Eastern Landscapes." In *Mapping Archaeological Landscapes from Space: In Observance of the 40th Anniversary of the World Heritage Convention*, edited by D. Comer and M. Harrower, 19–29. New York: Springer.

———. 2013b. "The Comparative Morphology of Neo-Assyrian Cities." *Subartu* 6–7: 11–22.

Vivian, J. 1978. *Building Stone Walls*. North Adams, MA: Storey.

Watson, P.J., and R. Gould. 1982. "A Dialogue on the Meaning and Use of Analogy in Ethnoarchaeological Reasoning." *Journal of Anthropological Archaeology* 1 (4): 355–81.

Weiss, H., S. Manning, L. Ristvet, L. Mori, M. Besonen, A. McCarthy, P. Quenet, A. Smith, and Z. Bahrani. 2012. "Tell Leilan Akkadian Imperialization, Collapse and Short-Lived Reoccupation Defined by High-Resolution Radiocarbon Dating." In *Seven Generations Since the Fall of Akkad*, 163–92. Studia Chaburensia 3. Wiesbaden: Harassowitz.

Wendrich, W. 2012. *Archaeology and Apprenticeship: Body Knowledge, Identity, and Communities of Practice*. Tucson, AZ: University of Arizona Press.

Winter, I. 1993. "'Seat of Kingship'/"A Wonder to Behold": The Palace as Construct in the Ancient near East." *Ars Orientalis* 23: 27–55.

Wittgenstein, L. (1977) 1980. *Culture and Value*. Edited by G. H. von Wright. Translated by P. Winch. Chicago, IL: Chicago UP.

Wulff, H. 1966. *The Traditional Crafts of Persia: Their Development, Technology, and Influence on Eastern and Western Civilizations*. Cambridge, MA: MIT Press.

Wylie, A. 1982. "An Analogy by Any Other Name Is Just as Analogical." *Journal of Anthropological Archaeology* 1 (4): 382–401.

Yokoyama, M. 1994. "The Administrative Structure and Economic Function of Public Service (Ilkum) of the Old Babylonian State in the Old Babylonian Period." Ph.D. Thesis, Los Angeles, CA: UCLA.

Zevi, B. 1972. *Architectura in nuce*. Firenze: Sansoni.

———. 1994. *Architettura concetti di una controstoria*. Roma: Newton.

Appendix: BlockGen Vademecum and Program Code

This appendix provides practical information regarding the BlockGen plug-in. The first section gives a vademecum explaining how to create the script files needed to generate a 3D model using this tool. The second section gives the program code for the plug-in itself; this plug-in was designed by this study's author and was improved in collaboration over several versions, but was coded by a professional programmer[199] experienced with AutoCAD. The coding was sponsored by IIMAS and the DFG through the Research Training Group "Value and Equivalence" at the Universities of Frankfurt am Main and TU Darmstadt. The code will be distributed as open source software under a GNU license and will also be made available as a compiled DLL. A link to the latest downloadable DLL will be made available on the publisher's website (www.undena.com) together with the reference to this volume as well as the Mozan / Urkesh Project Website (www.urkesh.com) on the pages dedicated to the AP Palace; a GitHub project page is also in development.

Vademecum

The scripts using BlockGen are designed to be called from within AutoCAD (version 2010 and later) as script files. These script files contain more commands than just the BlockGen calls, and it may be of use to someone else wanting to use this plug-in to understand what was used in the generation of the scripts generating the AP Palace. Three types of scripts were used: an initial script, followed by a series of scripts building specific walls of the palace, and a final script. Each of these will be described in the following sections.

Initial Script

```
;Initial Script
;
filedia
0
netload
```

199 The plug-in was written by Steve Kimling of CADfx thanks to the financial support of IIMAS and the Research Training Group "Value and Eqivalence" (DFG).

```
"c:\Program Files\Autodesk\AutoCAD 2012 –
English\BlockGen2\blockgen.dll"
vscurrent
Conceptual
zoom window 31200,44485 37900,40600
snap off
-layer new 3DPolylines
color truecolor 127,159,255 3DPolylines

;
-layer new Stone
color truecolor 153,153,153 Stone

;
-layer new RBrick
color truecolor 165,41,0 RBrick

;
filedia
1
;
;If you can't see dialog boxes, enter "filedia 1"
;Be sure all snap modes are off: F3 F4 F9 F10 F11
```

The initial script begins with a series of notes using a semicolon – any text beginning with a semicolon are ignored by AutoCAD. The command "filedia{enter}0{enter}" tells AutoCAD not to open a dialog box when running commands from the command line. "netload{enter}XXXX" calls the blockgen DLL, where XXXX is the path where the BlockGen DLL is located. "vscurrent{enter}Conceptual" starts the 'conceptual' view of AutoCAD, while "zoom window X,Y X,Y" zooms to a specific area of the virtual space, where X,Y X,Y are the upper left and lower right corners of the area to be viewed. "snap off" removes the 'snap' feature, which interferes with the positioning of the solids.

The next series of commands create new layers, which are very important for separating construction elements being modeled as well as reconstructed walls, for example. "-layer new 3DPolylines" creates a new layer called 3DPolylines, while "color truecolor 127,159,255 3DPolylines" gives a color attribute to the new layer. The following commands create two further layers, 'Stone' and 'Rbrick', and assign colors to them.

"filedia{enter}1" reinstates the dialog boxes, which are necessary for interfacing with the program outside of the scripts. Two further notes (using semicolons) remind the user that if the dialog boxes do not appear (if the script stops halfway through, for example) one must manually enter "filedia{enter}1" to get them back. The second note reminds the user that all snaps must be off, and that the F3,4,9,10,11 keys turn snaps on and off.

Wall Scripts

```
;11 - D2 NW
;
clayer Text
filedia 0
text 35088,43232,8590 7 -90 AP 507=Y1r18
text 34997,43276,8590 7 -90 AP 183
text 34968,43208,8590 7 -90 AP 594
text 35070,43175,8590 7 -90 AP 512
text 35088,43232,8590 7 -90 AP 507=Y1r18
filedia 1
;
clayer 3DPolylines
3dpoly
35088,43232,8590
34997,43276,8590
34968,43208,8590
35070,43175,8590
35088,43232,8590
Close
;
clayer Stone
WallGen
35088,43232,8280
34997,43276,8280
34968,43208,8280
35070,43175,8280
35088,43232,8280
;
35088,43232,8367
34997,43276,8366
34968,43208,8356
35070,43175,8369
35088,43232,8367

;
clayer RBrick
WallGen
35088,43232,8367
34997,43276,8366
34968,43208,8356
35070,43175,8369
35088,43232,8367
;
35088,43232,8392
34997,43276,8392
34968,43208,8392
```

```
35070,43175,8392
35088,43232,8392

;
clayer RecBrick
WallGen
35088,43232,8392
34997,43276,8392
34968,43208,8392
35070,43175,8392
35088,43232,8392
;
35088,43232,8590
34997,43276,8590
34968,43208,8590
35070,43175,8590
35088,43232,8590
```

This is an example of a script creating a wall segment. Typically many of these would be called in creating the model; this script calls wall segment 11, the NW wall of room D2. The next command switches to a certain layer (created already) through "clayer Text", turns off the dialog boxes (see the initial script section for more on 'filedia') and then AutoCAD writes the point name (AP 183) at a specific coordinate set: "text 35088,43232,8590 7 -90 AP 183". This is quite useful when checking the final model builds.

The next section creates a simple line through the points describing the wall, also as a way to check the data if the solid of the wall should not be able to be created. The command "3dpoly" is used.

The next sections use the command "WallGen" (the actual command of BlockGen) to create 3D solids of the particular wall segment, placing them on specific layers using the "clayer" command. The points are divided into two parts, the coordinates describing the base of the segment followed by the coordinates describing the top of the segment. These points must overlap: the first point of the base must be below the first point of the top and so on.

Final Script

```
-layer set 0

;
-layer off 3DPolylines

;
zoom
extents
;
```

```
vscurrent
Conceptual
;
-vports
mo
_d
_2
v
;
-view
_SWISO
zoom
extents
```

The final script aids in viewing the finished model. The initial commands brings the active layer to the 0 (root) layer, so that no unintended changes are made when initially viewing the model. The 3Dpoly layer is turned off, so that the line does not interfere with viewing the model – its primarily purpose is in troubleshooting mistakes, and will be described in the following section. The following commands zoom to the model itself, set the viewport to conceptual, sets the viewports to an optimal viewing position and an isometric view from the southwest.

Troubleshooting Errors

In general, two sorts of errors occur when running these scripts: errors within the AutoCAD commands and errors with the WallGen command (from BlockGen). The errors with the AutoCAD commands generally are due to the wrong number of spaces and/or carriage returns (enters) within the script file. Try entering the commands in the AutoCAD command line apart from the script file, and be sure that the enters/spaces are the same.

Problems with the WallGen command stem mostly from one of two causes: either the data or the position of the first point. The data can be easily checked by looking at the 3Dpoly line and the point numbers generated before the WallGen command is used: are there wild jumps in the coordinates, in the Z coordinate for example? Does the outline resemble the wall being modeled? Do the upper and lower sets of coordinates match?

The second common source of error in the WallGen command occurs when the initial point is not a clear corner – several problems were solved by moving the first point (of both lower and upper coordinate sets) to a different point along the wall.

Program Code

The program code itself was written in Visual Basic .NET; what follows is the programming code of the AutoCAD plug-in as written by a professional programmer[200] for this study – it was not written by this study's author. The plug-in will be distributed through the project (see www.iimas.org) and author's webpages as an OpenSource project and as a compiled DLL. The code is given here in printed format to ensure the durability of the code itself; the font selected is *OCR A Extended* in 9pt size, should it be necessary for future researchers to compile the plug-in from the published version. The following sections represent each a portion of the VB project.

BlockGen.vbproj

```
<?xml version="1.0" encoding="utf-8"?>
<Project                                                    DefaultTargets="Build"
xmlns="http://schemas.microsoft.com/developer/msbuild/2003" ToolsVersion="4.0">
  <PropertyGroup>
    <Configuration Condition=" '$(Configuration)' == '' ">Debug</Configuration>
    <Platform Condition=" '$(Platform)' == '' ">AnyCPU</Platform>
    <ProductVersion>8.0.50727</ProductVersion>
    <SchemaVersion>2.0</SchemaVersion>
    <ProjectGuid>{26311FA0-7289-42FE-80F2-B461F860AC78}</ProjectGuid>
    <OutputType>Library</OutputType>
    <RootNamespace>BlockGen</RootNamespace>
    <AssemblyName>BlockGen</AssemblyName>
    <MyType>Windows</MyType>
    <TargetFrameworkVersion>v3.5</TargetFrameworkVersion>
    <FileUpgradeFlags>
    </FileUpgradeFlags>
    <UpgradeBackupLocation>
    </UpgradeBackupLocation>
    <OldToolsVersion>2.0</OldToolsVersion>
    <TargetFrameworkProfile />
  </PropertyGroup>
  <PropertyGroup Condition=" '$(Configuration)|$(Platform)' == 'Debug|AnyCPU' ">
    <DebugSymbols>true</DebugSymbols>
    <DebugType>full</DebugType>
    <DefineDebug>true</DefineDebug>
    <DefineTrace>true</DefineTrace>
    <OutputPath>bin\Debug\</OutputPath>
    <DocumentationFile>BlockGen.xml</DocumentationFile>
     <NoWarn>42016,41999,42017,42018,42019,42032,42036,42020,42021,42022,42353,
42354,42355</NoWarn>
  </PropertyGroup>
  <PropertyGroup Condition=" '$(Configuration)|$(Platform)' == 'Release|AnyCPU' ">
    <DebugType>pdbonly</DebugType>
    <DefineDebug>false</DefineDebug>
    <DefineTrace>true</DefineTrace>
    <Optimize>true</Optimize>
    <OutputPath>bin\Release\</OutputPath>
    <DocumentationFile>BlockGen.xml</DocumentationFile>
     <NoWarn>42016,41999,42017,42018,42019,42032,42036,42020,42021,42022,42353,
42354,42355</NoWarn>
```

200 Steve Kimling of CADfx.

```
</PropertyGroup>
<ItemGroup>
  <Reference Include="AcDbMgd">
    <HintPath>External Modules\AcDbMgd.dll</HintPath>
    <Private>False</Private>
  </Reference>
  <Reference Include="AcMgd">
    <HintPath>External Modules\AcMgd.dll</HintPath>
    <Private>False</Private>
  </Reference>
  <Reference Include="System" />
  <Reference Include="System.Data" />
  <Reference Include="System.Xml" />
</ItemGroup>
<ItemGroup>
  <Import Include="Microsoft.VisualBasic" />
  <Import Include="System" />
  <Import Include="System.Collections" />
  <Import Include="System.Collections.Generic" />
  <Import Include="System.Data" />
  <Import Include="System.Diagnostics" />
</ItemGroup>
<ItemGroup>
  <Compile Include="BlockGenMain.vb" />
  <Compile Include="Extents.vb" />
  <Compile Include="Faces.vb" />
  <Compile Include="My Project\AssemblyInfo.vb" />
  <Compile Include="My Project\Application.Designer.vb">
    <AutoGen>True</AutoGen>
    <DependentUpon>Application.myapp</DependentUpon>
  </Compile>
  <Compile Include="My Project\Resources.Designer.vb">
    <AutoGen>True</AutoGen>
    <DesignTime>True</DesignTime>
    <DependentUpon>Resources.resx</DependentUpon>
  </Compile>
  <Compile Include="My Project\Settings.Designer.vb">
    <AutoGen>True</AutoGen>
    <DependentUpon>Settings.settings</DependentUpon>
    <DesignTimeSharedInput>True</DesignTimeSharedInput>
  </Compile>
  <Compile Include="Surfaces.vb" />
  <Compile Include="Triangle.vb" />
</ItemGroup>
<ItemGroup>
  <EmbeddedResource Include="My Project\Resources.resx">
    <Generator>VbMyResourcesResXFileCodeGenerator</Generator>
    <LastGenOutput>Resources.Designer.vb</LastGenOutput>
    <CustomToolNamespace>My.Resources</CustomToolNamespace>
    <SubType>Designer</SubType>
  </EmbeddedResource>
</ItemGroup>
<ItemGroup>
  <None Include="My Project\Application.myapp">
    <Generator>MyApplicationCodeGenerator</Generator>
    <LastGenOutput>Application.Designer.vb</LastGenOutput>
  </None>
  <None Include="My Project\Settings.settings">
```

```
    <Generator>SettingsSingleFileGenerator</Generator>
    <CustomToolNamespace>My</CustomToolNamespace>
    <LastGenOutput>Settings.Designer.vb</LastGenOutput>
  </None>
 </ItemGroup>
 <Import Project="$(MSBuildBinPath)\Microsoft.VisualBasic.targets" />
  <!-- To modify your build process, add your task inside one of the targets below and
uncomment it.
     Other similar extension points exist, see Microsoft.Common.targets.
 <Target Name="BeforeBuild">
 </Target>
 <Target Name="AfterBuild">
 </Target>
 -->
</Project>
```

BlockGen.sln

```
Microsoft Visual Studio Solution File, Format Version 11.00
# Visual Studio 2010
Project("{F184B08F-C81C-45F6-A57F-5ABD9991F28F}") = "BlockGen", "BlockGen.vbproj",
"{26311FA0-7289-42FE-80F2-B461F860AC78}"
EndProject
Global
	GlobalSection(SolutionConfigurationPlatforms) = preSolution
		Debug|Any CPU = Debug|Any CPU
		Release|Any CPU = Release|Any CPU
	EndGlobalSection
	GlobalSection(ProjectConfigurationPlatforms) = postSolution
		{26311FA0-7289-42FE-80F2-B461F860AC78}.Debug|Any CPU.ActiveCfg =
Debug|Any CPU
		{26311FA0-7289-42FE-80F2-B461F860AC78}.Debug|Any CPU.Build.0 =
Debug|Any CPU
		{26311FA0-7289-42FE-80F2-B461F860AC78}.Release|Any CPU.ActiveCfg
= Release|Any CPU
		{26311FA0-7289-42FE-80F2-B461F860AC78}.Release|Any CPU.Build.0 =
Release|Any CPU
	EndGlobalSection
	GlobalSection(SolutionProperties) = preSolution
		HideSolutionNode = FALSE
	EndGlobalSection
EndGlobal
```

BlockGenMain.vb

```
'Main class contains functions needed for connecting to AutoCAD

Imports Autodesk.AutoCAD.Runtime
Imports Autodesk.AutoCAD.EditorInput
Imports Autodesk.AutoCAD.DatabaseServices
Imports Autodesk.AutoCAD.Geometry
Imports Autodesk.AutoCAD.ApplicationServices

Public Class BlockGenMain
   Implements Autodesk.AutoCAD.Runtime.IExtensionApplication 'Ties this dll to AutoCAD

   'The following functions are required by AutoCAD extensions
                                   Public Sub Initialize() Implements
```

```
Autodesk.AutoCAD.Runtime.IExtensionApplication.Initialize
        'Report to the user that this dll has been loaded
        Dim uEditor As Editor = Application.DocumentManager.MdiActiveDocument.Editor

        uEditor.WriteMessage(vbNewLine & My.Application.Info.Title & " " & _
        My.Application.Info.Version.ToString & " Loaded" & vbNewLine)
    End Sub

                                    Public          Sub         Terminate()          Implements
Autodesk.AutoCAD.Runtime.IExtensionApplication.Terminate

    End Sub
    'End of required functions

    'AutoCAD command definition for "BlockGen"
    'On execution, the BlockGen command will prompt for 8 points
    'Example script (sample1.scr):
    '  BlockGen 0,0,0 5,0,0 5,0,5 0,0,5 0,5,0 5,5,0 5,5,5 0,5,5
    'Or each point can be on its own line like this (sample2.scr):
    '  BlockGen
    '  0,0,0
    '  5,0,0
    '  5,0,5
    '  0,0,5
    '  0,5,0
    '  5,5,0
    '  5,5,5
    '  0,5,5
    <CommandMethod("BlockGen")> _
    Public Shared Sub CBlockGen()
        Dim uEditor As Editor = Application.DocumentManager.MdiActiveDocument.Editor
                                              Dim      uDatabase      As      Database      =
Application.DocumentManager.MdiActiveDocument.Database
                                                    Dim      uTransactionManager      As
Autodesk.AutoCAD.DatabaseServices.TransactionManager                                    =
uDatabase.TransactionManager

        Dim PointList As New Point3dCollection
        Dim origon As New Point3d(0.0, 0.0, 0.0)
        Dim XDirection As New Vector3d(1.0, 0.0, 0.0)
        Dim YDirection As New Vector3d(0.0, 1.0, 0.0)
        Dim ZDirection As New Vector3d(0.0, 0.0, 1.0)

        'Get the points
        Dim OldOsMode As Object = Application.GetSystemVariable("osmode")
        Application.SetSystemVariable("osmode", 0) 'Turn off object snap modes during point
input
        For index As Integer = 1 To 8
                Dim result As PromptPointResult = uEditor.GetPoint(vbLf & "Enter Point " &
index.ToString & ": ")
            If Not result.Status = PromptStatus.OK Then
                Exit Sub
            End If
            PointList.Add(result.Value)
        Next
        Application.SetSystemVariable("osmode", OldOsMode)

        'Define all 6 faces (planes) used
```

```
        Dim uFaces As New Faces(PointList)

        'Find overal extents of entered points.
        Dim uExtents As New Extents(PointList)

        'Grow extents by 25% to make sure we have enough "material" to cut away from
        uExtents.Grow(0.25)

        Using uTransaction As Transaction = uTransactionManager.StartTransaction()
            Dim uBlockTable As BlockTable = DirectCast(uTransaction.GetObject(uDatabase.BlockTableId, OpenMode.ForRead), BlockTable)
            Dim ModelSpace As BlockTableRecord = DirectCast(uTransaction.GetObject(uBlockTable(BlockTableRecord.ModelSpace), OpenMode.ForWrite), BlockTableRecord)

            'Create a base solid from which to cut the faces based on the actual entered points.
            'This will accomodate any reasonable angle that each face plane creates.
            Dim box As New Solid3d
            box.CreateBox(uExtents.DeltaX, uExtents.DeltaY, uExtents.DeltaZ)

            Dim trans As Matrix3d = Matrix3d.AlignCoordinateSystem(origon, XDirection, YDirection, ZDirection, _
                uExtents.Center, XDirection, YDirection, ZDirection)

            box.TransformBy(trans)
            ModelSpace.AppendEntity(box)
            uTransaction.AddNewlyCreatedDBObject(box, True)

            'Cut the base solid down to the given points
            uFaces.CutFaces(box, uTransaction, ModelSpace, uExtents)

            uTransaction.Commit()
        End Using

    End Sub

    <CommandMethod("WallGen")> _
    Public Shared Sub WallGen()
        Dim uEditor As Editor = Application.DocumentManager.MdiActiveDocument.Editor
        Dim uDatabase As Database = Application.DocumentManager.MdiActiveDocument.Database
        Dim uTransactionManager As Autodesk.AutoCAD.DatabaseServices.TransactionManager = uDatabase.TransactionManager

        Dim PointList As New Point3dCollection
        Dim origon As New Point3d(0.0, 0.0, 0.0)
        Dim XDirection As New Vector3d(1.0, 0.0, 0.0)
        Dim YDirection As New Vector3d(0.0, 1.0, 0.0)
        Dim ZDirection As New Vector3d(0.0, 0.0, 1.0)

        Dim ppo As New PromptPointOptions("")
        ppo.AllowNone = True

        'Get the points
```

```
        Dim OldOsMode As Object = Application.GetSystemVariable("osmode")
        Application.SetSystemVariable("osmode", 0) 'Turn off object snap modes during point
input
        For index As Integer = 1 To 100
            ppo.Message = vbLf & "Enter Point " & index.ToString & "<enter to build>: "
            Dim result As PromptPointResult = uEditor.GetPoint(ppo)
            If Not result.Status = PromptStatus.OK Then
                Exit For
            End If
            PointList.Add(result.Value)
        Next
        Application.SetSystemVariable("osmode", OldOsMode)

        'Check for even number of points and split into two groups.
        If Not PointList.Count Mod 2 = 0 OrElse PointList.Count < 4 Then
                uEditor.WriteMessage(vbLf & "Number of supplied points is not divisible by 2,
Exiting")
            Exit Sub
        End If

        Dim PointList1 As New Point3dCollection
        Dim PointList2 As New Point3dCollection
        For index As Integer = 0 To (PointList.Count / 2) - 1
            PointList1.Add(PointList(index))
        Next
        For index As Integer = (PointList.Count / 2) To PointList.Count - 1
            PointList2.Add(PointList(index))
        Next

        'Initiate surface class
        Dim smanager As Surfaces = Nothing
        If PointList1(0).Z > PointList2(0).Z Then
            smanager = New Surfaces(PointList1, PointList2)
        Else
            smanager = New Surfaces(PointList2, PointList1)
        End If

        'Build Surface
        Try
            Using uTransaction As Transaction = uTransactionManager.StartTransaction()
                                                    Dim uBlockTable As BlockTable =
DirectCast(uTransaction.GetObject(uDatabase.BlockTableId,      OpenMode.ForRead),
BlockTable)
                                            Dim ModelSpace As BlockTableRecord =
DirectCast(uTransaction.GetObject(uBlockTable(BlockTableRecord.ModelSpace),
OpenMode.ForWrite), BlockTableRecord)

                smanager.GenerateSurface(uTransaction, ModelSpace)

                uTransaction.Commit()
            End Using
        Catch ex As Exception
            MsgBox(ex.Message)
        End Try


    End Sub
```

```
End Class
```

Extents.vb

```
'Class for handeling extents information

Imports Autodesk.AutoCAD.Geometry
Imports Autodesk.AutoCAD.DatabaseServices

Public Class Extents
    Private m_maxx As Double
    Private m_maxy As Double
    Private m_maxz As Double
    Private m_minx As Double
    Private m_miny As Double
    Private m_minz As Double
    Private m_Extents As Extents3d
    Private m_PointList As Point3dCollection

    Public Sub New(ByVal aPointList As Point3dCollection)
        m_PointList = aPointList

        GetMaxMin()

            m_Extents = New Extents3d(New Point3d(m_minx, m_miny, m_minz), New
Point3d(m_maxx, m_maxy, m_maxz))

    End Sub

    Public ReadOnly Property DeltaX() As Double
        Get
            Return m_maxx - m_minx
        End Get
    End Property

    Public ReadOnly Property DeltaY() As Double
        Get
            Return m_maxy - m_miny
        End Get
    End Property

    Public ReadOnly Property DeltaZ() As Double
        Get
            Return m_maxz - m_minz
        End Get
    End Property

    Public ReadOnly Property Center() As Point3d
        Get
            Return New Point3d(m_minx + (m_maxx - m_minx) / 2.0, _
                        m_miny + (m_maxy - m_miny) / 2.0, _
                        m_minz + (m_maxz - m_minz) / 2.0)
        End Get
    End Property

    Public ReadOnly Property LongestLength() As Double
        Get
                Return Math.Max(Math.Max(m_maxx - m_minx, m_maxy - m_miny), m_maxz -
```

```
m_minz)
      End Get
   End Property

   Private Sub GetMaxMin()
      'Must use this method due to a bug in AutoCAD's Extents3d functionality that
      'doesn't reset the minimum point of the extents correctly.
      m_maxx = Double.MinValue
      m_maxy = Double.MinValue
      m_maxz = Double.MinValue
      m_minx = Double.MaxValue
      m_miny = Double.MaxValue
      m_minz = Double.MaxValue

      For index As Integer = 0 To 7
         If m_PointList(index).X > m_maxx Then m_maxx = m_PointList(index).X
         If m_PointList(index).Y > m_maxy Then m_maxy = m_PointList(index).Y
         If m_PointList(index).Z > m_maxz Then m_maxz = m_PointList(index).Z

         If m_PointList(index).X < m_minx Then m_minx = m_PointList(index).X
         If m_PointList(index).Y < m_miny Then m_miny = m_PointList(index).Y
         If m_PointList(index).Z < m_minz Then m_minz = m_PointList(index).Z
      Next
   End Sub

   Public Sub Grow(ByVal aPrecentage As Double)
      Dim ExpansionLength As Double = LongestLength * aPrecentage

      m_maxx += ExpansionLength
      m_maxy += ExpansionLength
      m_maxz += ExpansionLength

      m_minx -= ExpansionLength
      m_miny -= ExpansionLength
      m_minz -= ExpansionLength

         m_Extents = New Extents3d(New Point3d(m_minx, m_miny, m_minz), New
Point3d(m_maxx, m_maxy, m_maxz))

   End Sub

End Class
Faces.vb
'Class for handeling face information and cutting

Imports Autodesk.AutoCAD.Geometry
Imports Autodesk.AutoCAD.DatabaseServices

Public Class Faces
   Private m_Bottom As Plane
   Private m_Top As Plane
   Private m_Left As Plane
   Private m_Right As Plane
   Private m_Front As Plane
   Private m_Back As Plane
   Private m_PointList As Point3dCollection

   'The following is a translation from the entered points as described in
```

```
'the "plug-in requriements.pdf" received from Federico Buccellati on July 3, 2007
'to the individual faces of the solid with the "bottom" and "top" being
'parallel to the world plane in AutoCAD.
Private m_BottomPointIndexes() As Integer = {4, 0, 1, 5}
Private m_TopPointIndexes() As Integer = {2, 3, 7, 6}
Private m_LeftPointIndexes() As Integer = {3, 0, 4, 7}
Private m_RightPointIndexes() As Integer = {5, 1, 2, 6}
Private m_FrontPointIndexes() As Integer = {1, 0, 3, 2}
Private m_BackPointIndexes() As Integer = {7, 4, 5, 6}

Public Sub New(ByVal aPointList As Point3dCollection)
   m_PointList = aPointList
   m_Bottom = New Plane(aPointList(m_BottomPointIndexes(0)), aPointList(m_BottomPointIndexes(1)), aPointList(m_BottomPointIndexes(2)))
   m_Top = New Plane(aPointList(m_TopPointIndexes(0)), aPointList(m_TopPointIndexes(1)), aPointList(m_TopPointIndexes(2)))
   m_Left = New Plane(aPointList(m_LeftPointIndexes(0)), aPointList(m_LeftPointIndexes(1)), aPointList(m_LeftPointIndexes(2)))
   m_Right = New Plane(aPointList(m_RightPointIndexes(0)), aPointList(m_RightPointIndexes(1)), aPointList(m_RightPointIndexes(2)))
   m_Front = New Plane(aPointList(m_FrontPointIndexes(0)), aPointList(m_FrontPointIndexes(1)), aPointList(m_FrontPointIndexes(2)))
   m_Back = New Plane(aPointList(m_BackPointIndexes(0)), aPointList(m_BackPointIndexes(1)), aPointList(m_BackPointIndexes(2)))
End Sub

 Public Sub CutFaces(ByRef aBox As Solid3d, ByVal aTransaction As Transaction, ByVal aModelSpace As BlockTableRecord, _
         ByVal aExtents As Extents)
   Dim PlaneCoords As CoordinateSystem3d
   Dim cutterBase As Circle
   Dim cutter As Solid3d
   Dim CurveList As DBObjectCollection
   Dim NewObjects As DBObjectCollection
   Dim uRegion As Region
   Dim FaceList As New List(Of Plane)

   FaceList.Add(m_Bottom)
   FaceList.Add(m_Top)
   FaceList.Add(m_Left)
   FaceList.Add(m_Right)
   FaceList.Add(m_Front)
   FaceList.Add(m_Back)

   For Each uPlane As Plane In FaceList
      PlaneCoords = uPlane.GetCoordinateSystem()
      cutterBase = New Circle(PlaneCoords.Origin, uPlane.Normal, aExtents.LongestLength * 2.0)

      CurveList = New DBObjectCollection
      CurveList.Add(cutterBase)
      Try
         NewObjects = Region.CreateFromCurves(CurveList)
      Catch e As Exception
         Continue For
      End Try
```

```
            uRegion = DirectCast(NewObjects(0), Region)

            cutter = New Solid3d
            If uPlane.Normal.Equals(uRegion.Normal) Then
               cutter.Extrude(uRegion, aExtents.LongestLength * 1.5, 0.0)
            Else
               'if the normals of the new region and the original plane don't match
               'we have to use a negative value for the extrusion distance. This was added
               'to deal with an AutoCAD bug.
               cutter.Extrude(uRegion, -aExtents.LongestLength * 1.5, 0.0)
            End If

            aModelSpace.AppendEntity(cutter)
            aTransaction.AddNewlyCreatedDBObject(cutter, True)
            aBox.BooleanOperation(BooleanOperationType.BoolSubtract, cutter)
         Next

   End Sub
End Class
Surfaces.vb
'Class for handeling surface conversions

Imports Autodesk.AutoCAD.Geometry
Imports Autodesk.AutoCAD.DatabaseServices
Imports System.Runtime.InteropServices
Imports Autodesk.AutoCAD.ApplicationServices

Public Class Surfaces
   Private TopPointList As Point3dCollection
   Private BottomPointList As Point3dCollection
   Private SurfaceObjs As New List(Of ObjectId)

   '<DllImport("acad.exe", CallingConvention:=CallingConvention.Cdecl, EntryPoint:="acedCmd")> _
   'Private Shared Function acedCmd(pResbuf As IntPtr) As Integer
   'End Function

   Public Sub New(ByVal pTopPointList As Point3dCollection, ByVal pBottomPointList As Point3dCollection)
      TopPointList = pTopPointList
      BottomPointList = pBottomPointList
   End Sub

   Public Sub GenerateEdgeSurface(ByVal aIndex As Integer, ByVal aTransaction As Transaction, ByVal aModelSpace As BlockTableRecord)
      Dim f As New Face(BottomPointList(aIndex), BottomPointList(aIndex + 1), TopPointList(aIndex + 1), TopPointList(aIndex), True, True, True, True)
      Dim surf As Autodesk.AutoCAD.DatabaseServices.Surface = Autodesk.AutoCAD.DatabaseServices.Surface.CreateFrom(f)

      SurfaceObjs.Add(aModelSpace.AppendEntity(surf))
      aTransaction.AddNewlyCreatedDBObject(surf, True)
   End Sub

   Public Sub GenerateSurface(ByVal aTransaction As Transaction, ByVal aModelSpace As BlockTableRecord)
      For index As Integer = 0 To TopPointList.Count - 2
         GenerateEdgeSurface(index, aTransaction, aModelSpace)
```

```
Next

Dim topTriangles As List(Of Triangle) = Tessellate(TopPointList)
Dim bottomTriangles As List(Of Triangle) = Tessellate(BottomPointList)

For Each t As Triangle In topTriangles
   t.GenerateSurface(aTransaction, aModelSpace, SurfaceObjs)
Next

For Each t As Triangle In bottomTriangles
   t.GenerateSurface(aTransaction, aModelSpace, SurfaceObjs)
Next

' best method for creating a solid from multiple surfaces
Using sol As New Solid3d()
   Dim surfaces As New List(Of Entity)
   For Each oid As ObjectId In SurfaceObjs
      Dim ent As Entity = aTransaction.GetObject(oid, OpenMode.ForWrite)
      If Not ent = Nothing Then
         surfaces.Add(ent)
      End If
   Next

   Dim flags As New IntegerCollection()
   sol.CreateSculptedSolid(surfaces.ToArray(), flags)

   For Each ent As Entity In surfaces
      ent.Erase()
   Next
   aModelSpace.AppendEntity(sol)
   aTransaction.AddNewlyCreatedDBObject(sol, True)
End Using

' Alternate method that works, but not quite as well
'SurfaceObjs.Reverse()

'Dim surf As Autodesk.AutoCAD.DatabaseServices.Surface =
aTransaction.GetObject(SurfaceObjs(0), OpenMode.ForWrite, False)
'Dim nsurf As Autodesk.AutoCAD.DatabaseServices.Surface = Nothing

'SurfaceObjs.RemoveAt(0)

'Try
'   For Each oid As ObjectId In SurfaceObjs
'      Dim s As Autodesk.AutoCAD.DatabaseServices.Surface =
aTransaction.GetObject(oid, OpenMode.ForWrite, False)
'      nsurf = surf.BooleanUnion(s)
'      s.Erase()
'      If nsurf = Nothing Then
'         Continue For
'      End If
'      aModelSpace.AppendEntity(nsurf)
'      aTransaction.AddNewlyCreatedDBObject(nsurf, True)
'      surf.Erase()
'      surf = nsurf
'   Next

'   Try
```

```
      '       Dim sol As New Solid3d()
      '       sol.CreateFrom(surf)
      '       aModelSpace.AppendEntity(sol)
      '       aTransaction.AddNewlyCreatedDBObject(sol, True)
      '       surf.Erase()
      '    Catch ex As Exception
      '        Application.DocumentManager.MdiActiveDocument.Editor.WriteMessage(vbLf +
"WallGen ERROR: Unable to convert surface to solid. Look for self intersection.")
      '    End Try
      'Catch ex As Exception
      '    MsgBox(ex.Message)
      'End Try
   End Sub

   Private Function asPnt2d(ByVal aPoint As Point3d) As Point2d
      Return New Point2d(aPoint.X, aPoint.Y)
   End Function

      Private Function ContainsEdge(ByVal aLine As LineSegment2d, ByVal aLineList As
List(Of LineSegment2d)) As Boolean
      Try
         For Each ln As LineSegment2d In aLineList
                                             If aLine.StartPoint.IsEqualTo(ln.StartPoint) AndAlso
aLine.EndPoint.IsEqualTo(ln.EndPoint) Then
               Return True
            End If
                                             If aLine.StartPoint.IsEqualTo(ln.EndPoint) AndAlso
aLine.EndPoint.IsEqualTo(ln.StartPoint) Then
               Return True
            End If
         Next
      Catch ex As Exception
         MsgBox(ex.Message)
      End Try
      Return False
   End Function

    Private Function IsLineInside(ByVal aLine As LineSegment2d, ByVal aLineList As List(Of
LineSegment2d), ByVal aPointList As Point3dCollection, ByRef isEdge As Boolean) As
Boolean
      Dim tol As New Tolerance(0.1, 0.1)
      Dim mid As Point2d = aLine.MidPoint
      isEdge = False

      ' if the test line is an edge segment, it's not inside
      If ContainsEdge(aLine, aLineList) Then
         isEdge = True
         Return False
      End If

      ' if the above point isn't contained within the polygon, then it's assured the line is
      ' at least partially outside the polygon
      If Not PointInPolygon(mid, aPointList) Then
         Return False
      End If

      For Each ln As LineSegment2d In aLineList
         Dim ipoints() As Point2d = ln.IntersectWith(aLine, tol)
```

```
        If ipoints Is Nothing Then
           Continue For
        End If

        ' count non end points
        Dim icount As Integer = 0
        For Each pt As Point2d In ipoints
           If pt.IsEqualTo(aLine.EndPoint, tol) OrElse pt.IsEqualTo(aLine.StartPoint, tol) Then
              Continue For
           End If
           icount += 1
        Next

        ' if the test line intersects with any other line it can't be used since at least
        ' part of it is outside.
        If icount > 0 Then
           Return False
        End If
     Next

     Return True
  End Function

  Private Function Tessellate(ByVal aPointList As Point3dCollection) As List(Of Triangle)
     Dim lines As New List(Of LineSegment2d)
     For i As Integer = 0 To aPointList.Count - 1
         lines.Add(New LineSegment2d(asPnt2d(aPointList(i)), asPnt2d(aPointList(i + 1 Mod
aPointList.Count))))
     Next

     Dim pivot As Integer = 0
     Dim epoint As Integer = 1
     Dim i2 As Integer = 0
     Dim i3 As Integer = 0
     Dim isEdge = False
     Dim Triangles As New List(Of Triangle)
     Dim stopAt As Integer = -1
     Dim stopAts As New Dictionary(Of Integer, Integer)

     While pivot >= 0
                         Dim testline As New LineSegment2d(asPnt2d(aPointList(pivot)),
asPnt2d(aPointList(epoint Mod aPointList.Count)))
        If Not IsLineInside(testline, lines, aPointList, isEdge) Then
           If isEdge AndAlso i2 = pivot Then ' represents the first side of the triangle
              i2 = epoint
           ElseIf isEdge AndAlso i2 = i3 Then ' represents the second side of the triangle
              i3 = epoint
               epoint -= 1 ' need to cancel out indexing of epoint next cycle will take care of
it
           End If
           epoint += 1
           If epoint >= aPointList.Count Then
              Exit While
              ElseIf epoint < aPointList.Count - 2 Then ' only continue while not at the last
triangle
              Continue While
           End If
```

```
        ElseIf i2 = pivot Then ' test line is inside polygon but don't have a 3rd point yet so
keep going
            i2 = epoint
            epoint += 1
            If epoint > aPointList.Count Then
                Exit While
            End If
            Continue While
        End If

        ' if we get here, epoint should close the triangle
        i3 = epoint
        Triangles.Add(New Triangle(aPointList(pivot), aPointList(i2), aPointList(i3)))
        If (i3 - i2) > 1 Then 'means there was a gap and we have missing triangles
            stopAt = i3
            If Not stopAts.ContainsKey(stopAt) Then
                stopAts(stopAt) = pivot
            End If
            pivot = i2 'temporarily shift pivot until reaching stop at
            epoint = pivot + 1
            If i3 = aPointList.Count Then
                epoint = pivot + 1
                i2 = pivot
                stopAt = -1 'we are at the end of the list so this no longer applies
            End If
        Else
            i2 = i3
            epoint = i3 + 1

            If i3 = stopAt Then
                If Not stopAts.TryGetValue(stopAt, pivot) Then ' shift pivot back
                    stopAt = -1
                End If
            End If
        End If
        If epoint >= aPointList.Count - 1 Then
            Exit While
        End If
    End While
    Return Triangles
End Function

'Only works for flat polygons parallel to the world plane
    Private Function PointInPolygon(ByVal apoint As Point3d, ByVal aPointList As
Point3dCollection) As Boolean
    Return PointInPolygon(New Point2d(apoint.X, apoint.Y), aPointList)
End Function

    Private Function PointInPolygon(ByVal aPoint As Point2d, ByVal aPointList As
Point3dCollection) As Boolean
    Dim polySides As Integer = aPointList.Count
    Dim polyX(polySides) As Double
    Dim polyY(polySides) As Double
    Dim i As Integer = 0
    Dim j As Integer = polySides - 1
    Dim oddNodes As Boolean = False
    Dim x As Double = aPoint.X
    Dim y As Double = aPoint.Y
```

```
        For Each vtx As Point3d In aPointList
            polyX(i) = vtx.X
            polyY(i) = vtx.Y
            i += 1
        Next

        For i = 0 To polySides - 1
            If (polyY(i) < y AndAlso polyY(j) >= y) OrElse (polyY(j) < y AndAlso polyY(i) >= y)
Then
                If polyX(i) + (y - polyY(i)) / (polyY(j) - polyY(i)) * (polyX(j) - polyX(i)) < x Then
                    oddNodes = Not oddNodes
                End If
            End If
            j = i
        Next

        Return oddNodes
    End Function

End Class
```

Triangles.vb

```
'Class for handeling triangles

Imports Autodesk.AutoCAD.Geometry
Imports Autodesk.AutoCAD.DatabaseServices

Public Class Triangle
    Private Point1 As Point3d
    Private Point2 As Point3d
    Private Point3 As Point3d

    Public Sub New(ByVal aPt1 As Point3d, ByVal aPt2 As Point3d, ByVal aPt3 As Point3d)
        Point1 = aPt1
        Point2 = aPt2
        Point3 = aPt3
    End Sub

    Public Sub GenerateSurface(ByVal aTransaction As Transaction, ByVal aModelSpace As
BlockTableRecord, ByRef aSurfaceObjs As List(Of ObjectId))
        Dim f As New Face(Point1, Point2, Point3, True, True, True, True)
        Dim surf As Autodesk.AutoCAD.DatabaseServices.Surface =
Autodesk.AutoCAD.DatabaseServices.Surface.CreateFrom(f)

        aSurfaceObjs.Add(aModelSpace.AppendEntity(surf))
        aTransaction.AddNewlyCreatedDBObject(surf, True)
    End Sub
End Class
```

AP Palace Wall Catalog

The following is a catalog of the 3D data used to create the 3D model of the AP Palace used in this study. The data is presented with an image of each 3D block together with its script file. The data is given here in printed format to ensure the durability of the code itself; the font selected is *OCR A Extended* in 9pt size, should it be necessary for future researchers to compile the plug-in from the published version. For more information on the commands used, see the appendix above. The data collection was organized, followed by, checked and corrected by the author.

Each wall is identified by a sequential number, which corresponds to the number of the sub-chapter within the catalog. It is followed by a capital letter that refers to the sector of the Palace, and a number that corresponds to the room number within the sector. This in turn is followed by a letter that refers to the cardinal point within the room where the wall is situated. Thus, for example: '004-D1 E' should be read as follows – '004' is the sequential number of wall, 'D1' is room D1, and 'E' is the east side of room.

Image and Scripts

001- F E-SE

```
;01 - F E-SE
;
filedia 0
clayer Text
text 36006,43362,8590 7 -90 AP 601
text  36015,43381,8590  7  -90  AP
600=Y1r13
text 35872,43434,8590 7 -90 AP 599
text 35814,43336,8590 7 -90 AP 598
text 35982,43228,8590 7 -90 AP 603
text 36027,43353,8590 7 -90 AP 602
text 36006,43362,8590 7 -90 AP 601
filedia 1
;
clayer 3DPolylines
3dpoly
36006,43362,8590
36015,43381,8590
35872,43434,8590
35814,43336,8590
35982,43228,8590
36027,43353,8590
36006,43362,8590

clayer Stone
WallGen
36006,43362,8284
36015,43381,8284
35872,43434,8284
35814,43336,8292
35982,43228,8284
36027,43353,8284
```

```
36006,43362,8284
;
36006,43362,8354
36015,43381,8354
35872,43434,8361
35814,43336,8345
35982,43228,8351
36027,43353,8349
36006,43362,8354

;
clayer Rbrick
WallGen
36006,43362,8354
36015,43381,8354
35872,43434,8361
35814,43336,8345
35982,43228,8351
36027,43353,8349
36006,43362,8354
;
36006,43362,8473
36015,43381,8473
35872,43434,8433
35814,43336,8433
35982,43228,8430
36027,43353,8409
36006,43362,8473

clayer Recbrick
WallGen
36006,43362,8473
36015,43381,8473
35872,43434,8433
35814,43336,8433
35982,43228,8430
36027,43353,8409
36006,43362,8473
;
36006,43362,8590
36015,43381,8590
35872,43434,8590
35814,43336,8590
35982,43228,8590
36027,43353,8590
36006,43362,8590
002- F S
```

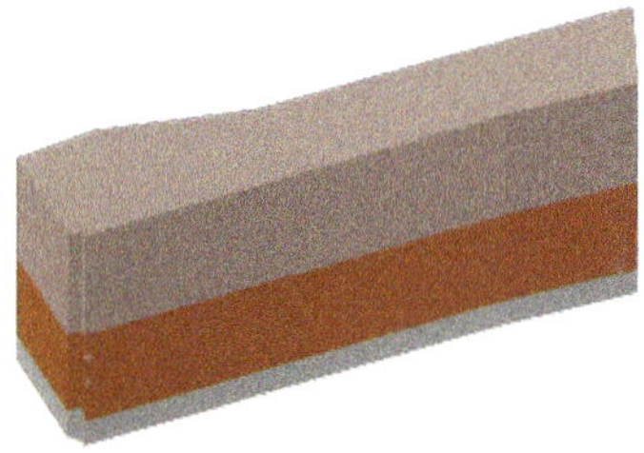

```
;02 - F S
;elevations reconstructed
;
filedia 0
clayer Text
text 35707,43362,8590 7 -90 AP 078
text 35640,43207,8590 7 -90 AP 099
text 35658,43201,8590 7 -90 AP 098
text 35655,43192,8590 7 -90 AP 097
text 36190,43008,8590 7 -90 AP 096
text 36346,42943,8590 7 -90 AP 084
text 36452,43059,8590 7 -90 AP 083
text 35982,43228,8590 7 -90 AP 603
text 35814,43336,8590 7 -90 AP 598
text 35707,43362,8590 7 -90 AP 078
filedia 1
;
clayer 3DPolylines
3dpoly
35707,43362,8590
35640,43207,8590
35658,43201,8590
35655,43192,8590
36190,43008,8590
36346,42943,8590
36452,43059,8590
35982,43228,8590
35814,43336,8590
35707,43362,8590

clayer Stone
WallGen
35707,43362,8301
35640,43207,8301
35658,43201,8288
35655,43192,8288
36190,43008,8288
36346,42943,8288
36452,43059,8288
35982,43228,8284
35814,43336,8292
35707,43362,8301
;
35707,43362,8337
35640,43207,8338
```

```
35658,43201,8339
35655,43192,8323
36190,43008,8323
36346,42943,8323
36452,43059,8323
35982,43228,8351
35814,43336,8345
35707,43362,8337

;
clayer Rbrick
WallGen
35707,43362,8337
35640,43207,8338
35658,43201,8339
35655,43192,8323
36190,43008,8323
36346,42943,8323
36452,43059,8323
35982,43228,8351
35814,43336,8345
35707,43362,8337
;
35707,43362,8448
35640,43207,8448
35658,43201,8448
35655,43192,8448
36190,43008,8448
36346,42943,8448
36452,43059,8457
35982,43228,8430
35814,43336,8433
35707,43362,8448

clayer Recbrick
WallGen
35707,43362,8448
35640,43207,8448
35658,43201,8448
35655,43192,8448
36190,43008,8448
36346,42943,8448
36452,43059,8457
35982,43228,8430
35814,43336,8433
35707,43362,8448
;
35707,43362,8590
35640,43207,8590
35658,43201,8590
35655,43192,8590
36190,43008,8590
36346,42943,8590
36452,43059,8590
35982,43228,8590
35814,43336,8590
35707,43362,8590
```

003- F S_Corner

```
;03 - FS Corner w/o Brick
;
clayer Text
filedia 0
text 36346,42943,8590 7 -90 AP 084
text 36380,42931,8590 7 -90 AP 085
text 36386,42943,8590 7 -90 AP 703
text 36403,42937,8590 7 -90 AP 702
text 36459,43036,8590 7 -90 AP 701
text 36444,43041,8590 7 -90 AP 700
text 36452,43059,8590 7 -90 AP 083
text 36346,42943,8590 7 -90 AP 084
filedia 1
;
clayer 3DPolylines
3dpoly
36346,42943,8590
36380,42931,8590
36386,42943,8590
36403,42937,8590
36459,43036,8590
36444,43041,8590
36452,43059,8590
36346,42943,8590

clayer Stone
WallGen
36346,42943,8280
36380,42931,8280
36386,42943,8280
36403,42937,8280
36459,43036,8280
36444,43041,8280
36452,43059,8280
36346,42943,8280
;
```

```
36346,42943,8456
36380,42931,8458
36386,42943,8454
36403,42937,8449
36459,43036,8462
36444,43041,8459
36452,43059,8457
36346,42943,8456

;
clayer RecBrick
WallGen
36346,42943,8456
36380,42931,8458
36386,42943,8454
36403,42937,8449
36459,43036,8462
36444,43041,8459
36452,43059,8457
36346,42943,8456
;
36346,42943,8590
36380,42931,8590
36386,42943,8590
36403,42937,8590
36459,43036,8590
36444,43041,8590
36452,43059,8590
36346,42943,8590
```

004- D1 E

```
;04 - D1 E
;
clayer Text
filedia 0
text 36190,43008,8590 7 -90 AP 096
text 36346,42943,8590 7 -90 AP 084
text  36115,42381,8590  7  -90  AP
086=Y1r10
text 35980,42415,8590 7 -90 AP 095
text 36190,43008,8590 7 -90 AP 096
filedia 1
;
```

```
clayer 3DPolylines
3dpoly
36190,43008,8590
36346,42943,8590
36115,42381,8590
35980,42415,8590
36190,43008,8590

;
;
;
clayer Stone
WallGen
36190,43008,8288
36346,42943,8288
36115,42381,8290
35980,42415,8293
36190,43008,8288
;
36190,43008,8323
36346,42943,8323
36115,42381,8323
35980,42415,8323
36190,43008,8323

;
clayer Rbrick
WallGen
36190,43008,8323
36346,42943,8323
36115,42381,8323
35980,42415,8323
36190,43008,8323
;
36190,43008,8458
36346,42943,8456
36115,42381,8502
35980,42415,8449
36190,43008,8458

;
clayer Recbrick
WallGen
36190,43008,8458
36346,42943,8456
36115,42381,8502
35980,42415,8449
36190,43008,8458
;
36190,43008,8590
36346,42943,8590
36115,42381,8590
35980,42415,8590
```

```
36190,43008,8590

005- D1 S
```

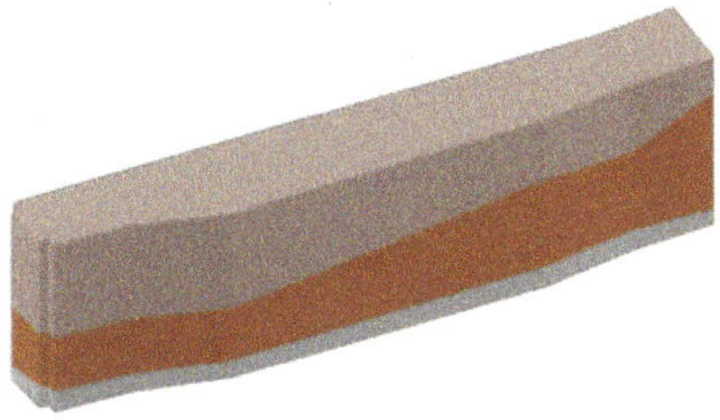

```
;005 - D1 S
;
clayer Text
filedia 0
text 35125,42715,8590 7 -90 AP 204
text 35087,42728,8590 7 -90 AP 604
text 35079,42705,8590 7 -90 AP 605
text 35065,42710,8590 7 -90 AP 606
text 35045,42634,8590 7 -90 AP 607
text 35060,42628,8590 7 -90 AP 608
text 35053,42611,8590 7 -90 AP 609
text 35169,42565,8590 7 -90 AP 573
text 35294,42480,8590 7 -90 AP 572
text 35783,42318,8590 7 -90 AP 242
text 35939,42291,8590 7 -90 AP 237
;text 36069,42252,8590
text  36115,42381,8590  7  -90  AP
086=Y1r10
text 35980,42415,8590 7 -90 AP 095
text 35125,42715,8590 7 -90 AP 204
filedia 1
;
clayer 3DPolylines
3dpoly
35125,42715,8590
35087,42728,8590
35079,42705,8590
35065,42710,8590
35045,42634,8590
35060,42628,8590
35053,42611,8590
35169,42565,8590
35294,42480,8590
35783,42318,8590
35939,42291,8590
36069,42252,8590
36115,42381,8590
35980,42415,8590
35125,42715,8590

clayer Stone
WallGen
35125,42715,8277
35087,42728,8309
35079,42705,8305
35065,42710,8297
35045,42634,8297
35060,42628,8297
35053,42611,8297
35169,42565,8297
35294,42480,8302
35783,42318,8297
35939,42291,8297
36069,42252,8297
36115,42381,8290
35980,42415,8293
35125,42715,8277
;
35125,42715,8323
35087,42728,8323
35079,42705,8343
35065,42710,8323
35045,42634,8335
35060,42628,8329
35053,42611,8332
35169,42565,8328
35294,42480,8332
35783,42318,8332
35939,42291,8332
36069,42252,8323
36115,42381,8323
35980,42415,8323
35125,42715,8323

;
clayer Rbrick
WallGen
35125,42715,8323
35087,42728,8323
35079,42705,8343
35065,42710,8323
35045,42634,8335
35060,42628,8329
35053,42611,8332
35169,42565,8328
35294,42480,8332
35783,42318,8332
35939,42291,8332
36069,42252,8323
36115,42381,8323
35980,42415,8323
35125,42715,8323
;
35125,42715,8449
35087,42728,8425
```

```
35079,42705,8425
35065,42710,8425
35045,42634,8425
35060,42628,8425
35053,42611,8425
35169,42565,8425
35294,42480,8422
35783,42318,8482
35939,42291,8467
36069,42252,8526
36115,42381,8502
35980,42415,8449
35125,42715,8449

clayer Recbrick
WallGen
35125,42715,8449
35087,42728,8425
35079,42705,8425
35065,42710,8425
35045,42634,8425
35060,42628,8425
35053,42611,8425
35169,42565,8425
35294,42480,8422
35783,42318,8482
35939,42291,8467
36069,42252,8526
36115,42381,8502
35980,42415,8449
35125,42715,8449
;
35125,42715,8590
35087,42728,8590
35079,42705,8590
35065,42710,8590
35045,42634,8590
35060,42628,8590
35053,42611,8590
35169,42565,8590
35294,42480,8590
35783,42318,8590
35939,42291,8590
36069,42252,8590
36115,42381,8590
35980,42415,8590
35125,42715,8590
```

006- D1 S-SW

```
;06,0,D1,S-SW
;
clayer Text
filedia 0
text 35236,42756,8590 7 -90 AP 202
text 35225,42763,8590 7 -90 AP
205=Y1r20
text 35236,42778,8590 7 -90 AP 616
text 35155,42787,8590 7 -90 AP 203
text 35125,42715,8590 7 -90 AP 204
text 35206,42686,8590 7 -90 AP
086=Y1r10
text 35236,42756,8590 7 -90 AP 202
filedia 1
;
clayer 3DPolylines
3dpoly
35236,42756,8590
35225,42763,8590
35236,42778,8590
35155,42787,8590
35125,42715,8590
35206,42686,8590
35236,42756,8590

clayer Stone
WallGen
35236,42756,8297
35225,42763,8288
35236,42778,8287
35155,42787,8280
35125,42715,8277
35206,42686,8288
35236,42756,8297
;
35236,42756,8319
35225,42763,8305
35236,42778,8319
35155,42787,8319
35125,42715,8323
35206,42686,8319
35236,42756,8319
```

```
;
clayer Rbrick
WallGen
35236,42756,8319
35225,42763,8305
35236,42778,8319
35155,42787,8319
35125,42715,8323
35206,42686,8319
35236,42756,8319
;
35236,42756,8500
35225,42763,8500
35236,42778,8500
35155,42787,8500
35125,42715,8449
35206,42686,8502
35236,42756,8500

clayer Recbrick
WallGen
35236,42756,8500
35225,42763,8500
35236,42778,8500
35155,42787,8500
35125,42715,8449
35206,42686,8502
35236,42756,8500
;
35236,42756,8590
35225,42763,8590
35236,42778,8590
35155,42787,8590
35125,42715,8590
35206,42686,8590
35236,42756,8590
```

007- D1 W

```
;07 - D1 W
;
clayer Text
filedia 0
text 35340,43311,8590 7 -90 AP 192
text 35282,43185,8590 7 -90 AP 193
text 35262,43191,8590 7 -90 AP 194
text 35235,43146,8590 7 -90 AP 195
text 35251,43136,8590 7 -90 AP 196
text 35246,43125,8590 7 -90 AP 197
text 35288,43100,8590 7 -90 AP 198
text 35275,43075,8590 7 -90 AP 199
text 35346,43026,8590 7 -90 AP 200
text 35349,43041,8590 7 -90 AP 201
text 35364,43035,8590 7 -90 AP 052
text 35444,43241,8590 7 -90 AP 051
text 35340,43311,8590 7 -90 AP 192
filedia 1
;
clayer 3DPolylines
3dpoly
35340,43311,8590
35282,43185,8590
35262,43191,8590
35235,43146,8590
35251,43136,8590
35246,43125,8590
35288,43100,8590
35275,43075,8590
35346,43026,8590
35349,43041,8590
35364,43035,8590
35444,43241,8590
35340,43311,8590
Close
;
clayer Stone
WallGen
35340,43311,8280
35282,43185,8280
35262,43191,8280
35235,43146,8280
35251,43136,8280
35246,43125,8280
35288,43100,8280
35275,43075,8280
35346,43026,8280
35349,43041,8280
35364,43035,8280
35444,43241,8280
35340,43311,8280
;
35340,43311,8378
35282,43185,8371
35262,43191,8370
35235,43146,8372
35251,43136,8360
35246,43125,8360
```

```
35288,43100,8365
35275,43075,8366
35346,43026,8367
35349,43041,8369
35364,43035,8370
35444,43241,8368
35340,43311,8378

;
clayer RBrick
WallGen
35340,43311,8378
35282,43185,8371
35262,43191,8370
35235,43146,8372
35251,43136,8360
35246,43125,8360
35288,43100,8365
35275,43075,8366
35346,43026,8367
35349,43041,8369
35364,43035,8370
35444,43241,8368
35340,43311,8378
;
35340,43311,8424
35282,43185,8420
35262,43191,8410
35235,43146,8410
35251,43136,8410
35246,43125,8410
35288,43100,8391
35275,43075,8410
35346,43026,8410
35349,43041,8400
35364,43035,8410
35444,43241,8410
35340,43311,8424

;
clayer RecBrick
WallGen
35340,43311,8424
35282,43185,8420
35262,43191,8410
35235,43146,8410
35251,43136,8410
35246,43125,8410
35288,43100,8391
35275,43075,8410
35346,43026,8410
35349,43041,8400
35364,43035,8410
35444,43241,8410
35340,43311,8424
;
35340,43311,8590
35282,43185,8590
35262,43191,8590
35235,43146,8590
35251,43136,8590
35246,43125,8590
35288,43100,8590
35275,43075,8590
35346,43026,8590
35349,43041,8590
35364,43035,8590
35444,43241,8590
35340,43311,8590

008- D2 SW
```

```
;08 - D2 SW
;
clayer Text
filedia 0
text 34953,42767,8590 7 -90 AP 586
text 34917,42777,8590 7 -90 AP 055
text  34884,42667,8590  7  -90  AP
579=Y1r21
text 34912,42654,8590 7 -90 AP 514
text 34916,42666,8590 7 -90 AP 513
text 34928,42662,8590 7 -90 AP 056
text 34962,42745,8590 7 -90 AP 056
text 34946,42749,8590 7 -90 AP 587
text 34953,42767,8590 7 -90 AP 586
filedia 1
;
clayer 3DPolylines
3dpoly
34953,42767,8590
34917,42777,8590
34884,42667,8590
34912,42654,8590
34916,42666,8590
34928,42662,8590
```

```
34962,42745,8590
34946,42749,8590
34953,42767,8590
Close
;
clayer Stone
WallGen
34953,42767,8280
34917,42777,8280
34884,42667,8280
34912,42654,8280
34916,42666,8280
34928,42662,8287
34962,42745,8280
34946,42749,8280
34953,42767,8280
;
34953,42767,8317
34917,42777,8353
34884,42667,8319
34912,42654,8345
34916,42666,8351
34928,42662,8353
34962,42745,8355
34946,42749,8355
34953,42767,8317

;
clayer RBrick
WallGen
34953,42767,8317
34917,42777,8353
34884,42667,8319
34912,42654,8345
34916,42666,8351
34928,42662,8353
34962,42745,8355
34946,42749,8355
34953,42767,8317
;
34953,42767,8410
34917,42777,8410
34884,42667,8410
34912,42654,8410
34916,42666,8410
34928,42662,8410
34962,42745,8410
34946,42749,8410
34953,42767,8410

;
clayer RecBrick
WallGen
34953,42767,8410
34917,42777,8410
34884,42667,8410
34912,42654,8410
34916,42666,8410
34928,42662,8410
34962,42745,8410
34946,42749,8410
34953,42767,8410
;
34953,42767,8590
34917,42777,8590
34884,42667,8590
34912,42654,8590
34916,42666,8590
34928,42662,8590
34962,42745,8590
34946,42749,8590
34953,42767,8590
```

009- D3 SW

```
;09 - D3 SW
;
clayer Text
filedia 0
text 35135,43233,8590 7 -90 AP 508
text 35121,43179,8590 7 -90 AP 509
text 35109,43180,8590 7 -90 AP 510
text 35107,43167,8590 7 -90 AP 511
text 35070,43175,8590 7 -90 AP 512
text 35088,43232,8590 7 -90 AP
507=Y1r18
text 35135,43233,8590 7 -90 AP 508
filedia 1
;
clayer 3DPolylines
3dpoly
35135,43233,8590
35121,43179,8590
35109,43180,8590
35107,43167,8590
35070,43175,8590
```

```
35088,43232,8590
35135,43233,8590

;
clayer Stone
WallGen
35135,43233,8280
35121,43179,8280
35109,43180,8280
35107,43167,8280
35070,43175,8280
35088,43232,8280
35135,43233,8280
;
35135,43233,8364
35121,43179,8364
35109,43180,8364
35107,43167,8364
35070,43175,8364
35088,43232,8364
35135,43233,8364

;
clayer RBrick
WallGen
35135,43233,8364
35121,43179,8364
35109,43180,8364
35107,43167,8364
35070,43175,8364
35088,43232,8364
35135,43233,8364
;
35135,43233,8410
35121,43179,8410
35109,43180,8410
35107,43167,8410
35070,43175,8410
35088,43232,8410
35135,43233,8410

;
clayer RecBrick
WallGen
35135,43233,8410
35121,43179,8410
35109,43180,8410
35107,43167,8410
35070,43175,8410
35088,43232,8410
35135,43233,8410
;
35135,43233,8590
35121,43179,8590
35109,43180,8590
35107,43167,8590
35070,43175,8590
35088,43232,8590
35135,43233,8590
```

010- D3 W

```
;10 - D3 W
;
clayer Text
filedia 0
text 35145,43370,8590 7 -90 AP 508
text 35088,43232,8590 7 -90 AP 509
text 34997,43276,8590 7 -90 AP 510
text 35038,43390,8590 7 -90 AP 511
text 35145,43370,8590 7 -90 AP 512
filedia 1
;
clayer 3DPolylines
3dpoly
35145,43370,8590
35088,43232,8590
34997,43276,8590
35038,43390,8590
35145,43370,8590
Close
;
clayer Stone
WallGen
35145,43370,8280
35088,43232,8280
34997,43276,8280
35038,43390,8280
35145,43370,8280
;
35145,43370,8372
35088,43232,8367
34997,43276,8366
35038,43390,8376
35145,43370,8372
```

```
;
clayer RBrick
WallGen
35145,43370,8372
35088,43232,8367
34997,43276,8366
35038,43390,8376
35145,43370,8372
;
35145,43370,8392
35088,43232,8392
34997,43276,8392
35038,43390,8392
35145,43370,8392

;
clayer RecBrick
WallGen
35145,43370,8392
35088,43232,8392
34997,43276,8392
35038,43390,8392
35145,43370,8392
;
35145,43370,8590
35088,43232,8590
34997,43276,8590
35038,43390,8590
35145,43370,8590
```

011- D2 NW

```
;11 - D2 NW
;
clayer Text
filedia 0
text  35088,43232,8590  7  -90  AP 507=Y1r18
text 34997,43276,8590 7 -90 AP 183
text 34968,43208,8590 7 -90 AP 594
text 35070,43175,8590 7 -90 AP 512
text  35088,43232,8590  7  -90  AP 507=Y1r18
filedia 1
;
clayer 3DPolylines
3dpoly
35088,43232,8590
34997,43276,8590
34968,43208,8590
35070,43175,8590
35088,43232,8590
Close
;
clayer Stone
WallGen
35088,43232,8280
34997,43276,8280
34968,43208,8280
35070,43175,8280
35088,43232,8280
;
35088,43232,8367
34997,43276,8366
34968,43208,8356
35070,43175,8369
35088,43232,8367

;
clayer RBrick
WallGen
35088,43232,8367
34997,43276,8366
34968,43208,8356
35070,43175,8369
35088,43232,8367
;
35088,43232,8392
34997,43276,8392
34968,43208,8392
35070,43175,8392
35088,43232,8392

;
clayer RecBrick
WallGen
35088,43232,8392
34997,43276,8392
34968,43208,8392
35070,43175,8392
35088,43232,8392
;
35088,43232,8590
34997,43276,8590
34968,43208,8590
35070,43175,8590
35088,43232,8590
```

012- D2 W

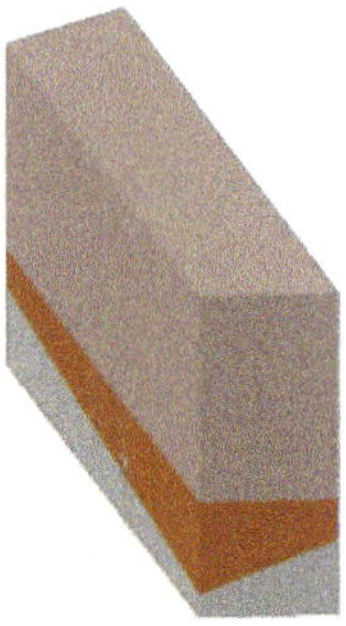

```
;12 - D2 W
;
clayer Text
filedia 0
text 34968,43208,8590 7 -90 AP 594
text 35070,43175,8590 7 -90 AP 512
text 34917,42777,8590 7 -90 AP 055
text 34834,42853,8590 7 -90 AP 593
text 34968,43208,8590 7 -90 AP 594
filedia 1
;
clayer 3DPolylines
3dpoly
34968,43208,8590
35070,43175,8590
34917,42777,8590
34834,42853,8590
34968,43208,8590
Close
;
clayer Stone
WallGen
34968,43208,8280
35070,43175,8280
34917,42777,8280
34834,42853,8280
34968,43208,8280
;
34968,43208,8356
35070,43175,8369
34917,42777,8353
34834,42853,8303
34968,43208,8356

;
clayer RBrick
WallGen
34968,43208,8356
35070,43175,8369
34917,42777,8353
34834,42853,8303
34968,43208,8356
;
34968,43208,8392
35070,43175,8392
34917,42777,8392
34834,42853,8392
34968,43208,8392

;
clayer RecBrick
WallGen
34968,43208,8392
35070,43175,8392
34917,42777,8392
34834,42853,8392
34968,43208,8392
;
34968,43208,8590
35070,43175,8590
34917,42777,8590
34834,42853,8590
34968,43208,8590
```

013- D2 SW

```
;13 - D2 SW
;
clayer Text
filedia 0
text 34917,42777,8590 7 -90 AP 055
text 34834,42853,8590 7 -90 AP 593
text 34791,42756,8590 7 -90 AP 506
text 34884,42667,8590 7 -90 AP
579=Y1r21
text 34917,42777,8590 7 -90 AP 055
filedia 1
;
clayer 3DPolylines
3dpoly
34917,42777,8590
34834,42853,8590
34791,42756,8590
34884,42667,8590
```

```
34917,42777,8590
Close
;
clayer Stone
WallGen
34917,42777,8280
34834,42853,8280
34791,42756,8283
34884,42667,8280
34917,42777,8280
;
34917,42777,8353
34834,42853,8303
34791,42756,8348
34884,42667,8319
34917,42777,8353

;
clayer RBrick
WallGen
34917,42777,8353
34834,42853,8303
34791,42756,8348
34884,42667,8319
34917,42777,8353
;
34917,42777,8392
34834,42853,8392
34791,42756,8392
34884,42667,8392
34917,42777,8392

;
clayer RecBrick
WallGen
34917,42777,8392
34834,42853,8392
34791,42756,8392
34884,42667,8392
34917,42777,8392
;
34917,42777,8590
34834,42853,8590
34791,42756,8590
34884,42667,8590
34917,42777,8590
```

014- C7 W

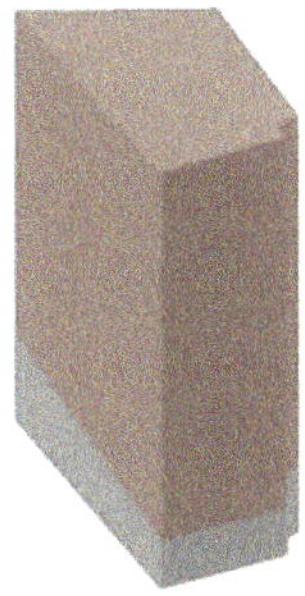

```
;14 - C7 W
;
clayer Text
filedia 0
text 34791,42756,8590 7 -90 AP 506
text 34884,42667,8590 7 -90 AP 579=Y1r21
text 34840,42549,8590 7 -90 AP 581
text 34824,42552,8590 7 -90 AP
text 34819,42539,8590 7 -90 AP 591
text 34735,42570,8590 7 -90 AP 582
text 34791,42756,8590 7 -90 AP 506
filedia 1
;
clayer 3DPolylines
3dpoly
34791,42756,8590
34884,42667,8590
34840,42549,8590
34824,42552,8590
34819,42539,8590
34735,42570,8590
34791,42756,8590
Close
;
clayer Stone
WallGen
34791,42756,8283
34884,42667,8280
34840,42549,8277
34824,42552,8276
34819,42539,8274
34735,42570,8276
34791,42756,8283
;
34791,42756,8348
34884,42667,8319
34840,42549,8333
34824,42552,8312
34819,42539,8309
34735,42570,8312
34791,42756,8348
```

```
;
clayer RecBrick
WallGen
34791,42756,8348
34884,42667,8319
34840,42549,8333
34824,42552,8312
34819,42539,8309
34735,42570,8312
34791,42756,8348
;
34791,42756,8590
34884,42667,8590
34840,42549,8590
34824,42552,8590
34819,42539,8590
34735,42570,8590
34791,42756,8590

015- D3 N
```

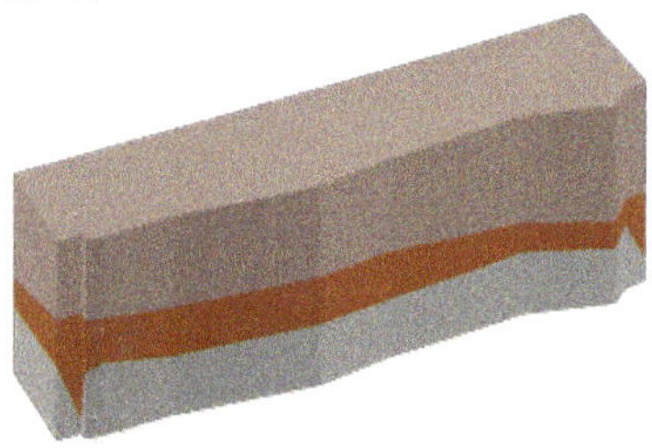

```
;15 - D3 N
;
clayer Text
filedia 0
text 35557,43415,8590 7 -90 AP 048
text 35508,43250,8590 7 -90 AP 049
text 35476,43255,8590 7 -90 AP 050
text 35444,43241,8590 7 -90 AP 051
text 35340,43311,8590 7 -90 AP 192
text 35145,43370,8590 7 -90 AP 191
text  35038,43390,8590  7  -90  AP
182=Y1r4
text  34854,43478,8590  7  -90  AP
181=Y1r3
text 34756,43511,8590 7 -90 AP 170
text 34734,43522,8590 7 -90 AP 020
text  34739,43534,8590  7  -90  AP
019=Y1r2
text 34705,43545,8590 7 -90 AP 018
text 34772,43693,8590 7 -90 AP 047
text 35557,43415,8590 7 -90 AP 048
filedia 1
;
clayer 3DPolylines
3dpoly
35557,43415,8590
35508,43250,8590
35476,43255,8590
35444,43241,8590
35340,43311,8590
35145,43370,8590
35038,43390,8590
34854,43478,8590
34756,43511,8590
34734,43522,8590
34739,43534,8590
34705,43545,8590
34772,43693,8590
35557,43415,8590
Close
;
clayer Stone
WallGen
35557,43415,8280
35508,43250,8280
35476,43255,8280
35444,43241,8280
35340,43311,8280
35145,43370,8280
35038,43390,8280
34854,43478,8280
34756,43511,8280
34734,43522,8280
34739,43534,8280
34705,43545,8280
34772,43693,8280
35557,43415,8280
;
35557,43415,8385
35508,43250,8314
35476,43255,8381
35444,43241,8368
35340,43311,8378
35145,43370,8372
35038,43390,8376
34854,43478,8374
34756,43511,8395
34734,43522,8385
34739,43534,8304
34705,43545,8397
34772,43693,8384
35557,43415,8385

;
clayer Rbrick
WallGen
35557,43415,8385
35508,43250,8314
```

```
35476,43255,8381
35444,43241,8368
35340,43311,8378
35145,43370,8372
35038,43390,8376
34854,43478,8374
34756,43511,8395
34734,43522,8385
34739,43534,8304
34705,43545,8397
34772,43693,8384
35557,43415,8385
;
35557,43415,8429
35508,43250,8420
35476,43255,8420
35444,43241,8410
35340,43311,8424
35145,43370,8446
35038,43390,8450
34854,43478,8450
34756,43511,8465
34734,43522,8467
34739,43534,8470
34705,43545,8471
34772,43693,8429
35557,43415,8429

;
clayer RecBrick
WallGen
35557,43415,8429
35508,43250,8420
35476,43255,8420
35444,43241,8410
35340,43311,8424
35145,43370,8446
35038,43390,8450
34854,43478,8450
34756,43511,8465
34734,43522,8467
34739,43534,8470
34705,43545,8471
34772,43693,8429
35557,43415,8429
;
35557,43415,8590
35508,43250,8590
35476,43255,8590
35444,43241,8590
35340,43311,8590
35145,43370,8590
35038,43390,8590
34854,43478,8590
34756,43511,8590
34734,43522,8590
34739,43534,8590
34705,43545,8590
34772,43693,8590
35557,43415,8590
```

016- B3 W

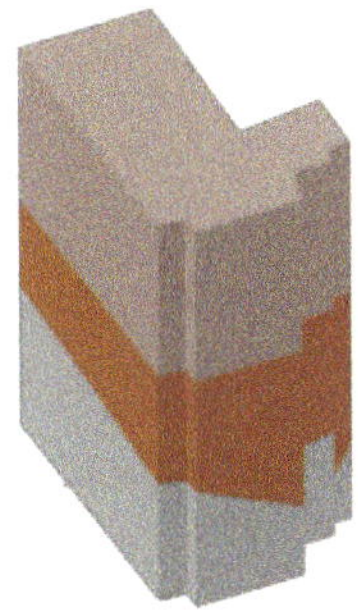

```
;16 - B3 W
;
clayer Text
filedia 0
text 34854,43478,8590 7 -90 AP
181=Y1r3
text 34756,43511,8590 7 -90 AP 170
text 34677,43296,8590 7 -90 AP 171
text 34696,43288,8590 7 -90 AP 172
text 34691,43272,8590 7 -90 AP 173
text 34770,43245,8590 7 -90 AP
174=Y1r5
text 34789,43273,8590 7 -90 AP
175=Y1r23
text 34818,43263,8590 7 -90 AP 176
text 34824,43275,8590 7 -90 AP 177
text 34841,43268,8590 7 -90 AP 178
text 34861,43319,8590 7 -90 AP 179
text 34796,43332,8590 7 -90 AP
text 34854,43478,8590 7 -90 AP
181=Y1r3
filedia 1
;
clayer 3DPolylines
3dpoly
34854,43478,8590
34756,43511,8590
34677,43296,8590
34696,43288,8590
34691,43272,8590
34770,43245,8590
34789,43273,8590
34818,43263,8590
34824,43275,8590
```

```
34841,43268,8590
34861,43319,8590
34796,43332,8590
34854,43478,8590
Close
;
clayer Stone
WallGen
34854,43478,8280
34756,43511,8280
34677,43296,8280
34696,43288,8280
34691,43272,8280
34770,43245,8280
34789,43273,8280
34818,43263,8280
34824,43275,8280
34841,43268,8280
34861,43319,8280
34796,43332,8280
34854,43478,8280
;
34854,43478,8374
34756,43511,8395
34677,43296,8377
34696,43288,8374
34691,43272,8375
34770,43245,8337
34789,43273,8360
34818,43263,8365
34824,43275,8311
34841,43268,8343
34861,43319,8366
34796,43332,8366
34854,43478,8374

;
clayer Rbrick
WallGen
34854,43478,8374
34756,43511,8395
34677,43296,8377
34696,43288,8374
34691,43272,8375
34770,43245,8337
34789,43273,8360
34818,43263,8365
34824,43275,8311
34841,43268,8343
34861,43319,8366
34796,43332,8366
34854,43478,8374
;
34854,43478,8465
34756,43511,8465
34677,43296,8465
34696,43288,8465
34691,43272,8465
34770,43245,8465
34789,43273,8465
34818,43263,8465
34824,43275,8465
34841,43268,8465
34861,43319,8465
34796,43332,8465
34854,43478,8465

;
clayer RecBrick
WallGen
34854,43478,8465
34756,43511,8465
34677,43296,8465
34696,43288,8465
34691,43272,8465
34770,43245,8465
34789,43273,8465
34818,43263,8465
34824,43275,8465
34841,43268,8465
34861,43319,8465
34796,43332,8465
34854,43478,8465
;
34854,43478,8590
34756,43511,8590
34677,43296,8590
34696,43288,8590
34691,43272,8590
34770,43245,8590
34789,43273,8590
34818,43263,8590
34824,43275,8590
34841,43268,8590
34861,43319,8590
34796,43332,8590
34854,43478,8590

017- B3 SE
```

```
;17 - B3 SE
;
clayer Text
filedia 0
text 34997,43276,8590 7 -90 AP 183
text 34945,43285,8590 7 -90 AP 184
text 34928,43244,8590 7 -90 AP 185
text 34939,43237,8590 7 -90 AP 186
text 34937,43223,8590 7 -90 AP 187
text 34968,43208,8590 7 -90 AP 594
text 34997,43276,8590 7 -90 AP 183
filedia 1
;
clayer 3DPolylines
3dpoly
34997,43276,8590
34945,43285,8590
34928,43244,8590
34939,43237,8590
34937,43223,8590
34968,43208,8590
34997,43276,8590
Close
;
clayer Stone
WallGen
34997,43276,8280
34945,43285,8280
34928,43244,8280
34939,43237,8280
34937,43223,8280
34968,43208,8280
34997,43276,8280
;
34997,43276,8366
34945,43285,8329
34928,43244,8302
34939,43237,8361
34937,43223,8360
34968,43208,8356
34997,43276,8366
;
clayer Rbrick
WallGen
34997,43276,8366
34945,43285,8329
34928,43244,8302
34939,43237,8361
34937,43223,8360
34968,43208,8356
34997,43276,8366
;
34997,43276,8392
34945,43285,8392
34928,43244,8392
34939,43237,8392
34937,43223,8392
34968,43208,8392
34997,43276,8392

;
clayer RecBrick
WallGen
34997,43276,8392
34945,43285,8392
34928,43244,8392
34939,43237,8392
34937,43223,8392
34968,43208,8392
34997,43276,8392
;
34997,43276,8590
34945,43285,8590
34928,43244,8590
34939,43237,8590
34937,43223,8590
34968,43208,8590
34997,43276,8590

018- B2 SE
```

```
;18 - B2 SE
;
clayer Text
```

```
filedia 0
text 34834,42853,8590 7 -90 AP 593
text 34812,42868,8590 7 -90 AP 501
text 34803,42839,8590 7 -90 AP 592
text 34793,42850,8590 7 -90 AP 502
text 34763,42784,8590 7 -90 AP 503
text 34770,42780,8590 7 -90 AP 504
text 34780,42762,8590 7 -90 AP 505
text 34791,42756,8590 7 -90 AP 506
text 34834,42853,8590 7 -90 AP 593
filedia 1
;
clayer 3DPolylines
3dpoly
34834,42853,8590
34812,42868,8590
34803,42839,8590
34793,42850,8590
34763,42784,8590
34770,42780,8590
34780,42762,8590
34791,42756,8590
34834,42853,8590
Close
;
clayer Stone
WallGen
34834,42853,8280
34812,42868,8280
34803,42839,8280
34793,42850,8280
34763,42784,8280
34770,42780,8280
34780,42762,8280
34791,42756,8280
34834,42853,8280
;
34834,42853,8303
34812,42868,8301
34803,42839,8325
34793,42850,8323
34763,42784,8329
34770,42780,8321
34780,42762,8329
34791,42756,8348
34834,42853,8303

;
clayer RecBrick
WallGen
34834,42853,8303
34812,42868,8301
34803,42839,8325
34793,42850,8323
34763,42784,8329
34770,42780,8321
34780,42762,8329
34791,42756,8348
34834,42853,8303
;
34834,42853,8590
34812,42868,8590
34803,42839,8590
34793,42850,8590
34763,42784,8590
34770,42780,8590
34780,42762,8590
34791,42756,8590
34834,42853,8590
```

019- B1 N

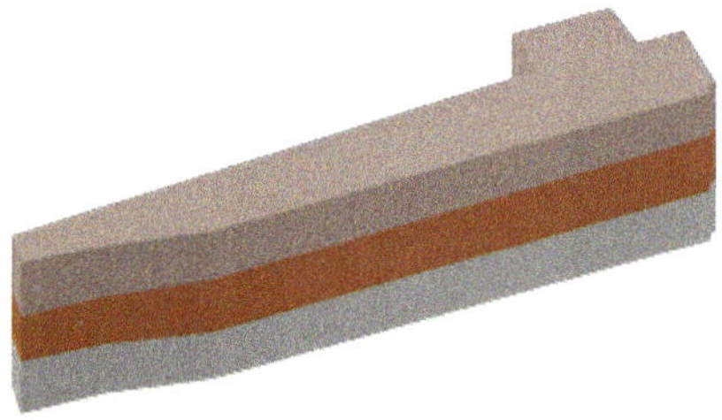

```
;19 - B1 N
;
clayer Text
filedia 0
text 34535,43595,8590 7 -90 AP 016
text 34539,43613,8590 7 -90 AP 500
text 34561,43608,8590 7 -90 AP 017
text 34627,43751,8590 7 -90 AP 015
text 34548,43779,8590 7 -90 AP 014
text 34586,43882,8590 7 -90 AP 013
text 34419,43944,8590 7 -90 AP 012
text 34371,43843,8590 7 -90 AP 011
text 33422,44132,8590 7 -90 AP 010
text 33378,44065,8590 7 -90 AP 009
text 33512,44001,8590 7 -90 AP 532
text 33672,43901,8590 7 -90 AP 531
text 34535,43595,8590 7 -90 AP 016
filedia 1
;
clayer 3DPolylines
3dpoly
34535,43595,8590
34539,43613,8590
34561,43608,8590
34627,43751,8590
34548,43779,8590
34586,43882,8590
```

```
34419,43944,8590
34371,43843,8590
33422,44132,8590
33378,44065,8590
33512,44001,8590
33672,43901,8590
34535,43595,8590
close
;
clayer Stone
WallGen
34535,43595,8296
34539,43613,8290
34561,43608,8296
34627,43751,8296
34548,43779,8296
34586,43882,8290
34419,43944,8296
34371,43843,8290
33422,44132,8296
33378,44065,8290
33512,44001,8296
33672,43901,8296
34535,43595,8290
;
34535,43595,8397
34539,43613,8389
34561,43608,8402
34627,43751,8401
34548,43779,8400
34586,43882,8391
34419,43944,8401
34371,43843,8396
33422,44132,8396
33378,44065,8396
33512,44001,8396
33672,43901,8390
34535,43595,8397

;
clayer RBrick
WallGen
34535,43595,8397
34539,43613,8389
34561,43608,8402
34627,43751,8401
34548,43779,8400
34586,43882,8391
34419,43944,8401
34371,43843,8396
33422,44132,8396
33378,44065,8396
33512,44001,8396
33672,43901,8390
34535,43595,8397
;
34535,43595,8507
34539,43613,8503
34561,43608,8502
34627,43751,8469
34548,43779,8447
34586,43882,8460
34419,43944,8485
34371,43843,8476
33422,44132,8480
33378,44065,8485
33512,44001,8490
33672,43901,8495
34535,43595,8507

;
clayer RecBrick
WallGen
34535,43595,8507
34539,43613,8503
34561,43608,8502
34627,43751,8469
34548,43779,8447
34586,43882,8460
34419,43944,8485
34371,43843,8476
33422,44132,8480
33378,44065,8485
33512,44001,8490
33672,43901,8495
34535,43595,8507
;
34535,43595,8590
34539,43613,8590
34561,43608,8590
34627,43751,8590
34548,43779,8590
34586,43882,8590
34419,43944,8590
34371,43843,8590
33422,44132,8590
33378,44065,8590
33512,44001,8590
33672,43901,8590
34535,43595,8590

020- B1 W
```

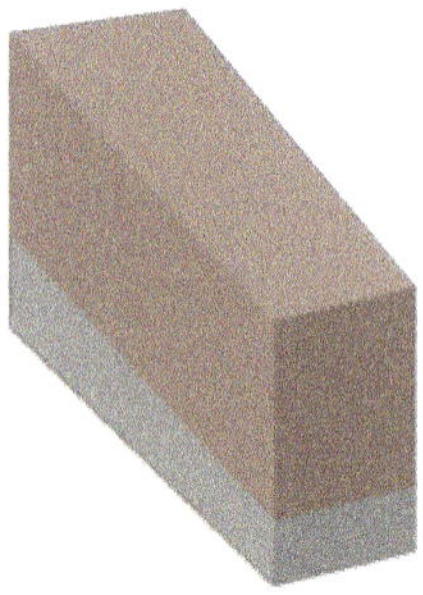

```
;20 - B1 W
;
clayer Text
filedia 0
text 33512,44001,8590 7 -90 AP 016
text 33672,43901,8590 7 -90 AP 500
text 33495,43382,8590 7 -90 AP 017
text 33347,43443,8590 7 -90 AP 015
text 33512,44001,8590 7 -90 AP 014
filedia 1
;
clayer 3DPolylines
3dpoly
33512,44001,8590
33672,43901,8590
33495,43382,8590
33347,43443,8590
33512,44001,8590
Close
;
clayer Stone
WallGen
33512,44001,8221
33672,43901,8258
33495,43382,8258
33347,43443,8258
33512,44001,8221
;
33512,44001,8341
33672,43901,8341
33495,43382,8341
33347,43443,8341
33512,44001,8341

;
clayer RecBrick
WallGen
33512,44001,8341
33672,43901,8341
33495,43382,8341
33347,43443,8341
33512,44001,8341
;
33512,44001,8590
33672,43901,8590
33495,43382,8590
33347,43443,8590
33512,44001,8590
```

021- A3 N

```
;21 - A3 N
;
clayer Text
filedia 0
text 34528,42044,8590 7 -90 AP 151
text 34252,42144,8590 7 -90 AP 150
text 34311,42306,8590 7 -90 AP 652
text 34289,42313,8590 7 -90 AP 651
text 34296,42336,8590 7 -90 AP 149
text 34184,42376,8590 7 -90 AP 148
text 34148,42278,8590 7 -90 AP 147
text 34043,42317,8590 7 -90 AP 146
text 33996,42179,8590 7 -90 AP 145
text 34095,42143,8590 7 -90 AP 144
text 34027,41946,8590 7 -90 AP 143
text 34143,41905,8590 7 -90 AP 142
text 34209,42065,8590 7 -90 AP 153
text 34452,41964,8590 7 -90 AP 670
text 34505,41941,8590 7 -90 AP
text 34528,42044,8590 7 -90 AP 151
filedia 1
;
clayer 3DPolylines
3dpoly
34528,42044,8590
34252,42144,8590
34311,42306,8590
34289,42313,8590
34296,42336,8590
34184,42376,8590
34148,42278,8590
34043,42317,8590
33996,42179,8590
34095,42143,8590
34027,41946,8590
34143,41905,8590
34209,42065,8590
```

```
34452,41964,8590
34505,41941,8590
34528,42044,8590
Close
;
clayer Stone
WallGen
34528,42044,8186
34252,42144,8186
34311,42306,8186
34289,42313,8186
34296,42336,8186
34184,42376,8186
34148,42278,8186
34043,42317,8186
33996,42179,8186
34095,42143,8186
34027,41946,8186
34143,41905,8186
34209,42065,8186
34452,41964,8186
34505,41941,8186
34528,42044,8186
;
34528,42044,8238
34252,42144,8232
34311,42306,8234
34289,42313,8232
34296,42336,8238
34184,42376,8238
34148,42278,8239
34043,42317,8238
33996,42179,8238
34095,42143,8222
34027,41946,8238
34143,41905,8238
34209,42065,8238
34452,41964,8254
34505,41941,8260
34528,42044,8238

;
clayer RecStone
WallGen
34528,42044,8238
34252,42144,8232
34311,42306,8234
34289,42313,8232
34296,42336,8238
34184,42376,8238
34148,42278,8239
34043,42317,8238
33996,42179,8238
34095,42143,8222
34027,41946,8238
34143,41905,8238
34209,42065,8238
34452,41964,8254
34505,41941,8260
34528,42044,8238
;
34528,42044,8340
34252,42144,8340
34311,42306,8340
34289,42313,8340
34296,42336,8340
34184,42376,8340
34148,42278,8340
34043,42317,8340
33996,42179,8340
34095,42143,8340
34027,41946,8340
34143,41905,8340
34209,42065,8340
34452,41964,8340
34505,41941,8340
34528,42044,8340

;
clayer RecBrick
WallGen
34528,42044,8340
34252,42144,8340
34311,42306,8340
34289,42313,8340
34296,42336,8340
34184,42376,8340
34148,42278,8340
34043,42317,8340
33996,42179,8340
34095,42143,8340
34027,41946,8340
34143,41905,8340
34209,42065,8340
34452,41964,8340
34505,41941,8340
34528,42044,8340
;
34528,42044,8590
34252,42144,8590
34311,42306,8590
34289,42313,8590
34296,42336,8590
34184,42376,8590
34148,42278,8590
34043,42317,8590
```

```
33996,42179,8590
34095,42143,8590
34027,41946,8590
34143,41905,8590
34209,42065,8590
34452,41964,8590
34505,41941,8590
34528,42044,8590
```

022- A6 N

```
;22 - A6 N
;
clayer Text
filedia 0
text 34553,42498,8590 7 -90 AP 159
text 34690,42443,8590 7 -90 AP
text 34667,42382,8590 7 -90 AP
text 34509,42443,8590 7 -90 AP 160
text 34378,42493,8590 7 -90 AP 161
text 34365,42456,8590 7 -90 AP 523
text 34341,42458,8590 7 -90 AP 524
text 34334,42449,8590 7 -90 AP 154
text 34228,42490,8590 7 -90 AP 155
text 34285,42657,8590 7 -90 AP 156
text 34405,42615,8590 7 -90 AP 157
text  34397,42600,8590  7  -90  AP
824=Y1r14
text 34413,42595,8590 7 -90 AP 522
text 34403,42557,8590 7 -90 AP 158
text 34553,42498,8590 7 -90 AP 159
filedia 1
;
clayer 3DPolylines
3dpoly
34553,42498,8590
34690,42443,8590
34667,42382,8590
34509,42443,8590
34378,42493,8590
34365,42456,8590
34341,42458,8590
34334,42449,8590
34228,42490,8590
34285,42657,8590
34405,42615,8590
34397,42600,8590
34413,42595,8590
34403,42557,8590
34553,42498,8590
Close
;
clayer Stone
WallGen
34553,42498,8200
34690,42443,8200
34667,42382,8200
34509,42443,8200
34378,42493,8200
34365,42456,8200
34341,42458,8200
34334,42449,8200
34228,42490,8200
34285,42657,8200
34405,42615,8200
34397,42600,8200
34413,42595,8200
34403,42557,8200
34553,42498,8200
;
34553,42498,8231
34690,42443,8238
34667,42382,8245
34509,42443,8254
34378,42493,8252
34365,42456,8243
34341,42458,8254
34334,42449,8254
34228,42490,8255
34285,42657,8260
34405,42615,8267
34397,42600,8317
34413,42595,8273
34403,42557,8257
34553,42498,8231

;
clayer RecStone
WallGen
34553,42498,8231
34690,42443,8238
34667,42382,8245
34509,42443,8254
34378,42493,8252
34365,42456,8243
34341,42458,8254
34334,42449,8254
34228,42490,8255
```

```
34285,42657,8260
34405,42615,8267
34397,42600,8317
34413,42595,8273
34403,42557,8257
34553,42498,8231
;
34553,42498,8320
34690,42443,8320
34667,42382,8320
34509,42443,8320
34378,42493,8320
34365,42456,8320
34341,42458,8320
34334,42449,8320
34228,42490,8320
34285,42657,8320
34405,42615,8320
34397,42600,8320
34413,42595,8320
34403,42557,8320
34553,42498,8320

;
clayer RecBrick
WallGen
34553,42498,8320
34690,42443,8320
34667,42382,8320
34509,42443,8320
34378,42493,8320
34365,42456,8320
34341,42458,8320
34334,42449,8320
34228,42490,8320
34285,42657,8320
34405,42615,8320
34397,42600,8320
34413,42595,8320
34403,42557,8320
34553,42498,8320
;
34553,42498,8590
34690,42443,8590
34667,42382,8590
34509,42443,8590
34378,42493,8590
34365,42456,8590
34341,42458,8590
34334,42449,8590
34228,42490,8590
34285,42657,8590
34405,42615,8590
34397,42600,8590
34413,42595,8590
34403,42557,8590
34553,42498,8590
```

023a- A4 EN

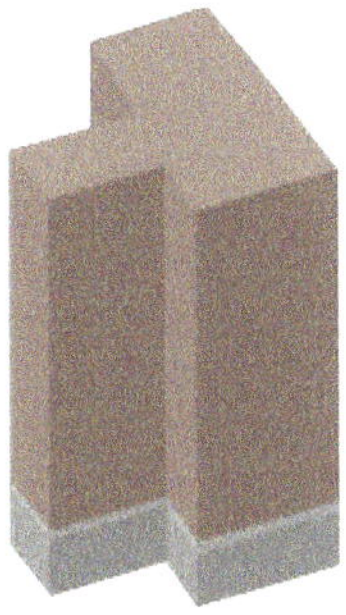

```
;23a - A4 EN
;
clayer Text
filedia 0
text 33722,42668,8143 7 -90 AP
text 33788,42847,8143 7 -90 AP 672
text 33819,42940,8200 7 -90 AP
text 33701,42979,8200 7 -90 AP
text 33662,42892,8143 7 -90 AP 673
text 33649,42864,8143 7 -90 AP 861=Y1r25
text 33524,42912,8143 7 -90 AP 862=Y1r27
text 33494,42829,8143 7 -90 AP
text 33611,42790,8143 7 -90 AP 860=Y1r26
text 33581,42717,8143 7 -90 AP
text 33722,42668,8143 7 -90 AP
filedia 1
;
clayer 3DPolylines
3dpoly
33722,42668,8143
33788,42847,8143
33819,42940,8200
33701,42979,8200
33662,42892,8143
33649,42864,8143
33524,42912,8143
33494,42829,8143
33611,42790,8143
33581,42717,8143
33722,42668,8143

;
clayer Stone
WallGen
```

```
33722,42668,8143
33788,42847,8143
33819,42940,8200
33701,42979,8200
33662,42892,8143
33649,42864,8143
33524,42912,8143
33494,42829,8143
33611,42790,8143
33581,42717,8143
33722,42668,8143
;
33722,42668,8203
33788,42847,8211
33819,42940,8205
33701,42979,8205
33662,42892,8205
33649,42864,8205
33524,42912,8205
33494,42829,8205
33611,42790,8205
33581,42717,8200
33722,42668,8203

;
clayer RecStone
WallGen
33722,42668,8203
33788,42847,8211
33819,42940,8205
33701,42979,8205
33662,42892,8205
33649,42864,8205
33524,42912,8205
33494,42829,8205
33611,42790,8205
33581,42717,8200
33722,42668,8203
;
33722,42668,8215
33788,42847,8215
33819,42940,8340
33701,42979,8340
33662,42892,8215
33649,42864,8215
33524,42912,8215
33494,42829,8215
33611,42790,8215
33581,42717,8215
33722,42668,8215

;
clayer RecBrick
WallGen
33722,42668,8215
33788,42847,8215
33819,42940,8340
33701,42979,8340
33662,42892,8215
33649,42864,8215
33524,42912,8215
33494,42829,8215
33611,42790,8215
33581,42717,8215
33722,42668,8215
;
33722,42668,8590
33788,42847,8590
33819,42940,8590
33701,42979,8590
33662,42892,8590
33649,42864,8590
33524,42912,8590
33494,42829,8590
33611,42790,8590
33581,42717,8590
33722,42668,8590

;,,,
023b- A4 ES
```

```
;023b - A4 ES
;
clayer Text
filedia 0
text 33651,42475,8143 7 -90 AP 137
text 33681,42557,8143 7 -90 AP
text 33538,42609,8143 7 -90 AP
text 33482,42470,8143 7 -90 AP 128
text 33277,42545,8143 7 -90 AP 129
text 33237,42442,8143 7 -90 AP 130
text 33465,42350,8143 7 -90 AP 131
text 33414,42191,8143 7 -90 AP 132
text 33531,42145,8143 7 -90 AP 133
text 33597,42321,8143 7 -90 AP
text 33703,42286,8143 7 -90 AP 135
text 33748,42430,8143 7 -90 AP 136
text 33651,42475,8143 7 -90 AP 137
```

```
filedia 1
;
clayer 3DPolylines
3dpoly
33651,42475,8143
33681,42557,8143
33538,42609,8143
33482,42470,8143
33277,42545,8143
33237,42442,8143
33465,42350,8143
33414,42191,8143
33531,42145,8143
33597,42321,8143
33703,42286,8143
33748,42430,8143
33651,42475,8143

;
clayer Stone
WallGen
33651,42475,8143
33681,42557,8143
33538,42609,8143
33482,42470,8143
33277,42545,8143
33237,42442,8143
33465,42350,8143
33414,42191,8143
33531,42145,8143
33597,42321,8143
33703,42286,8143
33748,42430,8143
33651,42475,8143
;
33651,42475,8203
33681,42557,8205
33538,42609,8205
33482,42470,8205
33277,42545,8205
33237,42442,8205
33465,42350,8205
33414,42191,8205
33531,42145,8205
33597,42321,8205
33703,42286,8205
33748,42430,8200
33651,42475,8203

;
clayer RecStone
WallGen
33651,42475,8203
33681,42557,8205
33538,42609,8205
33482,42470,8205
33277,42545,8205
33237,42442,8205
33465,42350,8205
33414,42191,8205
33531,42145,8205
33597,42321,8205
33703,42286,8205
33748,42430,8200
33651,42475,8203
;
33651,42475,8215
33681,42557,8215
33538,42609,8215
33482,42470,8215
33277,42545,8215
33237,42442,8215
33465,42350,8215
33414,42191,8215
33531,42145,8215
33597,42321,8215
33703,42286,8215
33748,42430,8215
33651,42475,8215

;
clayer RecBrick
WallGen
33651,42475,8215
33681,42557,8215
33538,42609,8215
33482,42470,8215
33277,42545,8215
33237,42442,8215
33465,42350,8215
33414,42191,8215
33531,42145,8215
33597,42321,8215
33703,42286,8215
33748,42430,8215
33651,42475,8215
;
33651,42475,8600
33681,42557,8600
33538,42609,8600
33482,42470,8600
33277,42545,8600
33237,42442,8600
33465,42350,8600
33414,42191,8600
33531,42145,8600
```

```
33597,42321,8600
33703,42286,8600
33748,42430,8600
33651,42475,8600

;
024- A4 W
```

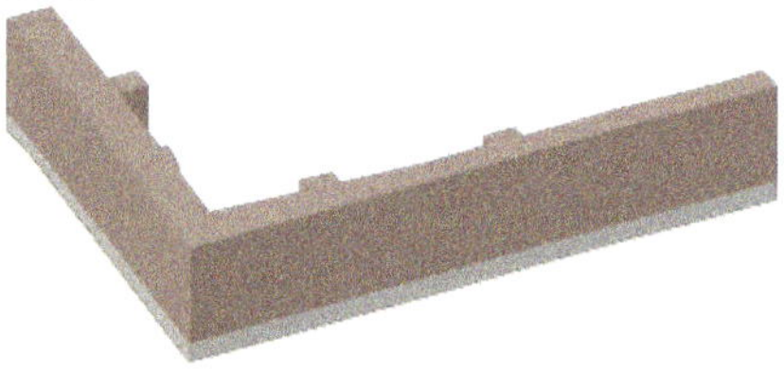

```
;24 - A4 W
;
clayer Text
filedia 0
text 33481,42012,8590 7 -90 AP
text 33503,42072,8590 7 -90 AP
text 33395,42118,8590 7 -90 AP
text 33372,42060,8590 7 -90 AP
text  33054,42202,8590  7  -90  AP
870=Y1r24
text 33156,42475,8590 7 -90 AP
text 33168,42460,8590 7 -90 AP
text 33218,42565,8590 7 -90 AP
text 33193,42575,8590 7 -90 AP
text 33310,42889,8590 7 -90 AP
text 33411,42850,8590 7 -90 AP
text 33441,42937,8590 7 -90 AP
text 33341,42971,8590 7 -90 AP
text 33430,43209,8590 7 -90 AP 525
text 33463,43299,8590 7 -90 AP 027
text 33495,43382,8590 7 -90 AP 022
text 33347,43443,8590 7 -90 AP
text 33325,43368,8590 7 -90 AP 530
text 33288,43263,8590 7 -90 AP 526
text 32865,42108,8590 7 -90 AP
text  33756,41785,8590  7  -90  AP
851=Y1r7
text 34219,41617,8590 7 -90 AP 654
text 34903,41364,8590 7 -90 AP 044
= A12r127
text 34928,41462,8590 7 -90 AP 043
= A12r128
text 34830,41493,8590 7 -90 AP 682
text 34482,41627,8590 7 -90 AP 681
text 34406,41655,8590 7 -90 AP 680
text 34246,41709,8590 7 -90 AP 653
text 34100,41762,8590 7 -90 AP 141
text 34116,41817,8590 7 -90 AP 138
text 34004,41858,8590 7 -90 AP 139
text 33985,41813,8590 7 -90 AP 140
text  33773,41883,8590  7  -90  AP
850=Y1r8
text 33481,42012,8590 7 -90 AP
filedia 1
;
clayer 3DPolylines
3dpoly
33481,42012,8590
33503,42072,8590
33395,42118,8590
33372,42060,8590
33054,42202,8590
33156,42475,8590
33168,42460,8590
33218,42565,8590
33193,42575,8590
33310,42889,8590
33411,42850,8590
33441,42937,8590
33341,42971,8590
33430,43209,8590
33463,43299,8590
33495,43382,8590
33347,43443,8590
33325,43368,8590
33288,43263,8590
32865,42108,8590
33756,41785,8590
34219,41617,8590
34903,41364,8590
34928,41462,8590
34830,41493,8590
34482,41627,8590
34406,41655,8590
34246,41709,8590
34100,41762,8590
34116,41817,8590
34004,41858,8590
33985,41813,8590
33773,41883,8590
33481,42012,8590
Close
;
clayer RecStone
WallGen
33481,42012,8140
33503,42072,8140
33395,42118,8143
33372,42060,8154
33054,42202,8154
33156,42475,8140
33168,42460,8140
```

```
33218,42565,8143
33193,42575,8154
33310,42889,8154
33411,42850,8140
33441,42937,8140
33341,42971,8143
33430,43209,8154
33463,43299,8154
33495,43382,8140
33347,43443,8143
33325,43368,8154
33288,43263,8154
32865,42108,8140
33756,41785,8140
34219,41617,8143
34903,41364,8140
34928,41462,8143
34830,41493,8154
34482,41627,8154
34406,41655,8140
34246,41709,8140
34100,41762,8143
34116,41817,8154
34004,41858,8154
33985,41813,8140
33773,41883,8140
33481,42012,8140
;
33481,42012,8215
33503,42072,8215
33395,42118,8215
33372,42060,8215
33054,42202,8215
33156,42475,8215
33168,42460,8215
33218,42565,8215
33193,42575,8215
33310,42889,8215
33411,42850,8215
33441,42937,8215
33341,42971,8215
33430,43209,8215
33463,43299,8215
33495,43382,8215
33347,43443,8215
33325,43368,8215
33288,43263,8215
32865,42108,8215
33756,41785,8215
34219,41617,8215
34903,41364,8215
34928,41462,8215
34830,41493,8215
34482,41627,8215
34406,41655,8215
34246,41709,8215
34100,41762,8215
34116,41817,8215
34004,41858,8215
33985,41813,8215
33773,41883,8215
33481,42012,8215

;
clayer RecBrick
WallGen
33481,42012,8215
33503,42072,8215
33395,42118,8215
33372,42060,8215
33054,42202,8215
33156,42475,8215
33168,42460,8215
33218,42565,8215
33193,42575,8215
33310,42889,8215
33411,42850,8215
33441,42937,8215
33341,42971,8215
33430,43209,8215
33463,43299,8215
33495,43382,8215
33347,43443,8215
33325,43368,8215
33288,43263,8215
32865,42108,8215
33756,41785,8215
34219,41617,8215
34903,41364,8215
34928,41462,8215
34830,41493,8215
34482,41627,8215
34406,41655,8215
34246,41709,8215
34100,41762,8215
34116,41817,8215
34004,41858,8215
33985,41813,8215
33773,41883,8215
33481,42012,8215
;
33481,42012,8590
33503,42072,8590
33395,42118,8590
33372,42060,8590
33054,42202,8590
```

```
33156,42475,8590
33168,42460,8590
33218,42565,8590
33193,42575,8590
33310,42889,8590
33411,42850,8590
33441,42937,8590
33341,42971,8590
33430,43209,8590
33463,43299,8590
33495,43382,8590
33347,43443,8590
33325,43368,8590
33288,43263,8590
32865,42108,8590
33756,41785,8590
34219,41617,8590
34903,41364,8590
34928,41462,8590
34830,41493,8590
34482,41627,8590
34406,41655,8590
34246,41709,8590
34100,41762,8590
34116,41817,8590
34004,41858,8590
33985,41813,8590
33773,41883,8590
33481,42012,8590
```

025- A3 E

```
;25 - A3 E
;
clayer Text
filedia 0
text 34406,41655,8590 7 -90 AP 680
text 34505,41941,8590 7 -90 AP
text 34528,42044,8590 7 -90 AP 151
text 34563,42106,8590 7 -90 AP
text 34708,42489,8590 7 -90 AP
text 34792,42462,8590 7 -90 AP
text 34655,42083,8590 7 -90 AP 671
text 34646,42063,8590 7 -90 AP
text 34682,42053,8590 7 -90 AP 554
text 34657,41989,8590 7 -90 AP 555
text 34622,41998,8590 7 -90 AP
text 34482,41627,8590 7 -90 AP 681
text 34406,41655,8590 7 -90 AP 680
filedia 1
;
clayer 3DPolylines
3dpoly
34406,41655,8590
34505,41941,8590
34528,42044,8590
34563,42106,8590
34708,42489,8590
34792,42462,8590
34655,42083,8590
34646,42063,8590
34682,42053,8590
34657,41989,8590
34622,41998,8590
34482,41627,8590
34406,41655,8590
Close
;
clayer Stone
WallGen
34406,41655,8182
34505,41941,8182
34528,42044,8182
34563,42106,8182
34708,42489,8182
34792,42462,8182
34655,42083,8182
34646,42063,8182
34682,42053,8182
34657,41989,8182
34622,41998,8182
34482,41627,8182
34406,41655,8182
;
34406,41655,8268
34505,41941,8268
34528,42044,8268
34563,42106,8268
34708,42489,8268
34792,42462,8268
34655,42083,8249
34646,42063,8268
34682,42053,8239
34657,41989,8239
34622,41998,8268
34482,41627,8268
```

```
34406,41655,8268

;
clayer RBrick
WallGen
34406,41655,8268
34505,41941,8268
34528,42044,8268
34563,42106,8268
34708,42489,8268
34792,42462,8268
34655,42083,8249
34646,42063,8268
34682,42053,8239
34657,41989,8239
34622,41998,8268
34482,41627,8268
34406,41655,8268
;
34406,41655,8320
34505,41941,8320
34528,42044,8320
34563,42106,8320
34708,42489,8320
34792,42462,8320
34655,42083,8320
34646,42063,8320
34682,42053,8320
34657,41989,8320
34622,41998,8320
34482,41627,8320
34406,41655,8320

;
clayer RecBrick
WallGen
34406,41655,8320
34505,41941,8320
34528,42044,8320
34563,42106,8320
34708,42489,8320
34792,42462,8320
34655,42083,8320
34646,42063,8320
34682,42053,8320
34657,41989,8320
34622,41998,8320
34482,41627,8320
34406,41655,8320
;
34406,41655,8590
34505,41941,8590
34528,42044,8590
34563,42106,8590
34708,42489,8590
34792,42462,8590
34655,42083,8590
34646,42063,8590
34682,42053,8590
34657,41989,8590
34622,41998,8590
34482,41627,8590
34406,41655,8590
```

026- C7 NE

```
;26,0,C7,NE
;
clayer Text
filedia 0
text 35169,42565,8590 7 -90 AP 573
text 35134,42459,8590 7 -90 AP 610
text 35140,42444,8590 7 -90 AP 611
text 35133,42435,8590 7 -90 AP 571
text 35259,42399,8590 7 -90 AP 570
text 35294,42480,8590 7 -90 AP 572
text 35169,42565,8590 7 -90 AP 573
filedia 1
;
clayer 3DPolylines
3dpoly
35169,42565,8590
35134,42459,8590
35140,42444,8590
35133,42435,8590
35259,42399,8590
35294,42480,8590
35169,42565,8590

clayer Stone
WallGen
35169,42565,8300
35134,42459,8300
35140,42444,8300
35133,42435,8300
35259,42399,8300
35294,42480,8300
```

```
35169,42565,8300
;
35169,42565,8320
35134,42459,8320
35140,42444,8320
35133,42435,8320
35259,42399,8320
35294,42480,8320
35169,42565,8320

clayer RBrick
WallGen
35169,42565,8320
35134,42459,8320
35140,42444,8320
35133,42435,8320
35259,42399,8320
35294,42480,8320
35169,42565,8320
;
35169,42565,8410
35134,42459,8410
35140,42444,8410
35133,42435,8410
35259,42399,8410
35294,42480,8410
35169,42565,8410

clayer RecBrick
WallGen
35169,42565,8410
35134,42459,8410
35140,42444,8410
35133,42435,8410
35259,42399,8410
35294,42480,8410
35169,42565,8410
;
35169,42565,8590
35134,42459,8590
35140,42444,8590
35133,42435,8590
35259,42399,8590
35294,42480,8590
35169,42565,8590

027- C4 NW
```

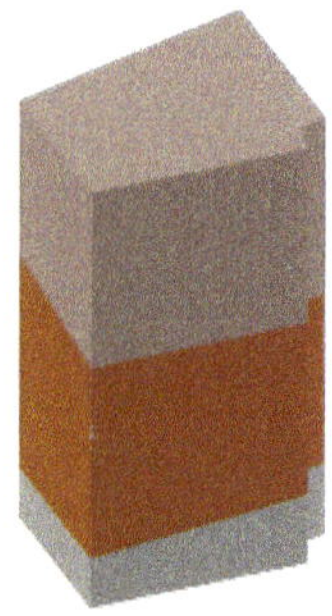

```
;27,0,C4,NW
;
clayer Text
filedia 0
text 35783,42318,8590 7 -90 AP 242
text 35748,42223,8590 7 -90 AP 241
text 35870,42165,8590 7 -90 AP 240
text 35880,42183,8590 7 -90 AP 239
text 35898,42179,8590 7 -90 AP 238
text 35939,42291,8590 7 -90 AP 237
text 35783,42318,8590 7 -90 AP 242
filedia 1
;
clayer 3DPolylines
3dpoly
35783,42318,8590
35748,42223,8590
35870,42165,8590
35880,42183,8590
35898,42179,8590
35939,42291,8590
35783,42318,8590
Close
;
clayer Stone
WallGen
35783,42318,8297
35748,42223,8297
35870,42165,8297
35880,42183,8297
35898,42179,8297
35939,42291,8297
35783,42318,8297
;
35783,42318,8332
35748,42223,8332
35870,42165,8346
35880,42183,8349
35898,42179,8347
35939,42291,8332
35783,42318,8332

clayer RBrick
```

```
WallGen
35783,42318,8332
35748,42223,8332
35870,42165,8346
35880,42183,8349
35898,42179,8347
35939,42291,8332
35783,42318,8332
;
35783,42318,8482
35748,42223,8467
35870,42165,8467
35880,42183,8467
35898,42179,8467
35939,42291,8467
35783,42318,8482

;
clayer RecBrick
WallGen
35783,42318,8482
35748,42223,8467
35870,42165,8467
35880,42183,8467
35898,42179,8467
35939,42291,8467
35783,42318,8482
;
35783,42318,8590
35748,42223,8590
35870,42165,8590
35880,42183,8590
35898,42179,8590
35939,42291,8590
35783,42318,8590
```

028- C4 ES

```
;28,0,C4,E,S
;
clayer Text
filedia 0
text 36231,42190,8590 7 -90 AP 750
text 36148,41876,8590 7 -90 AP 751
text 35828,41996,8590 7 -90 AP 246=Y1r11
text 35842,42036,8590 7 -90 AP 245
text 35830,42041,8590 7 -90 AP 244
text 35837,42054,8590 7 -90 AP 243
text 35719,42105,8590 7 -90 AP 258
text 35598,41823,8590 7 -90 AP 257
text 35509,41859,8590 7 -90 AP 256
text 35466,41728,8590 7 -90 AP 255
text 35570,41695,8590 7 -90 AP 254
text 35550,41646,8590 7 -90 AP 253
text 35568,41639,8590 7 -90 AP 252
text 35560,41617,8590 7 -90 AP 251
text 35674,41577,8590 7 -90 AP 250
text 35791,41892,8590 7 -90 AP 249
text 36318,41697,8590 7 -90 AP 713
text 36359,41815,8590 7 -90 AP 712
text 36250,41846,8590 7 -90 AP 711
text 36349,42146,8590 7 -90 AP 710
text 36231,42190,8590 7 -90 AP 750
filedia 1
;
clayer 3DPolylines
3dpoly
36231,42190,8590
36148,41876,8590
35828,41996,8590
35842,42036,8590
35830,42041,8590
35837,42054,8590
35719,42105,8590
35598,41823,8590
35509,41859,8590
35466,41728,8590
35570,41695,8590
35550,41646,8590
35568,41639,8590
35560,41617,8590
35674,41577,8590
35791,41892,8590
36318,41697,8590
36359,41815,8590
36250,41846,8590
36349,42146,8590
36231,42190,8590
Close
;
clayer Stone
WallGen
36231,42190,8285
36148,41876,8285
35828,41996,8285
35842,42036,8285
35830,42041,8285
35837,42054,8285
```

```
35719,42105,8282
35598,41823,8285
35509,41859,8266
35466,41728,8270
35570,41695,8280
35550,41646,8289
35568,41639,8285
35560,41617,8285
35674,41577,8285
35791,41892,8285
36318,41697,8285
36359,41815,8285
36250,41846,8285
36349,42146,8285
36231,42190,8285
;
36231,42190,8375
36148,41876,8375
35828,41996,8375
35842,42036,8375
35830,42041,8375
35837,42054,8375
35719,42105,8375
35598,41823,8375
35509,41859,8375
35466,41728,8375
35570,41695,8375
35550,41646,8375
35568,41639,8375
35560,41617,8375
35674,41577,8375
35791,41892,8375
36318,41697,8375
36359,41815,8375
36250,41846,8375
36349,42146,8375
36231,42190,8375

;
clayer RBrick
WallGen
36231,42190,8375
36148,41876,8375
35828,41996,8375
35842,42036,8375
35830,42041,8375
35837,42054,8375
35719,42105,8375
35598,41823,8375
35509,41859,8376
35466,41728,8375
35570,41695,8375
35550,41646,8375
35568,41639,8375
35560,41617,8375
35674,41577,8374
35791,41892,8375
36318,41697,8375
36359,41815,8375
36250,41846,8375
36349,42146,8375
36231,42190,8375
;
36231,42190,8526
36148,41876,8479
35828,41996,8405
35842,42036,8408
35830,42041,8401
35837,42054,8402
35719,42105,8405
35598,41823,8413
35509,41859,8401
35466,41728,8404
35570,41695,8402
35550,41646,8406
35568,41639,8402
35560,41617,8403
35674,41577,8406
35791,41892,8412
36318,41697,8443
36359,41815,8439
36250,41846,8503
36349,42146,8481
36231,42190,8526

;
clayer RecBrick
WallGen
36231,42190,8526
36148,41876,8479
35828,41996,8405
35842,42036,8408
35830,42041,8401
35837,42054,8402
35719,42105,8405
35598,41823,8413
35509,41859,8401
35466,41728,8404
35570,41695,8402
35550,41646,8406
35568,41639,8402
35560,41617,8403
35674,41577,8406
35791,41892,8412
36318,41697,8443
36359,41815,8439
```

```
36250,41846,8503
36349,42146,8481
36231,42190,8526
;
36231,42190,8590
36148,41876,8590
35828,41996,8590
35842,42036,8590
35830,42041,8590
35837,42054,8590
35719,42105,8590
35598,41823,8590
35509,41859,8590
35466,41728,8590
35570,41695,8590
35550,41646,8590
35568,41639,8590
35560,41617,8590
35674,41577,8590
35791,41892,8590
36318,41697,8590
36359,41815,8590
36250,41846,8590
36349,42146,8590
36231,42190,8590
```

029- C8 NE

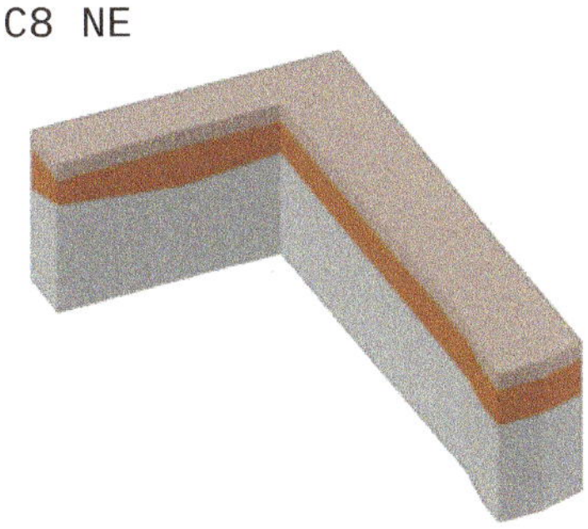

```
;29 - C8 N E
;
clayer Text
filedia 0
text 36069,42252,8590 7 -90 AP 750
text 36115,42381,8590 7 -90 AP 086=Y1r10
text 36801,42109,8590 7 -90 AP 578=Y1r12
text 36411,40968,8590 7 -90 AP 040
text 36301,40977,8590 7 -90 AP 286 = A12r160
text 36197,41013,8590 7 -90 AP
text 36222,41084,8590 7 -90 AP
text 36281,41195,8590 7 -90 AP 037
text 36570,42060,8590 7 -90 AP 576
text 36349,42146,8590 7 -90 AP 710
text 36069,42252,8590 7 -90 AP 750
filedia 1
;
clayer 3DPolylines
3dpoly
36069,42252,8590
36115,42381,8590
36801,42109,8590
36411,40968,8590
36301,40977,8590
36197,41013,8590
36222,41084,8590
36281,41195,8590
36570,42060,8590
36349,42146,8590
36069,42252,8590
Close
;
clayer Stone
WallGen
36069,42252,8200
36115,42381,8200
36801,42109,8200
36411,40968,8200
36301,40977,8200
36197,41013,8200
36222,41084,8200
36281,41195,8200
36570,42060,8200
36349,42146,8200
36069,42252,8200
;
36069,42252,8481
36115,42381,8440
36801,42109,8440
36411,40968,8454
36301,40977,8454
36197,41013,8454
36222,41084,8454
36281,41195,8448
36570,42060,8463
36349,42146,8444
36069,42252,8481

;
clayer RBrick
WallGen
36069,42252,8481
36115,42381,8440
36801,42109,8440
36411,40968,8454
36301,40977,8454
```

```
36197,41013,8454
36222,41084,8454
36281,41195,8448
36570,42060,8463
36349,42146,8444
36069,42252,8481
;
36069,42252,8544
36115,42381,8544
36801,42109,8544
36411,40968,8544
36301,40977,8544
36197,41013,8544
36222,41084,8544
36281,41195,8544
36570,42060,8544
36349,42146,8544
36069,42252,8544

;
clayer RecBrick
WallGen
36069,42252,8544
36115,42381,8544
36801,42109,8544
36411,40968,8544
36301,40977,8544
36197,41013,8544
36222,41084,8544
36281,41195,8544
36570,42060,8544
36349,42146,8544
36069,42252,8544
;
36069,42252,8590
36115,42381,8590
36801,42109,8590
36411,40968,8590
36301,40977,8590
36197,41013,8590
36222,41084,8590
36281,41195,8590
36570,42060,8590
36349,42146,8590
36069,42252,8590
```

030- C1-2 S

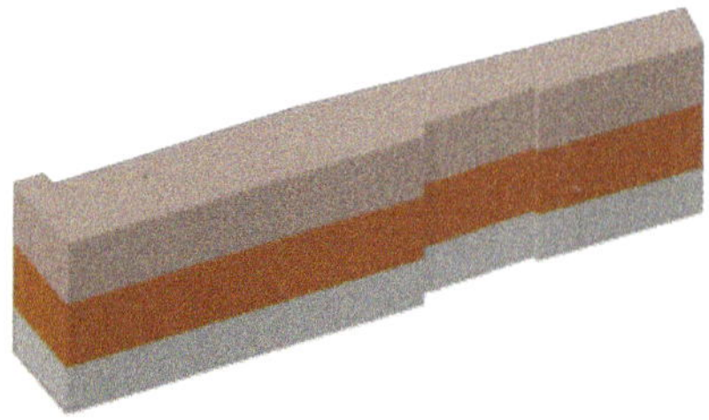

```
;30 - C1 C2 S
;
clayer Text
filedia 0
text 36222,41084,8590 7 -90 AP
text 35871,41199,8590 7 -90 AP
text 35878,41214,8590 7 -90 AP 410
= A12r153
text 35651,41272,8590 7 -90 AP 113
= A12r142
text  35632,41283,8590  7  -90  AP
041=Y1r30
text 35605,41252,8590 7 -90 AP 042
= A12r139
text 34928,41462,8590 7 -90 AP 043
= A12r128
text 34830,41493,8590 7 -90 AP 682
text 34902,41718,8590 7 -90 AP 541
text 34966,41698,8590 7 -90 AP 540
text 34957,41659,8590 7 -90 AP 539
text 35486,41502,8590 7 -90 AP 537
text 35623,41448,8590 7 -90 AP 687
text 36281,41195,8590 7 -90 AP 037
text 36222,41084,8590 7 -90 AP
filedia 1
;
clayer 3DPolylines
3dpoly
36222,41084,8590
35871,41199,8590
35878,41214,8590
35651,41272,8590
35632,41283,8590
35605,41252,8590
34928,41462,8590
34830,41493,8590
34902,41718,8590
34966,41698,8590
34957,41659,8590
35486,41502,8590
35623,41448,8590
36281,41195,8590
36222,41084,8590
Close
;
```

```
clayer Stone
WallGen
36222,41084,8184
35871,41199,8184
35878,41214,8184
35651,41272,8184
35632,41283,8184
35605,41252,8184
34928,41462,8184
34830,41493,8184
34902,41718,8184
34966,41698,8184
34957,41659,8184
35486,41502,8184
35623,41448,8184
36281,41195,8184
36222,41084,8184
;
36222,41084,8296
35871,41199,8296
35878,41214,8296
35651,41272,8296
35632,41283,8296
35605,41252,8296
34928,41462,8296
34830,41493,8296
34902,41718,8296
34966,41698,8296
34957,41659,8296
35486,41502,8296
35623,41448,8296
36281,41195,8296
36222,41084,8296

;
clayer Rbrick
WallGen
36222,41084,8296
35871,41199,8296
35878,41214,8296
35651,41272,8296
35632,41283,8296
35605,41252,8296
34928,41462,8296
34830,41493,8296
34902,41718,8296
34966,41698,8296
34957,41659,8296
35486,41502,8296
35623,41448,8296
36281,41195,8296
36222,41084,8296
;
36222,41084,8448
35871,41199,8448
35878,41214,8448
35651,41272,8448
35632,41283,8448
35605,41252,8448
34928,41462,8448
34830,41493,8448
34902,41718,8448
34966,41698,8448
34957,41659,8448
35486,41502,8448
35623,41448,8448
36281,41195,8448
36222,41084,8448

;
clayer RecBrick
WallGen
36222,41084,8448
35871,41199,8448
35878,41214,8448
35651,41272,8448
35632,41283,8448
35605,41252,8448
34928,41462,8448
34830,41493,8448
34902,41718,8448
34966,41698,8448
34957,41659,8448
35486,41502,8448
35623,41448,8448
36281,41195,8448
36222,41084,8448
;
36222,41084,8590
35871,41199,8590
35878,41214,8590
35651,41272,8590
35632,41283,8590
35605,41252,8590
34928,41462,8590
34830,41493,8590
34902,41718,8590
34966,41698,8590
34957,41659,8590
35486,41502,8590
35623,41448,8590
36281,41195,8590
36222,41084,8590

031- C2 ESE
```

```
;31 - C2 E SE
;
clayer Text
filedia 0
text 35486,41502,8590 7 -90 AP 537
text 35494,41518,8590 7 -90 AP 263
text 35510,41512,8590 7 -90 AP 262
text 35517,41527,8590 7 -90 AP 261
text 35628,41486,8590 7 -90 AP 685
text 35620,41475,8590 7 -90 AP 686
text 35631,41465,8590 7 -90 AP 260
text 35623,41448,8590 7 -90 AP 687
text 35486,41502,8590 7 -90 AP 537
filedia 1
;
clayer 3DPolylines
3dpoly
35486,41502,8590
35494,41518,8590
35510,41512,8590
35517,41527,8590
35628,41486,8590
35620,41475,8590
35631,41465,8590
35623,41448,8590
35486,41502,8590
Close
;
clayer Stone
WallGen
35486,41502,8184
35494,41518,8184
35510,41512,8184
35517,41527,8184
35628,41486,8184
35620,41475,8184
35631,41465,8184
35623,41448,8184
35486,41502,8184
;
35486,41502,8296
35494,41518,8296
35510,41512,8296
35517,41527,8296
35628,41486,8296
35620,41475,8296
35631,41465,8296
35623,41448,8296
35486,41502,8296

;
clayer RBrick
WallGen
35486,41502,8296
35494,41518,8296
35510,41512,8296
35517,41527,8296
35628,41486,8296
35620,41475,8296
35631,41465,8296
35623,41448,8296
35486,41502,8296
;
35486,41502,8448
35494,41518,8448
35510,41512,8448
35517,41527,8448
35628,41486,8448
35620,41475,8448
35631,41465,8448
35623,41448,8448
35486,41502,8448

;
clayer RecBrick
WallGen
35486,41502,8448
35494,41518,8448
35510,41512,8448
35517,41527,8448
35628,41486,8448
35620,41475,8448
35631,41465,8448
35623,41448,8448
35486,41502,8448
;
35486,41502,8590
35494,41518,8590
35510,41512,8590
35517,41527,8590
35628,41486,8590
35620,41475,8590
35631,41465,8590
35623,41448,8590
35486,41502,8590
```

032- C6 E

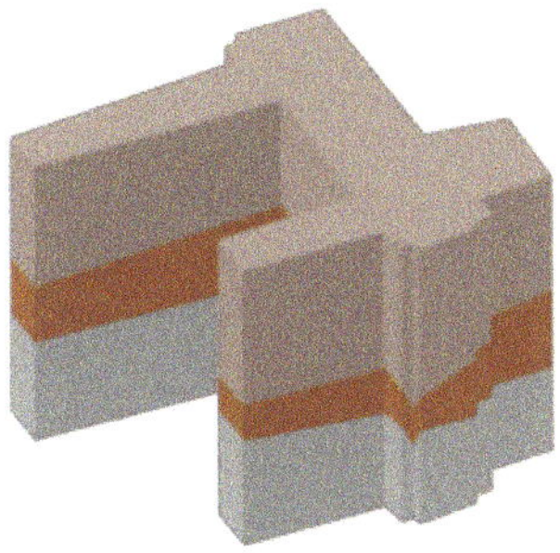

```
;32 - C6 E
;
clayer Text
filedia 0
text 35217,41946,8590 7 -90 AP 562
text 35120,41996,8590 7 -90 AP 563
text 35218,42270,8590 7 -90 AP 564
text 35105,42311,8590 7 -90 AP 565
text 35090,42300,8590 7 -90 AP 612
text 35076,42302,8590 7 -90 AP 613
text 35061,42272,8590 7 -90 AP 566
text 34755,42359,8590 7 -90 AP 0
text 34731,42295,8590 7 -90 AP 0
text 35046,42172,8590 7 -90 AP 551
text 34966,41966,8590 7 -90 AP 550
text 34783,42024,8590 7 -90 AP 549
text 34759,41954,8590 7 -90 AP 548
text 34939,41887,8590 7 -90 AP 547
text 34931,41848,8590 7 -90 AP 546
text 34947,41844,8590 7 -90 AP 545
text 34944,41830,8590 7 -90 AP 544
text 35024,41811,8590 7 -90 AP 561
text 35029,41824,8590 7 -90 AP 558
text 35057,41817,8590 7 -90 AP 559
text 35072,41851,8590 7 -90 AP 560
text 35168,41823,8590 7 -90 AP 543
text 35217,41946,8590 7 -90 AP 562
filedia 1
;
clayer 3DPolylines
3dpoly
35217,41946,8590
35120,41996,8590
35218,42270,8590
35105,42311,8590
35090,42300,8590
35076,42302,8590
35061,42272,8590
34755,42359,8590
34731,42295,8590
35046,42172,8590
34966,41966,8590
34783,42024,8590
34759,41954,8590
34939,41887,8590
34931,41848,8590
34947,41844,8590
34944,41830,8590
35024,41811,8590
35029,41824,8590
35057,41817,8590
35072,41851,8590
35168,41823,8590
35217,41946,8590

;
clayer Stone
WallGen
35217,41946,8184
35120,41996,8184
35218,42270,8184
35105,42311,8184
35090,42300,8184
35076,42302,8184
35061,42272,8184
34755,42359,8184
34731,42295,8184
35046,42172,8184
34966,41966,8184
34783,42024,8184
34759,41954,8184
34939,41887,8184
34931,41848,8184
34947,41844,8184
34944,41830,8184
35024,41811,8184
35029,41824,8184
35057,41817,8184
35072,41851,8184
35168,41823,8184
35217,41946,8184
;
35217,41946,8320
35120,41996,8314
35218,42270,8326
35105,42311,8330
35090,42300,8330
35076,42302,8334
35061,42272,8327
34755,42359,8330
34731,42295,8330
35046,42172,8326
34966,41966,8329
34783,42024,8340
34759,41954,8338
```

```
34939,41887,8323
34931,41848,8325
34947,41844,8291
34944,41830,8321
35024,41811,8314
35029,41824,8320
35057,41817,8324
35072,41851,8310
35168,41823,8307
35217,41946,8320

;
clayer RBrick
WallGen
35217,41946,8320
35120,41996,8314
35218,42270,8326
35105,42311,8330
35090,42300,8330
35076,42302,8334
35061,42272,8327
34755,42359,8330
34731,42295,8330
35046,42172,8326
34966,41966,8329
34783,42024,8340
34759,41954,8338
34939,41887,8323
34931,41848,8325
34947,41844,8291
34944,41830,8321
35024,41811,8314
35029,41824,8320
35057,41817,8324
35072,41851,8310
35168,41823,8307
35217,41946,8320
;
35217,41946,8391
35120,41996,8410
35218,42270,8410
35105,42311,8410
35090,42300,8410
35076,42302,8392
35061,42272,8397
34755,42359,8410
34731,42295,8410
35046,42172,8434
34966,41966,8410
34783,42024,8388
34759,41954,8390
34939,41887,8389
34931,41848,8378
34947,41844,8343
34944,41830,8369
35024,41811,8396
35029,41824,8398
35057,41817,8404
35072,41851,8409
35168,41823,8421
35217,41946,8391

;
clayer RecBrick
WallGen
35217,41946,8391
35120,41996,8410
35218,42270,8410
35105,42311,8410
35090,42300,8410
35076,42302,8392
35061,42272,8397
34755,42359,8410
34731,42295,8410
35046,42172,8434
34966,41966,8410
34783,42024,8388
34759,41954,8390
34939,41887,8389
34931,41848,8378
34947,41844,8343
34944,41830,8369
35024,41811,8396
35029,41824,8398
35057,41817,8404
35072,41851,8409
35168,41823,8421
35217,41946,8391
;
35217,41946,8590
35120,41996,8590
35218,42270,8590
35105,42311,8590
35090,42300,8590
35076,42302,8590
35061,42272,8590
34755,42359,8590
34731,42295,8590
35046,42172,8590
34966,41966,8590
34783,42024,8590
34759,41954,8590
34939,41887,8590
34931,41848,8590
34947,41844,8590
34944,41830,8590
```

```
35024,41811,8590
35029,41824,8590
35057,41817,8590
35072,41851,8590
35168,41823,8590
35217,41946,8590
```

033- B1 S

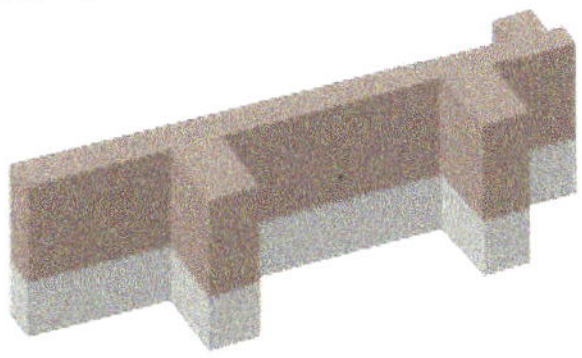

```
;33 - B1 S
;
clayer Text
filedia 0
text 33495,43382,8590 7 -90 AP 022
text 34583,42928,8590 7 -90 AP
text 34610,43002,8590 7 -90 AP
text 34698,42974,8590 7 -90 AP
text 34668,42893,8590 7 -90 AP
text 34703,42879,8590 7 -90 AP 676
text 34679,42817,8590 7 -90 AP 675
text 34495,42889,8590 7 -90 AP
text 34428,42710,8590 7 -90 AP
text 34322,42747,8590 7 -90 AP
text 34380,42935,8590 7 -90 AP
text 33892,43128,8590 7 -90 AP
text 33819,42940,8590 7 -90 AP
text 33701,42979,8590 7 -90 AP
text 33777,43173,8590 7 -90 AP
text 33463,43299,8590 7 -90 AP 027
text 33495,43382,8590 7 -90 AP 022
filedia 1
;
clayer 3DPolylines
3dpoly
33495,43382,8590
34583,42928,8590
34610,43002,8590
34698,42974,8590
34668,42893,8590
34703,42879,8590
34679,42817,8590
34495,42889,8590
34428,42710,8590
34322,42747,8590
34380,42935,8590
33892,43128,8590
33819,42940,8590
33701,42979,8590
33777,43173,8590
33463,43299,8590
33495,43382,8590

clayer RecStone
WallGen
33495,43382,8200
34583,42928,8200
34610,43002,8200
34698,42974,8200
34668,42893,8200
34703,42879,8200
34679,42817,8200
34495,42889,8200
34428,42710,8200
34322,42747,8200
34380,42935,8200
33892,43128,8200
33819,42940,8200
33701,42979,8200
33777,43173,8200
33463,43299,8200
33495,43382,8200
;
33495,43382,8340
34583,42928,8340
34610,43002,8340
34698,42974,8340
34668,42893,8340
34703,42879,8340
34679,42817,8340
34495,42889,8340
34428,42710,8340
34322,42747,8340
34380,42935,8340
33892,43128,8340
33819,42940,8340
33701,42979,8340
33777,43173,8340
33463,43299,8340
33495,43382,8340


;
clayer RecBrick
WallGen
33495,43382,8340
34583,42928,8340
34610,43002,8340
34698,42974,8340
34668,42893,8340
34703,42879,8340
34679,42817,8340
34495,42889,8340
```

```
34428,42710,8340
34322,42747,8340
34380,42935,8340
33892,43128,8340
33819,42940,8340
33701,42979,8340
33777,43173,8340
33463,43299,8340
33495,43382,8340
;
33495,43382,8590
34583,42928,8590
34610,43002,8590
34698,42974,8590
34668,42893,8590
34703,42879,8590
34679,42817,8590
34495,42889,8590
34428,42710,8590
34322,42747,8590
34380,42935,8590
33892,43128,8590
33819,42940,8590
33701,42979,8590
33777,43173,8590
33463,43299,8590
33495,43382,8590
```

034- R1 N

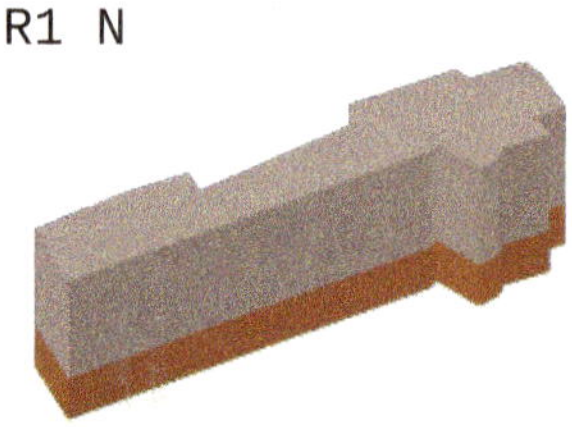

```
;34 - R1 N
;
clayer Text
filedia 0
text 36969,40444,8800 7 -90 AP 283
text 36441,40574,8800 7 -90 AP 282
text 36259,40618,8800 7 -90 AP 0
text 36326,40767,8800 7 -90 AP 0
text 36509,40734,8800 7 -90 AP 285
text 36629,40697,8800 7 -90 AP 536
text 36608,40645,8800 7 -90 AP 535
text 36926,40595,8800 7 -90 AP 534
text 36967,40638,8800 7 -90 AP 533
text 37165,40580,8800 7 -90 AP 757
text 37163,40545,8800 7 -90 AP 284
text 37270,40511,8800 7 -90 AP 746
text 37266,40506,8800 7 -90 AP
830=Y1r22
text 37259,40460,8800 7 -90 AP 756
text 37224,40369,8800 7 -90 AP 745
text 37161,40387,8800 7 -90 AP 744
text 37148,40332,8800 7 -90 AP 737
text 37059,40363,8800 7 -90 AP 736
text 37051,40351,8800 7 -90 AP 735
text 37046,40353,8800 7 -90 AP 734
text 37038,40345,8800 7 -90 AP 733
text 36991,40349,8800 7 -90 AP 732
text 36991,40450,8800 7 -90 AP 790
text 36969,40444,8800 7 -90 AP 283
filedia 1
;
clayer 3DPolylines
3dpoly
36969,40444,8800
36441,40574,8800
36259,40618,8800
36326,40767,8800
36509,40734,8800
36629,40697,8800
36608,40645,8800
36926,40595,8800
36967,40638,8800
37165,40580,8800
37163,40545,8800
37270,40511,8800
37266,40506,8800
37259,40460,8800
37224,40369,8800
37161,40387,8800
37148,40332,8800
37059,40363,8800
37051,40351,8800
37046,40353,8800
37038,40345,8800
36991,40349,8800
36991,40450,8800
36969,40444,8800

;
clayer Stone
WallGen
36969,40444,8520
36441,40574,8520
36259,40618,8520
36326,40767,8520
36509,40734,8520
36629,40697,8520
36608,40645,8520
36926,40595,8520
36967,40638,8520
37165,40580,8520
```

```
37163,40545,8520
37270,40511,8520
37266,40506,8520
37259,40460,8520
37224,40369,8520
37161,40387,8520
37148,40332,8520
37059,40363,8520
37051,40351,8520
37046,40353,8520
37038,40345,8520
36991,40349,8520
36991,40450,8520
36969,40444,8520
;
36969,40444,8524
36441,40574,8524
36259,40618,8524
36326,40767,8524
36509,40734,8524
36629,40697,8524
36608,40645,8524
36926,40595,8524
36967,40638,8524
37165,40580,8524
37163,40545,8524
37270,40511,8524
37266,40506,8524
37259,40460,8524
37224,40369,8524
37161,40387,8524
37148,40332,8524
37059,40363,8524
37051,40351,8524
37046,40353,8524
37038,40345,8524
36991,40349,8524
36991,40450,8524
36969,40444,8524

;
clayer RBrick
WallGen
36969,40444,8524
36441,40574,8524
36259,40618,8524
36326,40767,8524
36509,40734,8524
36629,40697,8524
36608,40645,8524
36926,40595,8524
36967,40638,8524
37165,40580,8524
```

```
37163,40545,8524
37270,40511,8524
37266,40506,8524
37259,40460,8524
37224,40369,8524
37161,40387,8524
37148,40332,8524
37059,40363,8524
37051,40351,8524
37046,40353,8524
37038,40345,8524
36991,40349,8524
36991,40450,8524
36969,40444,8524
;
36969,40444,8605
36441,40574,8605
36259,40618,8605
36326,40767,8605
36509,40734,8605
36629,40697,8605
36608,40645,8605
36926,40595,8605
36967,40638,8605
37165,40580,8605
37163,40545,8605
37270,40511,8605
37266,40506,8605
37259,40460,8605
37224,40369,8605
37161,40387,8605
37148,40332,8605
37059,40363,8605
37051,40351,8605
37046,40353,8605
37038,40345,8605
36991,40349,8605
36991,40450,8605
36969,40444,8605

;
clayer RecBrick
WallGen
36969,40444,8605
36441,40574,8605
36259,40618,8605
36326,40767,8605
36509,40734,8605
36629,40697,8605
36608,40645,8605
36926,40595,8605
36967,40638,8605
37165,40580,8605
```

```
37163,40545,8605
37270,40511,8605
37266,40506,8605
37259,40460,8605
37224,40369,8605
37161,40387,8605
37148,40332,8605
37059,40363,8605
37051,40351,8605
37046,40353,8605
37038,40345,8605
36991,40349,8605
36991,40450,8605
36969,40444,8605
;
36969,40444,8800
36441,40574,8800
36259,40618,8800
36326,40767,8800
36509,40734,8800
36629,40697,8800
36608,40645,8800
36926,40595,8800
36967,40638,8800
37165,40580,8800
37163,40545,8800
37270,40511,8800
37266,40506,8800
37259,40460,8800
37224,40369,8800
37161,40387,8800
37148,40332,8800
37059,40363,8800
37051,40351,8800
37046,40353,8800
37038,40345,8800
36991,40349,8800
36991,40450,8800
36969,40444,8800

;
035- R1 SW
```

```
;35 - R1 S W
;
clayer Text
filedia 0
text 36476,40027,8800 7 -90 AP 283
text 36922,39922,8800 7 -90 AP 282
text 36859,39741,8800 7 -90 AP 0
text 36622,39824,8800 7 -90 AP 0
text 36568,39860,8800 7 -90 AP 285
text 36432,39928,8800 7 -90 AP 536
text 35838,40079,8800 7 -90 AP 535
text 36197,41013,8800 7 -90 AP 534
text 36411,40968,8800 7 -90 AP 533
text 36326,40767,8800 7 -90 AP 757
text 36259,40618,8800 7 -90 AP 284
text 36081,40130,8800 7 -90 AP 746
text 36476,40027,8800 7 -90 AP
830=Y1r22
filedia 1
;
clayer 3DPolylines
3dpoly
36476,40027,8800
36922,39922,8800
36859,39741,8800
36622,39824,8800
36568,39860,8800
36432,39928,8800
35838,40079,8800
36197,41013,8800
36411,40968,8800
36326,40767,8800
36259,40618,8800
36081,40130,8800
36476,40027,8800

;
clayer Stone
WallGen
36476,40027,8520
36922,39922,8520
36859,39741,8520
36622,39824,8520
36568,39860,8520
36432,39928,8520
35838,40079,8520
36197,41013,8520
36411,40968,8520
36326,40767,8520
36259,40618,8520
36081,40130,8520
36476,40027,8520
;
36476,40027,8540
36922,39922,8540
36859,39741,8540
```

```
36622,39824,8540
36568,39860,8540
36432,39928,8540
35838,40079,8540
36197,41013,8540
36411,40968,8540
36326,40767,8540
36259,40618,8540
36081,40130,8540
36476,40027,8540

;
clayer RBrick
WallGen
36476,40027,8540
36922,39922,8540
36859,39741,8540
36622,39824,8540
36568,39860,8540
36432,39928,8540
35838,40079,8540
36197,41013,8540
36411,40968,8540
36326,40767,8540
36259,40618,8540
36081,40130,8540
36476,40027,8540
;
36476,40027,8605
36922,39922,8605
36859,39741,8605
36622,39824,8605
36568,39860,8605
36432,39928,8605
35838,40079,8605
36197,41013,8605
36411,40968,8605
36326,40767,8605
36259,40618,8605
36081,40130,8605
36476,40027,8605

;
clayer RecBrick
WallGen
36476,40027,8605
36922,39922,8605
36859,39741,8605
36622,39824,8605
36568,39860,8605
36432,39928,8605
35838,40079,8605
36197,41013,8605
36411,40968,8605
36326,40767,8605
36259,40618,8605
36081,40130,8605
36476,40027,8605
;
36476,40027,8800
36922,39922,8800
36859,39741,8800
36622,39824,8800
36568,39860,8800
36432,39928,8800
35838,40079,8800
36197,41013,8800
36411,40968,8800
36326,40767,8800
36259,40618,8800
36081,40130,8800
36476,40027,8800

;
036- R1 E
```

```
;36 - R1 E
;
clayer Text
filedia 0
text 36476,40027,8800 7 -90 AP 742
text 36922,39922,8800 7 -90 AP 743
text 36859,39741,8800 7 -90 AP 731
text 36622,39824,8800 7 -90 AP 732
text 36568,39860,8800 7 -90 AP 790
text 36432,39928,8800 7 -90 AP 283
text 35838,40079,8800 7 -90 AP 724
text 36197,41013,8800 7 -90 AP 742
filedia 1
;
clayer 3DPolylines
3dpoly
36907,40124,8800
36944,40117,8800
36999,40326,8800
36991,40349,8800
36991,40450,8800
36969,40444,8800
36948,40346,8800
36907,40124,8800
```

```
;
clayer Stone
WallGen
36907,40124,8520
36944,40117,8520
36999,40326,8520
36991,40349,8520
36991,40450,8520
36969,40444,8520
36948,40346,8520
36907,40124,8520
;
36907,40124,8540
36944,40117,8540
36999,40326,8540
36991,40349,8540
36991,40450,8540
36969,40444,8540
36948,40346,8540
36907,40124,8540

;
clayer RBrick
WallGen
36907,40124,8540
36944,40117,8540
36999,40326,8540
36991,40349,8540
36991,40450,8540
36969,40444,8540
36948,40346,8540
36907,40124,8540
;
36907,40124,8604
36944,40117,8604
36999,40326,8604
36991,40349,8604
36991,40450,8604
36969,40444,8604
36948,40346,8604
36907,40124,8604

;
clayer RecBrick
WallGen
36907,40124,8604
36944,40117,8604
36999,40326,8604
36991,40349,8604
36991,40450,8604
36969,40444,8604
36948,40346,8604
36907,40124,8604
;
36907,40124,8800
36944,40117,8800
36999,40326,8800
36991,40349,8800
36991,40450,8800
36969,40444,8800
36948,40346,8800
36907,40124,8800

;
080-082 R2 N1-3 Door
```

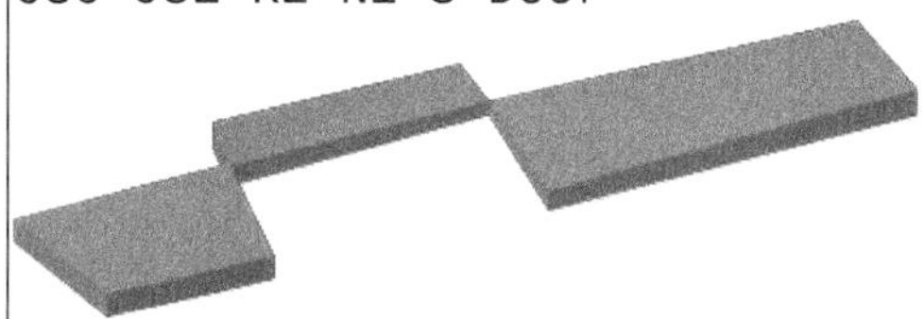

```
;80 - Door R2 N1
;
clayer Text
filedia 0
text 37420,40475,8530 7 -90 AP 748
text 37340,40498,8530 7 -90 AP 747
text 37330,40481,8530 7 -90 AP 0
text 37409,40452,8530 7 -90 AP 749
text 37420,40475,8530 7 -90 AP 748
filedia 1
;
clayer 3DPolylines
3dpoly
37420,40475,8530
37340,40498,8530
37330,40481,8530
37409,40452,8530
37420,40475,8530

;
clayer Installations
WallGen
37420,40475,8530
37340,40498,8530
37330,40481,8530
37409,40452,8530
37420,40475,8530
;
37420,40475,8531
37340,40498,8539
37330,40481,8537
37409,40452,8535
37420,40475,8531

;
```

```
;81 - Door R2 N2
;
clayer Text
filedia 0
text 37498,40363,8530 7 -90 AP 754
text 37514,40404,8530 7 -90 AP 753
text 37409,40452,8530 7 -90 AP 749
text 37388,40406,8530 7 -90 AP 0
text 37498,40363,8530 7 -90 AP 754
filedia 1
;
clayer 3DPolylines
3dpoly
37498,40363,8530
37514,40404,8530
37409,40452,8530
37388,40406,8530
37498,40363,8530

;
clayer Doorways
WallGen
37498,40363,8530
37514,40404,8530
37409,40452,8530
37388,40406,8530
37498,40363,8530
;
37498,40363,8539
37514,40404,8535
37409,40452,8535
37388,40406,8537
37498,40363,8539

;
;82 - Door R2 N3
;
clayer Text
filedia 0
text 37307,40439,8530 7 -90 AP 0
text 37330,40481,8530 7 -90 AP 0
text 37266,40506,8530 7 -90 AP
830=Y1r22
text 37259,40460,8530 7 -90 AP 756
text 37307,40439,8530 7 -90 AP 0
filedia 1
;
clayer 3DPolylines
3dpoly
37307,40439,8530
37330,40481,8530
37266,40506,8530
37259,40460,8530
37307,40439,8530

;
clayer Doorways
WallGen
37307,40439,8530
37330,40481,8530
37266,40506,8530
37259,40460,8530
37307,40439,8530
;
37307,40439,8538
37330,40481,8538
37266,40506,8538
37259,40460,8538
37307,40439,8538

;
083-084 Platform (X)
```

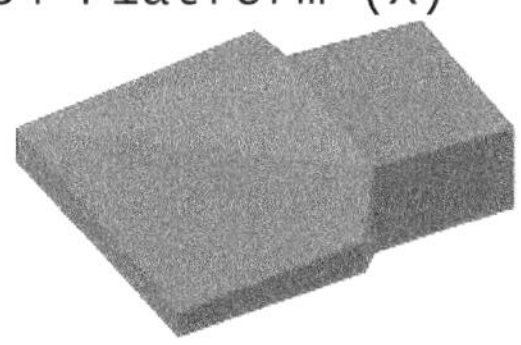

```
;083 - Platform 1
;
clayer Text
filedia 0
text 35651,41272,8150 7 -90 AP 113
= A12r142
text 35569,40992,8150 7 -90 AP 112
= A12r143
text 35750,40944,8150 7 -90 AP 409
= A12r145
text 35776,40958,8150 7 -90 AP 408
= A12r146
text 35838,41128,8150 7 -90 AP 405
= A12r149
text 35871,41199,8150 7 -90 AP 0
text 35878,41214,8150 7 -90 AP 410
= A12r153
text 35651,41272,8150 7 -90 AP 113
= A12r142
filedia 1
;
clayer 3DPolylines
3dpoly
35651,41272,8150
35569,40992,8150
35750,40944,8150
35776,40958,8150
35838,41128,8150
35871,41199,8150
```

```
35878,41214,8150
35651,41272,8150

;
clayer Installations
WallGen
35651,41272,8150
35569,40992,8150
35750,40944,8150
35776,40958,8150
35838,41128,8150
35871,41199,8150
35878,41214,8150
35651,41272,8150
;
35651,41272,8184
35569,40992,8174
35750,40944,8182
35776,40958,8238
35838,41128,8236
35871,41199,8210
35878,41214,8190
35651,41272,8184

;
;084 - Platform 2
;
clayer Text
filedia 0
text 35968,41090,8150 7 -90 AP 406
= A12r150
text 35838,41128,8150 7 -90 AP 405
= A12r149
text 35776,40958,8150 7 -90 AP 408
= A12r146
text 35911,40917,8150 7 -90 AP 0
text 35968,41090,8150 7 -90 AP 406
= A12r150
filedia 1
;
clayer 3DPolylines
3dpoly
35968,41090,8150
35838,41128,8150
35776,40958,8150
35911,40917,8150
35968,41090,8150

;
clayer Installations
WallGen
35968,41090,8150
35838,41128,8150
35776,40958,8150
35911,40917,8150
35968,41090,8150
;
35968,41090,8227
35838,41128,8236
35776,40958,8238
35911,40917,8231
35968,41090,8227

;
085-086 F ColorSteps
```

```
;085 - Color Stairs
;
clayer Text
filedia 0
text 35872,43434,8200 7 -90 AP 599
text 35936,43572,8200 7 -90 AP 800
text 35979,43553,8200 7 -90 AP
880=Y1r28
text 35927,43413,8200 7 -90 AP
881=Y1r29
text 35872,43434,8200 7 -90 AP 599
filedia 1
;
clayer 3DPolylines
3dpoly
35872,43434,8200
35936,43572,8200
35979,43553,8200
35927,43413,8200
35872,43434,8200

;
clayer Installations
WallGen
35872,43434,8200
35936,43572,8200
35979,43553,8200
35927,43413,8200
35872,43434,8200
;
35872,43434,8349
35936,43572,8284
35979,43553,8307
```

```
35927,43413,8307
35872,43434,8349

;
;086 - Color Platform
;
clayer Text
filedia 0
text  35979,43553,8307  7  -90  AP
880=Y1r28
text  35927,43413,8307  7  -90  AP
881=Y1r29
text  36015,43381,8307  7  -90  AP
600=Y1r13
text 36096,43500,8307 7 -90 AP 801
text  35979,43553,8307  7  -90  AP
880=Y1r28
filedia 1
;
clayer 3DPolylines
3dpoly
35979,43553,8307
35927,43413,8307
36015,43381,8307
36096,43500,8307
35979,43553,8307

;
clayer Installations
WallGen
35979,43553,8307
35927,43413,8307
36015,43381,8307
36096,43500,8307
35979,43553,8307
;
35979,43553,8354
35927,43413,8354
36015,43381,8354
36096,43500,8354
35979,43553,8354

;
087- Pebble Path
```

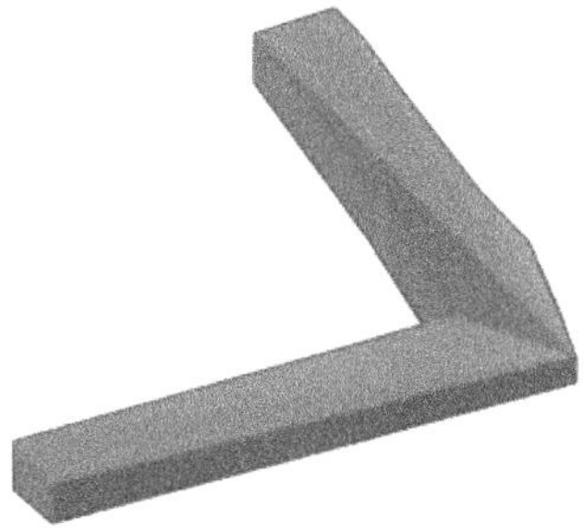

```
;087 - Pebble Path
;
clayer Text
filedia 0
text 35814,43336,8292 7 -90 AP 598
text 34864,43663,8319 7 -90 AP 809
text  34905,43798,8300  7  -90  AP
822=Y1r16
text 35693,43514,8287 7 -90 AP 806
text 35844,43872,8296 7 -90 AP 807
text 36023,44330,8300 7 -90 AP 0
text 36174,44285,8317 7 -90 AP 808
text 36148,44193,8343 7 -90 AP 805
text 35981,43737,8305 7 -90 AP 802
text 35936,43572,8284 7 -90 AP 800
text 35872,43434,8349 7 -90 AP 599
text 35814,43336,8292 7 -90 AP 598
filedia 1
;
clayer 3DPolylines
3dpoly
35814,43336,8292
34864,43663,8319
34905,43798,8300
35693,43514,8287
35844,43872,8296
36023,44330,8300
36174,44285,8317
36148,44193,8343
35981,43737,8305
35936,43572,8284
35872,43434,8349
35814,43336,8292

;
clayer Installations
WallGen
35814,43336,8292
34864,43663,8319
34905,43798,8300
35693,43514,8287
35844,43872,8296
36023,44330,8300
```

```
36174,44285,8317
36148,44193,8343
35981,43737,8305
35936,43572,8284
35872,43434,8349
35814,43336,8292
;
35814,43336,8345
34864,43663,8399
34905,43798,8400
35693,43514,8400
35844,43872,8400
36023,44330,8400
36174,44285,8400
36148,44193,8400
35981,43737,8400
35936,43572,8400
35872,43434,8361
35814,43336,8345

;
;clayer RBrick
;WallGen
;35814,43336,8345
;34864,43663,8399
;34905,43798,8400
;35693,43514,8400
;35844,43872,8400
;36023,44330,8400
;36174,44285,8400
;36148,44193,8400
;35981,43737,8400
35936,43572,8400
;35872,43434,8361
;35814,43336,8345
;
;35814,43336,8412
;34864,43663,8506
;34905,43798,8500
;35693,43514,8500
;35844,43872,8500
;36023,44330,8500
;36174,44285,8500
;36148,44193,8500
;35981,43737,8500
;35936,43572,8500
;35872,43434,8433
;35814,43336,8412
;
;
088- F1 E
```

```
;088 - F1 E
;
clayer Text
filedia 0
text 36148,44193,8292 7 -90 AP 805
text 35981,43737,8319 7 -90 AP 802
text 36144,43668,8300 7 -90 AP 803
text 36290,44145,8287 7 -90 AP
821=Y1r15
text 36148,44193,8296 7 -90 AP 805
filedia 1
;
clayer 3DPolylines
3dpoly
36148,44193,8200
35981,43737,8200
36144,43668,8200
36290,44145,8200
36148,44193,8200

;
clayer Stone
WallGen
36148,44193,8200
35981,43737,8200
36144,43668,8200
36290,44145,8200
36148,44193,8200
;
36148,44193,8343
35981,43737,8305
36144,43668,8298
36290,44145,8343
36148,44193,8343

;
089- D1 W Door
```

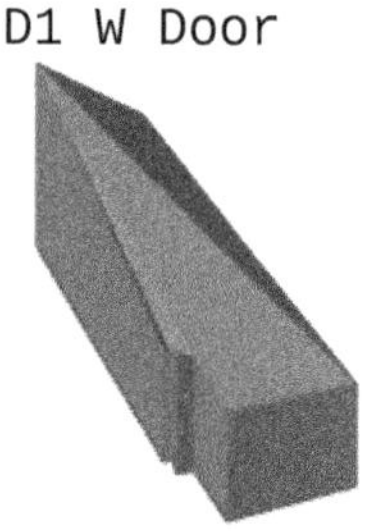

```
;089 - D1 W Sill
```

```
;
clayer Text
filedia 0
text 35346,43026,8357 7 -90 AP 200
text 35228,42778,8297 7 -90 AP 597
text 35236,42778,8287 7 -90 AP 616
text  35225,42763,8305  7  -90  AP
205=Y1r20
text 35236,42756,8297 7 -90 AP 202
text 35211,42697,8293 7 -90 AP 0
text 35305,42663,8288 7 -90 AP 596
text 35427,42999,8286 7 -90 AP 595
text 35346,43026,8357 7 -90 AP 200
filedia 1
;
clayer 3DPolylines
3dpoly
35346,43026,8200
35228,42778,8200
35236,42778,8200
35225,42763,8200
35236,42756,8200
35211,42697,8200
35305,42663,8200
35427,42999,8200
35346,43026,8200

;
clayer Doorways
WallGen
35346,43026,8200
35228,42778,8200
35236,42778,8200
35225,42763,8200
35236,42756,8200
35211,42697,8200
35305,42663,8200
35427,42999,8200
35346,43026,8200
;
35346,43026,8357
35228,42778,8297
35236,42778,8287
35225,42763,8305
35236,42756,8297
35211,42697,8293
35305,42663,8288
35427,42999,8286
35346,43026,8357

;
130- I
```

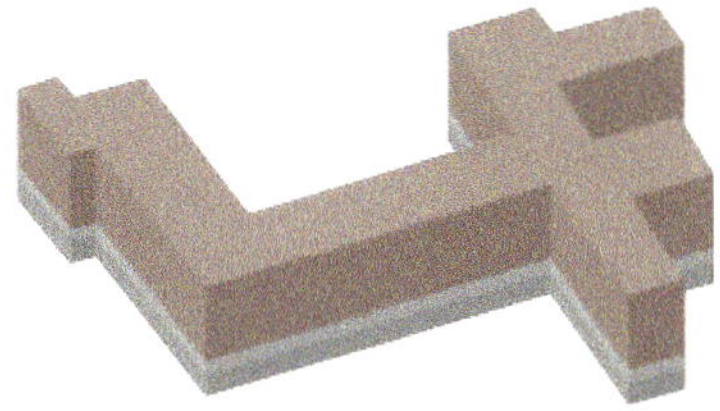

```
;130 - I
;
clayer Text
filedia 0
text 37569,39125,8520 7 -90 AP I-1
text 37724,39474,8520 7 -90 AP I-2
text 37910,39409,8520 7 -90 AP I-3
text 37876,39316,8520 7 -90 AP I-4
text 38094,39232,8520 7 -90 AP I-5
text 38040,39094,8520 7 -90 AP I-6
text 37758,39187,8520 7 -90 AP I-7
text 37670,38992,8520 7 -90 AP I-8
text 37854,38927,8520 7 -90 AP I-9
text  37763,38730,8520  7  -90  AP  I-
10
text  37583,38792,8520  7  -90  AP  I-
11
text  37456,38510,8520  7  -90  AP  I-
12
text  37334,38555,8520  7  -90  AP  I-
13
text  37495,38947,8520  7  -90  AP  I-
14
text  36730,39209,8520  7  -90  AP  I-
15
text  36914,39720,8520  7  -90  AP  I-
16
text 36859,39741,8520 7 -90 AP 295
text  36943,39980,8520  7  -90  AP  I-
17
text  37030,39951,8520  7  -90  AP  I-
18
text  37007,39875,8520  7  -90  AP  I-
19
text  37157,39818,8520  7  -90  AP  I-
20
text  36976,39325,8520  7  -90  AP  I-
21
filedia 1
;
clayer 3DPolylines
3dpoly
37569,39125,8520
37724,39474,8520
37910,39409,8520
37876,39316,8520
```

```
38094,39232,8520
38040,39094,8520
37758,39187,8520
37670,38992,8520
37854,38927,8520
37763,38730,8520
37583,38792,8520
37456,38510,8520
37334,38555,8520
37495,38947,8520
36730,39209,8520
36914,39720,8520
36859,39741,8520
36943,39980,8520
37030,39951,8520
37007,39875,8520
37157,39818,8520
36976,39325,8520
37569,39125,8520

;
clayer Stone
WallGen
37569,39125,8520
37724,39474,8520
37910,39409,8520
37876,39316,8520
38094,39232,8520
38040,39094,8520
37758,39187,8520
37670,38992,8520
37854,38927,8520
37763,38730,8520
37583,38792,8520
37456,38510,8520
37334,38555,8520
37495,38947,8520
36730,39209,8520
36914,39720,8520
36859,39741,8520
36943,39980,8520
37030,39951,8520
37007,39875,8520
37157,39818,8520
36976,39325,8520
37569,39125,8520
;
37569,39125,8570
37724,39474,8570
37910,39409,8570
37876,39316,8570
38094,39232,8570
38040,39094,8570
37758,39187,8570
37670,38992,8570
37854,38927,8570
37763,38730,8570
37583,38792,8570
37456,38510,8570
37334,38555,8570
37495,38947,8570
36730,39209,8570
36914,39720,8570
36859,39741,8580
36943,39980,8570
37030,39951,8570
37007,39875,8570
37157,39818,8570
36976,39325,8570
37569,39125,8570

;
clayer RecStone
WallGen
37569,39125,8570
37724,39474,8570
37910,39409,8570
37876,39316,8570
38094,39232,8570
38040,39094,8570
37758,39187,8570
37670,38992,8570
37854,38927,8570
37763,38730,8570
37583,38792,8570
37456,38510,8570
37334,38555,8570
37495,38947,8570
36730,39209,8570
36914,39720,8570
36859,39741,8580
36943,39980,8570
37030,39951,8570
37007,39875,8570
37157,39818,8570
36976,39325,8570
37569,39125,8570
;
37569,39125,8605
37724,39474,8605
37910,39409,8605
37876,39316,8605
38094,39232,8605
38040,39094,8605
37758,39187,8605
37670,38992,8605
```

```
37854,38927,8605
37763,38730,8605
37583,38792,8605
37456,38510,8605
37334,38555,8605
37495,38947,8605
36730,39209,8605
36914,39720,8605
36859,39741,8605
36943,39980,8605
37030,39951,8605
37007,39875,8605
37157,39818,8605
36976,39325,8605
37569,39125,8605

;
clayer RecBrick
WallGen
37569,39125,8605
37724,39474,8605
37910,39409,8605
37876,39316,8605
38094,39232,8605
38040,39094,8605
37758,39187,8605
37670,38992,8605
37854,38927,8605
37763,38730,8605
37583,38792,8605
37456,38510,8605
37334,38555,8605
37495,38947,8605
36730,39209,8605
36914,39720,8605
36859,39741,8605
36943,39980,8605
37030,39951,8605
37007,39875,8605
37157,39818,8605
36976,39325,8605
37569,39125,8605
;
37569,39125,8790
37724,39474,8790
37910,39409,8790
37876,39316,8790
38094,39232,8790
38040,39094,8790
37758,39187,8790
37670,38992,8790
37854,38927,8790
37763,38730,8790
37583,38792,8790
37456,38510,8790
37334,38555,8790
37495,38947,8790
36730,39209,8790
36914,39720,8790
36859,39741,8790
36943,39980,8790
37030,39951,8790
37007,39875,8790
37157,39818,8790
36976,39325,8790
37569,39125,8790

;
131- H3 Courtyard
```

```
;131 - H3
;
clayer Text
filedia 0
text 36762,41976,8520 7 -90 AP H-1
text 37801,41644,8520 7 -90 AP H-2
text 37633,40622,8520 7 -90 AP H-3
text 37514,40404,8520 7 -90 AP H-4
text 36326,40767,8520 7 -90 AP H-5
text 36762,41976,8520 7 -90 AP H-1
filedia 1
;
clayer 3DPolylines
3dpoly
36762,41976,8520
37801,41644,8520
37633,40622,8520
37514,40404,8520
36326,40767,8520
36762,41976,8520

;
clayer StoneCourtyard
WallGen
36762,41976,8485
37801,41644,8485
37633,40622,8485
37514,40404,8485
```

```
36326,40767,8485
36762,41976,8485
;
36762,41976,8520
37801,41644,8520
37633,40622,8520
37514,40404,8520
36326,40767,8520
36762,41976,8520

;
```

Alphabetical Index

3D model....204
3D Modeling Practices....210
3D printing....209
3D scanning....212
abi....15, 22, 24, 26, 37, 54, 56, 59, 61
abstraction in architectural theory....192
administrators....137
adobe....157
algorithms....173, 218, 231, 246, 248
Anastasiopolis....88
Animation....220
archaeological record....178
archéologie du bâti....83
architect....128, 183, 186
architectural orders....192
ash....118
AutoCAD....217
  functions....217
  measurements....218
basket....146
Bauforschung....186
BlockGen....212, 244, 257
brick carriers....147
brick form....100
brick piles....110
brick stacks....111
brick storage....105
builder....137, 183
CAD - Computer Aided Design....204, 215
carriage....142
Cave UT....221p.
chaff....96, 105, 118, 120, 155, 249
chaîne opératoire....80, 149, 231
  Bauforschung....83
  behavioral chain....81
  moment of discard....82
  nesting....82
  operational chain....80p.

operational sequence....80
skill diversity....82
chisels....90, 151
city gate....15
city planner....125
commissioning person....124, 187
communication....206
construction coordinator....130
corvée system....127, 134
Dara....88
data collection....214
deposition....224
design....182
didactic context....227
donkeys....147
doorways....165
drainage system....40, 67
drawings....204
durability....189
Egypt....89
emplacement....224
energetics....196p.
engineer....128
Ethics....85, 228
Drehem....85
Garshana....85
ethnoarchaeological experiment....85, 93, 112, 229, 256
Ethnoarchaeology....180
execution team....129
experience....207
extruded model....211
fill....122, 157
First-Person Interactive Environments....221
foreperson....136
foundation boxes....175
foundations....160
function....199
Garshana....85, 147p.
gender....147
GIS....219

Göbekli Tepe....89p.
gravel....88
gutter....167
gypsum....118, 145, 154, 172
half bricks....107
hammering tools....89
hermeneutic model....208
heuristics....195, 227
hole made for mudbricks....96
humidity....87
illustration....204
innovation....182
installations....61, 172
institution....191
interactivity....207, 229
iwan....27, 42, 50, 75
leveling....158
light source....208
lime....118p., 154
limestone....93
logging....144
manpower coordinator....126
master builder....129
material coordinators....129
materials....190
mauls....151
Mayan architecture....90
monumentality....182, 185, 206, 252
mortar....118, 145, 154
movable goods....172
mudbrick....94, 237, 249
  carrying....137
  drying-time....109
  gray bricks....97
  laying....163
  mudbrick production....153
  red bricks....97
  sizes....116
  storage....110
  temperature....94

timing........109
mudbrick deterioration........87
New Geology........180
niches........166
open spaces........209
overseer........129, 136
pack animals........147
palace........124
access........38, 51
entrance........26
footprint........72
mirrored architecture........47, 76
mirrored plan........26
position........14
royal........24
toilet........47
visibility........39
perception........33
philological considerations........113
Photo modeling........211
pisé........94, 182
planning team........125
plaster........117p., 145, 154, 172
plaza........191
postulates........178
Postulate 1: Ethnoarchaeological Link........85, 179
Postulate 2: Continuity of Experience........85, 180
pounders........151
prestige........253
primary data........177
process of construction........79
sources........83
proportion........30
quarry........88, 92
quarrying techniques........88
rabbeting........29, 92
rafts........144, 152
rations........112, 135, 175
reconstruction........208
reed matting........121, 155

reeds........144, 146
research questions........223
roof construction........121, 167
roofing beams........166
rooftop areas........170
seal impressions........189
second story........208
skilled workers........131
slaves........131, 133
sleds........138, 147
social institutions........199
social space........185
soil........105
standardization........182
stone........86, 137, 151
stone sub-structure........161
straw........96, 109, 118, 120, 146
style........194
surveyor........128, 187
tablet A15.231........56
tannur........49, 65
Tar'am-Agade........20p., 23, 72
Tell Chuera........89, 198
terracing........17, 75, 159
textual evidence........257
theoretical reflections........177
three dimensions........209
timeline........149
toilet........61
tools........122
    Egyptian quarrying tools........89
Tupkish........21p., 24, 53, 186
UFO problem........201, 223
Unap-[...]........21
uniformitarianism........86, 180
unskilled workers........131
Uqnitum........190
Ur-namma........122, 146
urban environment........183
urban texture........190

value..196p.
vernacular..182p.
visibility..251
volumetric measurements..246
volumetrics..208
wadi..140
wage..142, 175
wagon..147
walkthrough..220
water..106
wattle-and-daub..94
wedges..151
wheelbarrow..102
windows..165
wood..155
wooden beams..121, 137, 143, 168
work-crews..135, 149
Workforce..131
worksite..157
workspace..156
Zimri-lim..189

List of Illustrations

Illustration 1: AP Palace without the wall coverings, looking North..............13
Illustration 2: AP Palace showing Sectors and room numbers........................14
Illustration 3: AP Palace showing excavation unit designations....................15
Illustration 4: Elevations at Mozan..16
Illustration 5: The AP Palace with shading to indicate differences in elevation. Solid shading indicates the lower level, while dotted shading indicates the raised level...18
Illustration 6: AP Palace showing the installations; the main drain is marked with a dash-dot line running from NE to S..19
Illustration 7: Seal impressions of Tar'am-Agade and her court (G. Buccellati and Kelly-Buccellati 2002, 14-23)..20
Illustration 8: Unap-[...] impressions showing recutting of seal impression (G. Buccellati and Kelly-Buccellati 2002, 26)..21
Illustration 9: Administrative seal impressions found within the AP Palace (images are not to scale) (G. Buccellati and Kelly-Buccellati 1997, 81).....25
Illustration 10: AP Palace with possible entrances shown with arrows (upper right and upper left)...27
Illustration 11: Service Wing of the AP Palace with hatching to indicate the two iwan room groups A5-A2 and C5-C2...28
Illustration 12: Formal Wing and Sector C of AP Palace showing iwan room-pairs...29
Illustration 13: A graphic representation of the acoustic, haptic olfactory and optical spaces of perception. These do not completely overlap, thus, for example, what can be heard is not necessarily visible or touchable. A singing dancer (black dot in center) is perceived by various people through different senses in different spatial areas (adapted from Ankerl 1981, 156). 33
Illustration 14: Elevations at Tell Mozan...37
Illustration 15: Kite photo showing the spatial relationships within the monumental urban complex...39
Illustration 16: Oblique kite view of the excavations showing the excavated portions of the AP Palace (MZ V14k5042)..42
Illustration 17: Complete Plan of excavated portions of AP Palace showing sector and room designations...43
Illustration 18: AP Palace Service Wing, access analysis.............................45
Illustration 19: AP Palace with sector A highlighted....................................46
Illustration 20: AP Palace showing 'negative' sector A walls (MZ V13d8233). 47

Illustration 21: AP Palace with sector C highlighted......................................48
Illustration 22: AP Palace with sector B highlighted......................................49
Illustration 23: AP Palace with sector D highlighted......................................50
Illustration 24: AP Palace with sectors E and F highlighted............................51
Illustration 25: AP Palace with sector G highlighted......................................52
Illustration 26: AP Palace with sector H highlighted......................................54
Illustration 27: AP Palace with arrow indicating spot where the stone courtyard's perimeter wall backs onto area X outside of the palace............56
Illustration 28: AP Palace with sector I highlighted.......................................57
Illustration 29: Tablet A15.231 showing 1) measurement on tablet 2) equivalent in hexagesimal system and 3) possible relationship to measurement points (G. Buccellati 2005, 17-19).......................................58
Illustration 30: Statue of Gudea with plan of temple (Musée du Louvre).......59
Illustration 31: AP Palace with sectors Y, X and W highlighted.....................60
Illustration 32: Drain coming from C6 (lower left) and progressing through C3 to C2. Note change from baked brick to stone covering as drain goes deeper (V16d1172)...61
Illustration 33: Clay bin in room C2 (MZ V12d1408)...................................62
Illustration 34: Detail of bin, showing layering of clay (MZ V12d1429)........62
Illustration 35: Reconstruction of log position in C1 (MZ V16d1084)...........63
Illustration 36: overview of charred logs in room C1 (MZ V14d1205)...........64
Illustration 37: Detail of one of the logs in C1, showing lack of burning in surrounding accumulation and on wall (left) (MZ V12d0929)..................64
Illustration 38: Pebble path in F1 along southern and eastern edges of the courtyard (MZ V12d2913)...64
Illustration 39: Brick platform between F1 and G1. Note that bricks have been sprayed with water to enhance the coloring of the baked bricks (MZ V12d2714)..65
Illustration 40: Inside of the drain. Note stone lining above, on sides, and as bottom of the channel (MZ V16d1173)...66
Illustration 41: Brick platform looking SW (MZ V12d2715)..........................66
Illustration 42: Exit of drain to south of room C5 (MZ V16d1167)................67
Illustration 43: Drain channel in room C5 (MZ V16d1151)...........................67
Illustration 44: Closed drain access in room C8 (MZ V16d1166)...................68
Illustration 45: Drain in room H4, seen on right of image (MZ V14d3334)....68
Illustration 46: Stone Courtyard (H3) of the AP Palace (Photo: MZ V15d4117 Drawing: MZ W15d4510)...69
Illustration 47: Floorplan of AP Palace, with excavation limit shown as dotted line, projected walls in light gray...73
Illustration 48: Tell Chuera, Palace F (Tamm 2008, 101)..............................75

Illustration 49: Palace in Tell Beydar, Area F Level 3a (Lebeau and Suleiman 2003, Architectural Plan 6)....76
Illustration 50: Plan of Eridu from final publication (Margueron 1983, 227)..77
Illustration 51: A Stone construction element which was abandoned half excavated in a stone quarry near Göbekli Tepe (Schmidt 2006, 103)....91
Illustration 52: A reconstruction of stone quarrying near Göbekli Tepe, showing excavation, loading and transportation of a stone construction element (Kurapkat 2009, 75)....91
Illustration 53: Pisé construction technique with framing walls (Aurenche 1977, 138)....95
Illustration 54: Pit dug to mine dirt for mudbricks (Aurenche 1977, 129)....96
Illustration 55: Mud mixture for mudbrick production; note AP Palace in background (MZ V22i2235)....98
Illustration 56: Adding the mud-mixture to the brick form (MZ V22i2159)...99
Illustration 57: A trowel is used on the top (MZ V22i2161)....100
Illustration 58: Pressing mud-mixture into the form (MZ V22i2236)....101
Illustration 59: Removing the brick form (MZ V22i2162)....102
Illustration 60: Stages of drying – fresh bricks in background, lighter bricks are a day old, vertical bricks nearly dry (MZ V22i2702)....103
Illustration 61: Stacked bricks, ready for use, transport or storage (MZ V22i2237)....104
Illustration 62: Bonding along both longitudinal and latitudinal axes in a wall constructed using square and half-bricks (Sauvage 1998, 62)....108
Illustration 63: Opening a brick pile after a year (MZ V23i1102)....111
Illustration 64: Overhead of workspace at Mozan (MZ V22i2238)....113
Illustration 65: SIG4 after Deimel 1922....114
Illustration 66: SIG4 after Labat 1976....114
Illustration 67: SIG4 from Burrows 1935....114
Illustration 68: SIG4 from Green and Nissen 1987....114
Illustration 69: SIG4 from text#272 in Burrows 1935 – one of the earliest attestations of SIG4, from the EDI-II period (Cropped from CDLI image). 114
Illustration 70: Mixing dirt and water for plaster....117
Illustration 71: Adding chaff to the plaster....117
Illustration 72: Mixing the plaster with feet....119
Illustration 73: The lime cycle (Cornerstones Community Partnerships 2006, 133)....120
Illustration 74: Reed mats (Aurenche 1977, 155)....122
Illustration 75: Detail from stele of Ur-Namma; note tools in lower register (Canby 2001, Plate 31, fig. 14)....123

Illustration 76: Detail from drawing of Ur-Namma stele showing tools (after Canby 2001, Plate 33)....123
Illustration 77: Flowchart describing hypothetical working groups needed when building a palace....124
Illustration 78: Worker divisions within the texts from Garshana....132
Illustration 79: Stone sled (boat) (Vivian 1978, 68)....138
Illustration 80: Modern example of how to place heavy stone on top of a wall (McRaven 1999, 9)....139
Illustration 81: Google image with overlay showing the outer citywall of Urkesh and the wadi-bed (accessed December 2016)....141
Illustration 82: A Corona satellite image showing wadi-bed (Corona DS1104-1025DA012_12_b – cropped image)....141
Illustration 83: A workman at Mozan carrying two mudbricks on his back. Note the use of a cloth belt to support the back and the base of the bricks (MZ V22i2239)....143
Illustration 84: Transportation of Wooden Beams and Stone near MZ (hypothetical model) (Google Earth image, accessed December 2016)....144
Illustration 85: Two workmen at Mozan carrying a bucket using a stick (MZ V22i2242)....146
Illustration 86: Ur-namma of Ur carrying a basket of construction material (OI-Chicago website, accessed December 2016)....146
Illustration 87: Hypothetical administrative hierarchy for AP Palace construction....148
Illustration 88: Chaîne opératoire for the quarrying of stone. Materials needed during the various steps are indicated by boxes with a dashed line, link to further chaîne opératoire indicated by boxes with a dotted line....152
Illustration 89: Chaîne opératoire describing the production of mudbricks. Materials needed during the various steps are indicated by boxes with a dashed line, link to further chaîne opératoire indicated by boxes with a dotted line....153
Illustration 90: Chaîne opératoire describing the production of mud plaster and mortar. Materials needed during the various steps are indicated by boxes with a dashed line, link to further chaîne opératoire indicated by boxes with a dotted line....154
Illustration 91: Chaîne opératoire describing the production of gypsum and lime plaster. Materials needed during the various steps are indicated by boxes with a dashed line, link to further chaîne opératoire indicated by boxes with a dotted line....155
Illustration 92: Chaîne opératoire describing the construction project. Materials needed during the various steps are indicated by boxes with a

dashed line..156
Illustration 93: Wall terminology; drawing is meant as a comparative illustration, since it comes from a different cultural context (Cornerstones Community Partnerships 2006, 31)..157
Illustration 94: Overhead photo of the reconstruction project at the AP Palace. Note the mudbricks stacked in the top and right of the image, soil for plaster in the upper right, as well as the stones in the lower right (MZ V22i2240). 158
Illustration 95: High retaining wall with fill and drainage (Vivian 1978, 55). 159
Illustration 96: Elements of a stone foundation (Aurenche 1977, 79)...........160
Illustration 97: Typology of foundations (Birschmeier and Gasche 1981, 16). 161
Illustration 98: Note here the stonework (Ragette 1974, 23).........................162
Illustration 99: Example of a vertical run (McRaven 1999, 19)....................163
Illustration 100: Wall construction during the reconstruction of the destroyed walls of the AP Palace. Note the workman 'splitting' a brick into two half-bricks over a pole in the foreground (MZ V22i2241)..............................164
Illustration 101: Laying pattern for a wall with the width of a single brick (Ragette 1974, 23)..165
Illustration 102: A good example of well-laid brickwork (Aurenche 1977, 36). 165
Illustration 103: A modern doorway with wooden lintel visible. Note the stone substructure (Aurenche 1977, 111)...166
Illustration 104: Reconstruction of a roof (Ragette 1974, 23).......................167
Illustration 105: Roofing elements mentioned in the Garshana texts (Heimpel 2009, 173)..168
Illustration 106: Various stages of the roofing process: cross-pieces, straw, matting and dirt (Cornerstones Community Partnerships 2006, 185).......168
Illustration 107: Wooden beams and reed mats ready to be used in construction (Aurenche 1977, 97)..169
Illustration 108: House with second story in mudbrick (Aurenche 1977, 145). 170
Illustration 109: A second-story construction made of reeds (Aurenche 1977, 122)..171
Illustration 110: A flat roof accessed by means of a ladder (Aurenche 1981, 205)..171
Illustration 111: The plastered outer wall of a house; note the roof beams (Aurenche 1981, 135)..172
Illustration 112: Plaster can also be applied to stone (Aurenche 1981, 135). 172

Illustration 113: Doerpfeld's illustration of Troy (Schliemann 1891, Taf. III). 205
Illustration 114: Domus of the Mosaics, Roselle; prospective drawing (Medri 2003, 200)....... 205
Illustration 115: Domus of the Mosaics, Roselle; general plan (Medri 2003, 194)....... 206
Illustration 116: 3D Model of AP Palace showing existing stone walls - overhead view....... 233
Illustration 117: 3D Model of AP Palace showing existing and reconstructed stone walls - overhead view....... 234
Illustration 118: 3D Model of AP Palace showing existing and reconstructed stone walls - view to NE....... 235
Illustration 119: 3D Model of AP Palace showing existing and reconstructed stone walls - overhead view....... 235
Illustration 120: 3D Model of AP Palace showing existing stone walls - view to NE....... 235
Illustration 121: 3D Model of AP Palace showing existing stone walls and mudbrick - overhead view....... 236
Illustration 122: 3D Model of AP Palace showing existing stone walls and mudbrick - view to NE....... 237
Illustration 123: 3D Model of AP Palace showing existing as well as reconstructed stone walls and mudbrick - view to NE....... 237
Illustration 124: 3D Model of AP Palace showing existing as well as reconstructed stone walls and mudbrick - overhead view....... 238
Illustration 125: 3D Model of AP Palace showing existing as well as reconstructed stone walls and mudbrick - view to NE....... 239
Illustration 126: 3D Model of AP Palace showing existing stone walls and mudbrick - overhead view....... 239
Illustration 127: 3D Model of AP Palace showing existing as well as reconstructed stone walls and mudbrick - overhead view....... 240
Illustration 128: 3D Model of AP Palace showing existing stone walls and mudbrick - view to NE....... 241
Illustration 129: 3D Model of AP Palace showing existing as well as reconstructed stone walls and mudbrick, including installations - overhead view....... 242
Illustration 130: 3D Model of AP Palace showing existing as well as reconstructed stone walls and mudbrick, including installations - view to NE....... 243
Illustration 131: Block 088-F1 E generated with the erroneous script file....245
Illustration 132: Block 088-F1 E generated with the correct script file.........245

Illustration 133: Render of 3D model showing centrality of nodes A7 and C7. 250
Illustration 134: A render of the AP Palace 3D Model showing differences in elevation between formal and service wings....250

N.B. All illustration references beginning with "MZ" refer to field photos under copyright by the Mozan/Urkesh Archaeological Project.

List of Tables

Table 1: Phase sequence....23
Table 2: Proportion between the area and perimeter, sorted by room....30
Table 3: Proportion between the area and perimeter, examples....31
Table 4: Proportion between area and perimeter, sorted by area/perimeter proportion....32
Table 5: Square meters by sector....71
Table 6: Various suggested mudbrick compositions (Aurenche 1981, 46)....105
Table 7: Volume and weight calculations based on modern and ancient bricks from Tell Mozan....109
Table 8: Page numbers (right) refer to Salonen (1972)....115
Table 9: Formula to calculate transportation of materials....138
Table 10: Earth carriage over a 5 hour day (Coles 1973, 95)....145
Table 11: List of volumes of materials present (or reconstructed) for each wall portion....247